Roderick Heather

Following an honours degree in Economics from Sheffield University in 1967, the author spent almost thirty years working for various manufacturing businesses in the UK and overseas. In 1995 he moved to Tatarstan in Russia, leading a team of international consultants at a large automotive company and in 1997 he became an advisor to the UK Foreign Office and the Department for International Development covering Russia until 2002. He subsequently worked as a management consultant on various projects in Russia and Ukraine. Born in Royal Leamington Spa, the author has lived in Canada, Switzerland, France, the USA and Russia and has travelled to seventy different countries. The author has written two other books about Russia, *The Iron Tsar* and *Russia from Red to Black.* He is married with three adult sons and lives in Chester.

AN ACCIDENTAL RELATIONSHIP

The British in Russia, 1553 – 1920

Roderick Heather

AN ACCIDENTAL RELATIONSHIP

The British in Russia, 1553 – 1920

AUSTIN MACAULEY
PUBLISHERS LTD.

A CIP catalogue record for this title is available from the British Library.

ISBN 978 1 84963 586 8

www.austinmacauley.com

First Published (2014)
Austin Macauley Publishers Ltd.
25 Canada Square
Canary Wharf
London
E14 5LB

Printed and bound in Great Britain

Contents

"There is no greater folly circulating upon the earth .... than the disposition to undervalue the past, and to break those links which unite human beings of the present day with the generations which have passed away".

From a speech by William Gladstone, British Prime Minister, in August 1873.

Introduction

During man's time on this earth, many of his greatest inventions or discoveries have been accidental or unintended. Thus, the reputed accidental encounter of an apple with Newton's head ultimately gave us the theory of gravity and Columbus' search for a westerly passage to Cathay revealed the existence of the Americas. So it was with England's first encounter with Russia. Like Columbus, the English sailors that set out in 1553 were seeking a sea passage to the riches of the Orient, only in an easterly direction around the northern capes of Scandinavia. They had not intended to 'discover' Russia; it was totally accidental and unexpected. Yet this chance encounter was to lead to not only a remarkable relationship between Britain and Russia but also to the eventual involvement of thousands of British men and women in Russia's future social, military and economic development.

From the time the Bolsheviks brutally imposed their stranglehold on power across Tsarist Russia in the early 1920s, the country has been a relatively difficult place for foreigners to visit or in which to live or do business. Although things temporarily improved somewhat under President Yeltsin after the 1991 revolution, the Putin era has seen a renewed official distrust of foreigners and their activities in Russia. However, for over 300 years prior to the arrival of Communism, apart from the occasional period of war or political tension, Russia was as open to foreigners as any European country and the British increasingly took advantage of this situation. Driven initially by a desire for trade, the British relationship with and interest in Russia gradually expanded during the 17th, 18th and 19th centuries, mainly reflecting Britain's growing pre-eminence in the military, scientific, financial and industrial spheres. However, both nations benefitted from the relationship. For Britain, Russia not only provided a ready market for its goods and expertise but also an important political counterbalance to the threats from expansionary Spain and France. In return, Russia gained an increasingly powerful ally as well as access to vital skills and technology that it lacked for its future development. Over the course of some 360 years, the Anglo-Russian relationship would see friendship and rivalry, trade and blockade, alliance and war as the two nations developed into the world's two largest empires and competed on the international stage.

There were perhaps five main phases defining British involvement with Russia. The initial period of contact and trade between the governments of Elizabeth I and Ivan the Terrible, the expansion of relationships under Peter the Great and subsequently Catherine, the political tensions that led to the Crimean War and the so-called Great Game, the explosion of British industrial involvement in Russia in the latter half of the 19th century and finally the period of the First World War plus the subsequent British entanglement in the Russian civil war. Inevitably most British activity revolved around the two capital cities of Moscow initially and later St Petersburg. Since these two cities were the centres of political and economic power as well as the cultural hubs, many Britons living in Russia or visiting the country spent the majority of their time there. However, as we shall see, the British in the period covered by this book were active right across this vast country, not only as visitors or travellers but living and working in a wide variety of places from the Baltic to the Black Sea and from the Caucasus to Siberia. They were involved with Russian royalty and peasants; they ran the army and built theatres; they worked on the great estates and in the factories; some campaigned for social justice or became nurses in the Russian Army and a few became very wealthy and achieved high honours while others lost everything. Some loved the country and its people but others loathed it, finding the Russians uncultured and extremely corrupt.

The British were rarely the largest foreign presence in Russia but no other nation can claim to have had as great a continuous, diverse and widespread influence on Russia and its institutions as the British between the 16th and 20th centuries. Although many individual aspects of the broad gamut of British activities in Russia have been covered in various publications over the years, this book is an attempt to bring these stories together and give them some perspective and context. However, it is not my intention to draw any deep conclusions about the wider impacts of the contacts between the British and the Russians on their respective cultures and economic development, though clearly this was highly significant in various ways. This is a broad subject and beyond the scope of this book. Rather, the book is more a compendium of the experiences of the British in Russia, together with an overview of their reasons for going and what they achieved.

Sadly, the constraint of space has forced me to be highly selective about the stories and experiences of British people included in this book. There were hundreds of others that visited Russia or lived and worked there, each of whom in their own individual ways made a contribution to the unique Anglo-Russian relationship that evolved over some 360 years. Their stories will have to remain untold for the time being.

Over the course of more than 360 years, the British made a remarkable contribution to Russia in a wide variety of fields. Although their experiences in Imperial Russia were often difficult, they were also sometimes amusing (at least when viewed in retrospect) and the country steadily became a destination of choice for the British. Despite the fact that Britain's relationship with Russia would eventually overcome the traumas of the Bolshevik revolution and the Allied Intervention, it would never be the same as before. In particular, the large resident Anglo-Russian community, so embedded in the social, economic and cultural fabric of Russia had gone, mostly settling in Britain. Many of them had staked everything they had in Russia and most of them admired the country and its people. Their financial losses, coupled with their treatment by the Bolsheviks meant they would not return.

For some readers, the period covered by my book may perhaps appear arbitrary but the cutoff date of 1920 has been chosen because most of the existing British community resident in Russia had left the country by then and it marks the time when foreigners generally were unwelcome in what was soon to become the Soviet Union.

Chester: October 2013

Anthony Jenkinson's 1583 map of Russia

1
First Contacts

In the late summer of 1553 an English sailing ship, the *Edward Bonaventure*, having rounded the stormy capes off the northern end of Norway, headed south into the uncharted White Sea. The ship was captained by Richard Chancellor and he and his men were seeking a north-east passage to China on behalf of the recently formed Company of Merchant Adventurers. After a few days, they made landfall in the small harbour of the Nikolo-Korelsky monastery on the Dvina River, near what is now the Russian town of Archangel. As the 160 ton *Edward Bonaventure* approached, slicing easily through the dark, blue-black waters of the sound, local fishermen in their little wooden boats gazed in stunned awe at the unexpected sight of such a large ship. The English crew excitedly lined the deck, the brass buttons of their light blue company uniforms glinting in the northern sun's afternoon rays. The date was August 24th and this unexpected encounter marked the beginning of a unique relationship between people from the British Isles with those of Russia. A relationship that over the ensuing 360 years would see friendship and rivalry, trade and blockade, alliance and war as the world's two largest empires competed on the world stage.

Chancellor's ship was one of three that had left England in early July on the first expedition of the Company of Merchant Adventurers. The company, whose full title was *'Mystery and Company of Merchant Adventurers for the Discovery of Regions, Dominions, Islands, and Places unknown'*, was founded under Royal Charter in 1551 by Chancellor, Sebastian Cabot and Sir Hugh Willoughby, with the objective of finding a maritime passage around Scandinavia to the Orient. In the early 1500s England was heavily dependent on continental Europe for the supply of luxury goods. Merchants of the Hanseatic League, a group of powerful cities that controlled much of the North Sea and Baltic trade, enjoyed favourable trading privileges in England. Understandably, English merchants wanted a share of this lucrative trade and the growing production of woollen cloth for export encouraged them to search for routes to open up new markets. The idea of finding a northern polar passage to Cathay and the East Indies was first suggested by Robert Thorne, a Bristol merchant, in letters to both Henry VIII and Charles V in Spain in 1527. But his proposal was not followed up until the formation of the Merchant Adventurers in London.

This first Merchant Adventurers' expedition was actually led by Willoughby but although an experienced soldier, he had limited previous nautical or navigational experience so Chancellor was appointed pilot and navigator of the small fleet – the *Bona Esperanza* under Willoughby, the *Edward Bonaventure* captained by Chancellor plus the *Bona Confidentia*. Chancellor was from Bristol and gained his maritime and navigation skills from the explorer Sebastian Cabot and geographer John Dee. He was a well respected mariner and well liked by the men who served under him. As the three ships sailed north-east, entering the

Arctic Circle, they were hit by dense fog and a severe storm near the Lofoten Islands off northern Norway and were separated. Willoughby's ship and the *Bona Confidentia* managed to regroup and sailed east across the Barents Sea, eventually reaching the Russian islands of Novaya Zemlya[1]. Willoughby spent some time sailing along the coast, then turned back south and on September 14th he sailed into a bay to the east of present-day Murmansk. The ships decided to stay and rest for a while; fish and game initially seemed abundant so conditions weren't considered to be too hazardous but soon, the Arctic winter blew in trapping both ships in pack ice. Willoughby and his crew were neither prepared nor equipped for the extreme cold and conditions on board deteriorated rapidly. Despite a few desperate attempts, the men were unable to cross the ice to reach land and find help and soon the energy-sapping cold and night-filled days closed in on them. From the journals kept by Willoughby, it seems that he and the crew were still alive in January 1554. There is debate about their eventual fate; it is likely some or all succumbed to a mixture of starvation and freezing to death. However, it has also been suggested that the survivors were killed by carbon monoxide poisoning, following their decision to insulate their ships from the bitter Arctic cold. Whatever the eventual cause of their sad deaths, the following year the ships, laden with over sixty frozen corpses, were discovered by local Russian fishermen.

Chancellor was more fortunate. Having failed to rejoin the other two ships after the storm, he had sailed on, eventually turning south into the White Sea. The area where he first landed had only recently been added to the Russian kingdom of Muscovy and so there was great interest in the arrival of this western intruder. News of Chancellor's presence was soon relayed to the Russian court and Tsar Ivan IV immediately invited this unexpected explorer to visit him in Moscow. Leaving most of his crew behind, Chancellor made the journey of over 600 miles to Moscow on horse-drawn sledges, through a country blanketed in deep snow and ice. For Ivan, this intriguing and unexpected contact with the English was highly interesting. Like the British, the Russians under Ivan were then in the early stages of a major expansion of their empire that was to continue irregularly into the twentieth century. However, their desire to expand was severely constrained. To the west, they were hemmed in by the strong Swedish, Polish and Lithuanian kingdoms; to the south and east, the Tatars and their allies the Ottomans held sway. The Russians had no safe access to the important trading areas around the Baltic Sea and all overland trade with Europe was controlled by the Hanseatic League. So the opportunity to open up a sea route for trade with England and then potentially with other western European countries was particularly attractive to the isolated Muscovy. For Chancellor, the possibilities seemed no less encouraging. Although he had set out with the hope of finding Cathay, establishing a good market for English wool in the large Russian market and trading furs and other Russian goods in return seemed a good alternative. Both parties shared the common goal of eliminating the middlemen of the Hanseatic League and building on their accidental initial contact.

---

[1] For many years, these islands were depicted on later maps as Willoughby's Land.

Chancellor was impressed with the size of Moscow (it was then much larger than London) but thought it primitively built with few buildings of any note, most houses being constructed of wood. However, the palace of the Tsar was very luxurious, as were apparently the dinners he subsequently laid on for Chancellor. Ivan had only recently won a decisive victory against the southern Tatar Khanate after the siege of the strategically important city of Kazan where he earned the nickname of Ivan the Terrible[2]. However, Ivan failed to live up to his new name, instead inviting his English guests to the Russian court, hosting them lavishly and granting the English free trade in all his dominions. Chancellor's initial discussions with Ivan must have been rather tricky as his introductory letters and requests to trade would have been addressed to the anticipated potentates of Cathay. However, Chancellor obviously finessed this awkward problem as on his return to England in 1554, he carried with him letters from the Tsar to England's King Edward VI[3], welcoming English traders and promising them exclusive trade privileges. Communication between Ivan and Chancellor during these complicated trade negotiations must also have been difficult since neither spoke the other's language. It is possible they were conducted in German or Latin as they would seem to be the most likely languages of which each party might have had some knowledge at that time.

Soon after Chancellor's arrival back in England, the Company of Merchant Adventurers renamed itself the Muscovy Company and in 1555 he visited Russia again taking with him George Killingworth, the first of the Company's factors or agents to be based in Moscow. They spent the summer organizing trade deals with the Tsar's officials and trying to gather information on how India or China might be reached by the northern sea route. They also now heard the news of Willoughby's unfortunate end and the discovery of Novaya Zemlya. So, on his way back to England, Chancellor stopped en route near Murmansk to retrieve the body of Willoughby plus his two ships and goods as well as his personal papers. In addition to its growing trading activities, the Muscovy Company also now began to provide an important diplomatic link between Moscow and England with the Company's merchants increasingly carrying confidential correspondence between the Tsar and Queen Elizabeth I. On his third voyage to Russia, Chancellor was asked to take with him to England the first Russian ambassador, Osip Nepaya, accompanied by no less than sixteen Russian officials and traders. It seems that even as early as the 16th century, London was an attractive destination for the Russians. They were the first Russians officially allowed to leave the country, apart from an ambassador to the Danish court a few years earlier.

The group left Archangel in late autumn 1556 in the *Edward Bonaventure* plus Willoughby's two recovered ships and a new addition to the Muscovy Company's fleet, the *Philip and Mary*. Arriving off Trondheim in Norway in stormy weather, the fleet tried to take shelter in the harbour but the *Bona Esperanza* sank and the *Bona Confidentia* appeared to enter the fjord but was

---

[2] The meaning of Russian word then for 'terrible' had the sense of awesome rather than a reflection of the admittedly terrible and bloody events of the siege.

[3] Edward had died during Chancellor's voyage so the letters were handed to Queen Mary.

never heard of again. The *Philip and Mary* survived and successfully wintered in Trondheim, arriving in London the following April but Chancellor in the *Edward Bonaventure* did not attempt to enter, sailing on instead towards the Scottish coast. Sadly, Chancellor's navigational skills couldn't prevent him running into another sudden storm off the Scottish coast near Aberdeen and on November 7th, the ship capsized. Chancellor, along with most of his crew, was drowned but Nepaya, together with seven of the Russians plus the interpreter Robert Best, survived and managed to reach the coaSt According to Napeya's later testimony, his own life was saved by Chancellor, who drowned in attempting to carry the ambassador and his entourage to shore in the *Edward*'s boat. All of the cargo valued at £20,000 plus Napeya's papers and the Tsar's presents to Elizabeth were lost in the wreck. Despite some initial difficulties with the suspicious local Scots who tried to hold them hostage, the survivors made it to Edinburgh and eventually travelled safely on to London, arriving in March 1557. With only a few trifles saved from the wreck, it was not an auspicious start for the first Russian ambassador to England.

Chancellor had found a sea route to Russia and although in time this part of his legacy was largely superseded by travel overland through Europe, it remained for many years the only feasible route for the English. Almost as important a part of his legacy was the vast amount of information that he supplied to the Muscovy Company which formed a guide to doing business in Russia for the English merchants who followed him. In fact, it was deemed too valuable to be disseminated widely and the Company jealously guarded Chancellor's notes until 1589, when Richard Hakluyt reproduced them in the first edition of his *Principall Navigations*. The small harbour where Chancellor had first landed on the coast of the White Sea soon became known to the British as St Nicholas, after the name of the Russian monastery there. In 1584 it was officially incorporated by the Russians as the town of Kholmogory to service the growing trade with the Muscovy Company. The name of Archangel was not used until 1762 when the growing town was given equal trade rights with St Petersburg. Within a few years of Chancellor's death, the Muscovy Company had established small but growing settlements of British traders at St Nicholas and Moscow as well as starting to expand into other towns across Russia.

Chancellor was eventually succeeded as the Muscovy Company's main overseas trader by the remarkable Anthony Jenkinson who was to become a frequent visitor to Russia playing an important part in the development of relations between the two countries. Jenkinson came from a wealthy Leicestershire family and trained in his early years for a mercantile career, travelling widely in the Mediterranean region and in 1553 he reached Aleppo in Syria where he negotiated a trading licence with the Turks. In 1557, he was appointed captain-general of the Muscovy Company and he sailed to Russia with four ships carrying the returning ambassador, Osip Nepea plus a large quantity of war materials and accompanied by several experts in medicine and iron mining, skills that Russia was badly lacking. Jenkinson spent four months at the Company's northern factories before travelling on to Moscow where he was handsomely entertained by Ivan at banquets held on Christmas day and in early January.

In early 1558 the intrepid Jenkinson, accompanied by two brothers, Richard and Robert Johnson, headed south by boat, sailing down the Volga through the recently conquered Tatar lands around Kazan and then on to Astrakhan on the Caspian Sea. After a month of difficult sailing across the Caspian, his party eventually made landfall at the Mangyshlak peninsula on the north-east coast in modern-day Kazakhstan. From there they travelled south-east for four months, crossing the Tartar-held lands, enduring great hardship and danger, before arriving at the important trading city of Bukhara. Jenkinson spent the winter here but despite the fact that the city lay on the Silk Road to the east, his discussions with local caravan merchants persuaded him that the city offered little prospect for the Muscovy Company's eastern trade. In the spring of 1559 Jenkinson decided against travelling further to Persia and retraced his steps, eventually returning to Moscow in September. He brought with him six Tartar ambassadors and twenty-five Russians who had been enslaved by the Tatars that he had freed. He returned to a warm welcome from the Tsar who was happy to see him back in Moscow safely and grateful for the return of his countrymen. Although Jenkinson's first expedition had not succeeded in reaching Persia, he returned to England in the spring of 1560 with important new knowledge of the remote Caspian region and confirmation of the potential land route across Russia to Persia. His party were almost certainly the first European traders to explore this little known area and Astrakhan was soon to become an important trading base for the Muscovy Company as it strove to open up direct trade with Persia and the Ottomans. Despite the dangers and difficulties en route, Jenkinson also managed to make a map of the Russian territories they had traversed and his map was later incorporated into the atlas of Abraham Ortelius, the *Theatrum orbis terrarum*[4].

On his return to England from his first expedition, Jenkinson immediately began preparations for a second trip to Russia, with the objective of reaching Persia and then to try to find an overland route to Cathay. Carrying letters of recommendation from the new Queen Elizabeth to Ivan and the Shah of Persia, Jenkinson arrived back in Moscow in August 1561. Unfortunately, the Tsar's recent remarriage and an obstructive court official delayed his audience with Ivan until March 1562. Their eventual discussions however, were cordial and entrusted with a secret diplomatic mission by the Tsar, Jenkinson, accompanied by the Persian ambassador, travelled south once more across Russia and the Caspian Sea reaching Shirvan in the eastern Caucasus (now part of Azerbaijan). After a short stay there, he carried on into Persia, finally reaching the Persian court at Quazvin[5] in late summer. Unfortunately, a recently signed trade treaty between Persia and Turkey compelled Jenkinson to change his plans and he spent the winter months a virtual prisoner before he was allowed to return to Shirvan where he successfully negotiated favourable terms for English merchants. He reached Moscow on 20 August 1563 and soon afterwards delivered diplomatic messages from the rulers of Shirvan and nearby Georgia to

---

[4] Written by Abraham Ortelius and engraved by the Englishman Nicholas Reynolds, it was originally printed in Antwerp in May 1570 and is considered to be the first true modern atlas.

[5] Quazvin, located some 100 miles north of Tehran was then the Persian capital.

the Tsar who, in appreciation of the manner in which Jenkinson had discharged his tasks, granted a significant extension of trade privileges to the Muscovy Company. Jenkinson arrived back in London in July 1564, some three years after having set out in the knowledge that he had established an excellent rapport with Ivan and paved the way for the Company's trade with Persia.

In May 1565 Jenkinson petitioned to explore a north-east passage to the Far East, debating the issue with Humphrey Gilbert before the Queen and the Privy Council but without success. However, he was awarded a life annuity of £40 the following year for his services to the Crown. Shortly after, Jenkinson was sent to Russia for a third time as a special envoy to settle a dispute regarding the trading arrangements that had been made with Russia during his previous visit in 1564. Upon his arrival in June 1556, he found the situation in Russia very different from the one he had left just two years earlier. In a letter to William Cecil, Jenkinson described the country's wars with Poland and Sweden and mentioned Ivan's great cruelty towards the noblemen and gentry he suspected of plotting against him. When Jenkinson presented Ivan with Elizabeth's letter in September 1566, the Tsar, instead of responding directly to her request to reaffirm the trade privileges, wrote requesting an architect and medical experts. Unable to progress discussions regarding trade, Jenkinson had no choice but to sail back to England in October with the Tsar's new message for Elizabeth.

In the summer of 1567 he returned again to Moscow conveying Elizabeth's confirmation that she would send the experts requested by Ivan. Armed with this positive response, Jenkinson was then able to skilfully conclude a considerable extension of the trade privileges and consolidated the Muscovy Company's absolute monopoly in the White Sea area of Russia. He sailed back to England in late 1567 with secret correspondence from the Tsar for Elizabeth in which Ivan stressed his desire for a political alliance, to be mediated by Jenkinson at ambassadorial level plus a safe haven pact for both monarchs in each other's country. He also asked for men to build ships and sail them plus artillery to assist in his military campaign against the Swedes and their allies. By now Jenkinson was not only the Muscovy Company's most experienced mariner but had become a pivotal planner and researcher for the Muscovy Company as well as a trusted emissary between the English and Russian courts. Elizabeth had no wish to become involved in an alliance and side-stepped the issue when she replied to Ivan's new requests in 1568 but her letter firmly promised the offer of sanctuary should Ivan be forced to flee Russia:

'We offer that yf at anie time it so mishappe that you, Lord, our brother Emperour and great Duke, bee by anie casuall chaunce, either of secrite conspiracie or outward hostillitie, driuen to change your countries, and shall like to repaire into our Kingdome and Dominions, with the noble empresse, your wife, and youre deare Children, the Princes, we shall.... appoint you, the Emperour and great Duke, a place in our Kingdom fitt vppon your owne charges, as longe as ye shall like to remaine with vs.'

Although this clever diplomatic riposte by Elizabeth was never taken up, as the Tsar soon afterwards signed a peace treaty with his enemies, it was well received by him and helped to strengthen the position of the English in Russia. In July 1571, Jenkinson was sent back to Russia on his fourth and final expedition there. As a result of a breakdown in the reciprocal defence treaty, resulting from Thomas Randolph's abortive mission to Moscow in 1568 (see page xx), Ivan had revoked the trading privileges that Jenkinson had so successfully negotiated in 1566. Jenkinson was now appointed ambassador, replacing Randolph and sent back to Russia with the remit to reinstate the trade agreement. However, due to plague quarantines, he was held up at Kholmogory for over six months and was unable to reach Moscow until March 1572. Jenkinson wrote to William Cecil, now Lord Burghley, describing the devastating results of the plague in Russia and the attack by Crimean Tartars on Moscow in May 1571. Much of the city was burnt to the ground, resulting in many deaths, including some thirty of the Company's employees who were burnt to death in the English House. He also provided yet more evidence of atrocities perpetrated by Ivan the Terrible on his own people and the Tsar's murder of his own son. During the course of two meetings with the Tsar, Jenkinson, by hinting verbally at a political alliance without committing anything concrete to writing, brilliantly persuaded the Tsar to reinstate all the Muscovy Company's privileges. With relations restored and the English trading privileges once again agreed, Jenkinson finally left Moscow in July 1572 and returned to England – a successful culmination to a remarkable period of fifteen years at the centre of Anglo-Russian relations. Despite all his travelling, Jenkinson still found time to court and then in 1568 marry Judith Marshe, the daughter of John Marshe who was one of the original members of the Muscovy Company and an MP for London. Jenkinson retained an interest in exploration and trade matters and collaborated closely with both Martin Frobisher and Sir Humphrey Gilbert, who paid tribute to Jenkinson as '*a man of rare vertue, great travaile, and experience*'.[6] Jenkinson died at his Northamptonshire home in 1610.

As well as continuing to explore a north-east passage, the ambitious Muscovy Company was pushing more of its merchants south and east across Russia to open up new trading routes and missions were dispatched in 1565, 1568 and again in 1569, following in Jenkinson's footsteps. Despite the benefits brought by the growing new trade with Russia, the Muscovy Company's search for a north-east sea passage to the Orient continued and several new exploratory voyages were undertaken, mostly led by Steven Borough, a Devon man who had been master of the *Edward Bonaventure* on the initial journey with Chancellor in 1553. He led an expedition to Russia in 1556 in the *Serchthrift*, a relatively small ship with a crew of only eight men. Using the knowledge from Willoughby's doomed voyage, he sailed east and discovered the important Kara Strait between Novaya Zemlya and the Russian mainland which would ease significantly further progress eastwards for subsequent explorers. He made limited contact with local tribes on the mainland but found them barbarous and unfriendly and sailed on. However, by early autumn, his small ship became increasingly surrounded by ice and with his route east now completely blocked, Borough was forced to turn back and sailed south into the White Sea. He wintered near Archangel at the spot where Chancellor had originally landed and

---

[6] Sir Humphrey Gilbert, *Discourse of a Discovery for a New Passage to Cataia,* 1576.

eventually returned to England the following year. In 1558, he visited the Spanish navigation school in Seville and brought back a copy of Cortés de Albacar's *Breve Compendio* which Borough had translated and published as the *Art of Navigation* in 1561. This book became the first English manual of navigation.

In 1560 he was in charge of another expedition to Russia and these Muscovy Company trips developed into something of a family affair. Borough's younger brother, William, who had served as an ordinary seaman in the *Edward Bonaventure* on her 1553 voyage, subsequently made many voyages to Muscovy. Steven's son, Christopher Borough, wrote a description of a later expedition for the Muscovy Company from the White Sea across Russia to the Caspian Sea[7]. Borough, who was a skilled linguist, speaking fluent Russian and Persian, set out from England in June 1579 with four other senior merchants, Arthur Edwards, William Turnbull, Matthew Talboys and Peter Garrard with the objective of trading with the Persians. The group arrived at St Nicholas one month later and from there they travelled to Yaroslavl, north of Moscow and then down the Volga by boat to Astrakhan. This expedition was in fact building on an earlier mission undertaken by Edwards with three other English traders who sailed down the Volga in a Russian river boat renamed the *Grace of God* in 1568 and reached the Caspian Sea. Borough's group spent the winter in Astrakhan and, leaving Arthur Edwards and half of their goods behind, the rest set sail in May 1580 on what Borough describes as an English-built barque across the Caspian Sea. Unfortunately, Borough fails to elaborate on the intriguing fact of how this English sailing ship came to be in Astrakhan as the Caspian is landlocked. It is possible that one of the early English shipbuilding experts that Ivan requested was dispatched to build ships here, either by Ivan or the Russia Company.

After some difficult sailing in the shallow waters of the Caspian, they eventually landed a month later near Baku (the capital of modern-day Azerbaijan) which was then under the control of the Turks, not the hoped for Persians. Given the situation, they decided to trade with the Turkish Pasha of Baku, who received them favourably. Two of the group, Turnbull and Talboys, risked travelling a little further inland where they finally made contact with some Persian merchants and traded some silk before returning to Baku, together with several stragglers they found on the way, including two Spaniards who had escaped from captivity by the Barbary pirates[8] near Tunis. On returning to Astrakhan in December, they discovered that Arthur Edwards had died there from a fever during the previous year. With the arrival of spring, the party split up, some returning north in April 1581 to eventually sail home in the *William and John* laden with the proceeds of their trading and the others staying behind

---

[7] Christopher Borough, *Aduertisements and reports of the 6th voyage into the parts of Persia and Media for the Company of Merchants for the discouerie of new trades, in the yeares 1579, 1580, and 1581.*

[8] The Barbary pirates or corsairs were primarily based in Algiers and Tunis and raided for slaves around much of the Mediterranean and even up to northern Europe. It has been estimated that they captured more than one million people as slaves between the 16th and 19th centuries.

to sell what was left. Borough is thought to have stayed on in Russia for several years, visiting the various English trading houses between Astrakhan and Archangel, collecting information for a subsequent report he made to the Muscovy Company. He is known to have returned to England by March 1586 and he died the following year. Borough's nautical training enabled him to record the latitudes of various regions in which he travelled during his time in Russia and his maps are considered the first to have been written by a European with regard to the northern parts of Russia and Central Asia. His linguistic expertise also led him to bring back two Russian manuscripts which are both now at the Bodleian Library in Oxford. Borough's reports also showed that in the fifteen or so years since Chancellor returned to England with the news of his first contact with Russia, the trading tentacles of the Muscovy Company had already spread considerably across the country.

The extent of the growing wealth and ambition of the Muscovy Company is shown by the fact that while Borough was still away and his whereabouts unknown, another expedition was organized. Arthur Pet and Charles Jackman set out in 1580 commanding two vessels the *George* and the *William*, with instructions to sail through the Kara Strait discovered earlier by Steven Borough and from there to continue eastwards beyond the Obi River in western Siberia[9]. They sailed past through the Kara Strait, past the southern tip of Novaya Zemlya and reached Waigat Island on the 19th of July. While trying to push their way along its northern coast, they became increasingly closed in by late ice, which prevented any further progress. The ships became separated and for a time could only communicate with each other by beating drums or firing off muskets. They eventually managed to regroup and, roping the two ships together, they then attached themselves to an iceberg, surrounded by fields of ice and enveloped in fog. In this precarious fashion, they sat and waited for two weeks for an improvement in the weather. However, it was then mid August and Pet and Jackman rightly concluded that it was too late to try to make further progress eastwards and so turned around to make the long journey home. Pet returned safely to England but there is some dispute about the final stages of Jackman's voyage. One version claims that he wintered in a Norwegian port before sailing home in the spring when his ship with all on board was lost at sea[10]. More likely is a contemporary version by the British ambassador of the time[11] who stated Jackman and his crew were seized off the coast of Siberia and were seen by him in Moscow around 1590. Whichever version is correct, Pet and Jackman must be credited with having reached the most easterly point of the north-east passage by any Muscovy Company explorer. This was to be the last maritime expedition by the Muscovy Company to try to find a north-east route to the Orient; the financial and human costs were proving too high. They did however persist with several overland expeditions by their factors or agents based in Moscow.

---

[9] The mouth of the Obi or Ob forms the world's longest estuary and is usually ice-bound from the end of October until early June.

[10] Helen Wright, *The Great White North*, 1910.

[11] Sir Jerome Horsey, *Travels in Russia*, 1601.

Although the dream of finding a northern passage around Russia to the east began to fade with the failure of Pet and Jackman's voyage, periodic English and Dutch expeditions continued to venture north into the Arctic regions in the early 17th century, often with disastrous results. Although the focus of these voyages was on finding a northern passage, the increasingly attractive potential for whaling in the Arctic waters to the north of Norway and Russia provided an added impetus. The Muscovy Company had been granted a monopoly on whaling by Queen Elizabeth as early as 1577 but it was not until the turn of the 16th century that the Company expanded its operations to exploit the profitable northern whaling grounds, principally around Spitsbergen. In the spring of 1607, the experienced English mariner Henry Hudson was recruited by the Muscovy Company to seek a passage via the North Pole to Japan and China. He set sail with his son John and ten companions, striking due north where he believed he would find an ice-free sea. On reaching the edge of the polar ice pack, he followed it east until he arrived at the Spitsbergen archipelago but was unable to make further progress. A year later, the Company again sent Hudson to seek a north-east passage through the Barents Sea and past the islands of Novaya Zemlya but, once more, Hudson found his path blocked by ice and he returned to England.

In April 1609 Hudson made a final attempt to find a north-east passage though this time in the employ of the Dutch East India Company. He sailed in the *Half Moon* from Holland but strong headwinds and storms blocked his path. Whilst in Amsterdam, Hudson had heard reports of possible routes to the East around North America and now decided to change his plans and sail westwards reaching the Atlantic coast of America where he explored the area around what would become New York and the river that bears his name. That same year Sir Thomas Smith set out from England in the *Amity* to search for a polar passage but, like Hudson, he was unable to progress past Spitsbergen due to the density of the ice pack. Over the next decade the Muscovy Company sent a number of expeditions into the Arctic region to search for a northern passage and hunt for walrus and whales. In 1610 Jonas Poole sailed north in the *Amity* to Spitsbergen where he spent three months exploring the west coast, hunting walrus and collecting blubber from beached whales. He returned north on two subsequent voyages in 1611 and 1612 and arrived back in London after the latter voyage, his ships laden with 180 tons of whale oil. His success was followed up with further expeditions sent north by the Muscovy Company under Robert Fotherby as well as the Dutch. In 1634 a Dutch ship was sent to Spitsbergen in an attempt to establish a whaling base and seven unfortunate men were landed and left to overwinter there. Two of the party were English – Andrew Johnson from Middlesbrough and Adrian Johnson, possibly a relative then living in Delft in Holland. When Dutch ships returned the following year, the whole party was found dead in their hut. A collection of early traveller's tales relates the story of a group of forty-two sailors of mixed nationality whose ship became stuck in ice in May 1646 in the same region[12]. By the time a passing ship found the wreck in September, only four men were still alive. The group had run out of food and

---

[12] John Pinkerton, *Voyages and Diverse Travels*, 1811

these four had survived by eating a leather belt that they had cut up and shared a few inches at a time. Despite the best efforts of the rescuing ship's crew, three of them died soon after on board and only one, an Englishman, finally made it back home.

Relations between England, the Muscovy Company and Russia continued to develop and improve through the first half of the 17th century, although there were distinct ups and downs. Predictably, most of the problems were in one way or another about money. As trade with Russia grew and the number of merchants involved increased, there were various disputes about payments and debts. Much of this involved merchants dealing independently outside the structures of the Company or stealing from each other. As this was the age of lawless Elizabethan buccaneers, it's not surprising that some English traders tried to break the Company's monopoly and operate on their own account, believing they would be beyond the reach of any law. There were also problems with Ivan, who at one stage decided to try to make money by trading himself and insisting that the Company should give priority to his goods over their own. During the reign of Ivan, various accusations, claims and counter-claims were made in letters exchanged between the Company and the Russian or English courts but, although these caused some temporary diplomatic rifts, they were generally eventually resolved. There were clearly good relations between Charles I and Tsar Alexis as Charles sent English troops to fight with the Russians under Colonel Sanderson in their 1632 war against the Poles (see Chapter II) and Tsar Alexis sent money and corn to help Charles during his struggle with the Parliamentarians. However, when news of the arrest and execution of Charles I reached the Russian court, Alexis was horrified. As an absolute monarch, his views on the actions and religious beliefs of the English Parliamentarians were predictable and understandable. Diplomatic relations were broken off and in 1646 he expelled all English merchants from Russia. These outward manifestations of the Tsar's feelings about the events in England perhaps conveniently masked an underlying change that had been going on for some years in Russia. The English success in its trade with Russia had provoked an increasing interest on the part of Dutch merchants who were becoming a growing force on the international scene. The Muscovy Company found the Dutch increasingly snapping at their heels and by a mixture of offering the Russians higher prices for their goods and payment of customs dues plus some dubious dealings with Russian officials, the Dutch had taken an important slice of the market by the mid 1600s. Also, there was growing opposition on the part of Russian merchants to the favoured position of the Muscovy Company. Thus Alexis' expulsion of the English was probably driven as much by commercial opportunism as by his disgust with the new English Puritan government.

With the restoration of Charles II to the English throne in 1660, Anglo-Russian relations resumed and correspondence between the two rulers indicated a mutual respect and warmth of feelings towards each other. The Muscovy Company was once again welcomed back to trade in Russia and, soon after, the Company reorganized its structure and became more commonly known as The Russia Company. Although it continued to enjoy important privileges regarding taxes and duties and officially retained its monopoly over English trade with

Russia, it was unable to recover its former dominant position in the Russian market. In 1698 the Company lost its privileged position as a result of domestic political opposition stirred up by other British merchants envious of the Company's trade rights. During the 16th and 17th centuries, the main Muscovy Company trade was initially English woollen cloth for Russian furs, timber and tallow. Due to its high quality and cost, the market for English cloth was largely limited to the Russian court and richer segments of society. Over time, the exports from Russia expanded to include wax, tar, leather and hemp as well as grain. Hemp became particularly important to meet the needs of the growing British navy and shipbuilding industry. The Russia Company soon set up its own rope works near Archangel as it was more economical to export Russian hemp in a processed form. Tobacco, metals such as iron, copper and lead plus manufactured metal products, especially armaments of all kinds, were exported back from England in exchange. Russian caviar, which had already become a sought after delicacy, was also exported by the Company to Italian ports and the Ottoman Empire. In 1717, the Company relocated its Russian headquarters from Moscow to Archangel and in 1723 it changed again to the new Russian capital of St Petersburg. Its individual agents across the country were called factors and the term 'British Factory' came to be used for the large group of British merchants in St Petersburg. During the 19th century it maintained trading posts in Moscow, Archangel and Kronstadt as well as the headquarters in St Petersburg and continued in existence until the Bolshevik revolution in 1917, since when it has operated mainly as a charity.

The remarkable exploits and achievements of Chancellor and Borough stand comparison with their more famous Elizabethan compatriots, Drake and Raleigh. By establishing a maritime route to Russia and developing the ensuing trade monopoly, they laid the foundations for Britain to eventually build the strongest navy in the world. Without the Royal Navy, the subsequent British Empire would not have been possible. However, these English explorers were not the first Europeans to visit Russia, neither were they the first to arrive from what we now call the British Isles. That honour probably belongs to an early member of the Scottish Bruce family called Rognvald Brusason. Born around 1010, he was the son of Brusi Sigurdsson, then the Earl of Orkney[13] whose mother was Scottish, possibly a daughter of Malcolm II. As a child, Rognvald was taken by his father to Norway where he remained for many years under the protection of King Olaf. Following the overthrow of Olaf in 1031, Rognvald went into exile with Olaf's brother, Harald Hardrada, arriving at Kiev in Rus where they served in the army of Yaroslav I, the Grand Prince of the Rus. Rognvald returned to Norway in 1035 and soon after, went back to Orkney as Earl where he died in 1046. Brusason was soon followed by another British prince. When the English king, Edmund Ironside lost his throne to King Canute in 1016, his son Edward fled to Europe, eventually ending up in Kiev. Now known as Edward the Exile, he married Agatha, one of the Grand Prince of Kiev's daughters and after the death of King Canute, he returned to England in

---

[13] The Orkney Islands, off the north coast of Scotland, were then part of the kingdom of Norway.

1057 but died shortly afterwards. Agatha eventually settled in Scotland where her eldest daughter, Margaret, married King Malcolm III of Scotland around the year 1070. Malcolm was the son of King Duncan, famously murdered by Macbeth.

Harald Hardrada also eventually returned to Norway, becoming king in 1047. In 1066, he invaded England but was defeated and killed at the battle of Stamford Bridge in September by King Harold's forces. However, Harold's victory was short lived, as only a few weeks later he was defeated by William the Conqueror at the Battle of Hastings. The fact that Harold had to make a forced march north to fight Hardrada at Stamford Bridge and then speedily move back south to confront the Norman invasion, all in less than three weeks, was an important factor in Harold's defeat by William. Coincidentally, Harold's defeat was to also result in the first English arrival in Russia. His daughter, Gytha, along with Harold's two sons, fled the country after their father's death in 1066 and sought the protection of their uncle, the king of Denmark. He soon married Gytha off to the son of Yaroslav I, Vladimir Monomakh, who was now the Grand Prince of Kiev. We have no record of Gytha's feelings at being packed off to faraway Rus but she stayed on for several years, having at least five children with Vladimir and two of their sons subsequently succeeded their father as Princes of Kiev. After living many years in Kievan Rus, there are two different versions of her final years. One has it that she died in 1098, having become a nun in a monastery. The other states that she left the country to take part in the First Crusade and was buried in Jerusalem. What is certain is that one of Monomakh's sons, Prince Yuri Dolgoruki, went on to become the founder of Moscow and thus the city may have been established by a half English Prince.[14]

The land of the Rus that Rognvald, Edward and Gytha went to in the 11th century was a distant and difficult place to reach, especially for those coming from the north or west of Europe. With almost six months of winter, the few roads were all but impassable and the rivers totally frozen. In the summer months, political instability and frequent wars between the various principalities and kingdoms made any journey eastwards towards Russia extremely hazardous and unpredictable. However, over the course of the next three centuries an increasing number of Europeans successfully made their way into the lands of Russia. The Germans, Scandinavians and Austrians arrived through Hungary, Poland and Lithuania and intriguingly, Sir Richard Hakluyt mentions[15] the travels of an unnamed Englishman in Tartary, Poland and Hungary in 1243. Some like Marco Polo travelled into the southern parts of what was later to become the country of Russia on their journeys farther east. These initial contacts were mostly to places around the Black Sea – Tartary (Ukraine), Georgia and Azerbaijan. But the approach from the south through the Mediterranean and Black Seas became increasingly dangerous, especially after the capture of Constantinople by the Ottomans in 1453. The Black Sea region

---

[14] Since Monomakh remarried after Gytha's death, it is not certain whether or not Dolguruki was her son.

[15] Richard Hakluyt, *The principall Navigations, Voiages and Discoveries of the English Nation, 1589.*

effectively became a closed area for Europeans as most of the coastal areas were then held by the Turks and their vassals, the Tatars. In addition, for those attempting to cross the Mediterranean, there was the very real threat of being captured and sold into slavery by the Barbary pirates based in North Africa. This partly explains the prolonged search by the Muscovy Company for a navigable northern route to Russia and beyond into Persia and the near east. The easier and more obvious route for a maritime nation like the British would normally have been across the Mediterranean and on into the Black Sea.

Although Chancellor's accidental 'discovery' of Russia in 1553 soon led to a mutually beneficial trading relationship, the two nations had more in common than the simple desire to trade. Both were ruled by strong monarchs. Each country sat at the outer edges of Europe, on opposite peripheries and both suffered from aggressive neighbours who were stronger militarily and more advanced culturally and economically, although England was significantly more developed than Russia. In addition, the two kingdoms shared a traditional religious distrust and hatred of Roman Catholicism. Each country was on the cusp of major territorial expansions that would turn both of them into empires and the dominant reason behind these expansions was similar – a desire to increase the nation's wealth by gaining access to important resources and especially, in England's case, controlling the resultant trade. For the English, the discovery and exploitation of a maritime route to Russia brought not only a growth in maritime knowledge and confidence but also helped develop the vision of England as a nation that extended beyond its own shores.

2

A Tartan Army

Until the Act of Union was finalised in 1707, Scotland and England (together with Wales and Ireland) were separate countries with differing political and trading attitudes so it is only right to consider the Scots initial contacts with Russia separately from the English. Although there were several Scots[16] involved in the Muscovy Company's early activities in Russia, for most of them the path to this new world in the east was different. The first recorded Scot to visit Russia was a Peter Davidson. He was a herald at the Danish Court and was sent by King John of Denmark as an envoy to Tsar Ivan III around the year 1495. King John was attempting to persuade the Russians to attack Sweden and Finland, in return for which the Danish king promised to assist Russia against Lithuania. It seems Davidson was well trusted, visiting Moscow several times over the next few years with messages for the Tsar regarding the proposed alliance.

By the time that the Muscovy Company started exploring the northern shores of Russia in search of a passage to Cathay, Scottish merchants had already spread into Germany, Estonia, Latvia and Poland in significant numbers; for example there were over 30,000 Scots living in Poland by the 17th century[17]. However, few, if any, seem to have been tempted further east into Russia. The beginnings of the Scottish colony in Russia in the sixteenth century were very different from that of the English merchants. The early Scottish arrivals did not come for trade – they were essentially adventurers and men of war. Some came willingly but the majority of the early Scots arrived in Russia in a far from voluntary manner. During the 15th and 16th centuries, Scottish mercenary soldiers (plus a much smaller number of Englishmen) played an important role in the various wars in mainland Europe, serving kings and princes in France, Sweden, Denmark, Germany, the Low Countries, Poland and Austria. Literally thousands of Scots are recorded in these European armies and they gained a reputation as tough and disciplined fighters. Over the years, several things occurred. Some of these mercenaries were captured by the Tsar's forces during the various wars between Russia, Sweden and Poland. They were then taken back to Russia where a variety of fates awaited them. Many were drafted into the Tsar's army and either sent back to fight the Poles or south to join in campaigns against the Crimean Tatars. One of these was Thomas Garne who, along with several Scots, was part of a Polish garrison that surrendered to the Russians in 1613 in what is now Belarus. He then joined the Russian army, later taking part in the battle for Smolensk in 1628 and was promoted to the rank of

---

[16] Several Scottish names such as Gordon and Logan appear in the Muscovy Company's early papers.
[17] Eric Richards, *Britannia's children: emigration from England, Scotland, Wales and Ireland*, 2004

colonel. Others were imprisoned in Moscow and it seems some were sent to various towns across Russia and set to work. Reports written by the Muscovy Company's traders during the 17th century confirm the enforced presence in Russia of these unfortunate men, often living in quite miserable conditions. Although some eventually made their way home, many remained in Russia until they died. A few of them married local women and had children such as Garne but the subsequent fate of their families is unknown.

Another involuntary early military visitor to Russia was the English adventurer John Smith who left his home in Lincolnshire at the age of sixteen and fought as a mercenary in the French and Dutch armies before joining the Austrian forces for several years. In 1602, he found himself fighting the Tatars in Wallachia (now part of Romania) and after being wounded, was captured and sold as a slave being sent initially to Constantinople and then to the Crimea. After several months there, he was able to escape and made his way up the Don River, still in chains, until he reached a Russian military outpost. There, the Russian commander gladly removed his fellow Christian's iron collar and gave him letters of introduction to assist his journey across Russia and Poland. Following various adventures, he eventually arrived back in England in 1604. Smith subsequently joined the London Virginia Company and sailed to the New World to help found the first English colony at Jamestown in 1607. There, he achieved legendary fame when, after capture by the local Indians, his life was allegedly saved by the chief's young daughter, Pocohantas.

A few of the more adventurous or foolhardy Scottish soldiers drifted eastwards and voluntarily joined the Russian army such as David Gilbert and Richard Dunbar. They entered the service of Tsar Dmitry II in the early 1600s and formed part of a royal guard of several hundred British soldiers. One of the earliest recorded Scottish volunteer adventurers in Russia was John Carmichael, who joined the army of Ivan IV. Carmichael, in command of 5,000 men, greatly distinguished himself at the siege of the city of Pskov by Stephen, King of Poland. In 1558 Russia endeavoured to open up a foothold on the Baltic Sea in the region of present day Estonia and Latvia. This resulted in the prolonged Livonian War that involved at different times, Sweden, Denmark, Norway, Poland and Lithuania as Russia's adversaries. Although initially successful, the Russians were eventually forced into retreat, losing their Baltic lands and they fell back on Pskov, then the second largest city in Muscovy. A 70,000 strong Polish army led by the Polish king arrived to lay siege to the city in 1581. For five months the Polish forces strove to capture the city but were continually repulsed, thanks in large part to the efforts of Carmichael, who led an important part of the Russian defensive troops. In 1582, the Polish army withdrew and a peace treaty was eventually signed. John Carmichael was made governor of the city in recognition of his role in defeating the siege but he was not the only Scottish soldier to achieve this elevated status in Russia as we will soon see. There is no record of how long he remained in Pskov or his subsequent life.

As relations between the Russian court and the Stewarts in Scotland gradually developed in the 17th century, records show an increasing number of Scottish volunteer soldiers in Russia's armies. Indeed, as the century progressed, the Scots become so numerous that the list almost resembles a roll-call of the

Scottish clans and it is impossible to tell all their stories in a book of this nature. Some of them were to achieve spectacular victories for the Russians and rose to high office, becoming generals and governors. Between 1650 and 1700, there were fifteen Russian generals of Scottish descent and two (George Ogilvie and James Bruce) attained the highest rank of field marshal. In 1624 there were around 450 foreign officers in Russia[18], mostly Poles and Germans but including several Scots as well as a couple of English officers such as Fox and Sanderson. The latter led the English forces sent over by Charles I to assist the Russians in their war with Poland in 1632, referred to in Chapter I. Sanderson was joined in this campaign in 1633 by Sir Alexander Leslie and a Captain James Forbes who between them had recruited several hundred Scottish mercenaries for service in Russia. The fact that these men had been recruited for the Tsar's army at the request of King Charles shows the close relationship that existed then between England and Russia. Despite this intervention by British forces (along with many other foreign mercenaries), Tsar Michael's numerically superior army proved no match for the Polish-Lithuanian troops and was defeated at the battle for Smolensk in 1634. Many of the foreigners subsequently deserted the Russian cause and joined the Poles but Leslie stayed on in Russia for the rest of his life, fighting several campaigns in the Tsar's forces. He was later promoted to the rank of general when his pay was apparently four times that of Russian officers[19], a situation that was to become very common as more foreign mercenaries arrived in Russia. Leslie married a Russian and had a son called Theodorus and eventually became governor of Smolensk when the city was finally taken by the Russians in 1654, an exceptional honour at the time for a foreigner. He died in Russia in 1661 at the great age of ninety-five. Two other Leslies are recorded as officers in the Russian army at much the same time, as well as a George Leslie, an official for the Muscovy Company in Archangel. Interestingly, in the mid 17th century there were five generals of the Leslie clan commanding the armies of four different nations – Scotland, Germany, Sweden, and Russia.

Paul Menzies or Menesius as he later became known in Russia was born in 1637 and left Scotland as an impecunious youngest son to seek a living overseas. A staunch Catholic, he followed the path of many Scots before him and went to Poland where he joined the army around 1655. After fighting in several campaigns, he defected to the Russian army in 1660, where he was made an officer and later married a Russian woman. Menzies was fortunate to develop a friendship with a Russian officer in the Tsar's Guard, who became the father-in-law of Tsar Alexis in 1671 and this, together with the support of General Gordon (see below) was to give Menzies a favoured position at court. In 1672, when the Russians were seeking European allies to fight the Ottomans, Menzies was chosen as an ambassador and sent to Germany, Austria and Italy. During the visit to Rome in 1673, Menzies was charged with delivering a letter from the Tsar to the Pope requesting his help against the Moslem Ottomans. He was also asked to obtain the Pope's formal recognition of Alexis' title of Tsar, as at that

---

[18] Robert Bain, *The First Romanovs*, 1905

[19] William Tooke – *A View of the Russian Empire*, 1799

time Rome only recognised Alexis as the Grand Duke of Muscovy who had conferred the title of Tsar upon himself. However, the Pope's blessing of this elevation was not obtained because an audience was refused when Menzies refused to kiss the Pope's foot. Despite this failure, on his return to Russia in 1674 he was promoted to the rank of major-general and became a tutor on military matters to the young Peter I. In the same year, along with several fellow Scottish soldiers in the Tsar's service, Menzies obtained the Tsar's permission to open a Catholic church in Moscow. This was the first Catholic church to be built in Moscow since 1054 when the Orthodox and Catholic churches split. Menzies remained in Russia until his death some twenty years later in 1694.

There were two primary factors behind this surge in migration of the Scots and English into Europe and Russia. First, the protracted English civil war from 1642 to 1651 produced large numbers of men trained in the latest techniques of battle. With the ultimate success of the Parliamentarians under Cromwell, many of the defeated Royalist soldiers now sought (or were obliged to seek) opportunities and adventure elsewhere. Second, the extreme weather experienced in Scotland during the so-called Little Ice Age in the latter part of the 17th century. Harvests failed year after year and the sea was too cold for the traditional cod fishing. Desperate and starving, Scots fled their homes in huge numbers. The almost constant wars in continental Europe provided an outlet for their skills and ambitions and their availability coincided with important changes in the Russian army. During the wars with Poland, Tsar Alexis, who succeeded to the Russian throne in 1645, had realised the need to reorganise his infantry regiments on the European plan and in so doing, he gave the command of some of them to foreign officers, mostly Germans and Scots. One such was a General William Drummond who commanded the regiment of the First Moskovsky around 1648. He returned to England briefly to fight for the Royalists in the final battle of the Civil War at Worcester in September 1651 where the Parliamentarian's New Model Army defeated the mainly Scottish Royalist forces of King Charles II. After the defeat, Drummond escaped and went back to Russia, again serving in the Tsar's army and became the second Scottish governor of Smolensk, succeeding Sir Alexander Leslie until returning to Britain in 1655. Tsar Alexis' experiences with these foreign officers were very positive; they were more skilled than the Russians and proved to be disciplined and brave in battle. As a result, Tsar Alexis invited other Scots to join his reorganised army and some three thousand[20] of them arrived in Russia after the defeat of Charles I. They were very well looked after with an area of land assigned them close to Moscow where they built their own homes, many settling to become part of the growing city and forming the first real Scottish community in Russia.

One of these three thousand Scots who came to fight for the Tsar was Sir Thomas Dalziel who was born in Linlithglow, Scotland in 1599. As a fervent Royalist, he served in the army of King Charles I in Ulster as a colonel and had also fought in the battle of Worcester but he was captured by the Roundheads. He was imprisoned in the Tower of London but soon escaped and went into

---

[20] General Baron Manstein, *Memoirs of Russia*, 1773

hiding. When he heard the news of the execution of King Charles, Dalziel vowed never to shave again and eventually grew a beard that reached almost to his waist. In 1654 he took part in the unsuccessful Highland Rebellion, after which he fled for his life, finally ending up in Moscow. Here he was soon able to obtain an officer's rank in a Cossack regiment at the age of fifty-three, thanks to a letter of recommendation from Charles II to the Tsar. His subsequent ferocity in battles against the Turks and Tatars earned him the nicknames 'the Muscovite Devil' and 'the Muscovy Beast' and he gained promotion to the rank of general. These southern campaigns were bitterly fought with no quarter ever asked for, nor given on either side. Anyone unfortunate enough to be taken prisoner was either shot, beheaded, impaled or burnt to death over slow fires. The brutality and cruelty on both sides experienced by Dalziel were almost beyond imagination. With the restoration of the monarchy in 1666, Dalziel asked the Tsar for his release from service which was granted with great reluctance as the Tsar was sorry to lose such a faithful commander. On Dalziel's return home, he was made commander-in-chief of the forces of King Charles II in Scotland where he founded a new regiment called the Scots Greys. After eleven years of brutal fighting against the Turkish and Tatar hordes, it seems that on his return to Britain, he had lost none of his vigour and ferocity, cruelly and ruthlessly suppressing the Covenanter rebellions in Scotland. Dalziel is reputed to have introduced the thumbscrew, a Russian invention, into Britain during this campaign. Like many other returning Scots, Dalziel held a deep-seated resentment against those who had killed the king and forced them into long exile. He later became the representative for Linlithgow in the Scottish Parliament following the accession of James II but died shortly afterwards, in 1685.

One of the most noteworthy and influential Scots to go to Russia was James Bruce, from Stirlingshire, who was to become the founder of the Russian branch of the Bruce clan. During the period of repression by Cromwell in Scotland, James together with his cousin John decided to leave Scotland and try their luck overseas. They made their way to the port of Leith in 1647 and on finding ships that would soon set sail for the Baltic, they agreed to go there. But as luck would have it, the masters of two of these ships had the same surname and the two cousins ended up boarding different ships, one bound for Germany and the other for Russia. John Bruce arrived in Koningsberg and joined the army there while James ended up in Russia and went into the Tsar's army, later serving with distinction in an artillery regiment. John Bruce settled in Germany and James in Russia and sadly, the two cousins were never to meet again. James married and had a son William in Moscow and his son James Daniel, followed in his grandfather's footsteps, eventually becoming a count and field marshal under Peter the Great. We will learn more about James Daniel Bruce in the next chapter.

Although at times of war Russia was usually able to mobilise a larger army than any of its European neighbours due to its larger population, the country lost most of the battles. Prior to the arrival of men like Drummond, Dalziel and Ogilvy, the Russian troops were relatively poorly equipped, ill-disciplined and badly led. For the past one hundred years, the principal fighting unit in the

Russian army had been the Strelitzes, originally formed by Ivan IV in his capture of Kazan in 1552 and they continued to form the bulk of the professional Russian army through the 17th century. Numbering over 50,000 men, they provided an elite bodyguard to the Tsar as well as performing police and security duties in Moscow plus garrison duty in border towns. Until the early 1700s, few of them had firearms, most were equipped with a variety of bows, spears or battle-axes with the rest having only wooden clubs. They were also badly or irregularly paid which frequently led to corruption, robbery and extortion by the soldiers. The achievements of foreign officers, although impressive, did not fundamentally alter the structure and military capability of the Russian army. The necessary improvements would only finally be introduced under a new Tsar, Peter I or Peter the Great. Through regular training and military exercises, the Scottish (and other foreign) officers imported by the Tsar gradually brought discipline and improved military capability to the Russian troops, laying the foundations for an army that later, with some improvements in pay and equipment, would compete more effectively with the rest of Europe.

Inevitably, there were several Scots from the numerous Gordon clan that went to Russia as mercenaries including Captain William Gordon and Lieutenant-Colonel Alexander Gordon who served with Colonel Thomas Garne mentioned earlier. The most famous however, was Patrick Gordon who was born into a fervent Catholic family in Aberdeenshire in 1635. At the age of fifteen, his parents sent him to a Jesuit college in Danzig to further his studies, but after graduating he decided he wanted a more active life. He then travelled around on foot in several parts of what is today Germany, ultimately ending up in Hamburg where he enlisted in the Swedish army of Charles X in 1655. In the course of the next five years he fought first in the Swedish army and then subsequently joined the Poles and was taken prisoner by both armies. While fighting for the Poles against the Russians in 1660, Gordon was wounded and having heard of the Stuart restoration, he decided to return to Scotland but was unable to obtain military employment there. He returned to Europe and in 1661 joined the Russian army of Tsar Alexis I. He seems to have formed a good relationship with the Tsar as he was sent on a diplomatic mission to the English king, Charles II in 1665.

Gordon played an important role in reviving Anglo-Russian relations, especially in the area of trade which had been minimal since the expulsion of the English merchants from the Russia in 1649. He advised both the English government and the Russia Company on strategies to adopt in negotiations with Russia. On his return to Russia he served with distinction in several wars against the Turks and Tatars in southern Russia. Although Gordon initially disliked Russian military service, complaining of the corruption and venality of Russian officials, he proved to be a talented soldier and received regular promotions. He became a major-general in 1678; he was appointed to the high command at Kiev in 1679 and in 1683 was made a lieutenant-general. In 1687 and 1689 he took part as quartermaster-general in campaigns against the Tatars in Crimea after which he was promoted to a full general. During the absence of Peter the Great from Russia in 1698, Gordon commanded loyal troops to suppress the revolt of the Strelitzes, effectively deciding events in Peter's favour.[21] As a result, for the rest of his life he remained a favourite of the Tsar who made him general-in-chief and placed Gordon in command of the capital during subsequent absences.

Gordon became an important member of a tight-knit, influential group of Scotsmen who formed part of the early entourage of Peter the Great which included Paul Menzies, Peter's first military tutor, the brothers James and Robert Bruce, Dr Robert Erskine, the Tsar's physician plus Henry Farquharson, an outstanding teacher and modernizer (see page 45). Gordon took over from Menzies as Peter's teacher in matters military and naval, and lent him books and mechanical instruments. The adoption by Peter of a reverse saltire as the flag of his navy[22] and his institution the Order of St Andrew in Russia are indications of the Scottish influence. Gordon kept a diary, written in English, for the last forty years of his life, parts of which have been published, firstly in German and Russian and then in English in the mid 19th century. Towards the end of his life Gordon suffered from illness and was frequently visited by the Tsar who was with him when he died in November 1699 and is reputed to have closed Gordon's eyes with his own hands.

Gordon married while in Russia and his only daughter became the wife of a German colonel but she was left a widow a few years later when the colonel died. Around the time of her father's death she married again, this time to her father's clansman and namesake in Russian service Alexander Gordon. Alexander Gordon was born in Auchintoul, Scotland in 1669 and at the age of fourteen was sent to Paris to pursue his education. From there he joined a Scottish contingent of mercenaries raised to assist the French army with their war in Spain. He spent a year or so there and reached the rank of captain. He returned to Scotland briefly before travelling to Russia in 1693 to try his luck and soon met up with his compatriot and future father-in-law General Patrick Gordon through whom he obtained his first Russian commission as a captain. He was clearly a feisty young man as early on in his time in Russia when he was invited to a party at which several young Russian nobles were present, a fight broke out. Gordon, who felt he had been insulted by the (drunken) Russians, struck the man sitting next to him with a blow to the head immediately knocking him to the ground and in the general melee that followed Gordon severely wounded five others. News of the affair soon reached the ears of the Tsar and when summoned into Peter's presence, Gordon feared for the worst – a severe flogging or possibly exile in Siberia. But it seems Peter was so won over by Gordon's attitude and bearing during the meeting that he promptly promoted him to the rank of major, followed soon afterwards by that of lieutenant-colonel. In 1696, when only twenty-seven, he fought against the Turks in the siege of Azov on the Black Sea coast, during which he commanded 4,000 cavalry, 20,000 infantry and a large detachment of Cossacks. He fulfilled his instructions

---

[21] In 1682, the Strelitzes became involved in the succession struggle that led to the regency of Sophia but when she was replaced by Peter the Great, they revolted and were forcibly disbanded. Hundreds were executed or deported and the corps was gradually absorbed into the regular army.

[22] Peter chose blue on a white ground rather than the Scottish white on a blue background.

totally, defeating the Turks, levelling their fortifications and then marched back to Moscow. He subsequently fought in several other campaigns but was captured by the Swedes at the battle of Narva in 1700 and held prisoner in Sweden for several years. He was eventually released in exchange for a Swedish colonel held by the Russians. Soon after his return to active duty he was made a brigadier and later rose to the rank of major-general. On learning of the death of his father in 1711, Gordon resigned from the Russian army and returned to Scotland where he essentially lived a quiet life of retirement as a Scottish gentleman. In his later years he decided to write a book about the life of Peter the Great[23] which was published posthumously after Gordon's death in 1752.

Although this chapter has so far concentrated on the Scottish involvement in Russia, it is worth noting that there was also an Irish dimension. In the early 1600s there were Protestant Irish mercenaries fighting in the Swedish army and Catholics with the Poles (at least until their wages were left unpaid) during their respective wars with Russia. Like the Scots, large numbers of Irish also moved to Europe during the last half of the 17th century, following the repression of Ireland by Oliver Cromwell and the later failed Jacobite rebellion there against William of Orange in 1691. Although estimates vary, it appears that over 50,000 Irish soldiers as well as women and children left the country and this exodus became known in Ireland as 'The Flight of the Wild Geese'. The great majority were Catholic and so initially headed for Spain, France and Italy where the men were readily accepted into the respective armies. A few drifted further east to Poland and Austria and probably the most celebrated of these was Count Peter von Lacy who became one of the most successful Russian commanders of the period. During a military career that spanned half a century, Lacy claimed to have been present at a total of thirty-one campaigns, eighteen battles, and eighteen sieges.

He was actually born as Pierce Edmond Lacy in 1678 near Limerick, Ireland and at the early age of thirteen was involved in the unsuccessful Jacobite defence of Limerick against the forces of William of Orange. As part of 'The Flight of the Wild Geese' Lacy, together with his father and his brother fled to France and joined the Irish Brigade there. Following the death of both his father and brother while fighting for the French in Italy, Lacy moved on to Austria. After two years in the Austrian Army, he followed his commanding officer, Charles Eugene de Croy, into the Russian service of Peter the Great. His first experience of fighting with the Tsar's forces was in the disastrous defeat of the Russians by the Swedes at the battle Narva in 1700 in which Lacy commanded a unit of musketeers.[24] However, after this inauspicious beginning, Lacy steadily made a name for himself in several wars and despite being seriously wounded twice, he was promoted in 1706 to the rank of Colonel. In 1710 Lacy played an important part in the successful siege of Riga by Russian troops personally led by Peter the Great that resulted in Russia taking possession of the Swedish territories in Estonia and Latvia. Lacy was subsequently appointed the first

---

[23] Alexander Gordon, *The History of Peter the Great, Emperor of Russia*, 1755.

[24] The Russians avenged this defeat four years later when a larger and better-trained Russian force, partly under the command of the Scot Field Marshal George Ogilvy, captured the town.

Russian commander of Riga Castle. This did not end the war with Sweden however and in 1719, Lacy launched an attack by sea landing near Umea in northern Sweden with 5,000 infantry and 370 cavalry, laying waste to a large part of the region and paving the way for an eventual peace treaty in 1721.

With his reputation soaring, Lacy was soon promoted to a general, becoming part of the Russian Ministry of Defence in St Petersburg in 1723. Three years later, Lacy was appointed commander of all Russian troops in Livonia, the former Swedish territories and in 1729 he was appointed Governor of Riga. Under the new Empress Anna, his star continued to rise and he had reached the rank of field marshal by the outbreak of the Russo-Turkish War in 1735 during which he achieved spectacular success. In 1736 he took control of part of the southern Russian army and captured the key Black Sea fortress of Azov and in the following year his troops crossed into the Crimea, where his army, now 40,000 strong, routed the combined forces of the Turks and Tatars. Once peace had been restored, Lacy returned to his former position in Livonia where there was the potential threat of another Swedish attack. When the Russian-Swedish War broke out in 1741, he was appointed Commander-in-Chief of the Russian army as he was then the most experienced of all their generals. Lacy quickly moved into Finland (then part of Sweden) and achieved two major victories, the first at Lappeenranta in August 1741 and then near Helsinki the following year when he encircled more than 17,000 Swedes, effectively bringing the war to an end. Lacy then returned to Riga where he remained until his death in May 1751. He had earlier married an Austrian woman with whom he had two daughters and five sons, one of which Franz Moritz von Lacy, joined the Austrian army in 1743 and became an Austrian field marshal and a count of the Holy Roman Empire. Another significant Irish family that went to Russia at the same time as Lacy was part of the O'Rourke clan. They also served in the Tsar's army and one of their descendants, Joseph O'Rourke, rose to the rank of general in the 19th century. When he retired in 1849, he settled in the area of Minsk and was clearly a wealthy man, owning 20,000 acres of land as well as several villages.

When they originally left their homes in Britain, few of these Scottish and Irish émigrés would have anticipated ending up in Russia and certainly couldn't have expected the various fates that awaited them, both good and bad. The astonishing success of so many Scottish and Irish soldiers in Russia, which was largely due to their military skills, did not always go unchallenged by jealous Russian nobles and senior officers. On several occasions there were overt and covert plots and intrigues which attempted to blacken the reputations of the foreigners and have them dismissed or demoted. These schemes even extended to refusals to support them in battle, causing disaster for the Russian forces overall. However, memories of the Streltsy revolt, the foreigners' proven loyalty and their general indifference to the intrigues of Russian politics meant that they were always held in high regard by the Tsars. With the steadily rising numbers of Scottish mercenaries in eastern Europe and Russia during the 17th century, small Scottish communities gradually evolved around the garrison towns as the soldiers either brought out their wives or married locally and had children. Itinerant pedlars began to arrive, bringing goods from Scotland to sell to both the locals and the Scots. They were followed by Scottish traders and merchants, some of whom established businesses in towns around the Baltic coast buying and selling much the same goods as the English merchants of the Russia Company. Scottish fishermen also crossed the North Sea and sailed into the Baltic to fish and to trade along the coast. The history of these early British communities in Russia is now largely lost to us. Although some of these families eventually returned to their native land, those that stayed gradually adopted Russian versions of their names as they steadily merged into the local population.

3
The Age of Peter the Great

Peter the Great's rise to supreme power in Russia was not a smooth or easy one. When Feodor III died childless in 1682, his natural successor was his fifteen-year-old brother Ivan but he was sickly, half blind and deemed to be weak in the head, not fit to rule the country. Ivan's half brother, Peter, was only ten years old, so still a minor. After intense behind-the-scenes political wrangling between the various family factions, a deal was eventually struck whereby the two brothers were made joint Tsars and Ivan's elder sister, Sophie, was appointed as regent. This fractious situation, with Sophie constantly trying to side-track Peter, continued until Ivan V died in 1696, leaving Peter as the sole Tsar. With the succession problem apparently resolved, Peter and his advisors felt it would be beneficial for him to undertake a grand tour of several European countries. Peter was determined to undertake drastic reform in Russia and to lead the country, willingly or not, into the modern era and it was felt that a European tour would provide valuable information on scientific and military progress in other countries. Peter would be the first Russian monarch to leave the country in peacetime. The subsequent visit to England by a young Peter I in 1698 was another accidental, unplanned encounter between the British and the Russians, yet it was to unleash the next major invasion of Russia by the British.

A visit to England was only a possibility in the Tsar's original tour plans. The Tsar's party had travelled through Germany and on to Amsterdam in Holland where they expected to stay many months before travelling to Italy. The decision to curtail the stay in Holland and travel across the North Sea seems to have been an impromptu, last minute one resulting from a hastily organised meeting with the English king, William III, who had recently arrived in nearby in Utrecht. The two rulers got on well with each other, each side recognising the potential importance of their meeting and an invitation for Peter to visit England was quickly made and accepted. Peter fully understood Russia's urgent need to build strategic links with major European powers to balance the recent Grand Alliance between France and Russia's constant enemy, the Ottoman Empire. Peter had great respect for England which was clearly a rising power in Europe, sharing Russia's distrust of France and so he felt the English would make a useful ally. From his time studying shipbuilding in Holland, Peter had also come to recognise that the Dutch techniques were less advanced than the English ones. The importance of building a modern Russian navy and merchant fleet was paramount in his mind, so Peter was keen to explore the maritime science and technology that England seemed to possess. The fact that the English had arrived bearing a gift for Peter in the shape of a fine, twelve gun, twin-masted ship called the *Royal Transport* as an example of English design and craftsmanship no doubt helped to make the case for a visit.

For the English, the driving force behind their invitation was the desire to rebuild trading relationships which had never fully recovered after the expulsion of the Muscovy Company merchants some fifty years earlier. Although the English government supported the Muscovy Company, it was also under pressure from a new generation of aggressive entrepreneurs eager to break into the large Russian market. Of particular interest were the rapidly expanding stocks of tobacco grown in the new English colony of Virginia. For many years, the use of tobacco products had been forbidden in Russia (as in several other European countries) and in 1643 Tsar Michael had declared smoking to be a deadly sin and smokers were liable to be arrested and flogged or have their lips slit. Although this ban had been lifted in 1676, the Russian tobacco market remained largely untapped. English merchants also wanted to explore the export potential for both Scotch and Irish whiskey of which Peter was later to say '*Of all the wines of the world, Irish spirit is the best.*' England was also keen to have improved access to raw materials from Russia such as tar and hemp to meet demand from its growing shipbuilding industry.

The Tsar found the English proposals of great interest as the increase in trade would generate significant benefits for his exchequer from taxes that in turn would help finance his plan to modernise Russia and improve its military capabilities. So Peter accepted the English invitation and, leaving part of his entourage in Holland, he sailed with a small group to London, arriving in January 1698. Peter's experiences during the 105 days that he spent in England were to have a profound impact on both the Tsar and the British, as well as ultimately the rest of Europe. His visit proved to be a catalyst that would spark Peter's imagination, helping to drive forward his domestic reform agenda and it lit a long fuse that would see Russia become a true world power over the course of the 18th century. The English preoccupation with trade ensured that an agreement was quickly reached regarding the import of tobacco to Russia.[25] The deal did not go to the Russia Company but rather to a new consortium of independent merchants led by the Marquis of Carmarthen who was acting as one of Peter's hosts during his stay in England. Carmarthen made an advance payment of £12,000 for the right to import at least 10,000 barrels annually into Russia which, since the Tsar's treasury was in a desperate position at that time, swung the deal their way. Predictably, the Russia Company was furious at this outcome and they tried to obstruct it at every opportunity. Yet within two years, the deal collapsed and the Marquis of Carmarthen's consortium forfeited the contract, with a considerable loss on their hands. This trade in tobacco from the American colonies for Russian hemp and tar was an early example of England's growing international mercantilist policy that would eventually lead to its pre-eminence as a naval and trading power.

The initial plans for Peter's visit schedule – sightseeing, meetings at court, visits by the English nobility etc. – were quickly revised at his request. He was uncomfortable with the protocol of formal occasions and crowds, partly because he didn't speak English. Peter and his advisors wanted a low-key visit that

---

[25] Sourced from England's colony in Virginia, tobacco had become a major part of England's growing international trade system.

would allow him freedom to undertake at first hand his research into England's shipbuilding and scientific knowledge as well as its social and economic structures. Peter and his small group of advisors initially moved into rented lodgings near the Strand and among the early visitors was Admiral David Mitchell, who had captained *HMS York*, the ship that carried Peter on his voyage to England from Holland. As Mitchell spoke Dutch, this allowed Peter, who also spoke a little Dutch, the opportunity to converse more easily, especially regarding maritime matters. The two men had got on so well during the voyage that, at the Tsar's request, Mitchell was assigned as one of Peter's official escorts and translator during his stay in London. His other principal host was the Marquis of Carmarthen who had recently been promoted to Admiral of the Fleet and was a gifted designer of ships, having designed the *Royal Transport,* presented to Peter by William III in Holland. He had a lively personality and was also a hard drinker and these traits, together with his maritime skills, resulted in his forming a close bond with Peter. This relationship no doubt also helped Carmarthen in obtaining the tobacco deal mentioned above. From his base near the Strand, Peter was able to indulge his keen interest in science and scientific instruments by visiting the shops of the major clock and instrument makers in London where he purchased a fascinating mixture of mathematical and navigation instruments, clocks and pocket watches. He also bought a geographical clock that incorporated a thirty year almanac that cost £60 from the watchmaker John Carte on the Strand and spent £10 on carpenter's equipment, £250 on medical instruments and fifteen shillings on four books on fireworks. Many of these items were later to form the basis of the Imperial Collection in St Petersburg, some of which have survived to this day. Peter not only acquired these instruments but also spent time with some of the makers to learn how they were made as well as something of the science behind them. Peter also indulged himself by purchasing several curious souvenirs, including a crocodile and swordfish which he took back to Russia on his return and put on display.[26] The wealth of what was on offer in London astounded Peter; it surpassed what he had seen in Holland and revealed the relative backwardness of Moscow. The image of an excited child in a sweet shop comes readily to mind.

However, Peter's main reason for visiting England was his interest in British maritime technology and in particular its shipbuilding expertise. Peter wanted to compare this with what he had learnt during his stay in Holland and so, after four weeks in London, Peter and his retinue removed to Deptford so he could be close to the dockyards. With the help of Mitchell and Carmarthen, Peter was not only able to see all the latest English shipbuilding technology but also spent time working with many of the skilled craftsmen, some of whom he would subsequently hire to work for him in Russia. As well as spending time at the dockyard in Deptford, Peter also visited the Royal Navy's dockyards and its base at Portsmouth, the Royal Mint, the Royal Observatory at Greenwich, Oxford University and the Royal Society. The people that he met and the things that he observed and learnt during these visits were all to have an impact on his later actions in Russia. Peter also called on the Archbishop of Canterbury at

---

[26] Mentioned as being in Moscow in 1698 General Patrick Gordon's diaries.

Lambeth Palace, where he attended a service of communion in the Archbishop's private chapel before they breakfasted together and discussed church affairs. Peter evidently found in Anglicanism an appealing liberal quality compared to Russian Orthodoxy; he may also have been attracted by its acknowledgement of the monarch as its head and by the level of control exerted on its activities by Parliament. These experiences are thought to have played a formative role in the reforms that Peter was later to introduce and which broke the power of the Orthodox Church.

Peter's time in England quickly became a frenetic mixture of official engagements, trade negotiations, hands-on learning or observing and buying sprees interspersed by drinking bouts and high jinks at their rented house in Deptford. This was the house of diarist John Evelyn who was subsequently paid £350 in compensation by the Crown for the damage wrought by Peter and his group. This was for repairs to the building's structure, furniture and fittings, pictures, sheets and curtains as well as to Evelyn's garden where Peter had not only knocked a hole through the garden wall in order to gain direct access to the Royal Dockyard but also ruined the hedges by racing wheelbarrows through them. However, Peter's visit to England was prematurely cut short when news of a serious rebellion by the Streltsy reached him in London. Although General Gordon had already crushed the Moscow revolt, the situation was sufficiently worrying that Peter decided to return immediately. The reasons for the revolt are not entirely clear but were partly linked to poor pay and service conditions in the army as well as a possible attempt to reinstate Peter's older sister, Princess Sophie to the Russian throne[27]. Peter was so enraged by the actions of the Streltsy that he instituted savage reprisals; over 1,000 were executed, many were tortured publicly in the most gruesome fashion and the rest were sent to the provinces[28]. Peter attended some of the executions together with members of his court. He also divorced his wife, the Tsarina Eudoxia, who was suspected of complicity in the conspiracy and shut her away in a convent, together with his sister Sophia. Peter subsequently married his mistress Catherine who would ultimately succeed him as Catherine I in 1725. It is difficult to equate the harshness of Peter's actions with those of the intelligent young man so recently in London but these reprisals reflected his determination to establish his own dynasty as well as serving as an early declaration of his ruthless intent to reform Russia.

With the revolt crushed and his position as Tsar firmly established, Peter was able to commence his modernisation of Russia and the most urgent plans in his mind were building a modern navy and improving the country's scientific skills. Peter had seen in England the importance of science and maths for military success. The correct use of artillery needed a sound knowledge of angles; the building of fortifications needed an understanding of engineering and

---

[27] Sophie had been regent for several years prior to Peter's coming of age.

[28] The tortures included roasting the men over open fires, tearing their flesh out with iron hooks and crushing feet in wooden presses; the executions included being broken by the wheel and being buried alive. Many of the bodies were hung around the monastery where Sophia and Eudoxia were confined.

successful navigation required naval officers to study maths. Peter rapidly started to implement his ambitious plans and the full scale of the English involvement in these momentous changes is hard to overstate. In January 1701, the School of Navigation and Mathematics was founded in Moscow run by British teachers, initially by Henry Farquharson from Aberdeen. In the same year, similar schools were created for artillery and languages. In 1707, a School of Medicine was created and in 1712 a School of Engineering. Thirty maths schools were created in the provinces and in 1724, the year before Peter's death, a School of Science was established that was also largely staffed by foreigners. The School of Mathematics and Navigation was directly modelled on the Royal Mathematical School in London and was initially mainly staffed by lecturers recruited during Peter's visit to England.

The first principal was a twenty-five-year-old Scot called Henry Farquharson from Aberdeen. As well as a being a good teacher, Farquharson was a gifted mathematician with a strong practical streak that was to win him the respect and firm friendship of the Tsar. He was also a skilled astronomer (he was sent by Peter to Voronezh in 1709 to observe the solar eclipse) and a competent surveyor (he surveyed the highway from Moscow to St Petersburg). He was assisted by two recent graduates of the Royal Mathematical School, Stephen Gwyn aged only fifteen and Richard Grice aged seventeen. Between them they set out the curriculum for teaching navigation to every Russian naval officer for the rest of the century. Both Farquharson and Gwyn went on to become professors at the St Petersburg Naval Academy, founded by Peter in 1715 but, sadly, Grice was murdered in Moscow in 1709. The Moscow School was also the site of Russia's first astronomical observatory, established by Peter's trusted lieutenant James Bruce (see below). Graduates of these two institutions not only provided the majority of maths teachers in provincial schools but also most of the surveyors, engineers, architects, artillery officers, civil servants, clerks and officials for Peter's projects for an entire generation.

Peter was helped with implementing much of his modernisation programme by a Scotsman called James Daniel Bruce, or Jacob Bruce as he was called in Russia. Bruce, who effectively became the Tsar's right-hand man was born near Moscow in 1669 and was the eldest of two sons of William Bruce and the grandson of James Bruce who had left Scotland around 1647, referred to in the previous chapter. Close to the Tsar in age, James became a close friend and confidant of Peter and accompanied him on his grand tour of Europe. As a young soldier, he fought in both the Crimean (1687) and Azov (1695) campaigns against the Ottomans and in 1700, at the age of thirty-one, Bruce achieved the rank of major general and commanded Russian forces in the Great Northern War against Sweden. After the humiliating defeat by the Swedes at Narva in 1700, after which Peter reputedly wept, Bruce was one of the men Peter relied on to modernise his army and equipment. Bruce established foundries in Moscow and St Petersburg to manufacture new artillery pieces and he helped establish military schools at Moscow and St Petersburg to teach practical geometry, engineering and gunnery. The success of Bruce's work, along with several other foreign officers, was a major factor in the defeat of the Swedish army at the battle of Poltava in 1709 and the subsequent victories at

Narva and Vyborg. Bruce actually commanded the Russian artillery in the battle of Poltava and later that year he was awarded the Order of St Andrew for his decisive role in reforming Russia's ordnance. Bruce also invited one of his relatives, Henry James Bruce to join him in Russia, which he did in around 1710, becoming a captain of engineers. Henry had trained in Germany and became a distinguished engineer in the Tsar's army, staying in Russia until 1724 when he returned to Scotland. In 1717, James became a senator and president of the Moscow Colleges of Mines and Manufacture and later took charge of the Moscow print works plus the St Petersburg mint. As first minister plenipotentiary, Bruce negotiated and signed the Russian peace treaty with Sweden in 1721 and that same year he became a count of the Russian Empire.

Like most of Peter's close-knit group of advisors, Bruce was a man of boundless energy and broad interests and shared his time between his work for the Tsar and his many different areas of study – military, diplomatic and scientific. While Bruce was in England with Peter, he pursued several subjects, including Isaac Newton's then avant-garde philosophy of optics and gravity. On his return to Russia, Bruce enthusiastically established the first observatory in Russia in 1702 at Moscow's School of Navigation. Bruce stayed on in England after Peter's departure for Russia, spending the better part of a year there studying astronomy and mathematics and buying instruments that were to help cement his position in the Russian scientific establishment on his return. Bruce also later became a skilled instrument maker; a telescope and a speculum made by him survive in the Academy of Sciences at St Petersburg and he designed an instrument for drawing sunspots. In the early 18th century he supervised the first edition of the Russian civil calendar, which, besides astronomic information, contained an astrological forecast for 1710 through to 1821. The calendar and particularly its forecasts stirred up strong public interest and prompted numerous imitations. Although Bruce did not generate the contents, only supervising its production, the calendar became known as the Bruce Calendar. He went in for mathematics, physics, astronomy, carried out geographic research and translated academic books from German and English into Russian. Contemporaries described Bruce as a man of high intelligence, sharp wit and good memory and he was regarded as one of the best educated people in Russia at the time. His personal library containing more than 1500 volumes, largely compiled in the 1730s, became a substantial part of the Russian Academy of Sciences own library. Bruce was also the first Russian heraldist, designing not only his own coat of arms but those of several other prominent contemporary Russians. After Peter's death, Bruce retired in 1726 with the rank of field marshal and remained in Moscow until his own death in 1735. During Peter the Great's reign, James Bruce was probably the most influential and powerful man in Russia after the Tsar. It is possible that Bruce's brother Robert was appointed by Peter the Great as the first governor of St Petersburg.

As Peter's drive to modernise his country gathered pace, the numbers of skilled British craftsmen, especially shipbuilders, recruited to work in Russia rose dramatically. The situation became so serious that an Act of Parliament was passed in 1718 to try to prevent the loss of these valuable artisans to other countries. However, its effectiveness, at least as far as Russia was concerned, was limited, largely due to the very generous terms on offer from the Tsar. In 1719, Parliament had become so concerned at the loss of experienced shipbuilders and their contribution to the rapid expansion of the Russian fleet that they asked the British ambassador, James Jefferyes to look into the matter. He was instructed to contact as many of these craftsmen as possible and try to persuade them to return to Britain. In a report written in July 1719, he expressed his pessimism about his chances of success:

'These are people who have taken their all with them into this country', and 'who have . . . consequently nothing to lose in Great Britain.'

He went on to state that:

'they are come to this country with their families to seek their fortunes and have in some respects found the same, for their sallaries are considerable, two of them having 2000 rubles each p. annum, and the other three 800 each, besides presents upon occasion and other advantages . . . the respect paid to them is more than they could pretend to in any other country... on festival days they sit at the Tsar's own table, while persons of the best quality are forced to stand and wait ... in short the Tsar omits nothing that may endear himself to them or that may engage them to continue in his service for life.' [29]

Jefferyes described how the ships now being built under the direction of British craftsmen were as good as any in Europe and yet constructed at only one third the cost of a similar English ship. Significantly, he concluded ominously that:

'by teaching their people the way of building will do more damage to Great Britain than what a yearly expense of 20 times as much as the Tsar allows them will amount to.'

So who were these British shipbuilders who made such a contribution to developing the Russian navy? One of the earliest was Joseph Nye who, after working for many years at the Royal Naval dockyard in Portsmouth, set up a new shipyard with his partner, George Moore, in 1695 on the Isle of Wight. Nye obtained a commission from the Royal Navy to build a ship of the line in 1696, followed by another one in 1697. However, in the following year while working on the second ship, Nye experienced severe financial problems and was unable to pay the wages of his workers. Leaving his partner to sort out the situation, Nye fled to London, coincidentally arriving soon after the start of Peter the Great's visit. Nye's unhappy, unpaid workers discovered his whereabouts and chased after him to try to recover the wages owed to them, eventually filing a petition of bankruptcy against him. While in London, Nye must have become aware of Peter's desire to recruit British shipbuilders and, given his situation, it was probably an easy decision for Nye to quickly sign up in the Tsar's service. He received a handsome bounty of £100 from Peter while in London and in June 1698, Nye left England for Archangel. Once there, he joined up with John Deane, the only other English shipbuilder to have been recruited at that time and the two of them were sent to Peter's new dockyard at Voronezh to immediately start building warships in the English style. Deane was the son of a famous English shipwright of the time, Sir Anthony Deane who had been a master

---

[29] Arthur Macgregor, *The Tsar in England*, Ashmolean Library 2004.

shipwright at Harwich dockyard and subsequently fulfilled the same role at Portsmouth. Sir Anthony Deane was one of the first to apply scientific principles to the construction of naval vessels and he designed and built twenty-five ships for the Royal Navy. He would have been well known to the Marquis of Carmarthen who introduced Sir Anthony to the Tsar and he became an advisor to Peter on naval architecture during his stay in London. This contact undoubtedly led to the early recruitment of Sir Anthony's son, John, into the Tsar's service.

At first sight the selection of Voronezh as the initial location for Peter's new dockyards seemed strange as it is some 300 miles south of Moscow and a similar distance to the nearest point on the Azov Sea. However, this apparently odd location made sense as it was sufficiently far inland to be safe from attacks by the marauding Tatars and yet its situation on the mighty River Don would provide access to the Black Sea. Later, with the founding of St Petersburg, large naval dockyards were constructed there as well to provide a Baltic fleet. During his visit to England, Peter had quickly recognised that the English shipbuilding methods were superior to those he had seen employed in Holland. The Dutch tended to build their ships based on their own personal knowledge and preferences, using traditional techniques and "rule-of-thumb" measurements. Peter had experienced at first hand the fact that the English system was based much more on scientific principles, using carefully drawn plans with precise measurements. Any capable craftsman could construct a ship using this system and indeed Peter had been trained in this way in Deptford was able to not only build ships but also to prepare a design on paper. The English method was less reliant on the skill or personal opinions of the individual shipbuilder and so a good design was easier to replicate. For Peter, this also meant that Russian shipbuilders could be trained much more readily and work from plans prepared by his English craftsmen and Peter implemented a side by side training system almost from the start. John Deane described in a letter in 1698 how a Russian shipwright would set up a ship next to the site where an English shipbuilder was building one so that he could copy the measurements and techniques of the Englishman:

'*To give the Russians the better insight, it is usual when an English master begins a ship, to order the Russian master to set up one of the same dimensions, near at hand; and the Russian must be indulged the liberty of observing and measuring the Englishman's work*'.[30]

The system worked well and within a few years, the Russians increasingly had their own master shipwrights. Sadly however, Deane did not live to see the results of his training as he fell ill during the severe weather of his first winter and died in Moscow early in 1699.

Nye remained in Voronezh, busy building large ships of the line and in the summer of 1700 he was joined by another Hampshire shipwright, Richard Cozens. Although Cozens was younger than Nye, having been born in 1674, he was to prove equally as good at designing and building ships. Members of the Cozens family worked at the Portsmouth dockyard at the same time as Nye so

---

[30] Robert Martin, *Joseph Nye*, 2004

the two men may have known each other before they arrived in Russia. Like John Deane, Cozens was introduced by the Marquis of Carmarthen to Peter during his stay in London but declined to sign a contract to work in Russia immediately. He preferred to think the offer over but eventually agreed a contract some two years later. With the arrival of Cozens, the new Nye-Cozens partnership began to produce the finest ships in Peter's expanding fleet. Over the next couple of years they were joined by Robert Davenport (Cozens' future father-in-law) and Henry Bird as joint under-masters, together with an assistant Robert Hadley plus three apprentices, William Snellgrove, Francis Kitchen and Leonard Chapman. This key group of English shipbuilders remained in Voronezh until around January 1704, with Nye building the *Flower of War* a ship of sixty guns and the *Scorpion* before they were transferred to the nearby shipyards of Tavrov and Osereda. The rapid expansion of the Voronezh dockyards made the town the largest in southern Russia for a few years around this time. Hundreds of peasants from across the region arrived, essentially conscripted to work as labourers at the dockyard. Nye and Cozens completed fourteen ships in the southern dockyards and also laid down several more but these were later abandoned when the war with the Turks in the south came to a close following Russia's defeat by the Turks at the Battle of Azov.

In 1711 Nye and Cozens were moved north to start work in the new shipyards in the St Petersburg area, where Peter was eagerly preparing a fleet to take on the Swedish navy for mastery of the Baltic. Nye and Cozens were joined in St Petersburg by two more English shipbuilders, Browne and Ramsey and in 1721 the *Apostle Andrew* which had been built jointly by Cozens and Ramsey was launched by Peter personally. Browne and Ramsey went on to construct several ships for the Tsar in their own right. The types of ships built in this later period in the northern dockyards were much more varied than those constructed earlier in Voronezh. Although the building of ships of the line remained important, Nye also built twenty barquentines[31], a new style of ship for him, as well as several bomb-ships and frigates and even a yacht. Cozens was chosen to build Peter's new flagship the *Ingermanland*, launched at St Petersburg in 1715 and described by the Tsar as '*running faster than all other ships*' and '*one of the best sailing ships ever*'. The *Ingermanland* was later used by Peter in his role as Commander in Chief of the combined British, Danish, Dutch and Russian fleet that sailed into the Baltic in August 1716 during the Great Northern War against the Swedes.

The achievements of the British shipbuilders were recognised in Britain as early as 1715 when a British admiral, Sir John Norris, wrote to the Admiralty to complain about the Tsar's new English-built sixty-gun ships that were the equal in every way to the very best ships of the line that Britain possessed. This comment arose from first-hand knowledge as Norris had commanded a joint Anglo-Dutch fleet that was operating in the Baltic in June 1715 protecting merchant ships against the Swedes. Interestingly, when Norris arrived in the Russian-controlled port of Reval (now Tallinn in Estonia), he met Peter the Great who offered him command of the Russian navy. However, Norris refused

---

[31] A new type of ship, smaller and more manoeuvrable than ships of the line

the offer and returned to England in October. The British government finally realized that its own shipbuilders had effectively helped create for the Tsar a powerful navy that not only changed the balance of power in the Baltic but could also present a potential future threat to Britain. As a result of the pressure from the British government through Jefferys, their ambassador in Russia, Nye, Cozens and Davenport, sympathizing with Britain's concerns, initially agreed to return home, even though they were only offered half their Russian salaries. However, both Browne and Ramsey refused these terms and subsequently Nye, Cozens and Davenport all changes their minds and stayed on in Russia. Even if the Englishmen had all agreed to return home, it was probably too late, the damage had been done. Thanks to Nye, Cozens and the others, not only had a large Russian fleet already been built but a large number of Russians had received almost twenty years of instruction in the English style of shipbuilding. The foundations of an independent, domestic shipbuilding industry had now been established. By the time of Peter's death in 1825, Russia had forty-eight ships of the line and 800 smaller barques and galleys and for the first time, the new Russian Navy was able to defeat Sweden's navy under Charles XII.

Jeffreys' earlier comments were echoed in a report by another British observer who stated:

'These people ye Czar flatters and caresses as much as possible; their Salaryes are large and punctually pay'd, they eat in private with him , they Sitt at his Table in the greatest assemblies, and he hardly goes anywhere or takes any diversion but some of them accompany him; by these caresses ye Czar means to captivate their affection so as to engage them not to quit him;..."

Given this treatment, it is easy to understand why the English shipbuilders were only too happy to remain in the Tsar's service.

Although shipwrights from Holland and Italy were later hired by the Russians, Peter's appreciation of the skills of his English shipbuilders was evident from the wages they were paid. While Nye and Cozens received wages of about 1000 roubles, the highest paid Dutch shipwright was paid less than the most junior English shipwright, John Terpley. Peter spent a great deal of time at the shipyards with his English shipbuilders and a strong personal relationship developed between them, with Peter even inviting Nye and Cozens to participate in some of his infamous drinking bouts. When attending ship launches, Peter would often reserve his own table solely for them, where they would sit and talk to the exclusion of all others. Apart from such events, both Nye and Cozens seem to have led relatively quiet and inconspicuous lives, concentrating on their shipbuilding trade and never losing the favour of Peter, unlike some other foreigners. When affairs of state took Peter away from Voronezh or St Petersburg, he still kept in close touch with both of them through letters. In St Petersburg, Nye's lodgings must have been close to the dockyard as a Scottish traveller staying with Nye in 1714, recalled seeing the Tsar *'walking about the yard so early an hour & a very cold morning'*. Peter sent for Nye who rushed out and *'brought his Majesty into the house, where he stayd about half an hour'*. Peter had come to look over the ship Nye was building at this early hour because *'he wanted to give some directions about it'*. This close supervision of shipbuilding activities was characteristic of Peter's intense interest in and love of his new navy. Other indications of his close relationship with his shipbuilders was Peter's willingness to intervene on their behalf in occasional disputes and act as godfather to their children, as illustrated by the following story relating to Robert Davenport:

'Mr Davenport, an English Shipbuilder being employed in the yard about a ship, that was on the Stocks, the Czar came & ordered some alterations to be made. The Builder told him he could not do it that day, because his Wife was brought to bed, & he must go home and get the Child baptized. Well says Peter is it a boy, yes replied Mr Builder, then go directly and get the Parson & I will come and be God-father. Accordingly he came, as the custom is, Saluted the good Woman in the Straw, & made Her the usual Present of a piece of gold. The ceremony being over, the Czar asked if there was anything for dinner'.[32]

Robert Davenport, Cozens' chief assistant in Russia, was the father of Mary, Cozens' wife whom he had known since childhood and married in St Petersburg in the early 1700s. It is possible that Mary was the main reason for Cozens not accepting the Tsar's initial invitation to go to Russia, as Cozens was courting Mary at the time and probably didn't want to risk losing her by disappearing off to work in distant Russia. Cozens and Mary subsequently had six children, all born in Russia and the Cozens family grew and prospered there. In June 1723, in recognition of their services, Cozens, Nye and Browne were promoted to the rank of captain commander, which according to Peter's recently published 'Table of Ranks' also conferred on them the privileges of Russian nobility. The award of such a high honour was a clear indication of Peter's appreciation of what they had achieved as well as the high esteem which he had for them. Nye's strong links with Peter and his elevated position in Russian society was also highlighted in Peter's funeral ceremony of 1725. Noy had risen to such heights that he was given a privileged position in the funeral procession and he was one of the key people around Peter's coffin, standing next to Russia's new ruler, the Empress Catherine.

Following the death of Peter the Great, both Nye and Cozens remained in Russia, building yet more ships, some again in collaboration with Browne or Ramsey. Around 1724, Cozens was transferred to Archangel by Peter along with a team of some 150 carpenters and other workers, to assist in the construction of new Admiralty buildings. Cozens stayed in Archangel for a couple of years building four more ships before returning to St Petersburg where in 1733 he became a Russian citizen. In December 1735, having recently completed the thirty-two-gun gun frigate *Hector*, Cozens died suddenly at the age of sixty-one and was buried in the Russian Admiralty cemetery in St Petersburg. Cozens had by then completed thirty-five years of almost relentless work in Russia building ships for the Tsars. Nye had considered returning to England after Peter's death but stayed on with the encouragement and support of Catherine, Peter's successor and in 1737 he was rewarded for his long and faithful service of almost forty years as a shipbuilder with a pension of 500 roubles a year by the

---

[32] Dixon, *Britain and Russia in the Age of Peter the Great*, School of Slavonic & East European Studies, 1998.

Tsarina. However, Nye was by now sixty-eight and the combination of old age and some ill health meant that he was increasingly unable to carry out his work effectively. He requested permission from Catherine to be allowed to return to England which she reluctantly granted. He returned to Deptford, where his original encounter with Peter had set him on his long path in Russia and spent the last years of his life there with his wife. He eventually died in 1753 and was buried in St Nicholas's church, Deptford. Nye was the very first of the many English shipbuilders to be recruited by Peter and during his forty years in Russia had served as a shipbuilder but also as an instructor, advisor and friend to the Tsar. He had spent much of his working life in the company of a man who could, at one moment, be severely ruthless and authoritarian, while at other times he could be found drinking heavily with his shipwrights, ignoring ceremony, rank and propriety. Nye, Cozens and the other English shipwrights had made a massive contribution to Peter's goal of building a modern navy in Russia; they were the keel and anchor of this ambitious project.

The British not only helped build the ships for Russia's new navy, they also sailed and commanded them as well. In the same way that Russia lacked the skills to construct modern ships, they also found they lacked experienced officers to man them. The first British sailor to join the Russian Navy was probably John Deane (no relation to John Deane the shipwright mentioned earlier) who was born in Nottingham in 1679. John Deane joined Peter the Great's new Russian navy in 1714 and like many other British émigrés to Russia, he went because he had a past that he wanted to leave behind. In the autumn of 1710, Deane had been in command of the *Nottingham Galley,* a merchant ship from London bound for Boston in New England. Hit by severe storms, the fully-laden ship foundered on Boon Island, a barren rock outside the harbour of Portsmouth, New Hampshire and sank. Amazingly, the whole crew survived and landed on the island but with little more than the clothes on their backs – no food, no shelter and no means of lighting a fire. Several men died in the first few days and the remainder only survived until rescue came more than three weeks later through cannibalism. On his return to England, Deane not only had to live down the taint of this horrific tragedy but he also found himself accused of intentionally trying to wreck the ship for the insurance money. This was the scandal that he wished to escape by joining the Russian Navy.

Deane was commissioned as a lieutenant and his first command in late 1714 was a newly built fifty-gun frigate, the *Yagudil* that he was asked to sail from Archangel to the Baltic. His first voyage under the Russian flag soon brought back memories of Boon Island. The storm-filled winter journey around the North Cape proved extremely difficult and almost half the crew died before they were able to dock at Trondheim in Norway. Fortunately for Deane, his subsequent assignments proved much straightforward and over the next few years he established himself as a bold and effective officer. He captured more than twenty Swedish ships as prizes and was promoted to the rank of captain. However, at the end of 1719 he was court-martialled for losing two prize ships and demoted to a lieutenant and exiled to Kazan. The case against him was probably the result of scheming by some of his junior Russian officers who were jealous and wanted his command. At the conclusion of the war against the

Swedes, Peter the Great issued a pardon for all disgraced officers and Deane returned to England in 1722.

With little prospect of paid employment in England, he decided to use his detailed knowledge of Russian naval affairs to publish a pamphlet in 1724 entitled *A History Of The Russian Fleet During The Reign Of Peter The Great*. Deane used this to promote himself to the British government as an expert on Russian affairs and fortunately his timing proved to be good. A rupture in Anglo-Russian relations after the Great Northern War had left Britain with no ambassador in Russia and the government was concerned about its lack of intelligence. In short order, Deane found himself being appointed as commercial consul in St Petersburg but his real mission was to effectively act as a spy, gathering whatever intelligence he could, especially regarding any Jacobite activity in Russia. He returned to St Petersburg in the spring of 1725 but the Russians refused to accredit him and he was forced to leave after only sixteen days. Once back in London, he wrote two reports on the situation in Russia but was initially unable to provide any information about any possible Jacobite conspiracies there. However, during his short time in the Russian capital, he made the acquaintance of an Irish Jacobite courier and by later promising him a king's pardon and a financial reward, Deane was able to persuade the Irishman to help him. The pair were subsequently able to intercept important Jacobite correspondence and broke their codes. In 1726, Deane sailed with the British fleet that was sent to the Baltic to threaten the Russians and prepared reports on the current state of their navy. Over the next few months he also set up a network of agents to provide further information for when he returned to London. Two years later he was rewarded for his work with the post of commercial consul for the ports of Flanders in Ostend where he remained until his retirement in 1738.

The recruitment of Deane into the Russian Navy was soon followed by that of several other British sailors. In 1717, Thomas Gordon was signed up along with Captains Saunders and Hay and Lieutenants Urquhart and Serocoled. Unlike John Deane, Gordon who was born in Aberdeen in 1658 had an exemplary record as a naval officer, serving first with the Scottish Navy and after the Act of Union with the newly combined British Navy. Gordon was a Stewart loyalist and unhappy at swearing an oath of allegiance to George I and so resigned his commission in 1714. He was sympathetic to the Jacobite cause and went initially to France and then to Holland where he was recruited by the Tsar's agents. As an experienced senior officer, he soon gained promotion to the rank of rear admiral, one of three in the Russian service. In 1726 Gordon found himself confronting his former comrades when he was ordered to sea to meet a more powerful British fleet that had been sent into the Baltic. Fully recognising the limitations of his much smaller fleet, Gordon advised Catherine that an engagement with the British would be foolish and fortunately the encounter proved amicable enough with naval courtesies exchanged instead of cannon balls. In May 1727 he was promoted to admiral and in November he became Commander-in-Chief at Kronstadt from where he took part in several significant actions including commanding the Russian fleet against the French that brought about the surrender of Danzig (modern-day Gdansk) in 1734. Gordon retained his position at Kronstadt until he died there in 1741. He had two sons, one of whom became a merchant in St Petersburg and two daughters Anna and Mary. The latter married William Elmsall, the son of an English merchant in St Petersburg and their daughter went on to marry Admiral Mackenzie (see page 61). Little is known of Saunders except that he also rose quickly to the rank of rear admiral and in 1724 he married the Danish sister-in-law of Vitus Bering, who had also joined the Russian Navy and would go on in 1741 to explore eastern Siberia and the straits that were posthumously named after him.

Alongside the construction and manning of his new navy, Peter was not only anxious to survey and map his empire, especially the newly acquired territories, he also had ambitious plans for much-needed new waterways and roads. This surge in science-based activities raised a heavy demand for technical instruments that was largely met (at least in the early years) by English instrument makers. John Bradlee, for example, was recruited in June 1710 by Bruce to make instruments at the Artillery Department in Moscow at an inital annual salary of 168 roubles. He also received 100 roubles for successfully training each of two Russians in the skills of instrument making. Bradlee went on to make a number of different instruments for the Russians, including some sundials specifically ordered by Bruce. Apparently, these sundials led to a complaint by Bruce as Bradlee had calibrated them for latitude 60° whereas Bruce had specified their use at St Petersburg, which has a latitude of 59° 48′. Some of Bradlee's dials still survive in various museums in Russia, including a gunner's brass calliper in the Hermitage. Bradlee moved to St Petersburg in 1716 and remained there until his death in 1743.[33] Also of importance was the highly skilled John Rowley from London who arrived in Russia a few years after Bradlee. Several of his scientific instruments also survive in Russian museums and on one of them Rowley described himself as 'Master of Mechanics to the King'. When the Imperial Academy of Arts was set up by Catherine the Great, English-made instruments were strongly represented with items by John Rowley, Joseph Moxon, Edmund Culpeper, Richard Whitehead, Isaac Carver, John Marshall, Matthew Loft and Jonathan Sisson.

The results of Peter's visit to England were not solely military or scientific. Following in the footsteps of the British craftsmen and instrument makers that came to Russia in the 18th century a growing number of skilled British artisans, technicians and engineers began to penetrate various aspects of Russian life as we shall see in later chapters. Peter's impressions of England and its manners also quickly became apparent in areas of the Russian court and society in general. When he became Tsar, Peter decreed that all those attending court should appear in handsome clothes made after the English fashion with gold and silver trimmings for those who could afford it. He also ordered patterns for such clothing to be displayed at all the city gates of Moscow so that everyone (apart from the peasantry) could make their clothes according to the English patterns. The fact that these new rules applied equally to the ladies attending court was an

---

[33] V.L. Chenakal, John Bradlee and his Sundials, *Journal for the History of Astronomy*, Vol. 4, 1973.

early indication of a more fundamental review of the future role to be played by women in Russian society.

One of the men attracted to the opportunities in Russia under Peter the great was John Perry who has been described as *'one of those unfortunate men who, despite an apparent abundance of talent, perseverance, and even opportunity, never attain the success which fate seems to have intended for them'*.[34] His life and tragic career seem to have been marked by brief moments of success and achievement, interspersed with much longer periods of disappointment and frustrating failure. Born in 1670 in Gloucestershire, Perry's early career was in the Royal Navy where he became a captain in 1693 when still only twenty-three years old. Later the same year, he had the misfortune to be captured by two French privateers off Ireland which led to the humiliation of a court martial at which he was fined £1000 and jailed for ten years for losing his ship. Although later pardoned, his career in the Navy was finished and Perry was forced to turn his attentions towards fresh fields and he became a hydraulic engineer. His first job was building a dry dock in Flushing, Holland in 1697 but coincidentally the following year, with no new work in prospect, Perry met the Russian ambassador. He immediately recommended Perry to the Tsar and in short order he was offered a job as a hydraulic engineer in Russia with a captain's commission, a yearly salary of £300 and the promise of further substantial bonuses on completion of particular projects. With no other prospects in sight, Captain Perry, who was still only twenty-eight, seized the chance to pursue his dreams abroad and left for Russia immediately.

Perry's first Russian project was the construction of a navigable route joining the Don and Volga rivers in the south of the country, thereby providing a direct link between the landlocked Caspian and the Black Sea. Such a connection had been one of Peter's ambitions for some years and a previous attempt a few years earlier had failed miserably. The idea was typically ambitious, requiring the construction of a large number of locks and sluices along the one hundred miles of existing tributary rivers plus the excavation of a totally new canal link some three miles in length. Perry was asked to take on this enormous challenge and after drawing up some preliminary plans, he set off to survey the line of his preferred route eastwards from the Don. However, on arriving at the Volga near Astrakhan he ran into his first problem. At his initial meeting there with the region's governor and his new boss, Prince Golitsyn, Perry immediately found himself escorted to a gallows and threatened with hanging, unless he agreed to start the project there and then, exactly where it had been abandoned after the previous unsuccessful attempt. Not being a man to fall at the first hurdle, Perry managed to eventually talk the Prince into reluctantly accepting his own plan but the argument caused bad blood between the two men that was to haunt Perry for several years. As the construction work got underway, the combination of the terrain plus the Russian climate caused increasing delays and frustration for Perry. These problems were made worse by inadequate and irregular supplies of materials plus the fact that not only was he given less than half the labour force originally promised but they were totally

---

[34] Peter Putnam, *Seven Britons in Russia*, 1952

unskilled peasants. Perry struggled on until 1701, no doubt with one eye on the gallows and the other on his potential bonus, when the costs of Russia's prolonged war with Sweden meant the government could no longer finance the work. The entire project was halted and then abandoned in its partially completed condition.

Perry was then sent north to Voronezh, the shipbuilding centre on the Don created by Peter the Great, where Perry was appointed Comptroller of Russian Maritime Works. Here he was given the task of organising the refit of a fleet of fifteen ships that were only partially finished, their rotting keels left sinking into the riverbank mud. Whether these were the same ships mentioned earlier that had been abandoned by Nye and Cozens or a Russian-built fleet is unclear. However, the undaunted Perry now displayed his undoubted talent by coming up with an ingenious plan to refloat these hulks. By early 1703, he had successfully dammed the river Don, no mean achievement, so that all the ships could be refloated in one go. Then by letting out the excess water through sluices, he would be able to slowly lower the ships onto wooden support cradles built on the bank. Although Perry's concept was brilliantly simple, it unfortunately suffered from a single flaw – his reliance on the Russian workforce. When the spring floods duly arrived, Perry's men apparently ignored his instructions to keep the sluices partly open so as to enable the vast quantities of debris washed down in the flood waters to pass through. As a result, the water behind the dam filled up with sand and mud so that there was insufficient clear water to float the ships onto the cradles.

Given the constant problems and lack of success, a lesser man might have given up and returned to England. Yet Perry persevered and over the next two years he was involved in the construction of a new lock on the Don, upstream of Voronezh, to improve navigation of the river by larger ships. However, after this minor success, an apparently straightforward project to build some new dry docks on the river in 1709 was to bring Perry yet more trouble. Having surveyed and selected a suitable site for these docks, Perry's scheme was rejected in favour of that of a Russian engineer who proposed to build the docks on a poorly located sandbank. It was clear that the Russian engineer was in collusion with the owner of the sandbank who would be compensated by the government with a grant of better land elsewhere. Despite Perry's embittered protests, the foundations of the new dock were built with difficulty on the shifting sands of the river bank. The Russian shipwrights knew better however and refused to use the new dockyard but instead of being vindicated, Perry found himself accused by his commander of conspiring with the shipwrights' act of insubordination.

Perry's financial situation was now becoming increasingly precarious. Although he had been in Russia for more than ten years, he had not yet received a single salary payment other than basic living expenses. Perry's wages had persistently been withheld in a succession of evasive excuses, initially by Prince Golitsyn and later by his new commander in Voronezh, Admiral Apraxin. Despite appeals and petitions to the Tsar directly, Perry was unable to obtain any satisfaction and these only worsened his deteriorating relationship with Admiral Apraxin. The Russian's actions centred on a concern that Perry might return to England, abandoning the project as soon as he received any money. His predecessor had fled the country immediately on receipt of his first year's salary and so from the start, Golitsyn had insisted that Perry provide a bond guaranteeing his intention to remain until the canal was completed. As a foreigner, Perry had been unable to provide any satisfactory pledge and so he was effectively forced to agree to the accumulation of his salary arrears.

Perry's earlier success with raising the rotting river fleet onto cradles for repair gave him a new idea. He now proposed to store all inactive ships in specially sheds built on land in order to prevent premature decay during peacetime. Peter initially endorsed the plan but his subsequent prolonged absence during a Polish campaign prevented Perry from taking matters further so he applied for a short leave to England until some suitable work could be found for him. Not only was Perry's request immediately turned down on the basis that it was a ruse to escape his employment but he found himself accused by Apraxin of intending to pass his recently conceived idea to the British. Although Perry denied the charge, correspondence from Charles Whitworth, the British ambassador, indicated that Perry had in fact tried to contract with the British Navy for construction of such sheds. Although Perry's actions were probably motivated more by a need to generate some income rather than any disloyalty to the Russians, they simply provided Apraxin with yet further grounds for closely monitoring Perry's behaviour.

Perry's awkward and frustrating years of working for Apraxin in Voronezh were unexpectedly brought to a halt in 1711 when the Russian army was soundly beaten by the Turks and lost the port of Azov. As this was Russia's only outlet to the Black Sea, the value of the Voronezh dockyards and the projects on which Perry had been employed were largely negated. Still unpaid, he was transferred to St Petersburg to work on a major new scheme that Peter the Great was considering – a direct water link from the capital to the Volga. Such an ambitious undertaking would be considerably greater than anything Perry had so far attempted but glad to be out from under Admiral Apraxin, Perry readily accepted the task of carrying out the preliminary route survey. By the spring of 1712, Perry had completed his survey and gave his route recommendations to his new commander, Prince Menshikov who then paid him £300 for this work – Perry's very first salary. Surprisingly, given Perry's track record, the Prince now agreed to place the entire project under him but Perry, probably feeling that this was the moment to make a stand, refused to proceed until his wage arrears had been paid in full. Predictably, this intransigence on the part of Perry did not sit well with the Prince who became so incensed that he threatened to use force to make Perry comply. When the Tsar also expressed his disquiet with the situation, Perry became so alarmed for his own safety that he sought protection from the British ambassador, Charles Whitworth. A few weeks later, the penniless Perry, escorted under diplomatic immunity by Whitworth, sailed for England. After fourteen years of toil in Tsarist Russia, Perry had only received the single payment of £300.

Perry's experiences were in stark contrast to those of the English shipwrights like Nye and Cozens who were extremely well treated during much the same period in Voronezh. Their close relationships with the Tsar no doubt helped as did their success in completing the ships Peter wanted. Perry was clearly unlucky in the projects he undertook and not directly to blame for their failure. He was also not the only foreigner to encounter the Russian government's dilatory nature when it came to paying for imported skills. As with Perry, the problem was compounded by the Russians unwillingness to let the foreigners leave the country; they could neither afford to pay them nor lose their skills by letting them depart. Even a highly revered man like General Gordon suffered from this unfairness. During his forty years of service in the Russian Army, he requested permission to return home four times but each time was turned down with threats of demotion and exile to Siberia. His only success came when he was obliged to leave his wife and children behind in Russia as guarantors of his eventual return. Captain Peter Bruce, who joined the Tsar's forces in 1711, also had four requests for home leave rejected. When he finally succeeded at his fifth attempt to leave Russia after thirteen years of service, all of his possessions were seized and two years of back pay were withheld. In Perry's case, although he was clearly a skilful and determined man, it would seem that he was neither able to get the best out of the people with whom he worked nor fully appreciate the precarious situation of his employment.

Once safely back in England, Perry turned his hand to writing and in 1716 he published *The State of Russia, under the Present Czar*. This account of his years in Russia became popular and was widely read, eventually running to several editions. It was an influential book and, as a first-hand account, was long considered to be an accurate description of the situation in Russia during a fascinating period in its history. Despite errors of both fact and judgement, Perry's book remains of interest to the modern reader with its contemporary observations the country and its people. Perry also pursued his career as a hydraulics engineer, finally achieving some success when he repaired a gap in the flood defence wall on the Thames at Dagenham that was a hazard to London's important maritime trade. Over a period of five years, he designed and constructed a series of new defences able to withstand the tremendous water pressure at high tide and completed the works in 1719. With his reputation and self-esteem now somewhat restored, Perry went on to undertake various river and harbour projects across the country, eventually settling down in Spalding where he died celibate, aged sixty-three, in 1733.

4

Shipbuilding, Canals and Great Estates

After the death of Peter the Great in 1725, the manic years of transformation of Russian society and the expansion of its borders were over, at least for a time. St Petersburg was established as the country's new capital, the nation had obtained strategic outlets on the Baltic and Black Seas, a growing number of Russian scientists and technicians were emerging from the nation's new colleges and the army had been modernised, no longer needing so many foreigners to train or lead it. As a result, the number of Britons holding key positions in Russia gradually declined, especially in the armed forces. The increasing opportunities for adventure and advancement in the expanding British Empire also attracted men who might otherwise have considered going to Russia. However, the reduction in quantity was more than made up by the quality and achievements of those British military men who served in the Russian armed forces over the next few decades. In Chapter Two, we looked at the exploits of the Irish soldier Lacy, especially his campaign in the Crimea. In fact, there was a large group of British officers serving with General Lacy that helped make the Russian victories possible, including eight other generals – Douglas, Leslie, Keith, Forman, Bruce, Stuart, Johnston and Farmer as well as Colonel Ramsay, Major William M'Kenzie, Leslie's son Captain Leslie and Lieutenant Innes. This list is a remarkable panoply of talent and illustrates the continuing dependence of the Russian army on foreign, and in particular British, senior officers.

During the remainder of the 18th century, yet more talented British military men arrived in Russia, building on what had been achieved by their illustrious predecessors. In 1728, James Francis Edward Keith entered the service of the new Tsar Peter II. Born in Scotland in 1696, he joined the failed Stuart rebellion in 1718 and then fled to Spain and fought in the Irish brigade there for ten years. As Keith was not a Catholic, the potential for promotion in Spain was limited so he moved on to Russia, initially serving as an ordinary soldier in a regiment of guards. His leadership skills and valour were soon recognised and he was promoted first to the rank of lieutenant general in 1735 and then later to a full general. While in the Crimea, Keith played an important role in training and disciplining the local Cossack troops, laying the foundations of the key imperial fighting force that they were later to become. In the war between Russia and Sweden from 1741 to 1743, Keith briefly became the de facto ruler of Finland as the senior officer in charge of the occupying Russian troops. Although Keith was by then regarded as one of the ablest officers and administrators in Russian service, he was ambitious and feeling that he was undervalued he offered his services to Frederick II of Prussia in 1747, who immediately promoted Keith to a field marshal and soon after made him governor of Berlin. He died in battle in Prussia in October 1758 and was buried in Berlin.

As the 18th century progressed, the role of British military personnel in Russia steadily shifted from the army to the Tsar's navy. Having helped construct the ships, the British now took an increasingly important role in manning and leading the new Imperial Navy. Probably the most renowned Scot to serve in the Russian navy was Samuel Greig who is known as the father of the Russian navy. He was born in 1736 at Inverkeithing in Fife and joined the Royal Navy where as a lieutenant he established a strong reputation for his naval skills and passion in carrying out his duties. When the British government received a request from the Russians to send out some British officers to assist with training their navy, Greig was one of those selected. His outstanding abilities were quickly appreciated by the Russians and he gained rapid promotion to the rank of captain. He first saw major action in the Russian navy when war broke out with the Turks and in 1770 Greig was dispatched to the Mediterranean serving in a fleet under the command of Count Orlov and the Russian Admiral Spiridov. Following an indecisive encounter with a much larger Turkish fleet, the Russians pursued the Turks to their overnight anchorage in Chesma harbour which was well protected by land batteries. That evening Greig was promoted to commodore and ordered to mount a night attack with fire ships to destroy the Turkish fleet and together with another British officer, a Lieutenant Drysdale, he successfully launched the Russian fire ships[35] and annihilated the Turkish fleet. The Russians now opened fire on the shore batteries and town, reducing almost everything to rubble by the following morning. The scale of the victory was such that the Russians only lost eleven men with just minor damage to the fleet. The Turks lost eleven battleships, six frigates and over thirty small craft. As a result of this important action, Greig was immediately promoted to the rank of admiral. The vain and militarily inexperienced Count Orlov tried to minimise the contribution of the British in this engagement but he was rebuffed and forced to resign his post, returned home in disgrace at the end of the war with the Turks.

After peace was declared, Greig chose to remain in the Russian navy and put his talents and indefatigable efforts into improving the quality of the Russian navy, remodelling its code of discipline and, by personal example, infusing a modern esprit de corps throughout the service. Largely as a result of his efforts, the Russians finally achieved Peter the Great's vision of becoming one of the most formidable navies in Europe. Greig's vital contributions to the Russian navy's development were recognised by the Empress Catherine who rewarded Greig with the high rank of admiral of the Russian Empire and governor of Kronstadt, thus following in the footsteps of Gordon. Greig's achievements were also recognised in England and in 1782 he was elected a fellow of the Royal Society. However, Greig's fighting days were not yet over and in 1788 he was in action once more, this time against the Swedish navy. After an important victory over the Swedes at the Battle of Hogland in the Gulf of Finland, Greig was struck down by a violent fever and taken to the port of Tallinn. As soon as Catherine heard of his serious illness, she immediately dispatched her personal

---

[35] Two of the fire ships were also commanded by British officers, Dugdale and Mackenzie who also both became admirals in the Russia navy.

physician, Dr Rogerson (see page 81) to Tallinn to care for the nation's most revered and valuable mariner. However, despite the attentions of Rogerson, Greig died at the age of fifty-three on board his own ship in October 1788. The Russian nation went into mourning and after a magnificent funeral ceremony Admiral Greig was buried in Tallinn cathedral. Greig left behind his wife Sarah and four sons, all born in Russia. The eldest, Alexei also became an admiral in the Russian Navy and went on to have a highly successful career in his own right, becoming a Privy Councillor and Knight of all the Imperial Russian Orders. Greig's fourth son, Samuil served for a time as the Russian consul in London and married Mary Somerville, a scientist and writer who was also a distant cousin of Samuil's father. Mary and Samuil had two sons, one of whom, Woronzow Samuilovich Greig became a barrister and scientist. His grandson Samuil Alexeyvich Greig became a lieutenant general, taking part in the defence of Sevastopol against the British during the Crimea War and was later the Russian Minister of Finance from 1877 to1880.

Several other British naval officers were active in Russia at much the same time as Greig, assisting with the modernisation of the country's growing navy such as John Elphinstone and Thomas Mackenzie who were both with Greig at the battle of Chesma Bay. Elphinstone was a senior British naval officer who joined the Russian Navy as a rear admiral in 1769. He was highly experienced in commanding fire ships which served the Russians well at Chesma Bay. He returned to the Royal Navy soon after the end of the war with the Turks. Mackenzie, who was actually born in Archangel when his own father was also serving in the Russian Navy, rose to the rank of rear admiral and became commander-in-chief of the Russian Navy in the Crimea. He was responsible for establishing the new port of Sevastopol as the headquarters of the Black Sea Fleet in 1783 and was based there until his death in 1786. Mackenzie became a very wealthy man and lived in the best house in the small town and owned several farms in the Sevastopol area, one of which was probably the Mackenzie's farm in which Lord Raglan later found himself during the Crimean War. Mackenzie never forgot his Scottish roots as an inventory of his possessions made after his death included a wardrobe that held, alongside thirty coats and uniforms, a kilt and full accompanying Highland apparel. The list also showed a cellar boasting kegs of vodka and brandy, 374 bottles of wine plus 554 empty ones – he was evidently a man who enjoyed his drink. Another British officer who served in the Tsar's navy was Admiral Charles Knowles. Following a long and distinguished career in the Royal Navy, he resigned in 1770 and accepted an appointment in St Petersburg, advising on the development of the Imperial Navy during Russia's war with Turkey. Unlike Greig and Mackenzie, his role was primarily an administrative one based in St Petersburg and he returned to England in 1774.

When Knowles first arrived in Russia, he brought with him as his private secretary John Robison who was more of a scientist and engineer than an administrator. He had studied at Glasgow University where he had become friends with James Watt and they had worked together on aspects of steam engine design. The Russians soon became aware of his talents and in 1771 Robison was offered a job involving the modernising of Russia's northern dockyards. While in this role, he conceived the idea of replacing the Kronstadt yard's antique windmills with steam engines imported from Britain and Robison invited his friend James Watt to come to Russia to help him with the project. Watts refused the offer but Robison later successfully engaged the Carron Company of Glasgow to carry out the work and Charles Gascoigne and his engineer James Smeaton produced a plan to install a steam engine for draining the Kronstadt docks. Carron's chief engineer, Adam Smith, then went to Kronstadt with fourteen British workmen to do the work in 1774. Meanwhile, in 1772, Robison had been appointed inspector-general of the Imperial Sea Cadet Corps in St Petersburg with the rank of colonel. However, he held this position for less than a year, choosing to return to Scotland when he was offered a chair at Edinburgh University. He did not lose touch with Russia entirely as he was asked to take back to Scotland three of his former young cadets to study at Edinburgh University, one of whom was the son of Princess Dashkova (see page 83). Robison was paid 400 roubles a year by the Russians to look after the cadets during their three years of residence in Scotland.

The mantle of shipbuilder to the Imperial Navy then passed to another British adventurer named John Lambe Yeames who arrived in Russia around 1737. Like his father before him, Yeames was an experienced builder of warships having worked in the Royal Navy's dockyards. He was invited to Russia at the age of thirty to supervise the construction of the country's first frigates for the Baltic fleet at Archangel and later built many other ships. Yeames lived in Russia for fifty years and rose to the position of a major-general and Surveyor of the Russian Navy. He was held in great esteem by Catherine the Great and she had such confidence in his skills that she always insisted on being on board his ships when they were being launched. Yeames became the founder of an Anglo-Russian family whose direct descendants continued to live there until relatively recently[36]. The Yeames subsequently intermarried with the Wishaws (see page 239) and together they probably formed the longest continuously resident family in Russia with British roots. One of his Russian-born descendents was the famous artist William Frederick Yeames who painted *And When Did You Last See Your Father?* which was exhibited at the Royal Academy in 1878.

The Russians continued to recruit British naval officers during the 18th century such as Thomas Candler and George Hamilton, both of whom rose to the rank of vice-admiral. Candler came from Yorkshire and joined the Imperial Navy in 1788. He eventually became a knight of the Orders of St. Anne, St George and St. Vladimir. He married Jane Booker, the daughter of John Booker, the British consul at Kronstadt and the couple had six children in Russia. Hamilton entered Russian naval service in 1791, initially as a Captain in the Black Sea Fleet until he was transferred in 1801 to the Baltic Fleet. He fought against France during the Napoleonic War and during a remarkably long career of 49 years in the Russian navy, he achieved several high honours

---

[36] According to the Yeames' family history, it is possible that Yeames' wife Mary, who was born in 1718, was the natural daughter of Peter the Great, conceived when he was working in the Royal Navy dockyards.

including the award of the St George Cross. Both men died in Russia and were buried in St Petersburg.

The ending of the American War of Independence caused a glut of experienced British military men to seek alternative employment; some of them found their way to Russia and not all were as distinguished as the previous examples. One of the less reputable was Major James Semple, a Scot who had served in the British army during the American War of Independence and arrived in Russia as part of the entourage of the infamous Duchess of Kingston (see page 137). Semple was a rogue and a charlatan who, like many of his ilk, survived on his swagger and blarney and he was a fitting companion to the deceitful Duchess, who had recently rescued him from a French debtors' prison. By the time of his appearance in St Petersburg, he was already well known in England as an imposter and a swindler. After some months spent enjoying the high life in the Russian capital, he found employment in the army and in 1783 he served for a while in the Crimea during the campaign against the Turks. In his subsequent dissembling memoirs[37], Semple claimed to have been an aide-de-camp to Prince Potemkin in the Crimea, gave himself the credit for introducing changes to the design of Russian army uniforms as well as inaugurating the cropping of soldiers' hair (to reduce lice infestation) and the fixing of the bayonet only when about to charge (presumably to avoid unfortunate accidents). The real truth of Semple's claims is hard to verify as there is no indication that he ever held any senior or influential role in the Russian army. Semple returned to England in late 1784, abandoned his wife and two children leaving them destitute, took up with other women and generally reverted to his former roguish ways, moving between London and Paris. By 1786, Semple was sufficiently infamous that a book appeared about his multiple misdemeanours which became so popular it ran to at least nine editions.[38] He was eventually sentenced to transportation to Australia but in a way his luck held as he died peacefully in his sleep in 1815 a few days before he was due to sail with the transport fleet.

During the rest of the 18th century, although merchants and traders continued to form the bulk of the British presence in Moscow and increasingly in St Petersburg, their numbers were steadily supplemented by a new breed of British arrivals. As we will see later, medical men, professional people and visiting travellers or tourists steadily became more common in Russia as well as women who began to arrive in their own right rather than as wives accompanying their respective husbands. Among the merchants, probably the most celebrated during the 18th century was Jonas Hanway. Born in 1712, he was the son of a grocer and at the age of seventeen was apprenticed to a merchant in Lisbon. Some years later, having learnt something of the trade, he set up his own merchant business which he ran successfully for several years. In 1743, Hanway took the opportunity to become a partner in a business with John Dingle, one of the Russia Company's merchants in St Petersburg. It is unclear why Hanway gave up his own business and moved to Russia but the lure of

---

[37] *The Life of Major JG Semple Lisle*, 1799

[38] *Memoirs of the Northern Imposter*, 1786

adventure and the prospect of significant financial gain by working for the prestigious Russia Company were probably the key factors.

Since the early 1700s Britain's trade with Russia had expanded immensely, despite the fact that the Russia Company no longer enjoyed the special privileges originally granted by Ivan IV more than one hundred years earlier. Even though the political climate was less favourable and competition had greatly intensified, the number of British ships calling at Russian ports rose more than tenfold over the four or five ships a year in the 17th century. By the time of Hanway's arrival in Russia, the value of British trade with Russia had risen almost four times the level in 1700 and was equal to that of all other European nations combined. This growth largely came about due to the new Anglo-Russian trade treaty which was agreed in 1734. However, Hanway's initial focus was not the immediate trade between Russia and Britain but a problem that was brewing in Persia, largely caused by the activities of another English adventurer, Captain John Elton. Within a couple of months of his arrival in Russia, Hanway was selected by the Russia Company to travel to Persia to sort out the problem. In order to understand his mission, we need to step back and look at the activities of Captain Elton. In the thirty years after Chancellor's landfall at Archangel in 1593, the Russia Company's merchants had sent six expeditions across Russia to endeavour to open up trade with Persia and the countries beyond. None of these brought enduring success and over the ensuing 140 years, the dual problems of regional instability due to various wars and entrenched competition from the Turks and the East India Company, meant that the Persian dream remained exactly that. Even after the Anglo-Russian trade treaty of 1734, which gave the Russia Company new, exclusive privileges on Russian trade with Persia, the Company did nothing. All that changed however, in 1738 when an unexpected incident occurred that opened up a new chapter in the story of British commercial adventures in Russia.

Elton, like John Perry some thirty years earlier, resigned from the Royal Navy and enrolled in the Russian service with the rank of captain in 1735. He was soon dispatched on a military expedition to the eastern banks of the Volga. His mission was to construct a series of forts to secure the region and then to establish communications with the important silk trading centre of Bukhara in Uzbekistan. Although Elton failed in the latter task, his experiences in the region opened up new ideas in his mind so that by early 1738, completely dissatisfied with working for the Russians, he left the Tsar's service. He then travelled to St Petersburg where he obtained financial support from the Russia Company for his new venture – a small trading expedition to test the feasibility of opening up the trans-Caspian route. Elton duly set out from St Petersburg, accompanied by Mungo Graeme, one of the Company's merchants, and after a difficult journey south along the Volga, they reached Astrakhan from where they successfully crossed the dangerous Caspian, arriving in Persia in 1739. Elton clearly had a talent for negotiation because he won the confidence of the local potentate, Nadir Shah and returned to St Petersburg the following year with a valuable cargo of silk plus an agreement on trading rights for the British. Elton now set out another proposal for the Russia Company to exploit this excellent new opportunity which, after much debate between the Company, the British government and the Russians, was finally agreed and put into motion in late 1741. As part of the arrangement, the Russian government agreed that the Russia Company could build its own 180-ton ship for use on the Caspian but the ebullient and overconfident Elton actually had two ships constructed. It then seemed that his exotic surroundings began to cloud his judgement and fuel his imagination as he obtained the agreement of Nadir Shah to set up a Persian navy with himself in command. When the rumours reached St Petersburg that Elton was building a Persian warship on the Caspian, the alarm bells started to ring. Such a development caused great concern in the Russian government and would endanger the Russia Company's new trading arrangements. So in 1743, the Company decided to send an emissary to the buccaneering Elton to persuade him to cease his reckless action and Jonas Hanway was the man selected for this delicate task.

Hanway duly set out from St Petersburg in September 1743, travelling south at a fast pace past Moscow and then on to Astrakhan. Hanway was an observant and dedicated merchant and used his journey to take comprehensive, detailed notes on almost anything relating to trade that might be of future use[39]. The towns he passed through were described in terms of their economic activity, rivers were classified according to their navigability and Hanway even included references to the climate and its potential influence on maritime and land transport. Hanway used one of the Russia Company's new ships, the *Empress of Russia*, to sail across the Caspian. It was commanded by Captain Thomas Woodroofe, an English mariner now employed by the Company and based at Astrakhan. They arrived at the Persian port of Asterabad shortly before Christmas. Unsurprisingly, since this undertaking was being financed by the Russia Company merchants, Hanway had brought with him a supply of goods for trade but these were quickly seized by local rebels. Alone in the city, he now found himself in danger of being enslaved or murdered but through luck, perseverance and a stiff British upper lip, he eventually managed to obtain an armed guard to escort him to see Nadir Shah and Elton. Unfortunately, Elton refused to be swayed from his ambitious course of action but Hanway did succeed in recovering most of his lost goods which he then traded and reinvested in a cargo of raw silk.

He set out once again for Astrakhan in September 1744 but his troubles were not yet over and his return journey was full of incident. Due to a '*series of betrayals, a critical illness, an attack by pirates, an absurd episode in which he served as a guard for a Persian harem*' [40] plus six weeks of Russian customs and quarantine delays, Hanway didn't arrive back in St Petersburg until the following spring. Despite several entreaties from the Russia Company and the British government, Elton continued to cause mayhem in the Caspian region until 1746 when news reached St Petersburg that one of his warships had stopped a Russian merchantman for neglecting to salute the Persian flag. Understandably, the Russian government reacted by promptly cancelling the

---

[39] His notes were published in 1753 as *An Historical Account of the British Trade over the Caspian.*

[40] Peter Putnam - ibid

rights it had granted the British to the trans-Caspian trade and the Elton affair effectively terminated the Russia Company's direct trading activities with Persia. For Hanway, it seems the excitement and travails of his journey to Persia had satisfied his desire for adventure and he left Russia for good in July 1750, returning across Europe to reach England in October. The ultimate fate of the swashbuckllng Captain Elton is unknown. Unwelcome in both Russia and Britain, he presumably saw out his remaining days in the service of the Shah of Persia.

The rest of Hanway's very active life was mostly spent in London where he became well known for his book and involved in a wide range of philanthropic activities. In 1762, he was appointed a commissioner for provisioning the Royal Navy and held this office for some twenty years. He died, unmarried, on September 5th 1786. However, Hanway has one other claim to fame, that of reputedly being the first man in London to carry an umbrella. Early versions of the umbrella, essentially a waterproofed parasol, were first seen in Paris and it was Hanway who brought the concept to Britain. Although much ridiculed at the time, especially by the hackney coachmen who saw this contraption as a threat to their trade, the idea fortunately eventually caught on.

The accession of Catherine II or Catherine the Great as she became known in 1762, introduced another period of change in Russia. She took on the transforming mantle of Peter the Great and strove to build on his modernising agenda for Russia, particularly in the fields of education, medicine and administration. Although under Catherine the principle foreign influences still came from France and Germany, the British steadily assumed a greater role. The earlier influx of so many capable British officers into the service of the Russian army and navy had helped to promote British prestige in Russia as well as encouraging a wider interest in all things British. The fact that Catherine came to rely on a Scottish doctor as her personal physician and employed a Scottish lady, Countess Bruce, as a lady-in-waiting no doubt added to the standing of the British in Russia. Catherine, like Peter the Great before her, recognised the skills of the British and was keen to attract more of them to her country. A report in *The Times* in October 1786 stated:

'The greatest encouragement is held out by the Empress of Russia to settlers from this country, especially if they are artificers; the principal tradesmen, who at present do business for her Imperial Majesty and the Archduke, we are assured, by a Gentleman lately arrived from Petersburgh are either British or Irish.'

Catherine was encouraged and abetted in this strategy by her principal adviser and lover Prince Potemkin who was a leading Anglophile and directly responsible for bringing to Russia a number of British men and women. Other Anglophiles in Russia at the time included Count Nikolai Mordvinov who became an admiral in the Russian Navy, spoke fluent English and married an English woman, Henrietta Cobley. One of the first English specialists employed by Potemkin was Samuel Bentham who went on to have a varied and quite unexpected career in Russia. The young Bentham first visited Russia in 1780, aged only twenty-three. Bentham, a trained engineer and experienced shipbuilder, had high hopes of making his fortune in Russia and unusually journeyed initially to Russia's Black Sea coast before making his way north overland to St Petersburg. Born in 1757, Bentham came from a well-to-do family and his elder brother was Jeremy Bentham, the philosopher and legal reformer. Although the two brothers shared a brilliant intelligence and a driving ambition, their personalities were quite different; Jeremy who was almost twenty years older was shy and scholarly while Samuel was sociable and amorous.

When Samuel first arrived in St Petersburg in 1781, he went to visit Potemkin who at that time was probably the most influential man in Russia, a successful military leader, statesman and the lover of Catherine the Great. Potemkin was looking for talented engineers and entrepreneurs, especially Englishmen to develop the Empire and Bentham fitted the bill perfectly. As he wanted to travel and see more of Russia, Potemkin asked him to go to Siberia to carry out an analysis of its industries. Bentham spent almost twelve months on this endeavour, travelling as far as Irkutsk but soon after he returned to St Petersburg, he found his interest taken up by something quite different from industry. In early 1783 he became involved with Countess Sophia Matushkina, the attractive niece and ward of Field Marshal Prince Alexander Golitsyn, the Governor of St Petersburg. Bentham and the Countess were both roughly the same age but as Golitsyn did not approve his niece's attachment to a foreigner, they pursued their affair by a series of clandestine meetings. However, news of their relationship soon became public and Bentham's love affair with the pretty Russian countess was eagerly followed by St Petersburg's society. Far from stepping in to break up the relationship, Catherine made it known at Court that she was thoroughly enjoying the scandal. It seems Bentham was not only in love with the young Countess but also the potential benefits of her position and wealth, believing that the interest of the Empress might even be to his advantage. Although Golitsyn had banned the couple from meeting, Bentham passionately pursued the forbidden courtship in as discreet a manner as the keenly interested Russian Court would allow. But with Golitsyn's continued objection to the relationship, the affair was doomed and Catherine eventually signalled that it should end. The compromised Bentham was now obliged to seek new opportunities away from the capital.

In December 1783 Potemkin, aware of Bentham's predicament, summoned Bentham to his apartments in St Petersburg. At the meeting Potemkin offered Bentham the position of an army lieutenant-colonel at Kherson, a new port in Ukraine that was being developed by Potemkin for Russia's Black Sea fleet. Coincidentally, Bentham had seen Kherson on his initial journey round the Black Sea coast three years before. The job came with a generous salary of 1,200 roubles a year plus additional expenses and Bentham agreed to take up the offer, although his future duties were not made entirely clear. From now on, Bentham was always to be seen in his lieutenant-colonel's uniform, a green coat with scarlet lapels, scarlet waistcoat embroidered with gold lace and white breeches. As one of the most powerful and important men in Russia, Potemkin seemed to have a plethora of potential projects running through his mind at the same time, both civilian and military and Bentham was to eventually find himself intimately involved in several of these plans. The following spring,

Potemkin left St Petersburg for Moscow where Bentham joined him a few days later for the start of what was to be a six month long tour of southern Russia, visiting various projects that the Prince was working on. Bentham travelled each day in the same coach as Potemkin, a rare honour for a foreigner that illustrated the close bond that was developing between the two men. Somewhere en route, the Prince changed his mind about his earlier offer to Bentham of the position in Kherson and decided instead to send him back north to his sprawling estate at Krichev, near the border with Poland. Bentham was made the estate manager, effectively in sole control of an estate that covered more than 100 square miles, larger than any English county, with five large villages and 145 hamlets with around 14,000 male serfs. Krichev was also next to another Potemkin estate, Dubrovna, which was even larger in size. Together, the total population of these two estates according to Bentham was over 80,000.

When Bentham arrived at Krichev, he found it to be the centre of Potemkin's extensive Russian industrial empire with a brandy distillery, tannery, copper works, a large textile mill making sailcloth, a rope factory that supplied the Prince's shipyards in Kherson, a complex of greenhouses, a pottery, a shipyard and a mirror factory. This was Potemkin's imperial arsenal, his manufacturing and trading headquarters, his inland shipyard and the chief supplier of his new cities in the south. The estate lay at the centre of a booming trade network that stretched from Riga on the Baltic all the way south to the Black Sea and beyond with goods being transported along the river system. Due largely to its trading activities, Krichev was then a crossroads teeming with different nationalities including Russians, Tatars, Germans and Poles, especially Jews plus a small group of Englishmen. Bentham moved into Potemkin's own estate house but it was very basic and his new location was a far cry from the sophistication and amorous adventure that he had enjoyed in St Petersburg. However, Bentham's new duties and responsibilities were considerable, being in charge of the people, the land and all of Potemkin's production facilities. The latter were generally in poor condition and one of Bentham's first tasks was to use his engineering skills to put them in good order and improve them. He accomplished this to such good effect that after only two years, Bentham made a proposal to the Prince to divide the estate into two parts. Potemkin would retain the modernised and profitable factories and Bentham would personally take over the remainder and run them for ten years. Potemkin readily accepted and an agreement was signed in January 1786 in which Bentham took possession of the factories rent-free with a loan of 20,000 roubles as working capital to be repaid out of any profits made.

Bentham's primary role now in Krichev was to build ships of all types for Potemkin, frigates for the Navy, barges for the river trade and later a ship and luxury barges for the Empress Catherine. Bentham was largely given free rein to design and construct the various vessels as he thought, using his earlier experience in the Royal Navy dockyards in Portsmouth. Once when he did try to clarify the design of a ship by asking the Prince how many masts and guns were required, he was told: 'there might be twenty masts and one Gun if I pleased.'[41]

---

[41] Simon Sebag Montefiore – *History Today*, August 2003.

The inexperienced Bentham was more than a little confused and matters didn't improve when he was asked by Potemkin to train some of his men for service in the Navy and sent him a battalion of musketeers for the purpose. Despite being a colonel in the Russian army, Bentham had no idea how to train or command these men and his inability to speak Russian was a further barrier so when a major asked for orders on parade, Samuel replied: "*Same as yesterday.*" How was this manoeuvre to be conducted? "*As usual,*" ordered Bentham.[42]

It soon became clear that if he was to fulfil Potemkin's demands, Bentham would need to find many more skilled foreign workers to supplement the few he had already imported. Again Potemkin gave him carte blanche to recruit the experts he required on whatever terms he wanted and the Prince was especially keen to have British talent running the mills and factories in Krichev as well as his botanical gardens, dairies, breweries and shipyards across Russia. Potemkin told Bentham that he wished to create an English colony complete with its own church and privileges. Bentham managed to recruit several experts including the English landscape gardener John Ayton, nephew of the King's gardener at Kew but it was clear that in order to meet requirements, an extensive recruitment campaign was needed. This was soon organised by Bentham in conjunction with his father and brother in England and based on a series of advertisements in the British press. The Benthams recognised that they now had an opportunity to profit both from acting as middlemen in this Russian recruitment campaign as well as to engage in trade by exploiting Samuel's contacts. Over a period of several months, Jeremy Bentham and his father gradually assembled a disparate bunch of potential British skilled workers to fill the positions requested by Samuel and in June the first batch of candidates was dispatched to Russia. The advance party, mostly from Scotland and Newcastle contained gardeners, millwrights, mechanics and a Doctor John Debraw, the former apothecary of Addenbrooke's Hospital in Cambridge who had been offered the position of experimental chemist. The budget for this project seemed limitless and the necessary funds were readily supplied through Sutherland[43], Potemkin's banker in London. A month later, a second disparate group complete with dairymaids and a botanist was ready to depart and Jeremy Bentham, who was desperate to join the adventure in Russia, sailed with them from England.

The initial joy of the two brothers at seeing each other again in Krichev after some five years apart was soon marred by a mounting series of problems with the new recruits, few of whom seemed to have the skills they originally claimed. The estate became a true den of iniquity with drunkenness, frequent quarrelling, thieving and wife-swapping and the whole project rapidly assumed 'the absurdity of an eighteenth century situation comedy.'[44] This farce of comic confusion was no doubt added to by communication problems between the British and the local Russians, many of whom were Jews and only spoke

---

[42] Simon Sebag Montefiore - ibid

[43] Originally from Glasgow where his career had been distinctly unsuccessful, Sutherland became a powerful financier in Russia and was the favourite money-dealer of Empress Catherine.

[44] Simon Sebag Montefiore - ibid

German or Yiddish. One of the Newcastle workers, Beaty, who had never been abroad before, was quite amazed at the unexpected mix of people and languages in Krichev:

'I thought it a collection of the strangest sounds that ever invaded my English ears' and 'on a Market Day when I behold such an odd Medley of Faces and Dresses, I have more than once started and wondered what brought me amongst them.' [45]

Potemkin now instructed Samuel to produce thirteen yachts and twelve luxury barges in preparation for a cruise down the River Dnieper by Catherine to visit her new southern territories in the spring of 1787. Despite the problems with his labour force, Samuel not only succeeded in completing Potemkin's large order but also added a special barge of a new design that he had developed called 'the vermicular'. This was a series of six barges linked together into a single articulated floating train, over 250 feet long and propelled by 120 oars. The vermicular was successfully deployed for the visit of the Empress and must have been a spectacular sight rowing down the Dnieper. In order to test his boats, Samuel temporarily relocated to the Black Sea, leaving his brother in charge of the increasingly rebellious British gang at Krichev. Their behaviour continued to deteriorate, partly due to the management of the inexperienced Jeremy and partly because Potemkin, perhaps understandably, had not paid them yet. As the year wore on, most of the debauched recruits moved on or died, including Dr Debraw who died soon after being made a physician-general in the Russian army. Meanwhile Jeremy continued work on an idea of Samuel's – the construction of a Panopticon, an open factory built in such a way that the manager could see all his workers from one central observation point. Although this was Samuel's solution to supervising his rebellious rabble of workers at Krichev, the legal reformer in Jeremy recognised its potential value in prisons. The brothers also discussed the pursuit of their dream of becoming large landowners in the Crimea which Potemkin apparently supported by indicating a willingness to grant them land.

But suddenly in 1787 Potemkin decided to sell the Krichev estate in order to purchase even bigger estates in Poland and this marked the end of the Bentham's adventures in Krichev. Jeremy returned to England after a little over a year in Russia and the aspiration of being Crimean landowners faded. It was not the end of the association between Potemkin and Samuel who remained in the employ of the Prince in Russia and rose to yet new challenges. In 1782, Bentham travelled through Siberia to China and spent several weeks in the border town of Nerchinsk where he studied Chinese ship designs, especially those of junks. Then when war broke out with the Turks in 1787, Bentham went on to command a squadron of Potemkin's navy on the Black Sea and was decorated for his distinguished part in a decisive victory against the Turks. The following year he was sent to the Siberian border with China by Potemkin in charge of one thousand Russian troops and tasked with creating a regimental

---

[45] Simon Sebag Montefiore - ibid

school, building alliances with the Mongols and opening up trade links with Japan and Alaska.

After almost twenty years of remarkable adventure and service under Potemkin, the multi-talented Samuel finally returned to England in 1791. For the next few years he worked with his brother Jeremy in trying to promote his Panopticon concept, hiring an architect and even designing machinery for use in it. He also met his future wife, Mary Sophia Fordyce, a friend of his brother and the pair married in October 1796. In subsequent years, Samuel worked for the Admiralty, designing six innovative new ships and he was also appointed Inspector General of Naval Works at the royal dockyards. In 1805 Bentham returned to Russia, this time on government business and he stayed there for two years with his family. He chartered a whole ship to take his establishment of belongings, equipment, servants and companions. Although his government mission proved unsuccessful, while he was in Russia he was finally able to supervise the building of a *Panopticon School of Arts* in St Petersburg based on his designs originally conceived in Krichev almost twenty years earlier. Sadly, the building was later destroyed by fire. Bentham returned home permanently in 1807 and died in London in 1831.

Bentham was not the only Englishman involved at this time in the construction of docks and naval facilities for the Russians in the Black Sea region. Another was John Upton, although his reasons for going to Russia were less planned and more accidental than Bentham's. Upton was born around 1774 in Petworth in Sussex and became a capable and experienced civil engineer working on various canal, road and port projects in England in the early 19th century. However, his career took a turn for the worse in 1818 when he was dismissed from a canal project in Gloucestershire for improper procurement of construction materials. Despite this, in 1819 he managed to find employment as a surveyor on the Midlands section of the new London to Holyhead road working for Thomas Telford who seems to have had a high regard for Upton's skills. But an audit of the work on Upton's section of the road in early 1826 showed that he had defrauded the enterprise of more than £1000. It turned out that his financial improprieties went further as he was also accused of borrowing £3000 from his wife's relations which he had failed to repay and defaulting on a franchise for the Daventry post office leaving his surety to pay £300. Due to appear at Northampton Assizes in July on charges of forgery (a crime then punishable by hanging), Upton skipped bail the day of his trial and fled to London where he offered his services to the Russian embassy. Keen to recruit experienced engineers for work in Russia, Upton was immediately hired and sailed for St Petersburg where he was soon joined by his wife Mary and four sons.

The following year, he was commissioned as an engineering officer in the Russian army and sent to the Crimea where he joined a growing, eclectic mix of British expatriates, including doctors, architects, builders, missionaries and businessmen, some of whom we will encounter later. Here Upton undertook many important projects and was eventually promoted to the rank of Colonel Engineer. His largest and most important construction work was in Sevastopol where he successfully redeveloped the harbour so that it was accessible to large ships and improved the city's defences. The Grafskaya or Count's Quay had originally been constructed as a wooden dock in 1780 to provide a base for the Russian Black Sea fleet but proved inadequate. In the ensuing years, several attempts had been made by the Russians to enlarge the port but without success. By 1846, Upton had not only designed and built an impressive new stone quay and dry docks but he had also designed the water supply and road layout as well as many other features around the harbour and in the town of Sevastopol itself. This project took over twenty years to complete and at one stage, Upton had more than 30,000 men working for him.[46]

Upton also worked in Odessa where, in 1841, he completed the city's most recognizable landmark, a grand sandstone staircase leading down from the centre to the port below. Designed by Russian architects, the steps were built from stone imported from Trieste and cost an extravagant 800,000 roubles. They would later become visually world-renowned as the Potemkin Steps after the famous 'pram scene' in the Eisenstein propaganda film made for the Bolsheviks, the *Battleship Potemkin*. Upton became a successful, well-respected member of Crimean society and a relatively wealthy man. He was friends with the fabulously wealthy Count Vorontsov who until the age of nineteen had been raised in England where his father was the Russian ambassador[47]. Upton oversaw construction of his majestic, Tudor-style Black Sea palace which turned out to be another twenty year long building project for Upton. The building was designed by British architects and filled with the latest designs in furniture imported from England. During much of his later work in Russia, Upton was assisted by his sons John, William, Thomas and Samuel who went on to become an architect and Russian academic. When Upton died in 1851 he left a large estate and vineyards in the Crimea to his family. Unfortunately, much of this was damaged during the ensuing Crimean War and William Upton was held for a short time by the British military who accused him of being a Russian spy. He was released on Lord Raglan's orders but forced to provide details of Sevastopol's topography and harbour defences. [48] William was an eye witness to the tragic Charge of the Light Brigade and later acted as a translator for Florence Nightingale at the British military hospital in Scutari (see page 197). William had a gift for languages and spoke French, Russian, German and Italian plus several Slavic languages. Promises of post-war compensation by the British were largely reneged on when William returned to Britain, so he and his English wife subsequently moved to Canada, settling on a farm near the future capital Ottawa.

With the death of John Upton, the unofficial title of British shipbuilder to the Tsars eventually passed to Murdoch Macpherson who was born in Perth, Scotland in 1813. He studied engineering at Glasgow and went on to own a small shipbuilding yard on the River Clyde. When Nicholas I decided that he wanted a new yacht, it was Macpherson who submitted the successful tender

---

[46] Mark Jodoin – *Esprit de Corps*, February 2007

[47] Vorontsov's sister, Ekaterina, married the 11th Earl of Pembroke and their son, Sydney Herbert was Secretary for War at the time of the Crimean conflict.

[48] Frances Duberley, *Journal kept during the Russian War*, 1856

and when the boat was finished, he proudly delivered it to St Petersburg himself. Nicholas liked what he saw in terms of both the yacht and its builder and offered Murdoch the position of engineer for all the Imperial yachts. Murdoch decided to accept the job and quickly disposed of his yard on the Clyde and relocated to Russia in the early 1830s. At the time, Nicholas had four yachts all manned with a full complement of Russian engineers and Macpherson sailed in whichever yacht the Emperor chose to use, usually running the engine room.[49] In 1841, Murdoch Macpherson married Julia Maxwell, who was then aged just seventeen and had come to Russia with her parents some years earlier. Over the years in St Petersburg, Julia gave birth to fifteen children of which five sons and five daughters survived. After more than a dozen years as the Imperial Engineer, Macpherson established the Baltic Iron Works and Shipbuilding Yard in St Petersburg, in partnership with an Englishman called Carr, sometime in the early 1850s. With his connection to the Tsar, he received an order for a new Imperial Yacht, the *Livadia* which operated in the Black Sea and after she was lost, the *Livadia II*. Carr and Macpherson's yard became a major operation, building a large number of vessels and built the first iron-plated ship in the country in 1861. The company was taken over by the Russian Navy in 1895 and it built many Russian cruisers and battleships. Macpherson died at St Petersburg in 1879. His wife and most of his ten surviving children remained in Russia where they in turn married and brought up families. One of his grandsons, Arthur Macpherson would become a prominent figure in St Petersburg society before suffering a tragic death at the hands of the Bolsheviks (see page 265) and through another grandson, Kenneth, the Macphersons would also become linked by marriage to the Rogers, Websters and Woodhouse families of Russia.

---

[49] Nicholas ordered another Britsh yacht from the yard of Sir John Rennie around 1850 which Rennie delivered personally to St Petersburg.

5

A Dose of British Medicine

The initial driving forces behind the strengthening links between England and Russia following Chancellor's 1553 voyage were trade and politics. However, it soon became clear to both countries that England's relatively advanced medical and apothecary skills could also be of mutual benefit. For Ivan I, the acquisition of English knowledge in these fields would be of immediate use in countering the various agues and plagues of 16th century Moscow. For Elizabeth I, by acquiescing to Ivan's requests for experienced English doctors and apothecaries, this not only improved the Tsar's attitude to the Muscovy Company and its trading activities but it also helped her sidestep or forestall some of his other more demanding requests. Elizabeth's objective was to maximise trade by cementing cordial relations between the two countries without becoming entangled in a military alliance. This initially almost accidental relationship involving the export of doctors to Russia was to become an important part of her largely successful strategy. The arrival of British physicians in Russia heralded a dramatic improvement in medical knowledge in Russia and it is hard to overestimate their importance over the next two centuries. The first medical experts sailed from England in 1557 accompanied by Osip Nepea, Russia's ambassador to the English court. On board were Dr Ralph Standish, a Cambridge graduate plus two apothecaries Richard Elmes and the Dutchman Arend Claesen van Stellingswerfft. It seems likely that Standish, the very first doctor in Russia, died there some two years later but Richard Elmes, the earliest English apothecary at the Russian court, stayed on for twenty-seven years, until 1584 and Stellingswerfft tenure as pharmacist to the Tsars lasted an incredible forty years. In 1567, Dr Reynolds arrived together with another apothecary, Thomas Carver and two chests of apothecary wares. Elizabeth's strategy was working, as soon after their arrival, the Tsar granted further concessions to the Muscovy Company giving it a monopoly over all trade by the White Sea and importantly, permission to trade from Russia with Persia and Cathay. Unfortunately, Carver was killed during the sacking of Moscow in 1571 by the Tatars.

Although we know very little about the day-to-day work of these doctors and apothecaries, the fact that Ivan repeatedly asked Elizabeth for more of them indicates the value placed on their expertise in Russia. In 1581, yet another request from Ivan saw the arrival of the apothecary James Frencham, together with Dr Robert Jacob and several regimental surgeons. Jacob was already a distinguished doctor prior to going to Russia having been given the title of 'Physician to the Household' of Elizabeth I. Frencham would have an important role in developing Russia's medical/ apothecary system and is generally regarded as the founder of the first Moscow Court Pharmacy, effectively Russia's first chemist shop. The Court Pharmacy served the exclusive needs of the Tsar and his immediate family. One of their most important functions was to test and taste all medicines before they were administered due to the fear of poisoning. Jacob and Frencham worked closely together but the latter was specifically charged by the Tsar with establishing the pharmacy. Once it was running smoothly, Frencham left Russia in 1584 but would return seventeen years later. Jacob however, remained and his medical duties expanded to include the roles of scholar, diplomat and merchant. Whilst he may not have advanced medical science in Russia directly, his versatility and usefulness in other roles to Ivan and later, his successor Theodore, were undoubtedly of benefit to Anglo-Russian relations and British influence on Russian medicine generally.

It seems to have been Jacob who suggested to Ivan (who had recently married for the fifth time) that he find and English wife as a way of linking the two kingdoms more closely and Lady Hastings, the Queen's cousin, was eventually selected in England as the unfortunate bride. The proposal was never consummated as Ivan died in 1584 and Jacob returned to England where he was soon made a freeman of his home town Canterbury. However, he was sent back to Russia two years later at the request of Elizabeth to treat the wife of the new Tsar. Jacob arrived in Moscow with the new English ambassador, Sir Jerome Horsey, bearing rich gifts for the Tsar, for Boris Godunov the Protector, and for his sister the Tsarina. These gifts from the English court not only placed both men in a favoured position with both Theodore and Gudunov but also resulted in a further round of beneficial trading privileges for the Russia Company. Jacob was now able to use his position and contacts at the Russian court to expand his activities beyond his normal medical role. He obtained information about Russian territories in the north east and Siberia which he then passed to his close friend John Dee, the navigator, in England and in 1586 persuaded the Tsar and Boris Godunov to issue an invitation for Dee to visit Russia, although the invite was never taken up. It was Dee who trained Richard Chancellor and others in navigational techniques and whose son, Arthur, would later work as a doctor in Russia – see below. Jacob later took advantage of his contacts to circumvent the Russia Company's monopoly position by trading wax on his own account. This not only caused great annoyance but also considerable loss to the Company. However, as we shall see, this multifarious role of the English doctor in Russia would become the norm rather than the exception for many years to come.

Things didn't always run smoothly however for some of the English doctors and apothecaries that were sent to Russia. It had become the practice for incoming apothecaries and doctors to bring with them medicines, books and even surgical instruments as these were not readily available in Russia. When Dr Timothy Willis was sent to replace Dr Mark Ridley in 1599, he was dismissed within three weeks of his arrival at Moscow because he was unable to produce any books or drugs. He had made the simple error of travelling overland to Russia and sending his books and medicines by sea. Willis was one of the first Englishmen to make the journey by land across Europe and no doubt regretted his decision. When he became Tsar, Boris Godunov thought so highly of English doctors and apothecaries that in 1601 he requested Sir Richard Lee, the English ambassador, to help secure the re-appointment of James Frencham at the Court Pharmacy. A special envoy was sent to London to re-engage him and

Frencham returned to Moscow in November 1602 where he concentrated on placing the Court Pharmacy on a stronger footing, working with the other doctors in Moscow.

Boris Godunov died on 13 April 1605 and a turbulent period in Russian history followed that reduced the numbers of English doctors and apothecaries in the country. However, the accession of Michael in 1613 gradually restored a good measure of stability to the country though the medical profession remained constrained. During the whole of Tsar Michael's long, thirty-year reign, there were only seven doctors, thirteen regimental surgeons, eight apothecaries and three alchemists or chemists in Russia. Over the next few years, several events occurred that strengthened the reputation and influence of British medicine in Russia. Firstly, the Society of Apothecaries of London was incorporated in 1617; secondly, the *Pharmacopoeia Londinensis* was published in 1618 and thirdly, the visit to Russia the same year by the pioneering botanist John Tradescant during which he recorded various Russian flora and fauna then unknown in Europe.

In 1620, an Apothecaries' Board was established in Moscow, with the objective of controlling the work of the Court Pharmacy and regulating the import of foreign medicines, on which Russia was heavily dependent. Initially, the small Apothecaries' Board was controlled by a Russian apothecary but in 1621, Arthur Dee arrived in Russia as senior physician to the Tsar Michael and soon took on the role of overseeing the Board. Dee clearly had detailed knowledge of the apothecary side of the profession as in his early career he had been repeatedly accused by the College of Physicians for illicitly selling apothecary medicines in London. However, he seems to have overcome these nefarious problems as he became Queen Anne's doctor in 1615. As senior physician to Michael, Dee worked closely with the other English medical staff in Moscow such as Randolph Wardley, who came to Russia in 1624 and the apothecaries William Tewe and his son Robert. Dee's activities however, like Dr Jacob before him, seemed to expand beyond the purely medical function. He became responsible for examining the knowledge and professional competency of all new medical personnel; he transacted official business for the Tsar's visit to England during 1626-7, and he wrote treatises on alchemy which proved of great interest to the Russians. Dee was a polyglot and widely travelled; his experience, cosmopolitan outlook and adaptability all helped to make him respected at court and able to exert an influence well beyond the immediate medical sphere. These talents also helped in his careful development and growth of the Apothecaries' Board as well as in his important role of procuring drugs for the use of the Russian court.

During Dee's time in Russia, various members of the Society of Apothecaries in London were supplying medicines to Russia, including to the Tsar and his court. When Dee returned from his trip to England with the Tsar in 1627, it seems he endeavoured to introduce more personal control over the acquisition and shipment of medicines to Russia. Dee's involvement in this was not surprising, given the fact that he was not only a member of the Russia Company, along with his two sons-in-law, but also an energetic and enterprising merchant in his own right. His large house also became the Russia Company's

Moscow headquarters in 1636. Dee now increasingly organised the shipments of supplies for the Apothecaries' Board, usually by sea to Archangel (sometimes brought over by his sons-in-law) and thence to Moscow. Dee continued to hold a pre-eminent role amongst the medical experts in Russia for fourteen years until his departure in 1634. He returned to England to take up the post of Physician Extraordinary to Charles I.

During the reign of Tsar Alexis from 1645 to 1676, further changes were made to the Apothecaries' Board in Moscow. Some of these developments resulted from the constant spate of wars and the need to make medical provisions for the expanded army. In 1654 the Apothecaries' Board founded the first Russian medical school and several of the English and other foreign doctors in Moscow provided much of the instruction in surgery, anatomy, botany, pharmacology, practical diagnosis of internal diseases and ambulatory medicine. Despite the decline in British influence and trade in Russia following the Tsar's adverse reaction to the execution of Charles I, the bulk of medical supplies continued to come from England, some ordered through English merchants and some through the Russia Company. In 1659, Samuel Collins arrived in Moscow to take up the post of physician to Tsar Alexis. Born in Braintree in Essex, Collins was an experienced and learned doctor, having studied medicine in Germany and Italy. He was particularly interested in investigating the links between medicine and botany and frequently visited the three apothecary gardens that existed in Moscow at the time. From his research, Collins wrote two papers in 1665, one on obesity (which no doubt attracted the attention of the corpulent Tsar) and the other on the medical uses of the valerian and burdock plants. Both treatises, written in Latin, were highly regarded and carefully preserved, along with his prescriptions, for the instruction of other medical men at the Apothecaries' Board.

Like Jacob and Dee before him, Collins also became involved in a variety of undertakings outside of medicine both for the Russians as well as the English. In April 1662, Collins returned to England on leave, travelling with the two Russian ambassadors sent to re-establish friendly relations with England after the Restoration. Whilst in London he acquired medicines and books for the Tsar and arranged for copies of the *London Gazette* to be sent regularly to him by friends. Collins then periodically translated these for the Tsar in Moscow, thereby acquainting him with some knowledge of English life and culture. Collins returned to Russia from his leave in 1663 to resume his post in Moscow where he remained for a further five years before settling back in England where he died in 1670. His memoirs were released posthumously in 1671.[50]

The other principal contributor to the development of Russia's medical system at this time was the apothecary Robert Benyon. In 1656, the highly regarded apothecary Robert Tewe requested the Tsar's permission to return to England after more than thirty years of service in Russia. It was Tewe who recommended Benyon as his replacement and the latter arrived in Russia in 1656. He brought with him eight medical books that were to form the foundation

---

[50] Samuel Collins, *The Present State of Russia*, 1671

of the Apothecaries' Board library in Moscow.[51] Benyon worked closely with Collins and their combined expertise enabled them to restock the Apothecaries' Board with new drugs so as to prepare more sophisticated remedies as well as expanding its operations. Private individuals were now allowed to purchase medicines and the Board was run on a commercial basis. In 1673, the Tsar granted the Board a monopoly of purchasing medicines and the new pharmacy was allowed to sell spirits, alcoholic tinctures as well as medicines. These changes marked a real development in the progress of pharmacies in Russia. It is not certain how long Benyon, who married in Russia, stayed in the country but records show him still there as late as 1676.

We have already seen the wide range of interests of Peter the Great who became Tsar in 1689 and medicine was most certainly a subject that caught his attention. During his tour of Holland and England, he visited hospitals, anatomical theatres and apothecary's gardens. As in other areas, Peter recruited a large number of foreign medical personnel to work in Russia, eventually including seventeen doctors, eighty-seven surgeons, one ophthalmologist and nine apothecaries. Predictably, Peter reformed the entire Russian medical system during his reign and he turned to a remarkable Scottish doctor, Robert Erskine, to implement the changes. Erskine was born in 1677 and had extensive training and experience before arriving in Russia. He served a five-year apprenticeship to an Edinburgh surgeon-apothecary, studied anatomy, surgery, chemistry and botany for two years in Paris, then graduated as a doctor at Utrecht University in 1700. On his return to England, he became a distinguished anatomy lecturer in London where his skill in dissecting the human body led to public acknowledgement and his election to the Royal Society in 1703. A few months later, Erskine was made a freeman of the Russia Company and he left soon afterwards for Moscow, initially becoming house doctor to Prince Menshikov, the Tsar's principal aide. However, Erskine only held this position for a short time, as Peter made him his own chief physician later the same year.

Peter clearly recognised Erskine's abilities early on as in 1706 he was made director of the Apothecaries' Board with overall responsibility for all of Russia's medical services. Under Erskine's leadership a new central pharmacy was constructed in a converted building to the east of the Kremlin. The conversion work started in 1706 and took three years to complete. Once finished, it seems the new pharmacy was extremely impressive with two apothecary gardens and became a showpiece in Moscow. Close to fifty people were employed there under Erskine. In 1709, he prepared his own book on herbal plants found around Moscow (the oldest surviving herbal in Russia) and he extended and systemised the collection of plant samples from across Russia. The founding of St Petersburg in 1703 by Peter brought not only great changes to Russian society in general but also to the country's medical system and Erskine was actively involved. His initial task was to set up the first St Petersburg Garrison Pharmacy in 1704 which was established at the same time as one for the Moscow garrison. These were followed by the transfer to the new city of the Apothecaries' Board or Chancery as it was now called which became a major planning and

---

[51] Benyon's original books are now held in the Academy of Sciences library in St Petersburg.

organising task. Two more pharmacies were then established by Erskine in St Petersburg and he now carried overall responsibility for the running of all these pharmacies. In addition, both the Moscow and St Petersburg Apothecaries' Gardens which were established in Erskine's time in Russia came under his control. A complete system of growing selected herbs and turning them into the medicines required by the doctors was set up in these gardens under the direction of the resourceful Erskine.

Just about the only medical things that were not under Erskine's direct supervision initially were the hospital pharmacies which were under the control of Russia's Orthodox Church Synod. The frequent wars that interspersed Peter's first two decades as Tsar meant that the hospitals themselves and the quality of their treatment and care of soldiers became increasingly important. Moscow's military hospital which was modelled on Greenwich Hospital in London was founded in 1706 and the St Petersburg Naval and Military Hospital was built in 1717. Erskine was heavily involved in the administration of these hospitals as well as supervising soldiers' medical examinations and treatment by doctors plus the supply of medicines for the Navy. With the support of the Tsar, Erskine was the driving force behind organising Russian medicine on a war footing and as chief physician to the Tsar, Erskine accompanied Peter on many of his military campaigns and his frequent journeys abroad.

Although Erskine was naturally more comfortable in a medical environment, like his predecessors his activities also encompassed several other roles. As the highly respected chief physician to the Tsar and essentially Russia's chief medical officer, he had close relations with Peter and was able to exercise considerable influence. He successfully operated as a go-between and interlocutor in Anglo-Russian political affairs on several occasions. He interceded for his fellow countrymen with the Tsar and was often consulted by him on difficult questions relating to European politics. In 1716, in a letter to Charles Whitworth, Britain's envoy to Russia, Erskine wrote that he would rather 'write twenty receipts than one [political] letter'.[52] As a freeman of the Russia Company, Erskine was also an active commodities trader and investor, developing an extraordinary network of over two hundred contacts across Europe. In 1714, the Chamber of Curiosities, Russia's first natural history museum, was founded in St Petersburg with Erskine as its director and chief librarian. Erskine was actively involved in negotiating the purchases of world-famous collections for the museum, which later became the Academy of Sciences' Museum and Erskine donated his own large collection of curiosities, surgical instruments and anatomical specimens to it. Similarly, he purchased several significant medical libraries of the time adding them to his own which then formed the cornerstone of the future Academy's library.

As president of the Apothecaries' Chancery, Erskine planned Russia's first scientific expedition to Siberia and he also supervised all medical missions, including those of two of his compatriots – Thomas Garvine, a surgeon who visited China in 1715 and John Bell, another Scottish surgeon in both Russia and Persia. Finally on the medical front, both the Tsar and Erskine were very

[52] J. H. Appleby, *Medical History* vol 27, 1983.

interested in balneology (bathing in mineral waters) and Erskine discovered a spring containing iron on the outskirts of St Petersburg which was later developed into a spa treatment centre. Peter rewarded Erskine for his years of faithful service by raising him to the prestigious position of privy councillor in 1716. Robert Erskine died in November 1718, at the relatively young age of only forty-one and was buried with much pomp and ceremony at the Alexander Nevsky Monastery in St Petersburg. He was a remarkably talented man who as an innovator, organiser and developer, transformed and modernised the country's whole medical system. Russian medicine, botany and natural history in general owe more to his pioneering genius than to any other person of the period. Although many other British doctors followed Erskine to work in Russia, none would have the same diverse influence and widespread impact.

Erskine was only one of many Scottish physicians that worked in Russia during the 18th century and in some ways, this period seems to have been a time when the Russians caught 'Scottish fever' or maybe it was the other way round. The result was an injection of several skilled Scottish medical men into Russia, one of whom was James Mounsey. Born in Scotland in 1710, he worked in Russia from 1736–62. There is some confusion about him since although he was described as, and used, the title 'Doctor', there is no record of him ever having actually qualified. The fact that his initial position was as a regimental surgeon or *lekar* (a Russian term signifying a medical man with no degree) seems to confirm his lack of a formal qualification as a doctor. Mounsey served for several years in the Russian Navy before spending five years in private practice in Russia. He first rose to prominence when his compatriot, Field Marshal Keith was wounded by a gunshot to his leg which became so badly infected that Russian surgeons wanted to amputate. Mounsey, who was attached to Keith's forces as a doctor, disagreed and was able to successfully remove several pieces of cloth from the wound after which Keith made a complete recovery.

Mounsey had a keen interest in botany and natural history and travelled extensively in Russia for a while investigating the local fauna before returning to London where he was elected to the Royal Society in 1750. Perhaps on the basis of this and his success with Keith, Mounsey was appointed a physician to Empress Elizabeth and he returned to Russia. There he married Jean Grieve, the daughter of another Scottish doctor, James Grieve, in Moscow in 1754 and the couple had seven children in Russia[53]. Grieve had arrived in Russia in 1734 and initially spent several years as a physician in Kazan and Orenburg before moving to St Petersburg. There he worked first at the army hospital as a physician to the guards regiment and then as a city doctor. He finally relocated to Moscow in 1751 working in a similar capacity for several years when he also became a physician to Elizabeth. During his time in Russia, Grieve became fluent in Russian and is also known for his translation of *The History of Kamtschatka* in 1763.[54] His son, John Grieve, followed in his father's footsteps,

---

[53] The last of Mounsey's descendants in Russia died in Leningrad during the 1942 German siege.

[54] Stepan Krasheninikov - this book describes part of the 1733-1743 exploration into the vast eastern expanses of Asia initiated under Peter I and concluded during Elizabeth's reign.

also working as a doctor in Russia. Whether Mounsey replaced James Grieve or they worked alongside each other until Grieve's departure from Russia in 1763 is unclear. As Elizabeth was not a healthy woman, suffering from extreme obesity, dropsy and dyspnoea, it may well be that she required two doctors. In 1761 she began to have fits and died under Mounsey's care in 1762 from a heart failure linked to her obesity.

However, the death of Elizabeth under Mounsey did not adversely affect her husband and successor, Peter III who appointed him director of the Medical Chancery and of the whole medical faculty throughout Russia – the position that Erskine held previously. While in this post, Mounsey introduced several improvements to the Russian medical system, building on Erskine's earlier changes. However, just a few months later, Peter III was murdered at the instigation of his wife Catherine, who then seized the throne. Mounsey, perhaps prudently sensing that Catherine would want her own chief medical officer, chose to retire on health grounds and returned to Scotland. He built a mansion on a large estate that he had purchased in 1758 and in its garden cultivated the seeds of a medicinal plant he had brought back from Russia, later giving some to the Royal Physic Garden in Edinburgh. This plant was Siberian rhubarb[55] and Mounsey was the first to introduce it to Europe. There may have been another, more sinister reason for Mounsey's early departure from Russia. Mysteriously, for the rest of his life, Mounsey claimed he was under threat from Catherine's agents because of the many secrets of the Russian court known to him[56]. He apparently insisted that every room in his new house should be built with more than one exit so that if he were surprised in one of the rooms by his enemies he could more easily escape. These life-threatening secrets possibly related to events surrounding the assassination of Peter III by Catherine but whatever they were, Mounsey took them to his grave. He died in Edinburgh in 1773 having achieved much with remarkably few qualifications.

Mounsey was asked to recommend his replacement by the Russians and he chose Dr John Rogerson whose mother was Mounsey's half-sister. Rogerson was born in 1741 in Dumfriesshire, Scotland and graduated as a doctor in 1765 from Edinburgh.

He arrived in Russia in September 1766 and was appointed a court physician to Catherine the Great in 1769. Shortly before Rogerson's appointment, Catherine employed another British doctor when in 1768 she chose to use the services of an English Quaker physician, Dr Thomas Dimsdale. He was an experienced surgeon from Hertford who specialised in the newly discovered system of inoculation against smallpox and had published *The Present Methods of Inoculation for the Smallpox* in 1767. At the time, smallpox was one of the world's deadliest diseases and a severe epidemic was sweeping through Russia. Catherine became aware of the new inoculation process, possibly through Rogerson and asked her embassy in London to find a British doctor who would come to Russia to inoculate her as an example to demonstrate its success.

---

[55] Hannah Glasse is attributed with the first recipe in print for Mounsey's rhubarb in 1760 in the Compleat Confectioner.

[56] D Doyle – Royal College of Physicians Edinburgh Vol. 35, 2005

Dimsdale was selected for this high profile and potentially dangerous task and left for Russia in July 1768 with his son, Nathaniel who was a medical student at Edinburgh.

From the moment of their arrival in St Petersburg, they were treated very graciously; a large house with a coach and horses was placed at their disposal and Dimsdale was frequently invited to dine with nobility and had free access to the court. The call to inoculate Catherine came late one cold October night and the decision to proceed was a brave one on both sides. Dimsdale apprehensively carried out his work in strict secrecy with no other doctor present. After three weeks, the Empress had fully recovered, much to the relief of the court and no doubt Dimsdale himself. A few weeks later, Catherine's son and heir was also successfully inoculated and with a soaring reputation, Dimsdale now found himself inundated with clients among the rich and noble families. As well as his appointment as physician to the Empress, he received many honours and awards becoming a Baron of the Empire, a Councillor of State with the rank of major general plus an annuity of £500. Catherine presented him with a miniature painting of herself and a fee payment of £10,000 (worth over £1m today).

Over the next few months he continued his work in both St Petersburg and in Moscow, inoculating some two hundred people. When Catherine contracted a severe attack of pleurisy Dimsdale was again called to the palace to take charge of her treatment. This was a time of great strain for him as there were fears for the Empress's life and had she died under his care, it would have been very difficult for him. She eventually recovered however and in the spring of 1769, Dimsdale took leave of Russia and went home to Hertford where he continued with his inoculation work, becoming a Fellow of the Royal Society later that year and the MP for Hertford. He returned to Russia briefly in August 1781 accompanied by his newly acquired third wife, Elizabeth, to inoculate Catherine's two young grandsons Alexander and Constantine as well as several other members of the nobility. The Dimsdales were again extremely well treated during their stay in St Petersburg and the Empress provided them with private apartments in the royal palace of Tsarskoe Selo. In late September, the Dimsdales returned to England, eventually settling in Bath where Thomas died in 1801.

In 1756 Matthew Halliday went to Russia to work as a doctor, although it is not clear whether he was formally qualified. In December 1758, he married Anna Kellerman in St Petersburg and the couple apparently had numerous children between 1759 and 1781. For a while, Halliday was also employed as a physician to Catherine the Great, probably with Dimsdale but by 1768 he had moved on to take charge of the St Petersburg inoculation hospital where he practised for many years. In a notice in the St Petersburg News during 1791, Halliday was offering free treatment against smallpox, using the procedure pioneered some years earlier by Dimsdale. Halliday continued to practice medicine in St Petersburg until his death there in February 1809.

Rogerson now replaced Dimsdale as Catherine's senior physician and soon earned the respect and gratitude of the royal family by saving the life of Princess Dashkova's son (see below) who was seriously ill, probably with diphtheria which was endemic at that time. He was promoted some six years later and given the rank of Councillor of State, finally advancing to the level of a Privy Councillor in 1779, like Erskine over sixty years earlier. During his time in Russia, Rogerson gained a reputation as more of a socialite and gambler than an intellectual or physician. Indeed, he was spoken of as a *'usually fatal doctor'* by most others who saw the effect of his *'fatal laxatives and bleeding'*. When Field Marshall Prince Alexander Golitsyn died in Rogerson's care, bled and purged to death, Catherine is reputed to have jokingly remarked *'I'm afraid anybody who gets into Rogerson's hands is already dead.'* [57]

His primary duties it seems related not to medical care but rather preventing the libidinous Catherine from catching any venereal infection. If she saw a young man she fancied, he was first 'tried out' by her Scottish lady-in-waiting, Countess Bruce, then by Anna Protasova. Having made it to this point, the young man then received several weeks' instruction about the Empress's likes and dislikes from Potemkin, her principal adviser, her lover and, for a time, her husband. Finally, if the young man still seemed suitable he was thoroughly examined by Rogerson before being permitted to sleep with the Empress. Rogerson's closeness to the Empress, especially in this inspection role, inevitably caused jealousy at court which led to him being falsely suspected of spying, firstly for Sir James Harris (the British ambassador) and then for the Prussians. Later and more realistically, he was accused of having too much power and influence. Like most of his predecessors, Rogerson exercised considerable influence both over Catherine and the Russian court in general and undoubtedly used his position to profit financially from his time in Russia. As a paid servant of Catherine, he was not allowed to accept payments for services to other members of the Russian court but, apparently, presents were most certainly allowed. It seems Rogerson received many such gifts which he managed to convert into gold coin that he then sent home in sacks of grain with the help of his nephew, William Rogerson, who was a merchant in St Petersburg. Regardless of his medical skills, he seems to have made plenty of money during his time in Russia as he managed to purchase three homes in Scotland over the years, the last of which he purchased in 1810 for £90,000 (around £6m today). It was to this house that Rogerson finally retired in 1816 after fifty years work in Russia and he died in Scotland in 1823, aged eighty-two.

During Rogerson's period in Russia he associated with a close-knit group of fellow Scottish doctors and scientists who became close friends and were all linked to one another, either by birthplace, marriage, university and of course medicine. William Cullen was the personal physician to Princess Dashkova, a close friend and confidant of the Catherine the Great. He also worked closely with a Russian doctor, Samoilovich, on research into cholera. John Grieve, the son of James Grieve, was born in Edinburgh and studied philosophy, logic, mathematics and the classics prior to graduating in medicine in 1778. He arrived in Russia in June that year at the invitation of Rogerson who recommended him to his fellow Scotsman Admiral Greig. Greig appointed Grieve as a military doctor with the Voronezh Division, serving mostly in the Ukraine until March

---

[57] D Doyle - ibid

1783, when he returned home because of ill-health. He eventually settled in London where he worked in private practice and became a fellow of the Royal Society. However, in 1798, he returned to Russia as court physician, first to Tsar Paul and then to Alexander in St Petersburg. He died there suddenly, at only fifty-two years of age, in December 1805.

Matthew Guthrie was also born and educated in Edinburgh and graduated as a doctor in 1763. He initially worked for the East India Company and first visited Russia in 1770 with Admiral Charles Knowles and his private secretary John Robison. On leaving the East India Company he served in the Royal Navy until 1776 after which he returned to Russia and worked in St Petersburg from 1778 until his death 29 years later as chief physician to the Imperial Land Cadet Corps of Nobles there. A man of many interests outside medicine he was elected a fellow of the Royal Society of London in 1782, a member of the Societies of Antiquaries of both London and Edinburgh and wrote on subjects as diverse as music, scurvy, the plague, dances and history. Through his writings in various medical journals of the time, Guthrie also provided the British with a considerable amount of well-informed information about Russia's medical, natural and cultural history.

When Princess Dashkova expressed her keen wish to visit Britain and have her son Paul educated there, it was Cullen, Rogerson and Robison who helped with her visit plans and the arrangements for Paul's subsequent education at Edinburgh University.[58] She and her son spent several very happy years between 1775 and 1779 in Edinburgh and also took the waters at Buxton and Matlock in 1778 on the advice of Cullen. The Dashkovs' time in Britain had a very favourable effect on her subsequent views of the British. When Dashkova was later appointed as president of the Russian Academy of Sciences (becoming the first woman in the world to lead a national science academy) and then the Imperial Russian Academy, she helped secure the election of Rogerson to the Russian Academy of Sciences in 1776, the first person from Britain so honoured.

Although not part of the Scottish quintet, Sir James Wylie was also active in Russia at much the same time as Rogerson and rose to high office there. Born in 1768, he obtained his medical degree in Aberdeen and entered Russian service as senior surgeon in the Eletsky Regiment in 1794 and was on active duty at the Russian sieges of Warsaw and Krakow. During the campaign, he saved the life of the Danish Ambassador, Baron Otto Von Bloom, where other surgeons including the Scots had failed and Wylie's success led to his appointment as physician to the Royal Household in 1795. His reputation was further enhanced a couple of years later when Count Kutaisof, a close friend of the Tsar, suffered a choking fit. Wylie heard of the situation and offered to help but was rebuffed at first by the Count's own surgeons. However, when the Count's position became desperate Wylie was summoned and he saved Kutaisof's life by performing a tracheotomy, the first in Russia. As a result, Wylie achieved

---

[58] Prince Paul Dashkov was the first Russian to graduate from Edinburgh University in 1779 and he became a fellow of the Royal Society of London in 1781. He paved the way for a number of Russians who later studied at Scottish universities.

almost instant fame and was appointed as personal attendant by the appreciative Tsar Paul and provided with his own rooms in the Winter Palace. Years later, Wylie used to recount how he 'owed his promotion to cutting Count Kutaisof's throat'.[59]

This was not the only life or death incident involving Wylie and a tsar. A few years later when Wylie was out riding with Alexander I near Vilna, the pair came across a group of people struggling with what appeared to be the lifeless body of a young man rescued from the river. Apparently, the Tsar immediately leapt off his horse to assist in removing the wet clothes of the victim and then spent some time rubbing his body in an attempt to revive him but without effect. At the Tsar's direction, Wylie then tried to bleed him but after three hours, the body remained lifeless. However, Alexander urged Wylie not to give up and a short while later, the young man groaned and started bleeding – a clear sign of life. A report on the incident was sent to the British Royal Humane Society by James Grange, an English friend of Alexander who was probably riding with the Tsar's group. As a result, the Tsar was awarded a specially struck gold medal in 1806 by the Society which was presented to him in St Petersburg by the Marquis of Douglas. In 1799, Wylie became surgeon to the Tsar and physician to the heir apparent, the Grand Duke Alexander. When Paul was strangled by a group of army officers in 1801, Wylie and two other Scottish doctors embalmed the body and performed the post mortem examination. The resulting death certificate which concluded that Paul had died of apoplexy was probably produced under duress as it is unlikely Wylie would have been involved in the intrigue of Paul's murder.

Paul was succeeded by Tsar Alexander I who was also interested in developing Russia's medical services and under him Wylie flourished. In 1800 Wylie had played a leading role in establishing the Medico-Chirurgical Academy in St Petersburg and in 1804 he was elected president of the Academy, a position he held for thirty years. He became inspector-general of the army board of health in 1806 and worked hard to control a cholera epidemic in 1809 and to promote universal vaccination in Russia. Wylie served in the field during the Napoleonic Wars and was so horrified to see the carnage after the battles, especially at Austerlitz in 1805 when 30,000 died, he convinced Alexander to establish field hospitals. Until then, Russian officers received the undivided attention of the few doctors on the battlefield while the unfortunate ordinary soldier was left untreated. Wylie changed all that and transformed the medical services of the Russian army with the support of Alexander. The British and Foreign Medical Review later noted that '*the common soldier has to thank Sir James Wylie for such care and protection as his predecessors demanded in vain.*' During the course of the War, Wylie, who was himself wounded three times attended some twenty battles and travelled over 150,000 miles accompanying the Tsar. At the major battle of Borodino, where the Russians alone lost more than 45,000 men, Wylie operated on no less than 200 wounded in the field[60] and is the doctor mentioned by Tolstoy on the eve of the battle of

[59] Dr Peter Semple – paper given in St Petersburg, 2003.

[60] Mary McGrigor – Scottish Field, 2010

Borodino in his book *War and Peace*. He was appointed director of the medical department of the Ministry of War in 1812 but continued to serve in the front line to the end of the War in 1814.

Wylie accompanied the Tsar to England later that year and was knighted by the Prince Regent and in July, at the request of the Tsar, he was created a baronet. Wylie continued to travel everywhere with Alexander and was with him during his tour of the Crimea in 1825 where the Tsar died from a serious leg infection. As with Alexander's father, Wylie signed the death certificate. Wylie was now acknowledged as the leader of his profession in Russia and his *Handbook of Surgical Operations*, published in 1806, remained a standard textbook for over fifty years. He continued to enjoy imperial confidence under the next Tsar, Nicholas, becoming a privy councillor and receiving several Russian and foreign decorations. Wylie died celibate at St Petersburg in March 1854 and left most of his estate to the Russian state to fund the construction of a hospital in the capital to be attended by the pupils of the Medico-Chirurgical Academy and on Christmas day 1859, an imposing statue of Wylie was erected in the academy's courtyard in his memory. Wylie also left a sum of around £70,000 invested in British funds during his stay in London in 1814 which passed, after some litigation, to his Scottish relatives.

Wylie published a large number of books and articles on cholera, yellow fever and the plague based on his experiences in Russia. During his time in Russia of more than sixty years he had been a brave and loyal physician to three Tsars and brought significant improvements to both the military and civilian medical spheres. A contemporary British writer[61] described Wylie as:

'[O]*ne of the most notorious and powerful individuals in Russia.... With not very brilliant medical talents, with but very moderate scientific acquirements.... Sir James Wylie has risen from the most obscure parentage to be the first medical person in the Russian Empire.*'

Not all the British doctors that went to Russia worked for the imperial family in St Petersburg. Robert Lee was born in 1793 at Galashiels, Scotland and worked as a doctor in Edinburgh until he moved to the Crimea in October 1824. He was employed as the physician to Count Vorontzov, then the governor-general of southern Russia. Lee lived in Odessa which was then a relatively new town going through a period of rapid development under Vorontsov. The general living conditions for the rapidly expanding population of Odessa were difficult; typhus, malaria and meningitis were all common. Body lice were so commonplace that there was no seasonal fluctuation in the incidence of typhus.[62] For those living in the countryside, there were almost annual plagues of rats and locusts to deal with. Massive swarms of locusts devoured everything in their path and there was little Lee or anyone else could do to stop these devastating invasions. 'Millions of insects, their wings clacking and popping overhead, formed a black cloud that hung like thick smoke over fields and gardens'.[63] Lee remained in Odessa for a little over two years before

---

[61] Robert Lyall, *Travels in Russia*, 1825

[62] Norah Schuster, *English Doctors in Russia*, Royal Medical Society, Vol. 61, 1968

[63] Charles King, *Odessa*, 2011

returning to medical practice in Britain. He had clearly been well paid as he managed to save the substantial amount of £1,600 during his period in Russia.

There were many other medical men that played a part in this golden age of British physicians in Russia but in most cases we know little of their history. The names of at least thirty-three British medical men are noted in various records as being in Russia between 1770 and 1825. The influx of British medical men continued during the 19th century including Andrew Halliday who was born in Scotland in 1782 and qualified in medicine at Edinburgh University in 1806. After graduating, he travelled extensively in Russia hoping, no doubt, to emulate the success of other Scottish medical men. However, having failed to find a position to his liking, he returned home after a year to become a surgeon in the British army. Edward Morton left England in 1827 to work for Count Vorontsov, initially in St Petersburg and the following year at Vorontsov's sumptuous palace near Odessa. Sir James Leighton became head of the Russian Navy medical service in the 1820s and a court physician. Sir George Lefevre was physician to the British Embassy and to the English Hunt in Russia for sixteen years. He was one of first to regularly use a thermometer in his medical diagnoses and in 1836, while still in Russia, he published an account of the history and existing state of medicine in Russia.

There is one final, but important pair of Scotsmen in this prestigious list of British medical men in Russia and that is Alexander Crichton and his nephew Archibald Crichton who between them looked after the Russian Royal Family for almost thirty-five years. Sir Alexander Crichton (1763-1856) was from Edinburgh but qualified as a doctor in Holland in 1785. He later moved to England and did some important work on mental illness before becoming physician to the Duke of Cambridge in 1800. He arrived in Russia in 1803, having been recruited to work as the personal physician to Tsar Alexander and his family. He was also head of Russia's civil medical services, receiving several Russian honours and was elected an honorary member of the Academy of Sciences of St Petersburg. Crichton was interested in geology and during his travels in Russia he collected many important rock samples, some of which are now held at Leeds Museum. In 1819, he returned to England and was knighted in 1820 for his services to medicine. He continued to work as a doctor in Harley Street until his death in 1856, at the ripe old age of ninety-three.

Archibald Crichton, born in 1791, graduated as a doctor from Edinburgh University in 1810 and very soon after joined his uncle in St Petersburg. Through his uncle, the young Crichton obtained a post as medical supervisor, responsible for developing a mineral spa resort in the Caucasus mountains and he travelled to the region in 1811 to investigate potential locations (see also page 114). When Napoleon invaded Russia in 1812, Crichton volunteered for army service and in 1813 became physician at a hospital for French prisoners of war at Riga. Once the tide of war swung after Napoleon's disastrous retreat from Moscow, Crichton requested a transfer to his uncle's unit. As the Tsar Alexander's personal physician, his uncle was part of the Tsar's entourage at the front and Archibald then took part in the successful attack on the French capital in the spring of 1813. With the defeat of the French, the British hosted a dinner in April 1814 for their Russian allies that was attended by James Wylie,

Crichton (now promoted to physician-in-chief of the Russian hospitals in the city) and various senior Russian officers. In 1814 Crichton was awarded the campaign medal and the knight cross of the order of St Anne, as well as the Légion d'honneur by Louis XVIII. After a short period as a regimental surgeon in a guards regiment, he was appointed in 1816 as physician to the Grand Duke Nicholas, who became Tsar in 1825.

In addition to his medical duties Crichton often performed the role of a courtier and interpreter. He escorted Grand Duke Nicholas on his four month tour of Britain between 1816 and 1817, staying for part of the time at Chatsworth House as guests of the sixth Duke of Devonshire. In 1817 Crichton received honorary doctorates in medicine and law from Glasgow and Oxford universities respectively and he was knighted by the Prince Regent in the same year. He corresponded from Russia in 1818 with Russia's London ambassador Prince Lieven and the Duke of Devonshire about the birth of the Tsarevich Alexander, whom he safely vaccinated. In May 1820 he married in St Petersburg and his Russian bride, Sophia Louisa Kimmel, was the daughter of Nicholas Suthov, court physician and obstetrician. The couple had six children in Russia, although four died when still quite young.

Crichton played a significant part in monitoring the serious cholera epidemic that broke out in Russia during 1830-31. Strict containment measures such as local quarantines, armed cordons and restrictions on movement were introduced by the government which led to widespread riots. Rumours of deliberate contamination of ordinary people by government officials and doctors provoked mobs into raiding police stations and hospitals, resulting in many deaths. Crichton's medical advice on the subject was sought by his Russian colleagues and he co-ordinated information from all over Russia to compile a report on the epidemic for the Russian medical council towards the end of 1831. This report was used as the basis of two reports compiled by the Royal College of Physicians in London and these together with accounts from other British doctors about the epidemic in Russia were relayed to the board of health in London. These reports from Russia were particularly important as cholera reached Britain in 1831 and became an epidemic in 1832. Crichton also wrote to his uncle, Sir Alexander Crichton in England, describing the treatment of cholera by German doctors in St Petersburg hospitals.

In recognition of his cholera work, Crichton was awarded the knight cross of the order of St Vladimir and, soon after, the safe birth of Grand Duke Michael brought him the order of St Stanislas. Crichton was also given a special badge to mark twenty years of excellent service to the Royal Family two years later. However, by the mid 1830s, his health started to deteriorate and he was forced to relinquish his post of physician to Tsar Nicholas and he retired in 1837 with the rank of councillor of state, equivalent to a major-general, and presumably, with a handsome pension. Crichton remained in Russia with his wife and two surviving children, one of whom, Nicholas, became a councillor of state and married Helena Nieroth, a wealthy countess of German origin and their son, also Nicholas, served as a gentleman of the bed-chamber to the imperial court in 1911. Crichton was presented with a silver snuffbox on the Tsar's twenty-fifth wedding anniversary in 1847 and was elected an honorary member of the

Physico-Medical Society of Moscow University from 1838 to 1848. In addition to the honours mentioned already, he was awarded the Russian order of St Anne in 1837 plus a star of the grand cross of the order of the Red Eagle of Prussia. He was a member of the medical council in Russia and became a member of the Medico-Chirurgical Academy of St Petersburg in 1853. Crichton died in St Petersburg in February 1865 and was buried at the Smolensk evangelical cemetery.

The death of Archibald Crichton in Russia in 1865 brought to an end a remarkable, almost unbroken period of three centuries of British involvement in Russia's medical system. The British had acted as personal physicians to all the rulers of Russia as well as many of the country's leading noble and military families. Although there would be many other British medical personnel in Russia in future years, this marked the end of an era that not only brought great benefit to the Russian people but also to the British. The physicians themselves were mostly handsomely rewarded financially and many also received high honours. But through war and peace, epidemics and pestilence as well as climatic extremes their Russian experiences provided both countries with more than just improved medical skills. Many books by British medical writers were also translated into Russian. Perhaps the best known at the time was William Buchan's *Domestic Medicine*, published in Russian in four volumes by the Moscow University Press between 1790 and 1792. No Russian household was considered complete without a copy; indeed, Catherine was so pleased with it that she sent Buchan a gold medal and a complimentary letter.[64] In addition, the significant discoveries made by the British doctors in the fields of botany, geology and general scientific knowledge opened up a path for others to follow in future years.

---

[64] JH Appleby - ibid

TSARIST RUSSIA IN LATE 19TH CENTURY

6

Artisans, Architects, Artists, Authors and Artistes

Compared to its relationships with Russia in the areas of trade, the military, medicine and later on industry, Britain's impact and influence in the broad field of the arts was not nearly as great as that of the French, Germans and Italians. However, there were some noteworthy exceptions where British artisans, artists and architects made important contributions to cultural development in Russia. The earliest examples of British craftsmanship to arrive in Russia were those of English silversmiths which started to arrive in the late 16th century as gifts from either the English Court or the Russia Company to the Tsars. These early pieces were much admired by the Russian nobility who increasingly purchased similar items from the London silversmiths during the 17th and 18th centuries. Much of this silverware would later form part of the impressive imperial artwork collection at the Hermitage when it was built by Catherine and it remains one of the most important collections of early English silverware in the world. The visit by Peter the Great to England in 1698 drove home to the Russians how far behind Britain their country was, not only in terms of science or technology and the application of this knowledge in the fields of design and manufacture but also in the areas of education, culture and the arts generally. Along with the British soldiers and shipbuilders that Peter induced to come to Russia, we find several clockmakers, jewellers and design engineers arriving.

The growing reputation in Russia of the fine craftsmanship of British artisans led to the arrival of the Scottish clockmaker, Christopher Galloway. When, in the early 17th century, the Russians decided to rebuild the Moscow Kremlin from the ruins left after the Great Fire of 1571, the first tower to be rebuilt was the Spasskaya (Saviour's) Tower. The tower was part of the main entrance to the Kremlin and the Russians decided that it should be reconstructed so as to incorporate the city's first chiming clock. Galloway was invited to Moscow in 1621 to design and install the new timepiece. His design was both ingenious and original; he constructed two clocks, one facing out to the city and the other inwards to the Kremlin. Uniquely, instead of the hands rotating, the entire face of each massive clock moved round a static pointer. The clock was set at dawn and sunset by a duty watchman. Galloway explained that as the Russians did everything in a different way, their clock should be similarly unique. Not only was he was well rewarded for his original work but when a couple of years later, the tower and clocks were destroyed by fire, Galloway was re-employed at a similar handsome fee to rebuild them. His clocks continued to operate into the early 18th century. In 1633 Galloway also constructed a hydraulically-operated pump mechanism for the water tower of the Kremlin to supply water from the Moskva River direct to the Tsar's palace. Prior to this, every drop of water used had to be hauled up by hand from the river. Reputedly, some of the water was used for a rooftop pond where Peter the Great could sail his model boats. John Thaler arrived in Moscow at much the same time as Galloway and the pair worked together for around ten years restoring several palaces and cathedrals.

John Pateling came to St Petersburg in 1718, originally for only one year but ended up staying more than thirty years until his death in 1750. His first job was to install a set of steam pumps for the fountains in the Tsar's Summer Garden in St Petersburg. He also organised street lighting 'lanterns on posts in the English manner' along the city's main thoroughfare, the Nevskii Prospect as it would later become known.[65] Donald MacEwan was registered as a jeweller in St Petersburg in the mid 18th century and Robert Hynam was a British watchmaker who served the Russian royal court in St Petersburg in the early 1800s. One of the most celebrated creators of mechanical items of this sort in the second half of the 18th century was the London jeweller and goldsmith James Cox. His fertile imagination generated elaborate ideas that were then turned into reality by the skilled craftsmen of his company. Cox's firm produced a large number of sumptuously decorated, elaborate automata and he became internationally famous. His most well known creation was the Hermitage's famous Peacock Clock. Its history began in 1777, when the Duchess of Kingston visited St Petersburg (see page 137) and through her Prince Potemkin learned of Cox's magnificent mechanisms. In a gesture to impress his lover Catherine II, Potemkin commissioned Cox to make an expensive, spectacular automaton with a clock as the centrepiece. At the time, Coxe's financial affairs were in a poor state of health and in order to complete the order quickly, he used an existing mechanical peacock to which he added a cockerel, owl and a clock mechanism with a dial incorporated into the head of a mushroom. The newly concocted automaton was then shipped to Russia in pieces in 1781 and re-assembled at the Hermitage by a Russian technician. The Peacock Clock has remained one of the Hermitage's most well-known exhibits and is the only large 18th century automaton in the world to have survived unaltered and in a functioning condition. Despite the fact that it was ordered by Potemkin, the cost of the clock (11,000 roubles) was actually met by Catherine herself.

During the 18th century British landscape gardeners and their designs featured prominently in Russia, a trend that was initially led by Catherine. She became increasingly interested in all aspects of British landscape design and in the late 1760s started to introduce elements of the British formal garden style to her estates, especially at the gardens of Tsarskoe Selo palace. She sent her landscape architect and imperial gardeners to England to observe and copy the latest designs and techniques by visiting many of the notable gardens there. The knowledge they acquired was supplemented by careful study of various English books on landscape design and architecture, a few of which were published in Russian around this time. The first British landscape gardeners to arrive in Russia were Charles Sparrow and his brother John from Scotland, who were employed by Catherine in 1769 at the Gatchina estate near St Petersburg. Although John died shortly after arriving in Russia, Charles remained at

---

[65] Anthony Cross, *By the Banks of the Neva*, 1997.

Gatchina for many years gradually reworking the landscape into the style of a beautiful British garden. Sparrow went on to work for Prince Potemkin and was still in Russia in 1799 when the death of his wife was recorded in the register of the English church. Sparrow's trailblazing success was soon followed by the recruitment of an increasing number of gardeners from Britain by both Catherine and other wealthy Russians.

The undoubted enthusiasm and assiduous interest in British landscape design shown by the empress was inevitably subsequently followed by other members of the Russian aristocracy, some of whom observed them at first hand during their visits to Britain. This led to an almost insatiable demand for British gardeners[66] and one of the most influential was an English immigrant, the appropriately named Johann Busch or John Bush who ran a successful nursery garden in London. In 1771, he left England with his family and went to work for Catherine at Tsarskoe Selo where he remained for over eighteen years. Among many changes and improvements to the extensive gardens, he introduced the previously unknown concept of gravel walkways which delighted the Empress and the many visitors to her park. In time, Bush took on a wider role at the estate including supervising the greenhouses and hothouses where he grew a variety of exotic plants. Bush's two eldest sons and his first wife all died in Russia but when he returned to England in 1789, his son Joseph remained and took over his father's role as head gardener at Tsarskoe Selo. Joseph married twice and raised a large family in Russia though it is not known whether he remained or eventually returned to England.

Of comparable importance in the introduction of British-style landscaped gardens into Russia was the innovative William Gould. Gould was a colourful and popular figure in the British community in St Petersburg. Born in 1735, he arrived in Russia in 1776 and was initially employed by Prince Potemkin to work at the Taurida Palace gardens in St Petersburg. Gould worked in close cooperation with Potemkin's Russian architect, Starov to transform the previously flat featureless land around the palace into a remarkable and much praised example of British landscape design with covered walkways, extensive lawns, flower beds, mounds and ponds. Gould's work on the Taurida project was temporarily interrupted several times when he was dispatched to the Crimea by Potemkin to undertake landscaping there. In 1787 Gould was sent south to 'decorate' the route that Catherine II was to take on her Grand Tour of inspection in the region. Gould designed and erected a series of essentially overnight, pop-up gardens, some lit up at night with lanterns, creating an enchanting and magical atmosphere. It was pure theatre but Gould's instant gardens soon became the talk of Russia and he was given a grant of land in the Crimea by Potemkin in gratitude for his remarkable work. By 1790, the work at Taurida was largely finished and Potemkin hosted a magnificent party there in April 1791 for Catherine attended by some 3,000 guests. With Potemkin's death that same year, the palace passed to the empress and Gould was employed by

---

[66] Other British gardeners subsequently employed by Catherine include James Meader, Henry Mowat, John Munro and Francis Reid. Still more were recruited by Alexander I in the early 19th century.

her for a few years before returning to England to enjoy a comfortable retirement.

Architects and Builders

Russia's growing fascination with British landscape design inevitably led to a broader interest in British building and architectural design. Charles Cameron was outstanding among the British architects and craftsmen working in Russia during the latter part of the 18th century, receiving important commissions from Catherine 'the Great' and her son Paul, although the quantity of his surviving work is comparatively small. Cameron, who arrived in Russia in 1779, was a curious and somewhat dubious character. On arrival in St Petersburg, he made rather grandiose claims about his origins and background, stating he was a Scottish Jacobite descended from a famous Cameron clan as well as an experienced architect. In reality, he was born in London, probably around 1745, where he served an apprenticeship under his father who was a house builder. In 1768, Cameron was fortunate to be given a commission to travel to Rome to prepare a series of engravings for a book to be published by an English colleague on Roman imperial baths. However, Cameron chose to use some of the engravings to publish his own book *The Baths of the Romans* in 1772 but it was not a success. For the next few years, Cameron worked closely with his father on the renovation of a large house in central London and during this period, he developed his interior design skills in the neo-classical style. With the conclusion of this project, the pair fell out when Cameron senior ran into severe financial difficulties and ended up in a debtors' prison. With no immediate career prospects in Britain, Charles left his father to his fate in jail and decided to try his luck in Russia where he could put behind him the scandal of the court case and try to reinvent himself.

In many ways Cameron's timing could not have been better. During the last quarter of the 18th century more buildings were erected in Russia than in any previous period of the country's history[67] and this remarkable explosion in construction activity helped fuel a rising demand for foreign builders and architects. Also, the Empress Catherine had been exploring the idea of erecting a classical-style building in the grounds of her Tsarskoe Selo estate and soon after his arrival in St Petersburg Cameron obtained the commission to design such a building. Although it would be several years before his design was made reality, he clearly seems to have won the confidence of Catherine and quickly found himself busy with refurbishing the interior of the palace in the newly popular style of Classicism. Over the next few years, Cameron oversaw the conversion of several of the palace's apartments in a variety of styles, including Catherine's own private suite. By 1787, this major internal renovation work in the palace was complete (to the great satisfaction of the Empress) and Cameron turned his attentions to completing his original classical-style building in the grounds which was finished around 1786. Officially known initially as the Agate Pavilion and Colonnade, it housed a long glazed central gallery from which

---

[67] Miliza Korshunova, William Hastie in Russia, *Architectural History* Vol17, 1974.

Catherine was able to enjoy the fine views over her gardens, even in bad weather. It later became known as the Cameron Gallery, a considerable honour for its British designer.

In 1784 Cameron married Catherine, the daughter of John Bush, one of the landscape gardeners then employed in St Petersburg by the Imperial family. He then became involved in the design and construction for the Empress Catherine of the small model town of Sofia near Tsarskoe Selo. The centrepiece was the impressive Byzantine-style cathedral church of St Sophia, designed in imitation of the Hagia Sophia in Constantinople and consecrated in 1788. Sadly, much of the town was subsequently razed by Alexander I in 1808 but St Sophia still survives as a reminder of Cameron's capabilities and talent. He continued to work on other projects for Catherine, mostly designing parks and gardens until her death. When Paul took over from his mother in 1799, Cameron was initially dismissed from his post but was subsequently given several commissions to design various park buildings. With the accession of Alexander, Cameron was appointed chief architect to the Russian Admiralty and for the next three years he was as busy as under Catherine designing several naval buildings at Kronstadt and Oranienbaum, including a naval hospital for 400 patients which incorporated many of the ideas of Cameron's contemporary in Russia, the Quaker reformer John Howard (see page 147). In 1805, Cameron was again dismissed but remained in St Petersburg in quiet retirement together with his wife until his death there in 1812. Their only child, Mary, married James Grange, another English reformer, philanthropist and a governor of the Royal Humane Society who visited Russia several times and became a friend of Tsar Alexander. Although largely unrecognized in Britain for many years, subsequent biographers have described Charles Cameron as '*one of the greatest exponents of British taste and British Art abroad*'' and '*one of the major urban architects of the eighteenth century*'.[68]

The remarkable explosion in construction activity and landscape gardening under Catherine the Great helped fuel a rising demand for foreign builders and architects. Advertisements were placed by the Russians in various foreign journals and it was probably such a notice in the Edinburgh *Evening News* of January 1784 that enticed the Scot William Hastie to Russia. He joined Cameron as a junior stonemason, initially working at Tsarskoe Selo but Hastie had or developed excellent draughting skills and soon joined Cameron's design team. By 1792, Hastie was employed directly by Catherine and prepared a large portfolio of designs for classical villas, pavilions and other structures for the Empress. In early 1795, Hastie married Margaret Bryce, the daughter of another British stonemason and, in the same year, he was offered the job of chief architect to Count Zubov, the governor of Ekaterinoslav province in what is now Ukraine. Hastie was immediately thrown into the restoration of the former Khan's palace of Bakhchisarai on which he worked for some four years. He then returned north and became involved in the restoration of the important ironworks at Kolpino, then under the direction of fellow Scot, Charles

---

[68] Georges Lukomsky, *Charles Cameron, Architect*, 1943 and Howard Colvin, *A Biographical Dictionary of British Architects*, 2008.

Gascoigne (see page 235). In 1804, Hastie moved on to the Office of Waterways where he designed several new iron bridges for St Petersburg which were much acclaimed and set the standard for other bridge builders to follow in the city over the next twenty years.[69]

Eventually Hastie also replaced his former mentor, Cameron, as chief architect at Tsarskoe Selo in 1808, working for Alexander I and went on to produce a series of standardised plans for new town construction, complete with detailed designs for blocks, squares and buildings. After the great fire that devastated Moscow in 1812, Hastie prepared a plan for the reconstruction of the city featuring wide boulevards and vast open squares offering broad perspectives of the new city. In many ways, it was a forerunner of what Baron Haussmann was to achieve some fifty years later in Paris. Although endorsed by Alexander, Hastie's plan was eventually rejected as being too impractical and expensive. However, over the next twenty years, his standardised plans were adopted in many other towns and cities across Russia, from Onega in the north to Omsk and Tomsk in the east and Kiev and Ekarerinoslav in the south. Until his death in Russia in 1832, Hastie was the empire's master planner with enormous control and influence.

Adam Menelaws was another British stonemason who came out to Russia in 1784 to join Charles Cameron and whose career and responsibilities, like Hastie's, evolved during his time in the country. Born in Edinburgh, his primary skill was the construction of stone vaulting and Cameron employed him in this capacity at Tsarskoe Selo. However, after a year there Menelaws left and joined a Russian architect and landscape designer, Nikolai L'vov, with whom he was involved first in constructing two cathedrals and then more general building work. In between this activity, L'vov asked Menelaws to assist him in prospecting for coal in the Valdai Hills that lie between St Petersburg and Moscow. The unusual request in fact proved worthwhile and coal was found in the region in 1786 and for a while Menelaws found himself responsible for extracting the coal and sending it by barge to St Petersburg, assisted by other British workmen recruited from Tsarskoe Selo. In 1792, Menelaws married Elizabeth Cave and the St Petersburg ceremony was attended by L'vov and many prominent members of the British community. As well as continuing his cathedral building work, Menelaws was asked by L'vov to take charge of a new training for builders that L'vov had opened near Moscow as well as carrying out further searches for additional coal deposits. As L'vov's mining activities grew, his need for modern steam engines to power the mines led him to send Menelaws to England in 1800 to acquire the latest technology. By now, Menelaws was L'vov's right-hand man but the latter's death in late 1803 essentially brought to an end his varied enterprises and activities and Menelaws attempted to retire. However, possibly short of money and still only in his mid-fifties, Menelaws started work for the Razumovski family on their estates around Moscow and in Ukraine. Over a period of some eight years, he designed

---

[69] Hastie may well have acquired the necessary information on the latest iron bridge building techniques in England from Charles Gascoigne.

a wide range of buildings, parks and gardens, many in the then popular English style for the Razumoskis.

In 1814 Menelaws' wide-ranging skills were recognised by his appointment as a permanent member of the Russian government's Building Committee in St Petersburg. Menelaws continued to take other commissions and in 1818 he returned to his starting point of Tsarskoe Selo designing several new parks with their associated buildings and monuments over the ensuing decade. Menelaws worked for both Alexander I and his successor, Nicholas, who made Menelaws his house architect (and therefore de facto the leading architect in Russia) until his death from cholera during the Russian 1831 epidemic. His career in Russia had spanned a remarkable forty-seven years during which time he had evolved from a skilled stonemason into a talented builder, a creative designer and influential architect with a proven capability as a prospector and mining engineer.

The burst of activity overseen by men like Cameron, Hastie and Menelaws was not confined to the St Petersburg and Moscow regions. After Catherine the Great's seizure of the Crimea from the Ottomans in 1783, the Russians also embarked on a major building and reconstruction programme in the south, carried out at breakneck speed initially under Prince Potemkin and then later by Count Vorontsov, the governor of 'New Russia'. This led to the development of new ports such as Sevastopol as well as the expansion of existing settlements like Odessa and British architects and builders played a leading role in these projects. We have already seen the role played by John Upton and his sons in both of these towns as well as in the construction of Vorontsov's Black Sea palace. The original architectural designs for this lavish project were prepared by Thomas Harrison of Chester together with Francesco Buffo, an Odessan architect. Harrison was known to the Vorontsov family not only for his many fine classical-style buildings in England but also for some work for their estates in southern Russia.[70] Harrison's palace design, probably completed around 1822 was used for the ground plans and foundations when construction work first started in 1828. However, following a visit to England in 1831, Vorontsov changed his mind and after a year's delay, he decided to go with a largely mock-Tudor style building designed by Edward Blore. Harrison had died in 1829 and was therefore unable to oversee the project and at the time of Vorontsov's visit to England, Blore was very much in the ascendancy in the field of British architecture with a substantial portfolio in Britain and overseas. Vorontsov's change of heart was perhaps also influenced by the Gothic architectural vogue then prevailing in St Petersburg which was partly inspired by Walter Scott's novels which had recently become hugely popular in Russia. It was probably no coincidence that Blore had earlier also designed Scott's new mansion Abbotsford Castle near Edinburgh.

Vorontsov's new summer palace at Alupka, south west of Yalta, was finally completed to Blore's design in 1848. Overlooking the Black Sea, it was an exotic synthesis of the British Tudor-Jacobean revival style with local Crimean

---

[70] Yuri Pismak – The Influence of British Culture on the Formation of Crimea's Architectural Art Heritage.

Tatar or Muslim influences. The interiors included Gothic and Ottoman decor, a library modelled on Scott's at Abbotsford Castle plus the latest in British technology – twelve flushing lavatories. Externally, there were imposing gardens laid out in the current English style plus a steeply terraced park leading down to the sea. Blore never visited Alupka, the whole project was overseen by his assistant William Hunt and the work was carried out by Russian contractors and tradesmen under the supervision of English builders and craftsmen. As well as the Uptons, several other key skilled workers came out from Britain such as the Scot, Francis Heiton, who arrived in 1832 but sadly died from a fever the following summer and William Hunt from London. He remained in Count Vorontsov's employment as a builder and surveyor from 1833 to 1852. The joinery supervisor was Charles Wellington, who married a local girl and left many descendants; Edwin Rice made the furniture using trees that were imported from London.[71] Other architects such as Philip Elson were also working in the south of Russia at much the same time. Elson became the Russian provincial government's chief architect in the Crimean region in 1824 and worked on a variety of projects including Vorontsov's suburban house near Simferopol and later additions to the Alupka palace.

The final member of this panoply of influential British architects was William Walcot who was born in 1874 near Odessa, the son of Frank Walcot, a Scottish businessman in the town and a Russian mother. At the age of seventeen he went to St Petersburg to study architecture at the Imperial Academy of Art and continued his studies in Paris. He then returned to Odessa, practicing briefly as an architect before moving on to Moscow for six years where he designed the luxurious Hotel Metropol, completed in 1905, as well as several mansions for wealthy Russian clients. Due to his wife's illness, Walcot subsequently left for London where he settled in 1908, becoming a very successful graphic artist.

Painters and Sculptors

Richard Brompton was an English painter and portrait artist who, although quite successful, lived beyond his means and ended up in a debtors' prison in 1779. He was rescued from prison by the Russians who, possibly through the intervention of Sir James Harris the British ambassador, offered him a position as painter to the Russian Court. He was soon at work on portraits of the Empress as well as other members of the Royal Family and achieved popularity with the Empress with his allegorical portrait of the two young Grand Dukes Alexander and Constantine. Brompton's promising new career in Russia was literally short lived as he died some three years after his arrival in St Petersburg. Despite the significant money he had earned while in Russia, Brompton still managed to amass debts of 5,000 roubles which his widow was left to cope with. She soon married James Hill, a Russia Company merchant, in 1783 and the couple returned to England shortly afterwards. Contemporaries of Brompton as portrait painters in Russia at the time were Raphael Mengs and George Carter. The former arrived following an invitation by the Duchess of Kingston and the latter

---

[71] Sir Charles Brett, *Towers of Crim Tartary*, 2005.

possibly through an introduction by Baron Thomas Dimsdale. Neither seems to have had great success or influence in Russia and both returned home after a few years.

Catherine's interest in and enormous appetite for all types of works of art led her to not only employ British artists but also to acquire many originals directly from Britain, usually through the auspices of the Russian ambassador or consul in London. Perhaps her greatest coup was the acquisition of over 200 paintings in 1779 that had been collected by the British Prime Minister, Sir Robert Walpole. After his death, his family, deeply in debt, had put the art collection up for sale and through her ambassador in London, Catherine bought the lot for the Hermitage, paying £40,550 (around £60m today). She did however buy at least one work of art direct from a British artist in Russia. Thomas Banks was a talented English sculptor who was born in 1735 and studied sculpture, first at the Royal Academy and then in Italy, where he executed several excellent pieces, particularly a bas-relief representing a Cupid catching a butterfly. This remained unsold until Banks decided to take it with him on a visit to Russia where it was purchased by the Empress Catherine in 1781 for 4,000 roubles and placed in a grotto in Tsarskoe Selo gardens. Although Banks spent two years in Russia, he was unable to build on his successful sale to Catherine and he returned to England, where he was soon after made a member of the Royal Academy.

Joseph Hearn was a watercolour artist who arrived in St Petersburg in 1787 and enjoyed limited success with a series of six engravings of watercolours he painted of the Russian capital. James Walker was appointed imperial engraver in 1784 and enjoyed a relatively long and successful career in Russia. Walker is credited with popularising in Russia the English method of mezzotint engraving[72] and prints of his work became popular in both Russia and Britain. In 1794, in recognition of his achievements, he was made a full member of the St Petersburg Academy of Arts. Walker came to Russia with his wife Mary plus their daughter and young stepson, John Augustine Atkinson and the latter became an accomplished artist and engraver in his own right. The family returned to England in 1802 but unfortunately for Walker, the ship in which they were sailing was wrecked off the English coast and although the family survived, he suffered the tragic loss of all his engraved plates from Russia. In London, both Walker and Atkinson continued to publish popular works of Russian scenes and people.

One of the earliest established British artists to visit Russia was Sir Robert Ker Porter, an English artist and traveller who was born about 1775 at Durham and died in 1842. He became a student at the Royal Academy and became well known for the large, panoramic battle-pieces that he subsequently painted. In 1804, he was invited to Russia by Alexander I but his growing success and status in Britain caused him to initially hesitate in accepting. However, after further encouragement, he finally agreed to go and arrived in St Petersburg in September 1805. Alexander made him his historical painter and he completed several large historical murals for the Admiralty in St Petersburg. He formed a

---

[72] Anthony Cross – ibid, 1997.

close relationship with Alexander who he evidently much admired and respected. He left Russia in 1808 but subsequently returned briefly to marry a Russian princess. Porter was knighted by the Prince Regent in 1813 and in 1817 he was once more in St Petersburg on his way to Persia via the Caucasus. Although he was one of the most eminent painters of his time, he also achieved notable success as a writer. After his return to Britain, he published several books about Russia and his travels, including *Travelling Sketches in Russia and Sweden*, based on extensive correspondence with his family in England during his period overseas. His impressions of events, persons and the scenes that met his artist's eyes produced some of the finest word pictures in British travel literature.[73] He returned to Russia in 1841 to visit his daughter in St Petersburg who had married a Russian army officer there. In 1842, a few days before he was due to sail back to England, he died suddenly in his carriage as he was returning from a farewell visit to Alexander I and was buried in St Petersburg.

Sir Thomas Lawrence was born in Bristol in 1769 and for much of his life, Lawrence like his father before him, suffered from financial difficulties despite becoming one of the most acclaimed British portrait painters of his time. With the end of the Napoleonic wars, Lawrence travelled to Europe painting the Austrian Prime Minister Metternich, the King of Prussia and on his return to England, the Prince Regent and the Duke of Wellington. In 1818 he was invited to visit Russia where he painted Tsar Alexander and the Russian foreign minister Count Capo d'Istria as well as subsequently completing portraits of several leading members of Russian society, including Count Vorontsov, the governor of 'New Russia' (effectively modern-day Ukraine).

Another early artist to visit Russia was Edward Turnerelli who travelled extensively in the country under the patronage of the Tsar producing a popular series of fine pen and ink sketches of a wide range of scenes across the country. Born in London, Turnerelli was the son of a famous sculptor, Peter Turnerelli whose studio had been visited by Tsar Alexander in 1814 and Peter received orders for two busts from Alexander for the Hermitage. Edward arrived in Russia sometime in the mid 1830s and remained there for almost twenty years. Some of his most popular paintings were of the city of Kazan where Turnerelli lived for a five years and reproductions of these are still in print today. When he eventually returned to England in 1854 he published several books about Russia, including one about his experiences in Kazan.[74] Although he enjoyed his time in the city, there were clearly some things he didn't like such as the climate and in particular the local water which he describes in one of the most well known passages of his book:

'There are three different species of water in Kazan and the three degrees of comparison of the adjective bad serve perfectly to give an idea of each of these species. The first which is merely bad is the water of the Kaban, a lake that furnishes the whole town with this element. It is a stagnant pool which in the summer months becomes putrid. Even in winter it has an unpleasant taste and if left in a heated room for a short space of time, it becomes absolutely

---

[73] Peter Putnam – ibid.

[74] Edward Turnerelli, *Kazan, the Ancient Capital of the Tartar Khans*, 1854.

undrinkable. Every kind of filth and animal impurity is poured into this lake from the different sewers of the town.

The second species is obtained from the wells which are numerous in Kazan. This water is worse than the first, and although it may be employed for the kitchen, it is totally unfit for any other use.

The third species of water is that of the river Kazanka; this is bad to a superlative degree. It is impossible to employ it in consequence of the great quantity of sulphate of lime it contains. The inhabitants of Kazan employ this water for two purposes only – the washing of horses and the drowning of kittens.'

In fact Turnerelli was to discover a further important use for the river's water when he escaped across it to avoid a series of large fires that ravaged much of Kazan, including his own house and most of his possessions. Turnerelli then took refuge in another house but a few days later he woke up in the night to find this too was ablaze. Although the fires went on for almost two weeks and did great damage, Kazan was mostly rebuilt within a year. Perhaps it's not surprising that after his comments about the water in Kazan, Turnerelli ultimately retired to enjoy the clean and healthy waters of Royal Leamington Spa where he died in 1896.

One of the most successful and highest paid foreign artists to work in Russia was George Dawe, a talented English portrait painter and engraver. He was originally invited to St Petersburg by Alexander I and stayed in the country for ten years during which time he completed some three hundred portraits of the Russian royal family, nobility and various generals. Dawe was joined and assisted by his brother and his brother-in-law, Thomas Wright, who married Dawe's sister in St Petersburg in 1825. The rather sentimental and intimate portrait style used by Dawe for his royal family paintings became increasingly popular and Nicholas I also chose Dawe as a court painter and he was elected an honorary member of the Academy of Fine Arts in St Petersburg. Sir William Allan was a Scottish painter, born in 1782 in Edinburgh. He was originally apprenticed as a coach painter but later went on to study at the Royal Academy schools in London. After a spell in Russia between 1805 and 1814 he returned to Edinburgh and took to genre and history painting. In 1838 he was elected president of the Royal Scottish Academy.

Probably the only notable female British artist to visit Russia at this time was Christina Robertson who was born in Scotland in 1796 and became a successful portrait painter of Russian high society. From Scotland, she first moved to London where she set up her own studio and in 1829 became the first woman to become an honorary member of the Royal Scottish Academy. A few years later, she visited Paris where she painted portraits of several members of the Russian aristocracy and as a result of this work, Robertson was invited to St Petersburg in 1840 to paint a series of portraits of the Imperial royal family. She was made a member of the Russian Imperial Academy of Arts in 1841 and thereafter made a series of visits to the Russian capital, establishing a studio there in 1849 and producing a large number of portraits. Robertson died in St Petersburg in 1854.

Another English female artist with a tenuous but significant connection to the story of the British in Russia was Elizabeth Thompson. She was a young painter who in 1873 enjoyed modest success with a scene from the recent Franco-Prussian war, entitled *Missing.* She then announced her intention to portray a scene from the Crimean War that would depict the hardships endured by the ordinary soldier in as accurate a manner as possible. She diligently assembled a collection of the correct uniforms and military equipment and with the help of Crimean veterans, she embarked on her project. Her painting, entitled *Calling the Roll after an Engagement, Crimea*, was completed in March 1874 and tentatively submitted to the Royal Academy for exhibition. Her work was not the conventional, heroic depiction of war but rather a sombre scene of wearied, ordinary soldiers gathering together for a roll call in the snow after a battle. Thompson's painting, soon to be known as *The Roll Call*, was the first major Crimean War painting and immediately caused a stir at the Academy where the normally restrained selection committee greeted it with cheers. *The Roll Call* became an instant hit at the May exhibition and was received with excellent reviews by the press. It roused the interest of Queen Victoria who, pushing her royal prerogative to the limit, insisted on buying it from the Manchester industrialist who had originally commissioned the work. The painting went on a solo tour of the country generating great acclaim and long queues to see it and *The Roll Call* remained the most popular painting to have been exhibited at the Royal Academy during the 19th century. Thompson or Lady Butler, as she subsequently became, followed up this unexpected success with a series of war paintings from the Crimean, Napoleonic and Boer Wars and became the most famous female artist of her generation.

The talented sculptor Boris Edwards was born in Odessa in 1860, the son of an English father and a Russian mother. He studied in Odessa and St Petersburg before moving to Paris where he became adept at working with marble and bronze. In 1890 he was awarded a gold medal at the Paris World Exhibition. He then returned to Odessa where he married the Russian Princess Tatyana Uktomskaya. The couple lived a relatively quiet life there with Edwards teaching sculpture as well taking the occasional commission. In early 1914, he completed a monument to the courage of Russian soldiers made from the barrels of cannons used in the Russian-Turkish war of 1877-1878 which still stands in the grounds of Odessa University. The Edwards' tranquil life was shattered by the Bolshevik revolution during which the princess died, whether from illness or at the hands of the revolutionaries is unclear. Edwards stayed on in Russia until March 1919 when he escaped on board HMS *Marlborough*[75], together with his sister Lydia and her daughter Anastasia and they settled in Malta where he died in 1924.

---

[75] HMS *Marlborough* was sent to Yalta by the British government to rescue the Dowager Empress Marie Feodorovna, the mother of Tsar Nicholas II and other surviving members of the Russian nobility.

Authors and Writers

In the field of literature, the main interaction between British writers and Russia until late in the 18th century was the production of works about their travels and experiences in Russia. Although often widely read in Britain, they were rarely translated or circulated in Russia. The earliest literary work in English about Russia was written by George Turberville, an English poet born around 1540. The Turbervilles were an old Dorsetshire family and later provided the inspiration for the D'Urbervilles in Thomas Hardy's novel, *Tess of the D'Urbervilles*. In 1568, Turberville visited Russia as secretary to Thomas Randolph, the first English ambassador to the court of Ivan. On his return to England, Turberville published his *Poems describing the Places and Manners of the Country and People of Russia*, a rather negative commentary on his experiences there. Shakespeare certainly knew of and occasionally made reference to Russia in his plays. Ivan the Terrible's contacts with the court of Elizabeth I would have been well known in Shakespeare's London and the mention of *'a mess of Muscovites'* in *Love's Labour's Lost* may have been a reference to Ivan. Although Russian translations of Shakespeare's works were done in the mid 18th century, it was not until the Empress Catherine took the throne that any real interest in Shakespeare occurred in Russia. She adapted a couple of his plays into Russian but also banned both *Macbeth* and *Julius Caesar* because of their overt political themes. In fact, the interdiction on *Julius Caesar* remained in place for one hundred years. Alexander Pushkin, Russia's leading 19th century playwright, claimed to have based his most famous play *Boris Godunov* on the tragedies of Shakespeare. With the growth of British influence in Russia and a wider use of the English language in the latter half of the 19th century, Shakespeare's skills as a playwright were finally recognised and his works were increasingly read and performed.

Literary interaction between the two countries was further enhanced with the publication in Russian in 1792 of James MacPherson's *Ossian*. This series of epic poems, originally written in the early 1760s by MacPherson, had considerable impact on the works of many Russian writers including Pushkin and later Lermontov. The latter was descended from George Learmonth, an early 17th century British mercenary and Lermontov wrote several nostalgic poems in 1830 including *The Grave of Ossian*. An English translation of Pushkin's poems was published in 1835 by George Borrow who became a popular novelist in his own right some two decades later. Borrow was an accomplished linguist and had completed his translation of Pushkin's poems while he was working in St Petersburg for the Bible Society in 1834-35. Lewis Carroll also visited Russia for a few months in 1867 as part of a European tour and was impressed by both St Petersburg and Moscow. By this time, the reputation of Sir Walter Scott was also growing rapidly in Russia and probably exceeded that of any other foreign author during the 19th century. The other internationally famous Scottish author, Robert Burns, did not have any significant impact in Russia until the Soviet period when his works became widely read.

There was one other group of British writers that had significant influence on the opinions of the British and to a lesser extent, even the Russians. Over the course of the 19th and early 20th centuries, a growing number of correspondents representing the British press lived and worked in Russia. One of the first to arrive was James Longworth who first went to St Petersburg in 1838 as the Russian correspondent of *The Times* and returned again, along with many other newspaper men, during the Crimean War. One of his successors at *The Times* was George Forbes from Edinburgh who was sent to Russia in 1877 as their war correspondent with the Russian army during the Russo-Turkish war. He was subsequently awarded the Russian Order of St George. Forbes had actually visited Russia two years earlier on his return journey from Hawaii where he had led a British expedition to observe the Transit of Venus. Forbes decided to spend 1875 travelling back from Hawaii to Britain via Peking, the Gobi Desert, Siberia and St Petersburg. Although it took him twenty-five years to find time to write up and publish an account of his travels, he was one of the first astronomers to predict the existence of an additional planet fifty years before Pluto was discovered.

Henry Nevinson an experienced journalist and war correspondent was sent to Russia by *The Daily Chronicle* to cover the events of the 1905 revolution. He arrived in late October and filed his first report on December 4th. Nevinson was critical of the revolutionaries' opportunism yet recognized that they had "*struck the first blow at the heart of tyranny and made the old monster sprawl.*" He later attended the Central Strike Committee, met the leaders of the Bolsheviks, Mensheviks and Socialist Revolutionaries and also visited Leo Tolstoy at his home in Tula. On a visit to Moscow, Nevinson witnessed some of the awful atrocities of the struggle:

"*Officers began murdering in the name of the Tsar. Barricades were piled across the streets in the name of the people. The air crashed and whined with bullets and shells, and the snow was reddened with the blood of men and women.*"

A year after his return to England Nevinson published an account of his views and experiences of the 1905 revolution.[76] Some of the British correspondents lived in Russia for many years such as John Baddeley (*The Standard*), Harold Williams (the *Morning* Post and *Daily Chronicle*), George Dobson (*The Times*) and Robert Wilton (also *The Times*). Wilton, who was born in Norfolk, was the son of a British mining engineer employed in Russia and in 1889 he joined the European staff of the *New York Herald* where he worked for fourteen years. Wilton then became the Russian correspondent for *The Times* and gained a reputation as a keen observer of events in Russia during the last years of the Tsarist regime. He married a Russian but she sadly died in 1917 and he served with the Russian army during the First World War and was awarded the Cross of St George. After the Bolshevik revolution, he moved to Siberia from where he managed to escape from Russia in 1918, eventually arriving in

---

[76] Henry Nevinson, *The Dawn in Russia,* 1906.

Paris where he continued to pursue his journalistic career and completed two books on his time in Russia.[77]

Music and Theatre

In the domain of music British influence and involvement in Russia was limited but two men stand out. The first is John Field from Dublin who was a talented pianist and piano maker. He arrived in St Petersburg in 1802 where he became the manager of a shop selling pianos and also started to give private piano lessons to some of the capital's elite, including the Rachmaninov and Tolstoy families. In 1808, he married one of his Moscow pupils, a Frenchwoman, and his reputation in Russia and across Europe steadily grew. In 1819, he was offered the position of court pianist in St Petersburg but by then Field was sufficiently wealthy that he refused the post in order to concentrate on his own musical career. Following a European tour in the 1830s, he contracted pneumonia in Italy and returned to Russia. Although Field never fully recovered from his illness, he continued with his work until his death in Moscow in 1837. Field is recognised as having made a major contribution to the development of the Russian piano school through his concerts and teaching.

The second significant British influence on Russian music was Albert Coates who was born in St Petersburg, the youngest of seven sons. His father was Charles Coates who was a manager at the large British-owned Thornton woollen mills and his mother was Mary Gibson, who had also been born and raised in Russia by British parents. As a child in St Petersburg he learned the violin, cello and piano and then completed his education in England, eventually studying science rather than music at Liverpool University. Although Coates then returned to Russia to join his father's company, his love of music prevailed over business and he began studying with the famous Russian composer Rimsky-Korsakov and then took up a career as a conductor, first in Germany and then London. In 1910, following a debut performance with the London Symphony Orchestra, he was invited to conduct at the Mariinsky in St Petersburg and this led to his appointment as principal conductor of the Russian Imperial Opera, a post he held for five years. Despite the Bolshevik revolution in 1917, Coates was sufficiently admired that the Soviet government appointed him President of all Opera Houses in Soviet Russia, based in Moscow. However, living conditions in Russia were becoming increasingly desperate and most of the musicians with whom he worked were starving, with some even too ill to rehearse. In 1919 Coates fell seriously ill himself so he decided it was time to leave Russia and like many of his compatriots at the time, he escaped north with his family through Finland. After his arrival in England, he was appointed chief conductor of the London Symphony Orchestra.

The British were closely involved with the development of the theatre in both St Petersburg and Moscow. In the autumn of 1770, a group of English players paid their first visit to the capital and spent the winter there performing in a makeshift theatre converted from an old barn. Comfortable boxes were

---

[77] Robert Wilton, *Russia's Agony*, 1918 and *The Last Days of the Romanovs*, 1920.

provided for the nobility and their play was even attended by the Empress Catherine. In 1776, the English entrepreneur and impresario Michael Maddox arrived in Russia, following several years of success at the Haymarket Theatre in London. He formed a partnership with the Russian Prince Urusov who had been granted a ten-year monopoly on the operation of theatres in Moscow by Catherine the Great and by 1780 Maddox had erected the spectacular Petrovsky Theatre, which could seat 800 people. There were four levels of boxes, the more sumptuous costing up to 1,000 roubles to hire for an evening performance. Maddox became famous not only for his theatre but also as an organiser of large-scale balls and masquerades held in a rotunda attached to the theatre's main building. The walls of the rotunda were decorated with mirrors and here as many as 1,500 people would gather for one of his events. Maddox purchased a plot of land in Moscow and in 1783 created the 'Moscow Gardens' that were closely based on the successful Vauxhall Gardens in London. Despite charging an entrance fee, his gardens proved popular with open-air opera, dancing, firework displays and even billiard rooms. His gardens came to be known in Russian as a *voksal*, after the ones in London. Empress Maria later granted Maddox a lifelong pension of 3,000 roubles for his contribution to the development of the theatre in Moscow. His Petrovsky theatre continued in operation until 1805, when it was destroyed by a fire and replaced by the current Bolshoi Theatre.

7
Religion – Orthodox and Unorthodox

British Churches

While the Russians since the time of Ivan had gradually come to admire and absorb Britain's technology, scientific knowledge and its way of life, the subject of religion remained a deep-rooted area of difference between the two nations. The first discussions about religion between the Russians and the British occurred as early as 1583 when Tsar Ivan asked Dr Robert Jacob, a physician despatched to the Russian court by Queen Elizabeth and Humphrey Cole, a visiting English priest, to write down the main points of religion in England.[78] It is unclear whether Ivan was simply being inquisitive or trying to gain a deeper understanding of his new trading partners' beliefs and customs. Most likely, his real interest concerned the position of religion and the crown in Elizabethan England where the crown held the dual positions of head of state and of church. This was a subject that would continue to vex the Russian Tsars for many years and whatever Ivan's motivation was, it seems that this early discussion was not followed up by either side.

Russia's Orthodox Church was deeply embedded in its society, from the peasant commune through to the highest levels of the Tsarist state, although the levels of belief were perhaps not always as strong as the Church would have liked. The Orthodox Church was highly protective of its monopoly position with the Russian people but from early on the Tsars granted foreigners the right to practise their own religion. During the late 16th and 17th centuries, as the size of the British community in Russia waxed and waned in line with the state of trading and political relationships, its religious needs were met by a combination of churchmen intermittently dispatched from England by the Russia Company and through combined services with the Dutch Protestants. However, by the early 1700s, the British community was growing significantly following Peter the Great's drive to recruit foreign experts. As a result, the first English chapel in Russia was completed in Moscow in 1706 and its first chaplain was the Rev. Charles Thirlby who in that year recorded a congregation of fifty-three men and women.

The chapel's existence proved relatively short as it was closed when the Russia Company's headquarters relocated first to Archangel in 1717 and then to St Petersburg, the new capital, in 1723. Thirlby died in Moscow in 1715 and was replaced by the Rev. Thomas Consett who relocated with the Company to St Petersburg, retaining responsibility for the small British community left in Moscow. Consett remained as minister to the British in Russia for some ten years, conducting services in the capital in a chapel set up in the house of a

---

[78] John Appleby, *Medical History* Volume 27, pp 289-304, 1983

British merchant, Robert Nettleton. During his stay in Russia, Consett married and had three children. He was an academic and a scholar and became well known in Europe for various philosophical and theological works as well as his later book on the Russian Orthodox Church[79]. At a time when there was no official British diplomatic presence in Russia, he also provided the British government with reports on political developments within the country. For reasons that are not entirely clear, a dispute arose between Consett and the Russia Company that resulted in his departure in 1727. He was not replaced until 1737 when the Rev. Phillip Lernoult was appointed.

Despite various attempts to raise funds and seek Russian approval, the first English church in St Petersburg did not open until March 1754 when an empty building on the English Embankment was purchased and converted, largely at the expense of the Russia Company. The new Anglican church's first chaplain was the Rev. John King, who although still paid by the Russia Company, now operated under the administration of the Bishop of London. King was born in Suffolk and like most of his predecessors had graduated from Cambridge. He arrived in St Petersburg in 1763 with his young wife Anna who sadly died in Russia four years later, leaving King to raise their infant daughter. To divert his mind from this personal tragedy, King turned his mind to studying the Russian language and the Orthodox Church and in 1772 he published an extensive 500-page book on the subject[80] which remained the standard work in English for many years. He was elected to the Royal Society that same year. He resigned his position as chaplain in 1774, returning to England to settle in the London area where he married a second time. King returned briefly to Russia in 1781 when, acting on behalf of the widow of a close friend, he arranged the sale of a large collection of old English coins to a Russian nobleman.

King was quickly succeeded in St Petersburg by William Tooke who had originally come to Russia in 1771 to fulfil the role of chaplain to the English church at the port of Kronstadt. This position had been created around 1728 to look after the sizeable number of British merchants based there plus visiting seamen. Born in London in 1744, Tooke proved to be the longest serving Anglican chaplain in Russia staying on for eighteen years, caring for the growing British community until his return to England in 1792. He had a strong literary background, having already published two books prior to his appointment at Kronstadt and during his long stay in Russia Tooke continued to pursue his literary interests. He was also a skilled linguist, soon adding Russian to his existing knowledge of French, German, Latin, Greek and Hebrew. He took a keen interest in scientific matters, making close friends with members of the Academy of Sciences in both Russia and elsewhere in Europe. Tooke was elected to The Royal Society in London in 1783 and, shortly before his departure from Russia, he became a member of the Imperial Free Economic Society in St Petersburg. He regularly attended Catherine's annual *diner de tolérance* in St Petersburg held by the Empress for the clergy of all denominations which was presided over by Gabriel, the Metropolitan of Russia.

---

[79] Thomas Consett, *The Present State and Regulations of the Church in Russia*, 1729.

[80] John King, *Rites and Ceremonies of the Orthodox Church*, 1772.

In 1792 Tooke was left a fortune by a maternal uncle and understandably resigned his position as chaplain. He returned to England with his wife and three children and devoted himself to writing. During the next ten years Tooke became the foremost British commentator on Russian culture and history. By combining his literary and language skills, he drew on the writings of various foreign writers to compile revised and considerably extended versions of their works in English. Using this format, a succession of articles and books on Russia followed over the subsequent decade, including *The Life of Catherine II* in 1798, *View of the Russian Empire* in 1799 and a *History of Russia* in 1800. His work proved popular with the British public and his books ran into several editions, each with further additions. His intimate knowledge of Russia, especially Catherine's reign, plus his ability to carefully research his subjects gave his work an authority and level of detail lacking in previous writings on Russia. Tooke became chaplain to the Lord Mayor of London in 1814 and continued to work on editing and translating various publications until his death in November 1820.

Tooke's replacements as chaplain in St Petersburg continued to develop and expand the English Church in Russia. The Rev. London Pitt took over as chaplain in 1801 and became English tutor to Empress Elizabeth in 1807 and was also one of the early directors of the newly founded Russian Bible Society. In addition to the earlier appointment of a port chaplain in Kronstadt, the 19th century also saw the appointment of chaplains at Archangel, Riga and lastly Odessa. Edward Bindloss arrived as the Archangel chaplain in 1847 and married Maria Clark, the daughter of a local British merchant and together they had five children in Russia. Bindloss held the position until 1882 when his wife died and he returned to Britain. The church building in St Petersburg was extensively remodelled in 1815 (largely paid for by £4,000 from the Russia Company plus a grant of £5,000 from the British government) and had further reconstruction in the 1870s. A replacement for the original English chapel of 1706 in Moscow was not constructed until 1828 due to the low numbers of British residents there compared with St Petersburg. But by the 1820s, Moscow was developing fast as a manufacturing centre and so were the numbers of British traders and businessmen. In 1825, the Russia Company obtained permission from Alexander I to build a church in Moscow and following the Tsar's approval, the first resident chaplain, the Rev Charles Barlton, was appointed. He had previously been working as a locum in Kronstadt and this was to be the last independent chaplaincy established by the Russia Company. The Company supported the expansion of British churches in Russia not only to cater for religious needs but also because of its potential stabilising effect on the British expatriate community.

Apart from the senior Company merchants and the British diplomatic corps, the majority of British visitors and residents in Russia were young traders and sailors, far from home and family. They mostly lived in communal apartments sharing servants and expenses, generally pursuing a debauched, dissolute lifestyle with drinking as their main pastime and violent arguments and brawls were common. Apart from the wives of senior diplomats and merchants, the few British female inhabitants of St Petersburg or Moscow were mostly servants.

Russia was generally considered an unsuitable place for British women or children. There were no English schools and the limited social life generally revolved around the Russian Court so was only accessible to the most senior or wealthy British residents. By gradually adding primary schools and libraries, as well as organising occasional social functions, the British churches increasingly provided an incentive for men to bring out their wives and families, thus enjoying a less dissolute and more settled life.

The new British church in Moscow, or chapel as it was initially, saw a steady growth in its congregation and was gradually expanded to serve local needs. Some stables, a coach house and a hearse house were soon built in the grounds and the church committee even paid £200 to the Moscow authorities to build the first pavement outside the church. Successive chaplains became increasingly involved in charitable work in the wider community and in 1831 a foundling hospital or orphanage was established followed by a junior school for both boys and girls some years later. By the 1880s the chapel had become too small for the growing British community in Moscow and in 1882 it was decided to redevelop the site and construct a new church which was consecrated by the Bishop of London in 1885 as the British Church of St Andrew, Moscow. The new church building, designed in typical Victorian Gothic style by Neil Freeman of Bolton, was mostly of stone and brick and cost over 213,000 roubles. The Russia Company contributed around 10% of this with the remainder being raised by the congregation. St Andrew's could seat 300 and had a three-storey extension to the rear containing a library, meeting room plus the vestry and lavatories. St Andrews also boasted central heating, a mortuary, an organist's flat in the basement and even a strongroom in the tower for use by the congregation (the strongroom was to become particularly important during the Bolshevik revolution). A hostel was also added for the growing number of British nannies and governesses who were becoming very fashionable with both Russian and foreign families. However, the new church had nowhere for the chaplain and his wife to live. Due to a lack of funds, they had to stay in rented accommodation until a brick parsonage was built for them in 1894. Neither did the church have a belfry as only Orthodox churches at the time were allowed bells. An important part of the funding for the church and the later additions such as the parsonage and the governesses' hostel were provided by Robert McGill, a wealthy Moscow businessman and his wife Jane (see page 297 regarding the sad circumstances of her death).

Although the harsh winters caused at least one chaplain to leave prematurely, the Russia Company seems to have had no problems finding replacement clergy for the British churches as the salaries paid were quite attractive. The Company records show that in 1814 the Rev. Spencer's annual salary was £100 and similar amounts were paid to Rev. George Greaves in Archangel in 1823 and Rev. Law in 1826. In 1865 there were no fewer than 130 applicants for a vacant post in Moscow when the Company appointed the Rev. Robert Penny. Life for the chaplains was not easy however and relationships with the congregation sometimes proved difficult. The 19th century British communities in St Petersburg and Moscow reflected the mixed religious beliefs and prejudices of their home country with English Anglicans, Scottish

Presbyterians and a number of prominent Quakers. The Presbyterians in particular disliked the form of service based on the Anglican Prayer Book and heated disputes occasionally broke out.

Some of the Scottish 'dissenters' in St Petersburg broke away and attended services in the German Moravian chapel held by Dr John Paterson. He had arrived in Russia in 1812, working initially as an itinerant preacher and colporteur for the British and Foreign Bible Society but soon found an additional role at the Russian Bible Society with a handsome annual salary of 6,000 roubles paid by Tsar Alexander. Although the Russian Bible Society was not directly affiliated with the English Church or British and Foreign Bible Society, it received considerable support and encouragement from both as well as the British missionary societies. Based in St Petersburg, Paterson travelled across Russia extensively, helping to form many of the Bible societies that sprang up across Russia during Alexander's reign. He also worked closely with the Russians and various British missionaries in printing and distributing Bibles in Russian. Paterson married twice and his second wife was Jane, the daughter of Admiral Samuel Greig of the Russian navy. She had been born in Russia and her contacts, knowledge of the country and its language were of great help to Paterson in his work.

The other key player in the development of the Russian Bible societies was the English evangelist Dr Robert Pinkerton who, together with Paterson, helped found the Society with the Tsar's support in 1813. Like Paterson, he was based in St Petersburg and his wife, Dorothea, was also born in Russia. Pinkerton was employed as an agent of the British and Foreign Bible Society for almost eighteen years in the early part of the 19th century, working in both Russia and Finland. Within a few years of its founding, the Russian Bible Society had spread rapidly across the country. Pinkerton wrote that by 1818 there were '*One hundred and seventy-three Bible Societies in the Russian empire: Three hundred and seventy-one thousand six hundred copies of the Holy Scriptures, printed or printing in twenty-five languages and dialects; of which copies, One hundred and twenty thousand one hundred and five are already in circulation. The Receipts of the Society have been 1,361,499 roubles*' (over £160,000).[81] Despite its success, virtually all of the Society's operations ceased when it was dissolved by imperial decree in 1826.

The problems with the St Petersburg 'dissenters' lingered on into the 20th century but these were not the only disputes at the English churches. In 1903 the organist at St Andrews was sacked due to his inability to carry out all his functions properly. His failures were perhaps understandable as he was expected to combine the duties of organist, librarian and church caretaker all for a yearly salary of some £60. It is not surprising to find that after his departure, these jobs were divided up. Around 1908, Bousfield Lombard arrived as chaplain in St Petersburg, who later acted as chaplain to the British armed forces in Russia. His curate, Frank North took over as the chaplain in Moscow in 1911. He replaced Frederick Wybergh who resigned after being chaplain for some twenty three years. After an initial honeymoon period during which the congregation

---

[81] Robert Pinkerton, *Miscellaneous Observations on Russia*, 1833.

increased, North found himself facing many of the same problems as his predecessors with a divided congregation. While in St Petersburg, North married a member of the congregation, Margaret Birse who had been born in Russia of Scottish parents and was bilingual.[82] North never got round to learning any Russian (he was perhaps too busy dealing with his split congregation) and Margaret proved to be of considerable help to him in his later dealings with Russian officialdom.

With the outbreak of the First World War in 1914, the English churches provided important focus points, not only for the British community itself but also in helping to co-ordinate voluntary relief work with the Russians and North together with many of his congregation were heavily involved in these activities. Both churches also played an important role assisting British residents during the difficult period following the Bolshevik revolution of 1917. The Bolsheviks eventually closed all the Anglican churches in Russia during 1918, having first ransacked the strongroom at St Andrews and removed the congregation's 126 strongboxes with all their contents. The buildings were subsequently used for a variety of purposes. The parsonage of St Andrews was used for brief periods, first as the Finnish Embassy, and then as the Estonian Legation and the church itself was used as a hostel and later allocated to Melodiya, the State Recording Company, as recording studios and offices. After the Allied intervention in Russia in 1918 and the rupture of Anglo-Russian diplomatic relations, Frank North was effectively the only British man left in Moscow with any kind of recognised status and he became the unofficial leader of the much reduced British community of around 100. Mr Field, honorary treasurer of the Russia Company in St Petersburg performed a similar role there after the expulsion of Rev. Lombard. As the situation in Russia grew increasingly desperate, both men had to deal with a rising number of deaths among their respective British communities, mostly from starvation. Frank and Margaret North remained in Russia until March 1920, when, after arranging for the evacuation of the remaining British community, they were permitted to board the last train going to Helsinki. Both Norths were later awarded the CBE for their services to the community, and Frank North accepted the Helsinki chaplaincy which was renamed 'Helsinki with Moscow', a sign that St Andrew's was never relinquished.

Apart from the English churches and chaplaincies mentioned above, there was one other English church in Russia, that in Hughesovka in Ukraine. Arthur Riddle was appointed as the first Anglican chaplain there in December 1902, having arrived from St Petersburg with his wife Mary and their four children. The church had been built by the British-owned New Russia Company to serve the large British community in the town (see page 246). Riddle had been working for the English church in the St Petersburg region for several years and was known as 'Friar Tuck' due to his large girth and love of good food. Mary came from the Wishaw family who were well-established British

---

[82] One of Margaret's brothers, Arthur Birse CBE became a Russian interpreter for Churchill during World War II

merchants in St Petersburg. The Riddle family remained in Hughesovka until the death of Arthur in 1911 when they returned to England.

British Missionaries

The British churches in St Petersburg and Kronstadt, as well as those of other denominations, were well established by the early 19th century but their function was to look after their own local flock and not to actively proselytize in Russia. Indeed, they had only been tolerated on the basis that they adhered to the principle of not stepping on the toes of the Orthodox Church. There had been some limited evangelical activity during the 18th century by a few adventurous British missionaries largely following in the footsteps of the Russia Company's traders in the south and east but these had been intermittent and unsuccessful. There had also been periodic contacts between the Russians and the Society of Friends or Quakers and we will look at these later in this chapter.

In the latter part of the 18th and early 19th centuries, three events combined to significantly modify this situation. Firstly, the continued expansion of the Russian empire brought into its realm an increasing number of people with different beliefs; Catholics and Jews in Poland, Lutherans in Finland and the Baltic plus in the south and east Muslims, Buddhists, followers of the Dalai Lama and other more primitive sects. Secondly, the increased interest in the overall subject of religion by Alexander I who became Tsar in 1801. Thirdly, the growth in Britain of several increasingly well-financed and highly active missionary societies that felt it was their fervent duty to spread the word of God across the world. Although their proselytising activities were mainly directed to the newly discovered 'barbarian' people in Africa and Asia, the non-Christian population of Russia was not ignored. During the 19th century, these three events combined to induce a significant growth in foreign religious activities in Russia.

The first organised British missionary group to arrive in Russia were Scottish Presbyterians sent by the Edinburgh Missionary Society (renamed the Scottish Missionary Society in 1818) who travelled to the north Caucasus region in 1802 to work with the Muslim Nogay people. A petition by the Society to Tsar Alexander I for permission to '*turn various barbarian peoples to an enlightened position*' had been well received and the Tsar proved to be very supportive of their idea, generously granting the mission several thousand acres of farmland, free of taxes for thirty years. The Scottish missionaries were led by Reverend Henry Brunton and Alexander Paterson and initially consisted of fifteen persons, including family members[83]. They set up their base in the village of Karass within the Nogay lands, with the agreement of the local ruler, Sultan Mengli Geray. Although Karass was a somewhat isolated village, the Russian military base of Georgievsk was located nearby which was to prove of vital benefit in the years that followed plus the developing spa town of Piatygorsk with its hot springs.

---

[83] The additional male members of the party were Hay, Dickson, Hardie, Cousin and Frazer who actually arrived in 1803. Four more missionaries were sent out in 1805, Mitchell, Pinkerton, MacAlpine and Galloway.

Reverend Brunton, originally from Selkirk, had recently returned from West Africa where he had studied the languages of the local African tribes. He was an experienced though rather elderly man for this type of fieldwork and, although he had a good command of Arabic, neither he nor any of the missionary group had any knowledge of Russian or the local languages. Also they were seriously handicapped in their work initially by their lack of knowledge of the native people and their history, culture and traditions. However, with typical missionary zeal, they soon began to learn the local languages of Turkic and Adyge (used by the nearby Kabardian people), becoming sufficiently proficient that they were later able to publish religious pamphlets and the New Testament in Turkic. They also made an effort to study the history of the peoples they worked with and researched their culture. Paterson eventually learnt several languages including Tatar, Persian and Jewish (the missionaries saw the local Jews as additional potential converts). However, until the constraint of language was overcome and the missionaries could reach out to the people of Karass, it seems initially a good deal of their time was spent looking after their estate. Their land was mostly rich black soil and suitable for a variety of crops, both for the missionaries own use and for trade in the local markets. When Sir Robert Ker Porter, who had been appointed historical painter to the court of the Tsar in 1804 (see page 99), visited the station, he described it as more of an agricultural society than a theological college. The area was also visited in 1811 by the Scottish doctor, Archibald Crichton who was then working for the Russian civil medical service in St Petersburg and had been asked to look at developing a spa resort in this part of the Caucasus. Crichton met Alexander Paterson in Karass several times during his travels in the region.

The missionaries harboured the hopeful ambition that they might in time convert the Tartars and all other nations and tribes that lived to the south and east of European Russia, thus providing a 'corridor' of Christianity all the way to India. Sadly, this ambitious dream was to wither and ultimately die in Karass. Despite the dedication and hard work of Brunton and his group, they failed to make any substantial progress in achieving genuine converts among the local people. The problems encountered by the missionaries in Karass were common to all their fellow missionaries in other Muslim regions of the Tsarist Empire. The Society's missionaries *'approached their task as if they were introducing their message into a spiritual vacuum, tending to ignore the depth of the current well-established creed. It was quite apparent from their reports that once they were able to talk to a Muslim at some length, or especially to present him with any of the tracts they published, they were pretty confident that he would already be on the way becoming a Christian'.*[84] They misinterpreted their initial warm reception by the Muslims which usually derived from ignorance of the Scots true purpose, or from simple curiosity, or from fear because the missionaries were somehow connected with the Russian Government. Overall, the missionaries failed to appreciate the importance of religion to the non-Russian people which was deeply integrated into all aspects of their cultural and

[84] Hakan Kirmili, *Tatars, Nogays & Scottish Missionaries.*

social life as well as being a way of preserving their identity in the face of increasing Russian domination.

The troubles of the mission in Karass were by no means confined to their lack of success in finding converts among the local people. The Scottish group's presence in the northern Caucasus unfortunately coincided with a decade of political and social turmoil and the selected base of Karass proved to be far from ideal. When they first arrived, the population of Karass was around 500 but by 1810 it had declined to only forty people with hardly any Nogays left. Although it later recovered so that in 1813 there were 165 inhabitants in Karass including twenty-five from Britain (the missionary families), 122 German immigrants[85] and eighteen locals, it was still a small community. The decline in population was caused by the familiar scourges of pestilence and war. In 1804, the region was hit by an outbreak of plague from which many died, including the wife of Paterson who was the sister of Brunton. Then the latest round in the almost constant wars between the Russians and the Ottoman Empire broke out which lasted from 1806 to 1812. These disruptive events were compounded by an ongoing guerrilla struggle waged by the various tribes in the surrounding mountains. Armed warriors made periodic predatory attacks on Karass and other villages in the region, destroying some of the buildings and carrying off their cattle, sheep and horses as well as children. During such incursions, the inhabitants, including the missionaries, were forced to flee to the nearby garrison town of Georgievsk. Although a large number of Russian soldiers were eventually stationed on the edge of Karass to protect it, the local population became unsettled and semi-transient due to all the troubles and inevitably declined. This insignificant border settlement simply wasn't large enough to provide a suitable foundation for a successful mission and conversion campaign in the Caucasus.

However, the turmoil did provide one opportunity for the missionaries. Faced with their inability to generate conversions, the missionaries came up with a novel way to spread Christianity among the local Muslims. They decided to ransom local youths who had been captured by the surrounding mountain tribes during their raids and to educate them in Karass as Christians. The Scots were granted permission by the Russian authorities for their plan to redeem these captives provided that those ransomed were not older than sixteen and that they would leave the missionaries' care at twenty-three. This permission specifically excluded the purchase of Russian and Georgian prisoners from the mountain tribes for this purpose. The plan was put into effect and over the years more than thirty captives were rescued and brought up as Christians by the missionaries in Karass. Ten of them were eventually baptised and given a strange assortment of British-sounding names such as Abraham Warrend, Andrew Hunter, Walter Buchanan, Andrew Skirting Hay and James Peddy. Given their Caucasian tribal origins, the new lives of these converts must have seemed strange and taken some time for them to become used to. Perhaps the most successful was John Abercrombie, a Kabardian, who learnt the skills of a printer from the Karass

---

[85] In an attempt to speed up colonisation of the recently conquered southern lands, the Russians had welcomed immigrants from Europe, many of whom came from Germany.

missionaries and went on to work at the Society's station in Astrakhan in the early 1820s. He later tried to set up his own publishing business before moving on via Moscow and St Petersburg to Siberia where he worked as a printer with a group of British missionaries from the London Missionary Society in 1834.

Despite all their difficulties the missionaries, driven by their religious zeal and with the continued support of Sultan Geray, pushed on with their work and did achieve some progress. In late 1805 they set up a printing press using equipment sent out by the British and Foreign Bible Society and with a growing fluency in Turkic, they began their religious publishing work. Various tracts were produced and a translation of the New Testament into Turkish was eventually completed and published in 1813 with most of the translation done by Brunton, who tragically died a few months prior to its publication. In 1814, the Scottish Missionary Society decided to extend their activities to Astrakhan and Orenburg, sending several of the Karass missionaries to open up these new stations the following year. A school was also established by the Society in Astrakhan for the children of the missionaries to obviate the time and cost of sending them home to Britain for education. These new stations marked a change in the status of Karass as the centre of Scottish missionary work in Russia in favour of these two more easterly missions which were both located in more urban areas. The Society's work in Karass and elsewhere received much encouragement and support from Dr John Paterson in St Petersburg, as well as Rev Richard Knill, an English peripatetic preacher and evangelist who worked in Russia from 1820 to 1833. Based in St Petersburg like his friend Paterson, Knill at times worked on behalf of the London and the Scottish Missionary Societies, acting as an important point of contact between the missionaries and their societies. Knill also seems to have acted as paymaster for at least some of the missionary groups, drawing money from the Societies' accounts in St Petersburg and then sending it up country to the missionary stations. He married the Russian-born daughter of James Notman, a Quaker, who had worked for Alexander I in Kazan. The Knills had three children in Russia but two died, one daughter in 1826 and their son in 1831 from cholera. Knill also preached regularly in St Petersburg and seems to have been well known and liked by the British community there. Knill returned to England in 1833 to continue his preaching, ending up after some years in Chester in the early 1840s where he died in January 1857.

Although the missionaries only managed a handful of converts in the twenty odd years they were in Karass, there was one bright star that provided some consolation as well as great excitement amongst the group. A teenage boy called Katti Geray, a member of the Crimean branch of the Sultan Geray's family who had been orphaned at the age of four was brought to Karass in 1803 where he was apparently looked after by the missionaries. Inevitably, with close daily exposure to the Scots, Katti began to question his own faith and express an interest in Christianity. The missionaries were delighted with the hope of a member of the ruling Geray family embracing Christianity and attached a great deal of importance to his conversion. However, this was not viewed lightly by some of his countrymen who issued threats against Katti which resulted in him being placed under the protection of the local Russian military commander. By late 1805, Kattı had made rapid progress in reading and speaking English, in addition to his native Turkish and Russian and was openly talking about renouncing Islam and converting to Christianity. A few months later, he accompanied John Mitchell, one of the original missionary group, on a visit to St Petersburg. Disappointed to find out that St Petersburg was not the centre of the Presbyterian mission, Katti expressed a strong desire to visit their headquarters in Edinburgh. From St Petersburg, he sent a letter in English to the Edinburgh Missionary Society in his own handwriting asking permission to visit. Although Kattı's wish was favourably received by a somewhat surprised Society and they unanimously agreed to extend an invitation to him to come to Edinburgh, it would be a further decade before the visit occurred.

After his return to Karass, Kattı openly announced his decision to become a Christian and was baptised in July 1807. He wholeheartedly joined the missionaries' activities and began to work for the spread of Christianity among his countrymen, fervently defending his new religion against the Muslims. The latter, including his Geray relatives, were outraged by his decision, calling him an infidel and it was probably only due to the Russians' protection of Kattı that no violence ensued. Soon after his baptism, Katti left Karass to earn a living, going first to Georgievsk and then on to Nizhny Novgorod where he entered the Russian army. While serving in the army, he kept in constant touch with the mission in Karass either by letter or occasional visits and he continued to preach Christianity to every Muslim he happened to meet. In 1810, he wrote to Brunton offering to circulate missionary publications and later during a visit to Karass he expressed his strong desire to be employed in missionary work if he could be released from his military duties.

The lack of substantial progress by the missionary group in Karass, whilst discouraging, did not lead the Society to quit Russia. Instead it turned its attentions towards the Crimea, possibly encouraged by Geray who was keen to see a mission founded in his homeland. Both the Society in Edinburgh and the Scottish missionaries in Karass had been monitoring developments in the Crimea for some time and became increasingly convinced that it offered great potential for their work. Apart from its own significant non-Christian population of Muslims and Jews, the Crimea had the added attraction of providing a base to reach out across the Black Sea to Turkey and the southern Caucasus. In 1816, both Robert Pinkerton and Alexander Paterson travelled from Karass on separate visits to the Crimea to investigate the possibilities and develop contacts. They reported back positively and soon the Karass missionaries were supplying copies of the Turkish New Testament and other religious publications to the various Russian Bible societies that had recently been formed in Crimean towns such as Odessa and Simferopol. By 1818, the Society in Edinburgh had become convinced of the need to expand into the Crimea but sensibly recognised this could not be done without finding more suitably qualified missionaries. There was already a serious shortage of missionaries elsewhere in the Society's stations, especially in Karass where only three Scots remained out of the dozen or so sent out in the early 1800s. Several of the original group had died there (such as Brunton) and the others had mostly moved elsewhere. A further five years passed before the Society was able to set up a station in the Crimea.

While Geray was still in the Russian army, he had been fortunate to meet Tsar Alexander I and a warm relationship developed between the two of them. The religious nature of the Tsar no doubt made him both curious of and impressed by the idealism of this important Christian convert. When Geray left the army and the Society proposed to train him as a missionary with full theological training in Edinburgh, it was the Tsar who stepped in to cover Geray's costs in Britain with a generous annual salary of 6,000 roubles. Thus well provided for, Geray left Russia for his first visit to Scotland in the autumn of 1816. From the very outset, the whole story of Geray and his developing relationship with the missionaries had been regularly featured in *The Religious Monitor*, the monthly journal of the Scottish Missionary Society as well as in other missionary journals. So when Geray arrived in Scotland, he was already something of a celebrity and as one of the few converts of the Scottish missionaries in the Russian Empire he was warmly received in Edinburgh. His devotion to the Christian cause deeply impressed the Society and he was soon sent off to London where he began to his religious studies at Old Homerton College.

During his time in Britain, Geray developed a plan to launch a missionary educational project in his homeland that was based on establishing a Christian seminary for Muslim youth from the Crimea and beyond whose graduates would then return to their respective homelands to proselytise their kinsmen. Acting as religious 'agents provocateurs' they would gradually spread the Gospel throughout the Black Sea and Caucasus regions. On completion of his studies, Geray returned to Russia in 1817 and presented the outlines of his project to Alexander I in February 1818. Soon after, Geray returned on a second visit to Britain and was enrolled at the University of Edinburgh. Whilst there, he heard of the Tsar's approval of his project with a promise to provide any assistance required. Geray discussed the details of his project with the directors of the Society but although they were enthused and supportive, the Society's resources were then severely stretched. Maintaining the increasing number of missionary stations in the mostly Muslim parts of the Russian Empire had left the Society critically short of funds and it was unable to consider new projects such as the one now proposed by Geray. Thus with only moral support from the Society, the funds he needed would have to come primarily from his own efforts either in Britain or in Russia.

In the summer of 1819, Geray with the support of the Society, toured various towns in Scotland and Ireland with the objective of raising funds for his seminary as well as for a missionary station in the Crimea to be established by the Edinburgh Society. Geray's impassioned speeches about the millions of Tatar Muslims living in ignorance of the Gospel and the audacious simplicity of his plans seem to have been well received by his audiences. During his time in Edinburgh, Geray met and fell in love with Anne Neilson, the daughter of a wealthy Scottish businessman. The couple's marriage in Edinburgh in April 1820 created great sensation within the local Scottish society and various fanciful stories circulated regarding Anne's romance with an 'oriental Mogul prince'. Understandably, Anne's father found it difficult to accept his daughter's marriage to an oriental, who even if well educated and of good family, was planning to carry her off to a faraway land. Neilson disinherited his daughter. The couple left Scotland the following year and sailed to St Petersburg where Geray waited for an audience with the Tsar.

Meanwhile the Society, encouraged by the earlier promise of the Tsar to support Geray's project, had already established its first mission station in the Crimea with the Reverend J. Carruthers and his wife who arrived from Scotland. They were joined initially by William Glen from Astrakhan and Dr Robert Ross from Orenburg accompanied by James Peddie, one of the local youths ransomed earlier in Karass. Ross had worked at Orenburg for three years before his transfer to Astrakhan in 1821 and he served with distinction, developing a strong reputation as a medical practitioner and linguist. The Society's decision to proceed in the Crimea had also been influenced by enthusiastic support from Mary Holderness, an English traveller and writer resident in the Crimea from 1816 to 1820 who knew Geray and was aware of his plans. In her somewhat myopic, overly optimistic letters to the Society her view was that Geray's involvement might add great weight to enhancing the missionary cause among the Crimean Tatars and that the confidence of the Tatars could be won easily and once the schools planned by Geray were open. The missionaries duly set up their headquarters in Bahçesaray, the ancient capital of the Crimean khans, rather than at Simferopol, the Russian administrative centre of the Crimea at the time. It was expected that Geray, under the patronage of the Tsar, would join them there and his seminary which would be constructed in the region at the Russian government's expense would then be run by the missionaries.

In St Petersburg, Geray finally obtained an audience with Alexander who reaffirmed full financial support for the seminary as long as Geray remained engaged and active in the project and the local Muslims agreed for their children to be educated there. With the Tsar's support now assured, Geray left for the Crimea, arriving there in late November 1821. There was however, little evidence of any real progress at the missionary base and both Glen and Ross had by now moved on to Astrakhan, leaving Carruthers alone in Bahçesaray. In the early days the missionaries had fanned out across the Crimea distributing translations of the Bible but although there was some initial interest, the local attitude soon changed and the missionaries found themselves being branded as infidels and many of their books were returned. Carruthers was trying hard to master the Crimean Tatar language so as to be able to reach out to the Muslims and within two years he was to preach in Tatar. Nevertheless, his calls for conversion to Christianity found few receptive ears among the Crimean Tatars.

The first baptism of a Crimean Tatar would not occur until 1823 and although this was followed by three further baptisms of dubious converts, these would prove to be the end rather than the beginning of a successful mission. In fact, many local Tatars, encouraged by their mullahs, became outraged by these cases and now that they understood the real purpose of the Scots in their country, their attitude towards them changed totally. Carruthers found that people shunned him and in the street he could find very few Tatars who were willing to talk to him or receive a copy of the Scriptures. In fact, a whole year passed by without Carruthers being able to give away a copy of the New Testament. His wife also experienced a similar brick wall. At first, she was able to develop good relations with the local Tatar women who frequently visited her and she launched a teaching programme for Muslim children. Initially she made some progress with this, especially when she offered to compensate the parents for the loss of their children's labour whilst they were at school – an attractive proposition for the poorer families. But when Mrs Carruthers introduced the Scriptures into her lessons, the parents' attitude quickly changed and, like her husband, she found herself ostracised.

As the months and the years rolled on, the Carruthers encountered yet more problems. The sympathetic attitude of the Russian state towards the various Protestant missionaries in the country steadily receded during the 1820s. This was partly due to a decline in Alexander's interest in other religions and therefore his direct support and partly due to a more assertive Russian Orthodox Church that viewed the missionary activities of other religions as a threat and wanted them gone. Carruthers started to note a distinct change in the attitude of local officials, finding the Tsarist police would no longer allow the missionaries to baptise their converts and occasionally would even lead away his few precious converts to join the Orthodox Church. At the same time, Geray's dream of a seminary had stalled. The Russian government now reneged on its promised support and the Society was totally unable to underwrite the project as its funds were exhausted. Even the eternally optimistic Geray had to admit failure and he abandoned his proselytising work and closed his little school in mid 1823. With the failure of both parts of the Crimean project, the writing was on the wall for the Carruthers and in 1825 the Scottish Missionary Society closed down their operations there and moved the family to another assignment.

As the reign of Alexander I drew to a close the floodgates of what the missionaries called the 'Anti-Biblical Revolution in Russia' truly opened and the work of the foreign missionaries in Russia came under severe criticism and pressure. By 1824, the Russian Bible Society, which had been founded with the cooperation of the British missionaries and had played an important auxiliary role in their activities, was paralysed and moribund due to pressures from the Orthodox Church and State. The activities of the European missionaries in the area of printing the Testaments and tracts were severely curbed and made subject to the state and Orthodox Church censorship. With the death of Alexander I, the situation deteriorated further and the Russian Bible Society's already tenuous existence ended when its activities were "temporarily" suspended by Nicholas I in 1826. Part of the reason for the anti-Bible phobia of both the Orthodox Church and the Russian state was due to injudicious proselytising activities of some of the Society's agents and missionaries who failed to confine their evangelical work to the purely non-Christians in Russia. Perhaps this was out of frustration at their lack of success but it was against the original understanding with the Tsar when they were allowed to set up in Russia.

Alexander's death also terminated the important beneficial relationship that Geray and the Society had enjoyed with the Russian Tsar, finally removing all hope of success, not only in the Crimea but elsewhere in Russia too. In Karass, even before the 'Anti-Biblical Revolution', the mission had clearly entered a period of terminal decline. When Ebenezer Henderson visited the station in 1822, he found only two Scottish missionaries remaining – Alexander Paterson and James Galloway.[86] The lack of success seems to have led to a deterioration in relations between both the missionaries themselves as well as with the Society in Scotland which eventually resulted in the Society taking the grave step of severing its ties with Paterson. He was the elder statesman of the station, having arrived in 1803 with Brunton and had been its administrative head of the colony for over twenty years. After the death of his first wife, Brunton's sister, Paterson married again, this time to a German colonist, Helena who arrived in Karass in 1810. As well as being deeply religious, Paterson was clearly a talented man with a variety of interests. He operated an early meteorological station in Karass from 1811 onwards, recording pressure, weather and wind three times a day as well as noting comments in his personal diary about extreme weather and astrological events.

After the closure of the Karass mission in 1835, Paterson and his wife stayed on in Russia, moving to a town house in the nearby spa town of Pyatigorsk. Helena died in 1841 and was buried in the family plot in Karass along with Paterson who died in 1844. It is thought that the Patersons had seven children, four of whom died in Karass at relatively young ages and are buried in the family plot there alongside two of his other three children who lived on to adulthood. None of these three chose to go to the homeland of their father and take up a career there. Henrietta, who in her early years, had been educated at the missionary school in Karass went on to marry a Russian army officer. Edward became an officer in the Russian army and was stationed in the Ukraine for several years. Paterson's other son, Alexander, also educated at the Karass school and at university in Moscow, became a doctor and served in the Russian navy for six years. He then returned to the Karass area in 1841 to work first as a doctor at the Pyatigorsk military hospital and then as a local general practitioner for thirty-two years. He also held the positions of vice-president and treasurer of Russia's first Balneological Society. He died in 1873 and was buried in the Pyatigorsk cemetery close to the initial burial place of the Russian poet Lermontov, who was killed in a duel there in 1842.[87] Paterson also had a son called Alexander who followed in his father's footsteps, both as a doctor and joining the same Pyatigorsk Balneological Society, becoming its Secretary and Treasurer.[88]

Although Karass had experienced its own particular difficulties almost from the start, similar problems were encountered in all the Scottish missions across the Russian Empire and these had prevented the Society's missionary work with the Muslims from ever being successful. By 1825, the Scottish Missionary Society finally recognised the hopelessness of 'persevering in cultivating a field which appeared so barren and unpromising' [89] and most of the Scottish

---

[86] E Henderson, *Biblical Research & Travels in Russia*, London 1826

[87] Coincidentally, Lermontov also had Scottish ancestry - George Learmonth who came to Russia from Poland in 1613 and who in turn was descended from the Scottish 13th century poet, Thomas Learmount.

[88] Anton Grizenko - Karass - Little Scotland in North Caucasus, *Scotland-Russia Forum Review*, Dec 2008

[89] Hakan Kirmili - ibid

missionaries in the Russian Empire were withdrawn back home and their stations in Orenburg and Astrakhan were effectively mothballed. Only one missionary remained in Astrakhan to continue translation work on the Bible into Persian and he was funded by the British and Foreign Bible Society. The same year the Society also attempted to hand over their Karass operation to German missionaries who had arrived in Karass in 1821 but failed to obtain permission from the local Russian authorities. In the end, the Society's Karass mission struggled on until 1835 when Tsar Nicholas I finally approved its closure. Sadly, these closures did not happen early enough to prevent personal tragedies amongst the Scottish missionary families. Two of William Glen's children and one of John Mitchell's died of scarlet fever at the Astrakhan station in 1826 as did one of James Galloway's in Karass. When a British military officer, Captain Richard Wilbraham visited Karass in 1837 during a tour of the Caucasus, the Scottish missionaries had of course all left but he was greeted by a Mrs Lang. She told Wilbraham in a strong Scottish accent that she was the daughter of one of the original settlers and a Circassian mother (this was probably Margaret, the daughter of James Galloway and his wife Nancy, a ransomed Khabardian[90]). Mrs Lang left Karass a few years later, eventually settling in the Kherson area of the Ukraine where she died in 1873. However, she was not the last remaining link to the Scottish mission's presence in the area as the Society's records indicate that several of the missionaries married local girls and had children. James Galloway married an eighteen-year-old Kabardian girl who sadly died after giving birth to their child and two others, Davidson and Fraser, married Ossetian girls who had been ransomed out of slavery.[91] Unfortunately, there are no records confirming the subsequent fates of either of these families.

Before returning to conclude Katti Geray's story, it is worth noting that there was one other notable success of the Society's missionary's work among the Muslims. This was the case of Muhammed Ali Kasim Beg or Alexander Ivanovich Kazem-Bek (as he later became known) which holds many similarities to that of Geray. Muhammed was also descended from a noble family, though in his case it was Persian and his father had migrated to Astrakhan when Muhammed was a teenager. His fluency in several languages enabled him to gain employment teaching the Scottish missionaries in Astrakhan Turkish and Arabic. He gradually decided to convert to Christianity and in 1823, at the age of twenty-one, he was baptized. As with Geray in Karass, Muhammed's conversion outraged his kinsmen although it delighted the missionaries who were otherwise beset with problems and it provided them with a much-needed temporary revival. After his baptism, Kazem-Bek was compelled by the Russian authorities to leave the mission and join the army, much to the regret of the missionaries. He subsequently became a professor at Kazan and St Petersburg universities and an outstanding specialist on oriental languages and history. In his later life, like Geray, Kazem-Bek found that as a Protestant Christian he was detached from his former Caucasian or Persian identity but unable to fully be a part of Russian society and culture.

---

[90] Anton Grizenko - ibid

[91] Ahmat Musukayev - The mysterious world of the peoples of the Caucasus.

After the disbanding of the Scottish missionary organisations in Russia, Geray and his wife were alone in carrying forward his original joint project with the Society of converting the non-Christian peoples of the Russian Empire. Geray remained in contact with the Society, at least until early 1830s, partly in the hope of receiving some of the donations that had been made for his seminary project during his visits to Scotland and Ireland. But the Society felt that the fund had been donated to the Society for a specific purpose and not to Geray personally. As there was not the remotest possibility of resuming the Society's missionary work in the Crimea, it returned the donations or used them for other missionary activities. Geray carried on with his proselytising activities for a while but with no practical support from the Society and an unhelpful and suspicious Russian Orthodox Church, he met with complete failure and was unable to make a single convert. Geray still received the 6,000 roubles annual pension granted to him by Alexander I and so he and his Scottish wife were able to enjoy a fairly comfortable life in the Crimea, with a beautiful seaside villa near Simferopol and an estate in the mountains.

Following Geray's death in 1847, his wife Anne did not return to her native Scotland but continued to live quietly in Simferopol with her eight children. Over the years in Russia she had given birth to fourteen children but six had died in their early infancy. However, the family's peaceful life was dramatically disrupted by the outbreak of the Crimean War in 1853. Anne now not only faced the distress of finding her home country and her adopted one at war with each other but she also had to deal with the fact that at least two of her sons chose to fight for the Russians against her own countrymen. This was not the end of her problems however. The family home in Simferopol was close to the place on the coast where the Allies landed and the British sent a letter assuring her that in the event of Simferopol being taken by the Allied forces, she and her property would be protected. Unfortunately, this letter was intercepted by the Russians and they sought to remove Anne from her home and send her away from the Crimea to Yekaterinoslav (the modern Ukrainian city of Dnepropetrovsk) under escort. However, Anne boldly refused to make this journey into exile on the grounds of her poor health and the Russians eventually agreed that due to her sickness she could remain, placing her under surveillance instead.

Perhaps as a result of all this distress, Anne died at her home near Simferopol just a few months later in June 1855. All of the Geray children were baptised as Protestant Christians and indeed their first child, Alexandrine who was born in St Petersburg in 1821 and named after Alexander I was baptised by the Tsar himself at the Winter Palace. She became a lady-in-waiting at the Russian court to the wife of the Grand Duke Constantine and later married a German baron. She was also connected to the Danish court and a friend of the future British Queen Alexandra (the wife of King Edward VII). Another of the Geray's daughters married a British man called Thomas Upton and settled in Edinburgh. Of the other Geray children little is known of their lives except that the two sons who fought in the Crimean War, both survived.

The lack of success of the Scottish missionaries in Karass either failed to be relayed to other societies or was ignored as in 1814, the London Missionary Society (LMS) developed plans to send missionaries to 'the unnumbered hordes of Tartars who inhabit the immense regions of Siberia'.[92] The LMS had been formed in 1795 as a non-denominational society and had initially attempted to work in the Pacific region but ran into a series of problems that depleted their limited financial resources. But by 1814, they had recovered sufficiently for the Society to consider new regions of endeavour and one of those ultimately selected was Siberia. The Society accordingly approached Alexander I seeking his agreement for missions to Yakutia and Irkutsk which was readily granted in 1815. The Society's reasons for selecting these remote locations in Siberia as a new theatre of operations are unclear and it seems to have been almost accidental. The choice ultimately seems to have arisen from various contacts made by John Paterson and Robert Pinkerton in Russia that led them to erroneously conclude that *'the Buryats were ripe for conversion to Christianity'*.[93] There is also some evidence to suggest the Society thought it would be useful to have an outpost on the trade routes and lines of communication between Russia and China where they were also looking to expand their activities. This may have made some sense looking at a world map in London but the reality on the ground was very different and the decision would prove to be an expensive mistake.

Their first mission was to the Yakut people in eastern Siberia but this proved a disaster as those who were sent were never heard of again. Undeterred, the LMS then recruited Edward Stallybrass from Royston in Hertfordshire as leader and a Swede, Cornelius Rahm to accompany him to Irkutsk. The two men with their respective families set out from England in 1817, calling first at St Petersburg, where both men wisely studied Russian for several months and then at Moscow for an audience with Tsar Alexander who expressed strong support for their mission. They left Moscow for Siberia in the bitter cold of mid January on horse-drawn sledges to cover a distance of over 3500 miles that would take two months to complete. The description of their remarkable experience by the young wife of Stallybrass makes for fascinating reading.[94] Their journey eastwards took them through vast expanses of empty forest and across wide, frozen rivers. In good conditions they covered ten miles per hour or one hundred miles a day but on bad days, especially when their sledges broke down or overturned on the ice, progress was minimal. The temperatures were almost constantly well below zero but luckily it was mostly sunny with only a few days of snow. Their accommodation en route was varied, occasionally staying at inns, often in private lodgings and a few times even sleeping on their sledges. Amazingly, despite Rahm's daughter Hanna being only two years old and both Betty Rahm and Sarah Stallybrass pregnant, they all arrived safely and in good spirits at Irkutsk on Lake Baikal in March 1818. A Cossack guard accompanied

---

[92] LMS letter of December 1804 in the Stallybrass Collection, London School of Oriental and African Studies. The letters are interesting for not only their content but also they show the scarcity of paper as the reply to an incoming letter would often be written on the same piece of paper, usually at right angles to the original.

[93] C R Bawden, The English Missionaries in Siberia, *Asian Affairs* 16:2.

[94] Edward Stallybrass, *Memoir of Mrs Stallybrass*, 1836

the group for the whole journey but his intervention was only needed once during a minor altercation with some passing traders.

Both women successfully gave birth to their respective children later that year but Betty Rahm's health deteriorated in the extreme cold of the following Siberian winter and in May 1819, the Rahms relocated westwards to Sarepta, south of modern-day Volgograd to work among the Kalmuck people. That same year, Stallybrass concluded that the Irkutsk region was unsuitable for his work and moved on with his family to establish a mission station at Selenginsk, near the Mongolian border and close to the Buryat people. Here, there was good support for their intended work from the governor of Siberia and they were given seventy-two *desiatin* (about 175 acres) on which they built two homes and their mission. They were joined in Selenginsk by two Scots, William Swan[95] in the late summer and Robert Yuille and his wife the following year. Both men played important roles in helping with the mission work of preaching, tract distribution, visiting local schools and translation of the Scriptures into the Buryat language. However, the missionaries' location in Selenginsk was not the best as they were across the river from the main Buryat settlements and so contact and communication with the locals would always be difficult. In an account of a visit paid to the mission by Captain John Cochrane in 1822 (see page 146) he was quite explicit in his criticism of both their location and prospects. Despite this problem, it is clear from the missionaries' letters that they did succeed in making a few conversions in Selenginsk and in 1825 two Buryats were married in a Christian ceremony. However, this small progress was marred when some form of epidemic hit the missionary community and both the Stallybrass and Yuille families each lost a young child. Yuille's wife gave birth to their second child later in 1825 but she herself then died just two years later.

The cost of the mission was modest with Stallybrass and Yuille each receiving £250 a year and Swan, who had private resources, somewhat less. In the late summer of 1828, the Stallybrass family moved to a new location at Khodon with Swan going to nearby Ona, leaving Yuille in charge at Selenginsk. Stallybrass told the Society that the move to Khodon was because it was a more central location for working with the Buryats but it seems the real reason was a growing tension between the very different personalities of the three missionaries and *'they could not bear to live together any longer'*.[96] Stallybrass bought a house in Khodon for his family to live in. Apparently, this was the only house in the settlement and when in December, the wooden house caught fire and burnt down, the group had no choice but to move into a surviving barn. As the Buryats all lived in tents, there was no alternative accommodation in the area until they built a new house a year later. Both mission stations increasingly found themselves in strong competition with Buddhist missionaries plus the traditional local shamans or priests and conversions remained limited. The missionaries' opinions of the competition were low; Swan described the

---

[95] There is also a reference to a George Swan working as a missionary in Siberia around this time. It isn't clear whether he was a relation, the same man or an entirely different person.

[96] C R Bawden – ibid.

situation as '*the blind leading the blind*' and the shamans were drunk much of the time. The main success was their little schools run by Yuille in Selengirsk and Sarah Stallybrass in Khodon. The support and encouragement of the evangelists, John Paterson and Richard Knill in St Petersburg, both through correspondence and Paterson's occasional visits were important in maintaining the small missionary group's spirits at this time. Swan and Stallybrass collaborated on translating the Bible into Mongolian for publication by the Russian Bible Society. Swan returned to Britain in 1831 to marry but when he and his wife, Hannah Cullen arrived in St Petersburg on their way to Siberia, Swan was arrested and detained until 1833 before being allowed to continue on to Khodon.

Another missionary, William Carey, joined Stallybrass in Khodon around this time; he may have been a temporary replacement for Swan during his visit home. Famine struck the region in 1832 and 1833 causing great hardship to the Buryats as well as the missionaries and sadly, Sarah Stallybrass died early in 1833. It seems she had caught typhus the year before from a Buryat woman and although she initially recovered, a recurring bout caused her death and she was buried at Khodon. By 1834, Yuille had set up a printing press and with the help of John Abercrombie who had arrived from Karass, they started publishing translations of the Old Testament. In 1835, Stallybrass, together with his two Russian-born sons, returned to England, marrying his second wife, Charlotte Ellah in Copenhagen en route. Soon after, the couple left for Russia, arriving in Khodon in 1836 where they subsequently had three children, although sadly Charlotte died unexpectedly in 1839. Understandably, this tragic death left Stallybrass with a deep sense of loss which is evident from a harrowing letter he wrote to his sister relaying the news. But his trials were not over as a few months later one of the three children he had with Charlotte also died. On reading the often lengthy, handwritten correspondence of the missionaries with both their families and the Society, it is hard not to sympathise with their problems and frustrations. But despite all the difficulties and challenges they faced, they maintained a strong sense of evangelical optimism and belief in God's will.

Stallybrass and Swan continued their work on translating the Bible into Mongolian in Khodon and they completed a translation of the Old Testament which was published in 1840[97]. In that same year, the work of the LMS in Russia was suppressed by a decree of the Orthodox synod and Stallybrass and the other British missionaries were forced to close their two mission stations. Stallybrass and Swan returned to England and although they both subsequently retired from the LMS, they co-operated on a revision of the Mongolian version of the New Testament (originally produced by the Russian Bible Society in 1824) that was published in 1846. Despite the official closure of the Selenginsk mission, Yuille somehow managed to remain there (unpaid) for several more years, continuing to work with some of the converts and trying to find one of

---

[97] Although not credited in official accounts, it seems Hannah Swan was also an able translator and assisted in this work. One of the early converts, Ihagdur wrote to Hannah's mother praising her translation skills in 1835.

them to replace him. He also tried to sell their land and buildings to raise badly needed funds but was unable to do so and when in October 1845, he was finally forced to leave by the regional authorities, the station was abandoned. Yuille went first to St Petersburg and then eventually returned to Scotland in 1847 when he was still writing to the Society requesting (unsuccessfully) to return to Russia as a missionary.

There were other British missionaries and evangelists who visited Russia during the first half of the 19th century, either under the auspices of a foreign missionary society or independently but none of them had any notable or lasting success. For example, in 1803 Charles Fraser of the Scottish Missionary Society arrived in Karass before moving on to Orenburg where he became the first person to work on translating the Bible into Kazakh. His translation of Matthew was published in 1818 (this was based on Brunton's earlier translation work in Karass) and the complete New Testament in 1820, printed by the Russian Bible Society in Astrakhan. The Reverend Blyth also went to the Caucasus in 1821 with James Galloway from Karass to work with the Ingush people in Nazran but in less than a year they were ordered to leave by the local governor. Another was Peter Gordon, a retired sea captain, entrepreneur and freelance missionary who travelled across Russia from Siberia to Astrakhan in the early 1820s. He wrote several letters to the missionary societies in Britain describing his encounters with the local people and encouraging the missionary efforts in Russia. A Calvinist Scotsman, John Melville worked as a colporteur and evangelist in the Ukraine and Caucasus from 1860 almost until his death in 1886. In 1870, an unsuccessful attempt was made by James Gilmour to reopen the Siberian mission under the auspices of the Society's operations in northern China. He visited the former mission stations and although he found some of their pupils still alive, there was no other evidence of the missionaries' thirty years of effort.

It is hard some two hundred years after these events unfolded to fully comprehend the difficulties and challenges faced by these early missionaries in Russia. Like many other missionaries around the world in the 19th century, the great hardships, language barriers, suspicion and isolation they faced were compounded by a high mortality rate. In most cases, their religious fervour and remarkable dedication to their task, often sustained over many years of unrewarding toil and disappointment, can only be admired. The work of these missionaries ensured that 'the Divine Word was eventually published in as many as twenty languages' across the Russian Empire.[98] Some hundreds of thousands of Bibles were distributed in Russia by the missionaries and their supporters together with a much larger quantity of tracts and pamphlets. Once the so-called anti-Bible revolution occurred, they operated under even greater difficulties, often in fear of violence, arrest or deportation. A Captain Drury, a British officer serving in the Russian army was actually imprisoned for distributing Bibles in 1830. It is unfortunate that all this hard work and commitment over so many years neither achieved its objectives nor left behind any significant legacy. At the time, the missionaries justified the situation by viewing their activities as more like sowing seeds than gathering crops but, sadly, they never managed to

---

[98] Rev Charles Birrell, *The Life of Rev Richard Knill*, London 1860

reap what they had sown. The repressive anti-Bible movement in Russia not only put paid to the activities of the foreign missionaries and the Russian Bible societies, it also froze religious relations between the Russian Orthodox Church and European churches for the rest of the century. Things did not improve until the early 20th century when a revival in relations following the Anglo-Russian Convention in 1907 brought a renewed interest in Russia and the Orthodox Church.

The Quakers

The British Quaker movement or Society of Friends, although relatively small in number and with only limited resources was to have a significant, if sporadic involvement in Russia. The very first Quaker contact with Russia occurred when the principal founder of the Quakers, George Fox, wrote letters to Tsar Alexei I in 1656 and 1661 attempting to spread word of their beliefs. There is no record of any reply from the Tsar and Fox's letters were not followed up by any Quaker visits to Russia. However, the term 'Quaker' had certainly become known and used in Russia by the end of the 17th century and was often adopted in regard to Russian sects that shared some of the Quaker moral and religious beliefs. George Fox in an account of a group of some 200 Russians living near Moscow in the 1670s stated that they were labelled 'English Quakers'.[99] Thirty-six of them were apparently executed for failing to remove their hats and bow to the Tsar. Despite these inauspicious beginnings, the persistent Quakers sought out Tsar Alexei's son Peter the Great during his visit to London in 1697 and after meeting with them, he attended several Quaker meetings for worship while in England. Although Peter took a keen interest in the Quaker's views and never forgot his Quaker 'friends' in later life, he also looked at other faiths including the Church of England and the Jesuits. His interest was simply part of his insatiable quest for knowledge whilst in England.

There was no further significant contact between the Quakers and Russia until the reign of Catherine II when in 1768 she chose to use the services of the English Quaker physician, Dr Thomas Dimsdale to successfully inoculate her son, Alexander, against smallpox. When Alexander became Tsar at the relatively young age of twenty-four in 1801 following the murder of his father Paul I, he soon became embroiled in the intense struggle for power between the major European powers which eventually led to the Napoleonic War. Following the defeat of Napoleon, Alexander was invited to visit London in 1814 together with the King of Prussia and as with Peter the Great, the Quakers felt it important to take advantage of this opportunity to try to meet with the Russian ruler. Alexander had played a key role in the Allied victory over the evil forces of Napoleon and he was now viewed by many, including the French and the Quakers, as a magnanimous liberator and a man of peace. Through the Russian ambassador in London, Count Lieven, two London Quakers, William Allen and

---

[99] Richenda Scott, *Quakers in Russia*, 1964

Luke Howard[100] passed an address to the Tsar and requested a meeting. Much to their surprise, a few days later the Tsar expressed a wish to attend one of their meetings of worship after which he agreed to receive a small deputation of Quakers at his hotel. The resulting discussion covered not only the religious practices of the Quakers but also topics such as slavery, circulation of the Bible in Russia and elementary education for the masses. It seems that Alexander was impressed not only with the Quakers evangelical and spiritual approach but also their reformist views on society in general. For their part, the Quakers saw the Tsar as a powerful religious leader who could provide a channel for the spread of true Christianity across the Russian Empire as well as helping to promote more philanthropic activities such as the Russian Society for Care of Prisons (which was set up in St Petersburg in 1819 with the active approval of Alexander), the Russian Bible Society and the British and Foreign Schools Society.[101]

Nothing tangible immediately followed from Alexander's meetings with the Quakers in England until 1817 when the Tsar decided to revive a project to reclaim part of the desolate marshes that then surrounded St Petersburg. He recalled his earlier conversations with the Quakers and their high level of agricultural knowledge so he sent a request to England for a Quaker with good experience in land reclamation and drainage. The position was taken up by Daniel Wheeler, a married farmer from Sheffield with six children whose wife was also a Quaker. It was not an easy decision for either of them to move to Russia with their young family but strangely, several years before, Wheeler claimed he had a premonition that he would be called to serve the Lord in St Petersburg. Wheeler visited St Petersburg that summer to examine the terrain and formulate his plans for the work which were then presented to the Tsar who agreed to fund the whole project, including the expenses of Wheeler, his family and equipment. Wheeler only asked for the very modest sum of £5,000 to complete what would clearly be a considerable and lengthy job. A year later, Wheeler sailed from Hull for Russia with his wife and children together with two other farmers and their families, a young tutor for his children called George Edmondson plus a variety of cattle, seeds and agricultural implements. The small English group settled first in the Okhta region, later moving to Shushary (near today's Pul'kovo airport). At Okhta, a house on the banks of the Neva had been prepared for the Wheelers and it was here that Daniel started work on the first several thousand acres, implementing the modern English methods that he would deploy in subsequent operations. He had a workforce of some 180 men, mostly soldiers who, although fed and clothed at the Tsar's expense, were paid a daily labourer's rate by Wheeler. The Russians also provided an interpreter who had been educated in England as well as a surveyor who turned out to be totally

---

[100] Howard, a chemist and amateur meteorologist, was the first person to propose the current nomenclature system for clouds (cirrus, cumulus etc.) in 1802.

[101] The British and Foreign Schools Society supported the Quaker educationalist Joseph Lancaster whose 'monitorial' system of mass education was discussed with Alexander I during his London visit in 1814 and from 1818-28 schools on the Lancastrian model were set up across the Russian Empire.

inexperienced. The young tutor, Edmondson, soon stepped into the breach and, assisted by Wheeler's eldest son, was able to replace the Russian surveyor. In the early days, the scheme provoked a good deal of curiosity in St Petersburg and an almost daily procession of distinguished visitors arrived to observe the work. Wheeler's wife, Jane, found herself having to provide refreshments for a various members of the nobility and highly placed officials, including the Tsar and Tsarina, a princess and ministers of state. The group of Quakers worked long hours, usually from dawn to dusk during the summer months and had little time for other activities. On Sundays and Thursdays, winter and summer, the small Quaker group gathered for worship, occasionally joined by an English visitor such as William Allen and Stephen Grellet who came out to Russia in 1818. They were seeking an audience with the Tsar to ask for his support for the Bible Society and for his agreement to their intended tour of non-Orthodox and sectarian communities in the south of Russia.

Another visitor was Thomas Shillitoe who travelled out to St Petersburg in 1824 at the advanced age of seventy. Shillitoe was a remarkable character, a tailor by profession and deeply religious to the point of rashness. He had come to the Russian capital in response, as he saw it, to the promptings of the Holy Spirit and ultimately to seek a meeting with the Tsar. While in St Petersburg, he visited Wheeler's house in Okhta a couple of times to pray with the family. He also witnessed the deadly St Petersburg flood of that year, almost drowning himself while trying to help a girl in distress. He eventually had two interviews with Alexander I during which he spoke of Christ's love and the Tsar's responsibilities to his people, especially in the areas of penal reform and serfdom. The fact that Shillitoe had two meetings with the Tsar indicates the latter's respect for the Quakers and his interest in what they had to say. Another Quaker who witnessed the great flood was Sarah Kilham, a friend of the Wheeler family from Yorkshire who lived with them for a time when she first arrived in 1820. She ran a Lancastrian school in the city where she was trapped upstairs for several days with her pupils until the flood subsided. Sarah later left the Quakers and attended the English chapel of Rev Knill where she married an Englishman called Samuel Biller. Apparently, Tsar Nicholas held Sarah in such high regard for her dedicated work at the school that, in 1844, he had a hospital built for her to manage. She died in St Petersburg in 1852.

With the arrival of winter however both the Wheeler's work and their visitors largely ceased. The soldiers returned to their barracks and the English retreated to their houses and spent the long, dark evenings in study, letter writing and planning for the new season. Although they were not far from St Petersburg, they led a lonely life, cut off from the other British residents in the city during the winter and unable to fully communicate with the locals due to the language barrier. Their second winter at Okhta proved to be exceptionally harsh. Wheeler in his memoirs described how starving wolves would prowl around their perimeter fence, attacking anyone foolish enough to go outside. The children fell ill with scarlet fever but fortunately recovered. In the early years, in typical Quaker fashion, Wheeler tried to implement ideas to improve the life and conditions of his Russian workforce. To encourage productivity, he sought to introduce a plan of payment by results rather than a simple daily rate, regardless of the amount work done. He also proposed building cottages for workers and giving them plots of land to work in return for a set payment but neither of these projects came to anything. By the early summer of 1819, the first reclaimed plot of land was bearing a variety of excellent crops. Wheeler was amazed at how much quicker things grew in the warm Russian summer weather than in England. The Quaker farmers sold their produce in the St Petersburg markets and they soon found demand outstripped supply. The annual profits they made were significant, amounting to tens of thousands of pounds at today's value and in line with the original agreement with the Tsar were paid over to the Russian treasury. With honest accounting and no bribes deducted, the Russian officials were both surprised and delighted with what they received. Neighbouring landowners noticed the results of Wheeler's methods and quickly began to imitate them, though probably with less honesty as far as their taxes were concerned.

Later that year, Wheeler began reclamation work on a second tract of land at Volkova to the south of the city, estimated at 50,000 acres, which belonged to the Dowager Empress, the mother of Alexander. Wheeler placed young Edmondson in charge of the new site while he himself remained at Okhta some ten miles away. It was too far for Edmondson to travel each day so lodged in a peasant hut near the work site and fended for himself, cooking all his own meals. Although he was now in charge of some 200 Russian workmen, he was essentially alone, only seeing his compatriots for the bi-weekly service of worship. Prior to his arrival in Russia, Edmondson had become engaged and at the end of the summer having sought permission from the Tsar to return to England, he sailed home and married. He arrived back the following spring with his bride, Anna Singleton and her sister Sarah and they moved into a new log house constructed at Okhta where Edmondson was now to be the manager. The Wheeler family moved across to Volkova, living in a very dilapidated house where they all constantly suffered from sickness. Because of this, Wheeler sent his wife Jane and children back to England to recuperate, remaining in Volkova for a year with his son William.

Wheeler then fell seriously ill and did not fully recover until his family returned in May 1824 but more sickness followed. In the autumn of 1825, Edmondson's wife and young daughter fell ill and the family decided to return to England permanently. Then the health of two of Wheeler's sons, Daniel and Joshua seriously deteriorated and they too went back home. Through all his time at Okhta and Volkova, Wheeler had remained in close touch with the Tsar who regularly visited the project to view progress as well as occasionally to join in a short period of quiet worship. At the end of 1825 the death of Alexander, coming on top of all the other problems left Wheeler greatly saddened and depressed. Not only because he had lost a friend but also because he could see how the reactionary forces in Church and State were now turning against the Tsar's more liberal views. As with the men of the Edinburgh Missionary Society, the close relationship with the Russian Tsar was now ended and the Wheeler family never enjoyed the same contact with his successor. Wheeler struggled on and in 1826 started on an even larger reclamation project at

Shushari, leaving his second son, Charles, at Volkova and Robert Worthy, one of the farmers that originally came out in 1818, at Okhta.

The living conditions for Wheeler and his wife at Shushari were even worse than at Volkova. Their house was miles from any other, sitting on the edge of a huge marsh and had no water supply other than the rain collected from the roof. Wheeler was now fifty-seven and the years of hard physical labour in Russia were taking their toll. His sight was failing and he suffered from rheumatism but he persisted in his work until 1830 when his wife's poor health finally forced the pair back to England for several months' rest. They returned the following summer to find cholera raging through the region but fortunately both their sons, William and Charles had escaped the epidemic, probably due to their isolated locations. Within a year, Wheeler concluded that his work in Russia was almost at an end and he felt the call that it was time to move on and in October 1832, he sailed back to England to prepare for his next venture. After much deliberation and with great sadness, he left behind in Russia his wife and daughter, Jenny, plus his sons who took charge of the St Petersburg projects. A month later, a bout of serious illness hit the whole family and although the children eventually recovered, Jane Wheeler died in December 1832. Coincidentally, when news of the tragedy reached Wheeler in England, he was also lying ill at a friend's house in Norwich and was unable to return to Russia to comfort his children until the following spring when Jane was finally buried (the frozen ground had prevented this being done any earlier).

The death of Jane proved to be a watershed in the life of the Wheeler family. Wheeler himself now left Russia for the last time, bound ultimately for the South Seas, accompanied by Charles who had decided to join his father in his new adventure. William was still too weak from his illness to remain in charge of the reclamation work so his younger brother, Daniel junior came back from England to assist him. However, William's interest in the work had waned and in 1835 he left to help run a cotton mill in Finland that had been started by a Scot, James Finlayson but his health never fully recovered and he died in Finland two years later. His younger sister, Jenny died in 1837 in Shushari and was buried alongside her mother. Young Daniel soldiered on but by 1840 with failing health, he resigned his position and returned to England. The small plot of ground where Jane and Jenny were buried was assigned to the Quakers by Tsar Nicholas I as a permanent burial ground in gratitude for their work. In a period of twenty two years, the Wheeler family had drained well over 100,000 acres of marshy wasteland and brought more than 5,000 acres into profitable cultivation[102]. In doing so, they had notably improved agricultural practices in the region as well as making an important contribution towards improving the health of St Petersburg by reducing the fevers emanating from the swamps. But all this had come at great personal cost. Of the eight family members that had originally arrived in Russia in 1818, only three were still alive.

The only other direct contact between the British Quakers and a Russian Tsar occurred in 1854 when a group of Friends was sent to St Petersburg in the cause of peace. Fears about Russia's intentions in central Asia and her potential

---

[102] Richenda Scott – ibid.

threat to the Indian sub-continent were looming large in the public's mind in Britain. As war with Russia loomed ever closer, the Society of Friends decided to send a delegation to the Tsar with an address regarding the need for peace. Accordingly Joseph Sturge and Robert Charleton, together with Henry Pease, were chosen to travel to St Petersburg in January 1854 to seek an audience with the Tsar. Initially they were met with great courtesy and in February succeeded in meeting with Nicholas I. Their discussions were cordial and frank with both sides making known their views regarding the danger of war as well as the suffering that might ensue and the Tsar seemed genuinely moved by what they had to say. The three Quakers also met with the Tsarina and her daughter, the Grand Duchess Olga who received them warmly after their meeting with Nicholas and according to Charleton, she told them 'I have just left the Emperor, there were tears in his eyes'.[103] A few days passed while the three men waited for the Tsar's official written response to their address and during this time, the mail arrived from London with news of a hardening of attitudes in Britain. The atmosphere in St Petersburg now cooled distinctly and the Quakers were no longer welcome. They returned home in late February in deep disappointment knowing that they had failed to avert the almost now certain war between Britain and Russia. The Crimean War broke out just a few months later.

In the latter half of the 19th century, several other groups of British Quakers visited St Petersburg to seek an audience at the Russian court to promote their ideas on various civil rights but none were successful in meeting the Tsars. Other Quakers travelled to different parts of the Tsarist Empire in an attempt to reach out to some of the dissenting Russian sects that held similar views to the Society of Friends. In 1853 John Yeardley and William Rasche visited the Mennonites and Lutherans in the south; Isaac Robson and Thomas Harvey crossed the steppe to reach the Molokans north of the Azov Sea in 1867 and James Neave with John Bellows (both were over sixty years old) travelled to the Stundists and Doukhobors in the Caucasus in 1892. The latter pair made contact with the Tolstoy family in Moscow during their visit and Tolstoi's daughter-in-law, Olga, became a member of the Society of Friends. However, none of these visits resulted in any significant or lasting impacts on either Russian society or the Quaker movement.

The most important interventions of the Society of Friends in Russia during the second half of the 19th century related to their activities in disaster relief work. During the Crimean War, a British fleet was based in the Baltic, largely in order to blockade northern Russian ports but as St Petersburg was well protected by the offshore fortifications of Kronstadt, the British were unable to inflict much harm. However, the coast of Finland (then part of the Russian Empire) was unprotected and during the course of the British fleet's operations, some parts of this coast were raided and pillaged. Many villages were destroyed along with farms and fishing boats, disrupting the Finns traditional means of livelihood. The situation was made worse by a severe winter and the failure of the harvest the following year. As soon as the war ended, the Quakers resolved to help the Finns recover and Joseph Sturge together with Thomas Harvey was

---

[103] Richenda Scott – ibid.

sent to Finland to assess the situation and develop a plan of assistance. They found great poverty and suffering and on their return to London, a relief fund was established (Joseph Sturge and his brother donated £1,000) and in June 1858, the Quakers set up work relief schemes to pay the Finns to manufacture new farm implements and fishing equipment as well as reclaiming land for new farms (a small-scale replication of Wheeler's earlier work in St Petersburg). These Quaker projects did much to repair relations between the Finns and Britain.

The Quakers were again involved in relief work in Russia during the early 1890s when a series of poor harvests in the Volga region had resulted in famine conditions across a wide area. The Society of Friends resolved to provide assistance and in late 1891 two Quakers, Edmund Brooks and Francis Fox, left for St Petersburg to discuss with the Russian government how they might help. The Russians proved to be unenthusiastic about accepting any official, external aid but were willing to assist the Quakers as individuals in anything they chose to do. The pair then travelled down to the disaster area, spending time in Saratov and Kazan where they found the situation particularly acute. In a region larger than the whole of England, hundreds of thousands of people were at risk of starvation. There was virtually no food, no nearby railway connection to bring in supplies and most of the horses were dead or eaten so there was no local transport. When Brooks and Fox reported back to London another relief fund was started which quickly raised almost £40,000 (equivalent to around £3.5m today), some of it coming from Friends in the USA. The following year, Brooks returned to tour the Volga region, accompanied by another Quaker, Herbert Jones and they visited Samara, Kazan, Simbirsk and Nizhny Novgorod. In each location, they tried to find local people already carrying out relief work to whom they could give funds to help them and where there were none they set up new committees to start providing relief. In Nizhny, Brooks renewed the Quaker's acquaintance with the Tolstoy family and stayed at their home. The Tolstoys were already very active in the region's relief efforts having opened 270 soup kitchens in Samara financed by donations from around the world. Although there was no way that the Quakers' funds could feed all the hungry people, the work of Brooks and Jones did help to encourage and sustain local efforts as well as galvanising some regional officials into doing more. For a while, the Society of Friends became a household name in Russia and much public gratitude was expressed for their work.[104]

A few years later, the Quakers were again involved in humanitarian relief work in Russia, though this time it was to assist members of the Doukhobor religious sect to leave the country. After many years of persecution, the sect had been banished to the Caucasus where in 1896 they mounted a series of demonstrations against service in the military. The Russian administration attempted to exterminate the Doukhobors by attacking them with Cossack troops and through widespread starvation. The barbaric situation in the Caucasus was brought to the Quakers' attention by an article in *The Times* signed by Leo

---

[104] The Volga region suffered another major famine in 1906-07 when twenty million were at risk of starvation and Edmund Brooks was again involved in a Quaker relief effort there.

Tolstoy and they quickly sought to bring relief to the Doukhobors. An appeal was sent to the Tsar to allow the sect to leave Russia and funds were taken to the Caucasus by Captain Arthur St John, a former Royal Navy officer. He travelled there at his own expense and managed to distribute the money before the authorities expelled him. In 1898, the Tsar finally agreed that the Doukhobors could leave and with the help of Tolstoy and many other Russian sympathisers, sufficient money was then raised to evacuate most of the remaining Doukhobors. Some 7,000 Doukhobors then emigrated, some initially to Cyprus and the majority to Canada where the government granted over 270,000 acres of prairie on which they could settle. The final part of the story of the Quakers in Russia as far as the period covered by this book is concerned, came with the First World War and we will look at this later in Chapter Fifteen.

8

An Age of Enlightenment and Travel

On the eve of the Napoleonic wars, Napoleon Bonaparte is reputed to have remarked disparagingly that the British were a nation of shopkeepers – '*L'Angleterre, c'est une nation de boutiquiers.*'[105] He might have been just as accurate if he had said that the British were turning into a nation of travel writers as during the 18th and 19th centuries, British travellers suddenly seemed to embrace the world and began visiting almost every known and unknown corner within it. Having done so, a large number of them then wrote books and memoirs of their various travels on their return home. Russia was not spared this traveller's invasion and the number of publications dating from this period by both men and women is astonishing (cf. the bibliography in Appendix II). This upsurge in overseas travel arose largely due to the rising general wealth and education of the British which combined to generate both the time and the money for foreign visits as well as the inquisitiveness to undertake them. This was the age of Enlightenment and the Grand Tour and these foreign visitors were the tourists of the 18th century. They were not like the soldiers, physicians and traders who had largely come to Russia to seek their fortunes or the diplomats and missionaries who had been sent to Russia to perform a specific role. The primary objectives of these tourists were travel in its own right and the satisfaction of their own personal curiosities.

Their experiences and observations on Russia vary considerably as do the quality and reliability of their accounts. However, these publications give us fascinating glimpses of life in Imperial Russia as well as the impressions of the British regarding Russia and the Russians at the time. Inevitably, many of these are centred on St Petersburg and Moscow but the intrepid nature of some of these travellers also took them to most corners of the Tsarist Empire. Of course, travelling in Russia at this time was not easy. The country's road system was poor to non-existent and travel by river, at least in the summer months, was generally the preferred method of covering long distances. In winter however, the rivers, sometimes half a mile wide, froze and were therefore not navigable but conversely it was then easier to cross them and the previously dusty roads and tracks also became much easier to travel over by horse-drawn sledge in the snow and ice. Many visitors to Russia recorded sledge journeys covering more than one hundred miles in a day. The added danger from prowling wild animals in the open countryside such as bears and wolves simply added to the sense of adventure.

Most of the earliest British visitors to Russia were men who one way or another already had links with the country being related either to ministers and

---

[105] Napoleon was probably simply echoing remarks by Adam Smith, the economist, in his famous book *The Wealth of Nations* first published in 1776.

diplomats or merchants of the Russia Company. Although their stays in Russia were usually only a few weeks, their reports of the country gradually raised awareness and later led to visits undertaken purely out of interest and curiosity. Lord Baltimore was one of the very first such independent travellers to visit Russia, arriving in St Petersburg in June 1739 in his personal yacht, the *Augusta* as part of a grand maritime tour of the Baltic. Over the next couple of decades a steady trickle of curious Britons followed Baltimore to Russia, though they arrived in rather less style. Some 18th century visitors to Russia however, came not to broaden their minds but to escape from public notoriety following criminal proceedings in Britain. Indeed, the son of Lord Baltimore, Frederick Calvert, followed in his father's footsteps exactly thirty years later for this reason. After an unexpected and questionable acquittal on an abduction and rape charge, he fled England for Europe where he hoped he could avoid the scandal surrounding his London trial. He arrived in St Petersburg in July 1769 and was received by the British ambassador and introduced to Empress Catherine, his title evidently still offering him some respect and social standing.

Two of the first independent women travellers to Russia also fell into this category of travelling to Russia to escape notoriety at home. Elizabeth Justice left for St Petersburg following the conviction and transportation of her husband for stealing books in Cambridge. She spent three years in the mid 1730s as a governess with the family of Hill Evans, a British merchant in St Petersburg and later published a short account of her observations of Russia in a limited edition called *Voyage to Russia*. The second was Elizabeth Chudleigh, the Duchess of Kingston, who sailed into St Petersburg aboard her own luxury yacht in the summer of 1777 and the unusual presence of a wealthy duchess in the Russian capital caused an immediate stir. Born into a genteel but impoverished family in 1720, her rise to fame and fortune was largely based on '*a career of seduction, marriage, deception, exhibitionism and theft.*' [106] Having secretly married the heir to the Earl of Bristol, she later became the mistress of one of England's richest peers, the Duke of Kingston and openly remained in this relationship for many years. In 1769, Elizabeth bigamously married the wealthy old Duke and thereby was able to access a large part of his fortune. On his death a few years later, the truth of her bogus marriage came out and she was convicted of bigamy at a famous trial in London. The canny Elizabeth managed to hold onto her wealth plus her questionable title and fled her infamy, initially to Calais, where she sumptuously equipped her new yacht, partly with items stolen from Kingston Hall and recruited a French crew. She eventually set sail with a motley band of hangers-on and arrived in St Petersburg where she possibly hoped to become a lady at the court of Catherine the Great and thus restore her standing in European society.

Although initially well accepted by a curious St Petersburg society, the dissolute behaviour of the Duchess and her companions soon scandalised the locals. Although she did indeed meet with Catherine and Potemkin, neither was overly impressed with Elizabeth and her attempts to use both her wealth and skills as a brilliant conversationalist to enter the court eventually came to

---

[106] Simon Sebag Montefiore, *Catherine the Great*, 2000

nothing. The Empress Catherine offered the excuse that that a foreigner could not become her lady-in-waiting. In the late autumn, the disappointed Duchess tried to set sail for France but her yacht ran aground in a storm that hit St Petersburg and her French crew mutinied, all much to the amusement of the residents of the city. Although repairs were quickly carried out and a replacement crew recruited, the imminent arrival of winter weather persuaded Elizabeth to leave for France overland. She did however return to Russia some two years later, once more sailing back into St Petersburg in grand style in her personal yacht. She soon set herself up in a mansion in the capital which she furnished in the most elegant and luxurious fashion. In 1781, in an attempt to emulate the Russian aristocracy, she spent £100,000 acquiring an estate near St Petersburg, overlooking the Baltic Sea, which she then named *Chudleigh*. Once more, her estates in England were raided to furnish the new property as well as providing farm animals and implements. A young farmer from Lincolnshire, Richard Maws, was hired to run the estate and a business to manufacture vodka and brandy that Elizabeth had decided to set up. But the aging Duchesses' antics no longer impressed and she failed to gain favour at Court or make many friends among the city's society and by 1784 she had 'sunk into neglect, nobody thinks of her'.[107] She finally returned to France in 1785 where she lived until her death in 1788. Elizabeth did, however, unwittingly leave a legacy to Russia in the form of the many treasures stolen from Kingston Hall and used in her St Petersburg townhouse and *Chudleigh*. After her death, these were acquired by the Russians and some eventually made their way to the Hermitage where they can still be seen today. The remains of her distillery also survived until the Bolshevik revolution, along with the huge anchor from her yacht.

The trail blazed by the Duchess to St Petersburg was followed a few years later by another almost equally infamous and scandalous well-born lady, Elizabeth Craven. Born in London in 1750 to the Earl of Berkeley, Lady Craven was a society beauty, famous for her published plays and her apparently excruciatingly bad verse but equally famous for her indiscreet love affairs. In 1780 she left her husband, Lord Craven, and moved initially to Versailles in France. However, she was restless and unable to settle and soon set out on a lengthy tour around Europe, including Russia from 1783 to 1786. Not as opulently rich as the Duchess of Kingston, Lady Craven was nonetheless a wealthy woman and arrived in some style at St Petersburg in her liveried coach, accompanied by her servants. However, she was significantly more adventurous than the Duchess and after a few weeks enjoying the social scene of the Russian capital, Elizabeth left her carriage and retinue behind and set out alone for the south in early March using a locally hired small carriage. She made her way via Moscow (which failed to impress her) and arrived in the Crimea, en route to Constantinople, a couple of weeks later. Her travels in this part of the world were not easy for a single woman. There were few hotels or inns and she mostly found overnight accommodation in local homes and on the road, she seems to have survived on a diet of fresh milk and chocolate. Elizabeth spent several weeks exploring the Crimea, which she much enjoyed and often travelled

---

[107] Anthony Cross – ibid.

around on horseback, riding side-saddle. Indeed, at one stage she wrote to Prince Potemkin that she would happily settle in the region, though she never followed up on this idea.

Intriguingly, Lady Craven was not the first Englishwoman to arrive in the Crimea as she mentions an encounter with another Englishwoman living in Kremenchug with her Russian husband and children. Elizabeth was visited at her lodgings by this woman who 'flung her arms round my neck and almost smothered me with kisses.' [108] Lady Craven was the first fellow countrywoman that this English exile had seen since her arrival in the Crimea – sadly Elizabeth gives us no more details of this woman's history. In Sevastopol, she stayed in the fine home of Admiral Thomas Mackenzie who was the founder of the city and had recently died. Mackenzie was a wealthy man and his home was full of handsome English furniture and fittings as well as a well-stocked wine cellar. On her return to England in 1787, Robert Walpole suggested that Elizabeth should publish an account of her travels and her book, *A Journey through the Crimea to Constantinople*, appeared in 1789. It was also published in Russian in 1796 and became very popular in both countries. Craven's descriptions of the country are among the earliest published in English and her accounts of the Tatars in the Crimea are especially interesting as they show local people and life before their later inevitable assimilation by the Russians.

As Russia increasingly became an accepted extension to the Grand Tour, it was added to the itinerary of a growing number of well-to-do students or recent university graduates, often accompanied by their tutors. One of the latter was William Coxe, born in London in 1747 and, as the son of the physician to the King's Household, his family had sufficient wealth and social standing to organise an excellent education for him including Eton and King's College in Cambridge. In 1771, he joined the Anglican clergy but quit only a few months later and after a period as tutor and chaplain to the Duke of Marlborough's household at Blenheim, he went to work for the Duke's sister, Lady Elizabeth Pembroke in 1775. There he became the tutor to her sixteen-year-old son, George, with the primary objective of accompanying him on a lengthy continental tour that was then being planned. The tour would be as comprehensive as it was long, covering all the social, intellectual and physical accomplishments necessary for a well-rounded young man of the period. The five-year itinerary included visits to the Low Countries, Germany, Switzerland, Poland, Russia, Sweden, Denmark, Italy and France and through the family's connections, the travellers were to meet the best society in every country. During the winter months when travel would be difficult, George would spend most of his time in serious study covering lessons in French, Italian, Latin and Greek, geography, history, mathematics, fortifications, astronomy, experimental philosophy, literature, music and drawing. Local experts were hired to assist Coxe to deliver this broad curriculum. The final element was George's physical education and a second instructor was recruited to join the party, a Captain John Floyd, who was to assist with George's riding, shooting, swimming, tennis, fencing, dancing and even billiards.

---

[108] Lady Elizabeth Craven, *A Journey Through the Crimea*, 1789.

This triumvirate duly set off in late 1775 and spent almost three years travelling in Europe before crossing over the Polish border into Russia in August 1778. Coxe's subsequent account of his journey became one of the most successful and widely regarded travel books of the time, eventually extending to multiple editions in English and several foreign languages.[109] How the group's route was selected in unclear but it undoubtedly gave them a wider experience of the country than any of their predecessors since Jonas Hanway in 1744. Indeed, once they had crossed the Polish frontier, the Russians that Coxe and his party met said they were the first Englishmen to have passed this way. They travelled by carriage towards Smolensk crossing undulating, open countryside on decent, tree-lined roads. They stayed at comfortable post houses along the way and surprisingly found English beer and their suppers served on Wedgewood dishes. However, their accommodation in the town Smolensk was not so agreeable and Coxed described it thus:

'This inn, the only one in the town, was a wooden building, in a ruinous state, formerly painted on the outside. The apartment which we occupied had once been hung with paper, fragments of which here and there covered a small portion of the wainscot, a patchwork of old and new planks. The furniture consisted of two benches and as many chairs, one without a bottom, and the other without a back; a deal box served the purpose of a table. We were inclined to conjecture that there was a heavy tax upon air and light; for all the windows were closed with planks, except one, which could not be opened, and could scarcely be seen through, on account of the dirt.'

Coxe had taken the precaution of hiring a German servant who spoke basic Russian to accompany them on their trip but when they met with the governor and a local bishop, they were able to converse in Latin. Later in the day, they dined with a judge and his family, all of whom spoke French, followed by a few hands of whist. These were unintended but sound examples for George of the need to pay attention to his language lessons. Moving on in the direction of Moscow, they crossed the River Dnieper on two wooden rafts – one for their carriage and the other for the horses. Their route to Moscow would be followed some twenty-five years later in very different circumstances by Napoleon's invading army. After several days of slower travel due to the poor condition of the roads, they eventually crested a rise and saw Moscow laid out before them in a splendid crescent of gilded spires, copper-topped domes and tall towers gleaming in the sunlight. Moscow was then the largest city in Europe with a population of 250,000 plus a further 50,000 in the immediate area and beckoned them forward with a promise of comfort and sophisticated hospitality. Arriving in Moscow on September 1st, they were initially confused to receive an invitation from the city governor to dinner on August 22nd. They thought there must be a mistake as they had already passed the 22nd in Lithuania but then realised that the Russians still followed the old calendar so that, rather like crossing the modern International Date Line, they were able to enjoy the same day all over again. Coxe was not disappointed in the hospitality and entertainment provided by the Moscow nobility and he was also impressed by

---

[109] William Coxe, *Travels in Poland, Russia etc.*, 1784

the style and grandeur of their mansions and palaces, many of which featured gardens built by English landscape designers. Here they resided 'as independent princes, like the feudal barons in early times, have their separate courts of justice, and govern their vassals with almost unlimited sway'.[110]

In his book, Coxe describes some of the lavish functions he attended. These don't appear to have been laid on especially for him – rather they were the norm in terms of the sumptuous entertainment arranged by the Moscow nobility.

'*A large semicircular table was covered with all kinds of provision, piled in different shapes, and in the greatest profusion. Large slices of bread and caviare, dried sturgeon, carp, and other fish, were ranged to a great height, in the form of pent-houses and pyramids, and garnished with craw-fish, onions, and pickles. In different parts of the grounds were rows of casks full of spirituous liquors, and still larger vessels of wine, beer, and quass. Among the decorations, I observed the representation of an immense whale in pasteboard, covered with cloth and gold or silver brocade, and filled in the inside with bread, dried fish, and other provisions.*'

When Coxe uses the phrase 'greatest profusion' he was not exaggerating as this particular winter's feast was attended by 40,000 people and it's hard to imagine the cost, planning and organisation required to cater for such a vast number. In addition to the food, a variety of fairground-type amusements had been erected, including an ice skating rink. But these excesses had deadly results with violent drunken quarrels and many inebriated guests simply freezing to death overnight on the ground where they had collapsed; others were robbed and murdered as they made their way home late at night. Coxe estimated that at least 400 people had lost their lives through attending this event and he claimed to have personally seen no less than forty bodies collected the following day in two sheds near the place of entertainment. Interestingly, Coxe's comments on Moscow were the first detailed accounts of the city by a British writer.

After two weeks, the triumvirate left for St Petersburg, perhaps in fear of their own lives had they stayed longer to participate in more such frivolities. Sadly, Coxe does not record the views of the teenage George on their Moscow experiences – it would have been interesting to what the young man made of it all. In St Petersburg, they again enjoyed excellent hospitality and James Harris, the British Ambassador, took the time to personally show them many of the sights in the city. Whilst there, Coxe entered into correspondence with Catherine regarding the conditions in Russian prisons and she was courteous enough to reply in her own hand to a list of questions he sent her. After an extended stay of four months, Coxe and his group left Russia to continue their Grand Tour in Sweden in February 1779. However, Coxe returned to Russia again in late 1784, spending six months there this time as tutor to a recent Cambridge graduate, Samuel Whitbread, son of the founder of the eponymous English brewery. Coxe was clearly an intelligent and careful observer during his Russian travels, providing, as one might expect from such an educated man, a balanced and conservative account of his time in Russia. He also drew heavily on other

---

[110] Coxe - ibid

sources to produce what was in effect an excellent travel guide to the country that was probably keenly studied by some of our subsequent travellers.

One of these was a young man called James Brogden who spent some two years in Russia during 1787 to 1788. Brogden was born in Leicestershire in 1765 but moved to London as a child, living with his parents in Clapham Common and attending Eton school in 1780-81. We know of his travels and experiences from eighteen handwritten letters that were sent home from Russia by Brogden and which form part of a bound volume of forty letters covering a tour through Europe undertaken 'to improve himself'. His primary reason for going to Russia was to learn at first hand the fundamentals of the Russia Company's business in St Petersburg. Brogden's father, who had also spent some time in Russia, had long worked as a merchant for the Company which Brogden was also destined to join on his return. As the elder son of old John Brogden, James had already begun the process of succeeding to his father's business interests and this visit to Russia was probably viewed as the final stage of his apprenticeship. Through his father's contacts, Brogden was able to quickly settle into the British community in St Petersburg and was soon ensconced in a room on the English Embankment.

Although the purpose of his visit was not to play the tourist, it was intended as a study tour to allow him to learn Russian and study the Russia Company's operations, the young man soon found other more sociable activities to be of greater interest. Whilst he expressed a concern in one of his early letters that his father's generosity *'shall seldom contribute to folly & never to vice'*, he seems to have spent more time dining out and dancing than he did visiting boring factories or studying languages. However, this was to be to the benefit of posterity as his letters, mostly written to his father or sister Susan, provide an account of life in Russia, particularly that of the British community, which have an informality and breadth of interest rare in other writers of the time. Brogden was generally content to report and describe his impressions without attempting to interpret or digress into prejudiced comments. He stayed with the family of John Cayley, a merchant who had recently become agent of the Russia Company and the British Consul-General and was therefore well placed to observe the day-to-day life of both the British community and Russian society. As well as the usual comments about life in St Petersburg, the glitter of the Imperial Court and the difficulties of travelling in Russia, Brogden's letters are interesting for the perceptive remarks he makes regarding the '*deep cultural cleavage between the recognisably European upper classes and the impoverished mass of ordinary Russians*' and '*the peculiar mixture of Asiatic and European elements in Russian civilisation*'.[111] These are matters that have continued to intrigue foreign observers of Russia into the 21st century. Three months after returning to London, Brogden was admitted to the Russia Company 'by patrimony' and he remained a senior member of the Company for over fifty years until his death at Friar's Oak, his home in Sussex, in 1842.

---

[111] James Brogden in Russia 1787 – 1788 by James Cracraft, *The Slavonic and East European Review*, Vol XLVII No 108 January 1969.

Another perceptive commentator on Russian society was William Richardson who travelled to Russia as secretary to Lord Cathcart when he was appointed as British ambassador to the Court of Catherine II in 1768. The young Scot was also to act as tutor to the Cathcart family's two sons in St Petersburg. During his four years in Russia, Richardson set down his experiences and observations in a series of fifty-six letters which he later had published as a book.[112] His relatively privileged position as the ambassador's secretary gave him access to all levels of Russian society and his letters deal with the lives and customs of both the nobility and the peasants. One of his better known comments was in his description of the Russian winter of 1769 and the layers of winter clothing that men wore outdoors:

'fine gentlemen, adorned with silver and gold, and purple, and precious stones, starting forth from their rough external guise, like so many gaudy butterflies, bursting suddenly from their winter incrustations.'

These letters were later recognised as a very accurate perception of Russian society. Indeed, the vivid descriptions by writers such as Richardson of the magnificent opulence of Catherine the Great's court and capital increasingly attracted other travellers to Russia. After returning to Scotland in 1772, Richardson was appointed professor of humanities at the University of Glasgow.

It seems Russia was now so firmly established as a part of the European tour for the British that George Norman, a visitor to Moscow in 1784 wrote *'there are parties continually going to Moscow, Astracan, Warsaw & Constantinople, to which a man might join himself.'* [113] As visits to St Petersburg and Moscow became more commonplace by the turn of the 18th century, British travellers' itineraries became increasingly ambitious and adventurous. The idea of either crossing Russia southwards to the Caspian Sea and the Caucasus or eastwards through Siberia and possibly on to China gradually took hold. Samuel Bentham had already travelled to Siberia on Imperial business but the first British tourists seem to have been John Parkinson, an Oxford don and Edward Bootle. In 1793, the pair travelled as far as Tobolsk, then the capital of Siberia, as part of an extensive tour through Russia.[114] Parkinson's pioneering path was subsequently followed by many, including James Holman, one of the most remarkable and ambitious early British travellers. Holman was not only blind but also suffered from other physical disabilities. Born in 1786 in Exeter, he joined the Royal Navy in 1798 and reached the rank of lieutenant in 1807 but thereafter his health started to deteriorate so that within three years he became totally blind with a serious stiffness in his joints. He was invalided out of the Navy at the age of twenty-five and given a lifetime grant of care at Windsor Castle. However, he found his new life there so confining and boring that he took two leaves of absence, first to study at Edinburgh University and then to take a Grand Tour through western Europe visiting six countries between 1819 and 1821.

---

[112] *Anecdotes of the Russian Empire; in a series of letters, written, a few years ago, from St Petersburg*, 1784.

[113] Anthony Cross – ibid.

[114] Parkinson's detailed accounts of his travels *A Tour of Russia* were not formally published until 1971.

He set off again in 1822 with the ambitious idea of going around the world in a clockwise direction from west to east. At the time, such a feat had hardly ever been contemplated let alone achieved by a healthy and fit traveller. To consider undertaking such a risky and difficult journey when alone, blind and disabled was truly remarkable. Holman left Gravesend by ship bound for St Petersburg where he spent several weeks and from there travelled to Moscow and then on across Russia for six months until he reached the Siberian frontier town of Irkutsk. In the early 19th century, the town was a flourishing trading and administrative centre on the Angara river and had recently benefitted from the opening of the Siberian Trakt, a direct road link from Moscow. This was no paved highway but, rough as it was, it meant there was regular transport moving along it and Holman was able to hire a simple carriage and driver to reach Irkutsk. Part of his journey across Siberia was through extensive marshes full of malaria-carrying mosquitoes, which Holman successfully countered by wearing a beekeeper's gauze netting carried all the way from London for just such an occasion. In his book, the intrepid Holman describes the unhealthy conditions of the marshes that lay in wait for the unwary traveller:

'the insalubrious quality of its atmosphere, loaded with malaria, or miasmatic impregnation, is not only abundantly productive of typhus and intermittent fevers, but gives rise to a disease peculiar to this horrid Steppe. This is a tumour, that commencing on some part of the head, but more commonly on the cheek, continues to enlarge until it bursts and frequently proves fatal. This district gives birth also, to immense swarms of poisonous flies, and other insects, that almost literally overwhelm the unfortunate subject exposed to their attack; they penetrate into the mouth, ears, eyes, or any part that is not carefully guarded against them; the irritation of their bites is so great, that the face of the traveller requires to be covered with gauze, to protect him from serious injury.' [115]

He went on to outline the challenges faced in taking care of that important but most fundamental traveller's need – his daily food:

'Throughout the whole of this journey my arrangements for refreshment were as simple as possible. Breakfast, from the frequent difficulty of procuring water, or the necessary means of heating it, was generally the more complex meal. The ingredients, as tea, sugar, butter, and bread, I always took care to be provided with. Dinner was dispatched with more celerity and simplicity as it was only necessary to open the provision-basket, and place its contents on the table, the accompanying quass [traditional Russian alcoholic drink] *being generally served up in a large wooden bowl or a bucket, out of which myself and the postillion* [coachman] *were obliged to drink indiscriminately. The Tartar often wanted to prepare dinner for me, particularly when fish was to be met with, but having heard that his countrymen were in the habit of stirring up their cookery with a candle in order to give it good taste, I could not reconcile myself to take advantage of his culinary talents. Bread - in general, it is so heavy and gritty as to require nearly the stomach of an ostrich to digest it.'*

---

[115] James Holman – *Travels Through Russia, Siberia etc.*, 1825.

Once in Irkutsk, Holman spent some four months exploring the region and travelled as far as the Chinese border. He had to wait until Lake Baikal froze over so he could get a passage across and continue with his journey eastwards. In the town, he was liberally entertained by the local governor and also by a wealthy English widow, a Mary Bentham, originally from London, who lived there with her twelve-year-old son. Mary had met her Russian husband when he was on business in London some twenty years earlier and at the age of only fifteen she had gone with him to St Petersburg where they married. Her husband, who had been a prosperous trader in Irkutsk, had died some ten months previously but had left her well provided for. Mary would willingly have returned to England but was unable to sell her Siberian assets to raise money. Coincidentally, when Holman first arrived, Mary's sister-in-law who was on a visit had also died the day before from apoplexy. Despite the somewhat gloomy circumstances, Mary and Holman got on well with each other and both were probably glad of the chance to spend time with a fellow countryman. Holman was no doubt good company for Mary but it seems he also had an eye (albeit a blind one) for the ladies. In his book, he describes stealing kisses from another group of Russian women that he later met but he doesn't elaborate on the time he spent with Mary. With Christmas approaching, Mary and the governor organised a series of entertainments including fancy dress parties with native Buryats attending in their colourful festival clothes and visits to local places of interest.

Meanwhile, as Holman was enjoying this seasonal hospitality, the suspicious governor had sent a message back to St Petersburg querying the presence in Siberia of this blind Englishman. The local authorities were probably concerned he might discover too much about the commercially sensitive activities of the Russian American Company should he travel further east to the coast. Just after New Year's Day in 1823, an army officer arrived from St Petersburg with orders to escort Holman back to Moscow immediately so that he could then return home. The Russian officer claimed the government was concerned for the well-being of Holman as he was blind, spoke no Russian and didn't know the country. Holman was no spy and knew this was nonsense. He tried to prevaricate, proposing a change of route south to the Volga and then claiming a lack of immediate funds to pay his way back to Moscow but to no avail. The governor advanced him 500 roubles to help defray his travel costs and Holman was finally forced to go back with the army officer. The return journey proved to be something of a nightmare for Holman. He was unwell several times but forced to go on by his impatient escort. The officer drove their sledge at such a pace that a couple of the horses died along the way and to add insult to injury, Holman was told he would have to pay the cost of the dead horses. Once in Moscow, Holman was essentially confined to his hotel and prevented from visiting any of his contacts in the city. He did manage to smuggle out notes to tell friends of his plight but he was spied on continuously both by the army officer and a very menacing chief of police. He was escorted to his bank, Gillibrand and Holidays, where he was obliged to withdraw the money to repay the governor's loan as well for the cost of the trip to escort him out of Russia. After a journey of close to 5,000 miles as a prisoner, he was finally taken across the Polish border from where he was able to make his way home across Europe. Once back in England he wrote a book of his experiences, which was published in 1825 and ran to four editions. Holman was not the first Englishman to be ejected from Russia in such a dramatic and unreasonable fashion; exactly the same fate had happened to John Ledyard, a British naval officer who was falsely accused of being a spy in Siberia in 1788 and also hauled across Russia to be thrown out across the Polish border (see page 180).

Whilst Holman was in Moscow preparing for his onward journey to Siberia, he met another Royal Navy officer, a Captain John Cochrane who amazingly had also planned to travel round the world on foot. He had got as far as the Kamchatka peninsula, near the Bering Sea, when he fell in love with the fourteen-year-old daughter of a native chief (Cochrane was forty-four at the time) and was heading back home with his bride when he and Holman met. Cochrane admired Holman's courage in undertaking such a journey but was doubtful that a blind man could really gain much from going to such a bleak part of the world, let alone write about it. However, he passed Holman letters of introduction to his contacts along the way and wished him luck. On his return to England, Cochrane published a book about his own travels in 1823[116]. Despite the presumed attractions of his young wife, Cochrane was soon off on another journey through South America but he died in Venezuela in 1825. Holman however, always hopeful of a cure for his blindness, was determined to continue travelling the world. As he said in his book, '*in my case, the deprivation of sight has been succeeded by an increased desire for locomotion*'. He set out again in 1827 but this time using a different route through Africa and Asia. He succeeded in completing a circuit of the world in 1832 and published an account of his remarkable achievement in four volumes during 1834-1835 with the title of *A Voyage Round the World*, including *Travels in Africa, Asia, Australasia, America, etc.*

Holman recorded the notes of his experiences during his travels by using a device called a noctograph, invented by Ralph Wedgewood in 1806 as a device for writing in the dark for military purposes. It used a wooden frame with parallel wires across as guides and metal clips holding down a piece of carbon paper that was placed face down over normal paper. By writing on the carbon paper with a special metal stylus, the words were transferred to the sheet of ordinary paper which could then be read by a sighted person. This process however, generated large volumes of paper which although Holman claimed he then committed to memory, were more likely packaged up and send back home whenever he passed through a large town. Holman's ability to take in the world and sense his surroundings solely through the sounds he heard or the reverberations of a tapped cane was quite extraordinary. Holman was later elected a Fellow of the Royal Society and subsequently made another solo journey to Spain, Portugal and the Near East but died shortly after returning to London in 1857.

---

[116] Captain John Cochrane, *A Pedestrian Journey Through Russia and Siberian Tartary to the Frontiers of China, the Frozen Sea and Kamchatka*, 1823

Probably the earliest British married couple to travel as curious tourists in Russia was Thomas Atkinson and his wife Lucy. Atkinson was an architect and stonemason from Yorkshire and met Lucy while on a speculative visit to St Petersburg in 1846. The pair then seems to have spent an unusual, extended honeymoon travelling thousands of miles around much of eastern Russia during the ensuing six years. Atkinson documented his travels through several hundred sketches and watercolours and in 1858 he published the first volume of his journals and topographical drawings, followed by a second volume in 1860.[117] He was made a Fellow of the Royal Geographical Society in 1858 and of the Geological Society in 1859.

Not all the early British travellers to Russia came out of a sense of curiosity and adventure or to escape some scandal at home; some arrived with a much more focused purpose. William Willes, the son of the Bishop of Bath and Welles arrived in St Petersburg in 1751 with the sole intention of learning the Russian language. After some seven months in Russia, Willes returned to England where he worked in the government's Deciphering Branch (then part of the Post Office), presumably translating intercepted Russian correspondence. He was followed by John Maddison some ten years later who took a little longer to master the language, staying just over a year in Russia. He also returned to work for the Post Office in a similar role as Willes. In complete contrast was John Howard, an early prison reformer of independent means, who spent much of his life touring foreign prisons and hospitals. He came to be recognised internationally as an independent monitor and public benefactor and foreign prisons were readily made available for his inspections. In his book[118], he graphically described the terrible conditions he encountered.

Howard travelled to Russia twice, first in 1781 and again in late 1789 as part of an extensive European tour and he spent more than a year touring Russian prisons and hospitals. He exposed the miserable conditions he found, especially in the south of the country. Unlike some of his contemporaries who also visited southern Russia, Howard witnessed the oppressive results on the local population of the region's annexation by the Russians. Howard shunned the Imperial Court and officials and pursued his own agenda with vigour and focus. Sadly, Howard contracted typhus while visiting a military Russian hospital near Kherson during the Russo-Turkish War and died on 20th January 1790. Despite his manifest criticisms of the Russian prison system, when Prince Potemkin heard of Howard's illness, he sent his own doctor to look after him. His burial site in Ukraine became a place of pilgrimage for subsequent British visitors to Russia and, later in Alexander's reign, a large cenotaph was erected in his memory at the new prison in Kherson. In 1866, the Howard League for Penal Reform was named in his honour.

Howard's pioneering work was subsequently followed up by two brothers, Walter and John Venning, who were born into a Quaker family from Devon.

---

[117] *Oriental and western Siberia: a Narrative of Seven Years' Explorations and Adventures* and *Travels in the regions of the upper and lower Amoor*.

[118] *The State of Prisons in England and Wales... and an Account of Some Foreign Prisons*, 1777.

John Venning started work in 1790 for Jackson & Co. a London firm of merchants trading with Russia and three years later he came to St Petersburg where he became a successful merchant. Meanwhile, Walter had become involved in prison reform and was a member of the London Society for the Improvement of Prison Discipline. Probably at the invitation of his brother, Walter also came to Russia and became involved in prison reform there, helping to establish with his brother the St Petersburg Society for the Improvement of Prisons. Sadly, Walter contracted a fever during a visit to one of the city's prisons and died at St Petersburg in January 1821. John then took up his brother's mantle and toured prisons in Russia, England and several other European countries. He produced reports for the Imperial government and had meetings with both Alexander I and Nicholas I to discuss his ideas for improvement. The Vennings were well known to Rev Knill who states in his book[119] that John Venning and Alexander became close friends and for many years the Tsar regularly visited the Venning family home outside St Petersburg. Following the great flood of the city in 1823, in which large numbers of people were left stranded without food or clothing, Venning led much of the subsequent Russian charity work, helped by a donation of £1000 from the Imperial family. Part of this money was used to establish a permanent house of refuge for the poor and destitute of St Petersburg. He returned to settle permanently in England in 1830 and became involved in charity and evangelical work.

Roderick Murchison also came to Russia with a very specific purpose. He arrived in St Petersburg in 1840 at the invitation of the Tsar to conduct scientific research. Murchison was an eminent scientist and a leading geologist who developed the early classification of historical rock formations and identified the Silurian, Devonian and Carboniferous systems from his work in Britain. The Tsar's invitation to travel in Russia was a welcome and timely opportunity for Murchison to extend his system to cover Europe. He arrived in St Petersburg then spent several months travelling south through Moscow to Kazan, then east to the Urals and he returned to Britain in 1841. As a result of his work in Russia, Murchison was able to classify the Permian and Paleozoic periods and in 1845 he published a detailed book of his findings.[120] In 1846 he was knighted and he devoted much of his later life to the affairs of the Royal Geographic Society of which he was president for many years. The moon crater Murchison is named after him as well as at least fifteen geographical locations on Earth. He kept a daily journal during his travels in Russia in which he recorded his thoughts and experiences along the way, including lively accounts of life in Russia, meeting the Tsar and members of the Imperial Court, the difficulties and hazards of travel as well encounters with various ethnic groups. He kept this journal with the idea of publishing it on his return to Britain but never did.

Another British visitor who did manage to publish a book on his travels in Russia was a young Scottish writer, journalist and politician called Laurence Oliphant. Born in 1829 at Cape Town, South Africa, where his father was the attorney-general, he travelled extensively in his youth and first visited Russia in

---

[119] Rev Knill – ibid.

[120] *The Geology of Russia in Europe and Ural Mountains.*

1851. He journeyed through the Don River basin, on into Ukraine and then sailed around the Black Sea coast, ending up in Sevastopol in the Crimea. On his return to Britain, he wrote *The Russian Shores of the Black Sea,* published in 1853 which became very popular with the outbreak of the Crimean War soon afterwards. As well as a gentleman traveller, Oliphant was possibly also acting as a spy for the British during this journey as he went to a lot of trouble to enter Sevastopol which was then essentially a closed military city. After several years in Britain, Oliphant visited Russia once more as a companion to the Duke of Newcastle at the time of the Crimean War and he also acted as a correspondent for the *Daily News* during their tour. They were briefly at the siege of Sevastopol before heading off on a secret mission on behalf of the British government to the Caucasus where they unsuccessfully tried to make contact with local rebels who were in armed revolt against the Russian occupation. There were also several women visitors to Russia who published books on their travels at the time such as Elizabeth Rigby who wrote *A Residence on the Shores of the Baltic Told in Letters*, published in 1841 and Rebecca McCoy whose book *The Englishwoman in Russia: Impressions of the Society and Manners of the Russians at Home* was published anonymously in 1855. Rigby's letters describe her time in Estonia, then under Russian control and heralded the beginnings of a significant subsequent literary career. McCoy had gone to Russia to work as a governess and teacher of English and as her book came out during the Crimean War, her publisher recommended that she should not reveal her identity in Russia due to the risk of adverse reaction from the authorities.

Travel into and around Russia was never easy for a foreigner. The climate, both in winter and summer, was always a major hurdle to overcome and the sheer size of Russia meant long journeys had to be planned carefully. In a biography of the painter William Frederick Yeames[121] who was born in Russia in 1835 (see page 62), his nephew described a great journey made by his uncle's family from Taganrog in Ukraine right across Russia to visit relatives living in St Petersburg. This remarkable undertaking entailed over a month of sledge driving, during the coldest period of the year when the days were at their shortest. The winter was chosen because progress was quicker and easier on good hard snow than on the quagmire roads of spring or in the dust and heat of summer. The party consisted of Yeames' father, mother, and six children, the youngest being only six weeks old plus a couple of nurses and coachmen, all travelling together on two sledges. Each child spent the day in a fur-lined bag, tied up at the mouth, to protect them from frostbite.

Their sledge journey of over one thousand miles took them on a Russian panorama – across windswept steppes; through vast, primitive forests inhabited only by wolves, bears and foxes; over icebound lakes and rivers on which the only sign of life was a solitary fisherman's hut pitched on the ice itself. Occasionally, the snow-buried countryside revealed a small village, with coloured roofs and brightly painted wooden door frames providing a welcome contrast to the monotone white scenery. Here, if they were lucky, they found a post-house for the night. These places were usually so filthy and lacking in the

---

[121] M Stephen Smith, *Art and Anecdote*, 1900.

basic comforts that Yeames' mother refused to trust the bedding and ordered bundles of sweet smelling hay on which to sleep. On one occasion she saw what she at first took to be a black skirting to a room but then realized that it was a mass of fleas. Sometimes, during a very heavy snowfall, they had to spend an extra night at the post-house as roads and signposts quickly became covered over, making travel dangerous. It was easy to lose the way on the open steppe and an unwary traveller, after a hard day's driving, could well find himself back at his morning's starting-point, having driven in a circle. It was not unusual to discover the occasional sledge driver when the snows melted. Such were the joys of Russian travel in those days.[122]

For those foreign visitors entering or leaving Russia, the suspicious and tardy manner of border guards and local officials, usually looking for escaping prisoners or a bribe, often led to frustrating delays and bad-tempered exchanges. Captain Richard Wilbraham who was on an official mission in the Caucasus in 1837 wrote:

'I was detained for some hours by the non-arrival of the officer who was to serve as my guide, and my patience being at length exhausted, I set out without him. I crossed the Arpachai, and threw my well-fingered Russian passport into the stream. It was a pleasure to me to set foot once more on Turkish soil, for I was heartily tired of the vexatious forms to which the traveller is exposed in Russia'. [123]

One of the worst inconveniences for travellers arriving in Russia by sea during the 18th and early 19th centuries was the quarantine system. The system was introduced in an attempt to limit the spread of disease, especially the plague and was in operation in several European countries as well as Russia. For those caught up in this process during a suspected infectious outbreak, it was an annoying and frustrating period of isolation about which and during which they could do little. The isolation system varied as did the period of confinement. Ships arriving from a suspect destination were required to spend a week or more anchored off shore in quarantine before they were allowed into port. Their passengers and any cargo would then be allowed ashore for a further period of quarantine that could last anywhere between fourteen and forty-five days. To qualify for the shorter isolation time, the traveller had to strip naked on arrival and hand over all his possessions, which were then taken away and hung out in storage sheds, open to the air until the visitor was deemed to be clean from infection. The chances of seeing all of one's possessions again at the end of this period were fairly remote so most travellers took the second, longer option. In this case, the passengers did not have to strip and were allowed to hang on to their possessions during the lengthy period of isolation. They were mostly confined in what was called a *lazaretto*, usually a guarded building well away from the port area. One British visitor described his quarters as follows:

'The cell which I occupy with my servant is only sixteen feet by thirteen, and ten feet high; with two windows, four feet by two each. A common Russian oven, made of brick-work, in one corner, with two dirty bedsteads, and a fir table

---

[122] M Stephen Smith - ibid.

[123] Captain Richard Wilbraham, *Travels in the Trans-Caucasian Provinces of Russia*, 1839.

three feet by two, composed the furniture of the cell. We found it very damp and cold the first night; but the second day we made considerable improvement, by heating the stove, stopping up the holes in the floor to keep out rats and mice, and ordering provisions, &c. from the town.'

Inmates were not allowed to mix with one another, unless they were off the same ship and they were guarded by day and locked in their cells all night. If the traveller was healthy on arrival, the dirty, unhealthy conditions in the *lazaretto* were themselves likely to cause sickness. The same traveller described how his cell was *'usually damp, and the free circulation of air is prevented: in wet weather, it becomes a pool of stagnant water, to the great annoyance of those confined in the cells.'* [124]

The final trio of travellers in this chapter were each unusual visitors to Russia but for different reasons. Florence Crauford Grove was a gentleman traveller of independent means and an experienced alpinist, one of the best British climbers of his day. He was one of the founding members of the Alpine Club of London in 1857 and later served as its President from 1884 to 1886. He visited Russia in 1874 to undertake a walking tour of the Caucasus and to make the first successful ascent of Mt Elbrus, a dormant volcano that at 18,510 feet forms the highest peak in Russia and depending on one's definition, the highest in Europe. Grove was probably the first foreigner to go mountain climbing in Russia purely for pleasure and his subsequent book[125] was the first to be written on recreational sport in Russia.

George Forbes' visit to Russia in 1875 was unusual because he made his journey across Russia from east to west whereas almost all previous British travellers had proceeded in the opposite direction. Although only twenty-four years old, Forbes was already a leading astronomer in Britain (he predicted the existence of Pluto fifty years before it was actually discovered) and had travelled out to Hawaii in 1874 in charge of a British expedition to observe the transit of Venus. He was now returning alone to his home in Scotland via the overland route through China, the Gobi Desert, Siberia, Kazan, Moscow and St Petersburg. It was a remarkable journey that covered some 5,000 miles and took four months to complete and it was twenty-five years before he found time to write up and publish an account of his travels. As Forbes was crossing the remote Mongolian/Siberian border, he was introduced to a seventeen-year-old Scottish girl called Miss Campbell. How or why she is in this out of the way location was not made clear by Forbes but she apparently asked for his assistance to help her return to Scotland, to which he agreed. The pair travelled together as far as Irkutsk where they met up with some Poles, exiled there by the Russian government. The young lady then fell in love with one of them, a Josef Szlenker, but according to Forbes, the local administration prohibited the wedding unless she promised never to try to escape from Russia. The amorous Miss Campbell duly gave her promise and the wedding took place in the Catholic church in Irkutsk.

---

[124] Robert Pinkerton – ibid.

[125] F C Grove, *The Frosty Caucasus*, 1875.

Despite some misgivings about leaving the couple behind, Forbes then continued his journey alone but when he arrived back in England he wrote to the Duke of Saxe-Coburg (previously the Duke of Edinburgh until he married the daughter of the Tsar in St Petersburg) who interceded and successfully obtained the Szlenkers' release from exile in Siberia. In 1877, Forbes returned to Russia at the request of *The Times* newspaper to act as their war correspondent with the Russian army in the Caucasus during the Russo-Turkish war. On his way to the front, he met up with the Szlenkers again, now happily settled in St Petersburg. During his time in the Caucasus, he actually became involved in the conflict and he was subsequently awarded the Russian Order of St George for his leadership and acts of bravery. Soon after his return to Britain, he moved to live near London in 1880 and devoted himself to electrical engineering projects, including the electrification of the London Underground.

The visit to Russia by Charles Wenyon, an English doctor, was also made in the same east to west direction that Forbes had taken almost twenty years before. Wenyon had been visiting China on a medical mission and arrived at Vladivostok in 1893 on his way back to England. Although the port was the terminus of the Trans-Siberian Railway, Wenyon decided to take the original post road across southern Siberia and his journey home, later described in his book[126] was full of interest and incident. Particularly striking are his haunting descriptions of the gangs of exiles under armed escort that he occasionally encountered trudging along the road in the opposite direction:

"There were seldom less than two hundred persons in a gang - women as well as men. They wore long coats of coarse, earth-coloured frieze, and were chained together as they walked. A file of soldiers with fixed bayonets marched on either side; there were vehicles in front for those who were sick, and for the little children of the exiles; and so, beneath the shadow of the pines, without a word, and with no sound but the confused tramp of feet, and the mournful clanking of the chains, the procession wended its way eastward, never to return........"

Although Wenyon found many of the Russian people he met were friendly and generally helpful, he sensed a malaise and discontent in the country that the government's policies merely suppressed rather than solved:

"There is no doubt that opinions subversive of social order and political stability are particularly rife in Russia, but the Government has yet to learn that its policy of severe repression is increasing the evil it wishes to destroy. It is illegal to give a public lecture in Russia, or to call together more than a very limited number of people for any private purpose whatever, even for a dinner-party in one's own house, without the special permission of the police, and, if such permission is granted, it is the express understanding that detectives shall be admitted to the assembly. The intelligence of the Russian populace is increasing in vigour and activity, and thought cannot be much longer denied utterance."

Having finally made his way safely right across Russia, Wenyon was arrested and held for three days at the border while the police checked by

---

[126] *Across Siberia on the Great Post-road*, 1896.

telegraph to make sure that he was not an escaped Siberian exile. When he finally crossed over into Germany, the soldiers at the frontier post said that if he had crossed Russia from Siberia, he must have had his full share of annoyances and wished him a quick and pleasant journey home to England.

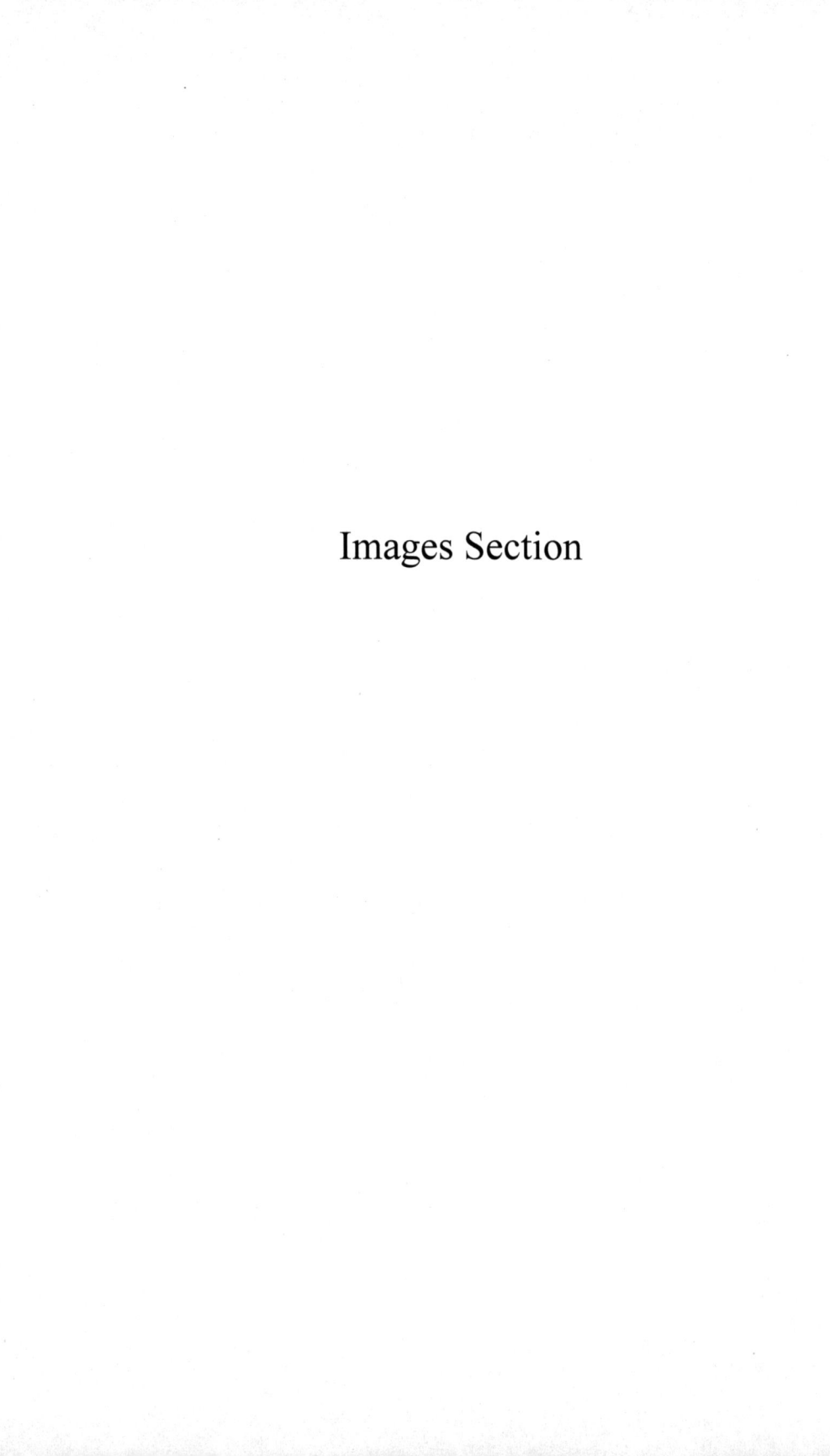

Images Section

General James Bruce

Admiral Samuel Greig

Dr Thomas Dimsdale

Jonas Hanway

Dr John Rogerson

Samuel Bentham

Charles Cameron and below his Agate Pavillion at Tsarskoe Selo Palace, St Petersburg.

Sir Thomas Lawrence 1788

Christina Robertson

Elizabeth, Duchess of Kingston

James Holman 1830

Lady Elizabeth Craven

Sir Roderick Murchison

Captain James Cook

Captain Charles Clerke

Lord Raglan 1855

William Howard Russell

The Allied Camp at Sevastopol 1854

The Seige of Sevastopol 1855

Roger Fenton and below his evocative photo of the Valley of Death strewn with cannonballs after the Charge of the Light Brigade

Florence Nightingale

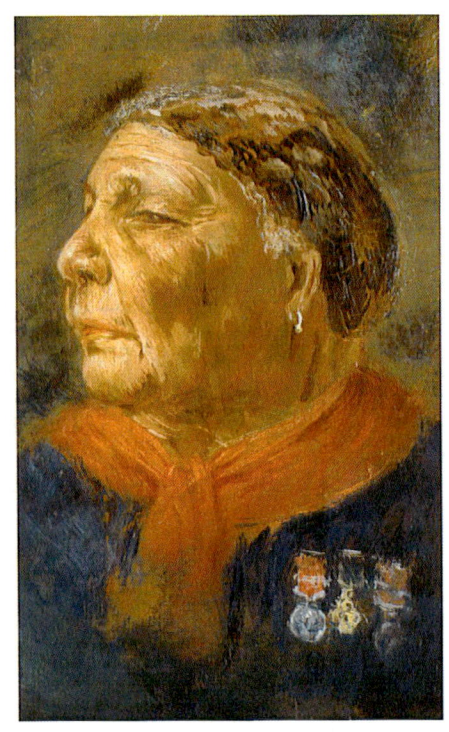

Mary Seacole

Sir James Horsey at the Court of Ivan the Terrible

James I's 1604 Gift to Tsar Boris Godunov

Sir James Harris

Arthur Conolly

Sir George Buchanan

Paul Dukes

Charles Gascoigne

John Hughes (Courtesy of GRO)

Arthur Macpherson with his children Robert, Arthur, Victor and Ellinor

The English Court Moscow, original home of the Muscovy Company

The English Embankment, St Petersburg 1835

Theodora Platts in Local Costume Odessa 1915

Muir & Mirrielees Store Moscow

Landrin Store St Petersburg

St Andrews Anglican Church Moscow c. 1884

Hughesovka English Football Team 1912 (Courtesy of GRO)

Margaretta Eagar and the Grand Duchess Olga

Charles Sydney Gibbes with the Grand Duchess Anastasia

British Workers Leaving Russia to Enlist 1914 (Courtesy of GRO)

First World War Russian Propoganda Poster

Petrograd-England in 6 days

via KRYLBO - HALLSBERG - BERGEN.

1st day	dep.	**Petrograd** Finland station		7.40 a. m.
"	"	dep. {Valkeasaari / Bjeloostrov} (custom)		9.41 a. m.
"	"	dep. Riihimäki		1.19 p. m.
"	"	dep. Tammerfors		7.07 p. m.
2nd day	dep.	Uleaborg		9.10 a. m.
"	"	arr. **Torneo** (custom)		12.20 noon
"	"	dep. Haparanda (custom)		7.30 p. m.
3rd day	dep.	Boden		7.33 a. m.
"	"	dep. Langsele		8.25 p. m.
4th day	arr.	Krylbo (change)		7.10 a. m.
"	"	dep. Krylbo		7.56 a. m.
"	"	arr. Hallsberg (change)		12.07 noon
"	"	dep. Hallsberg		12.28 noon
"	"	dep. Laxa		1.24 p. m.
"	"	arr. Charlottenberg		6.31 p. m.
"	"	dep. " (custom)		6.39 p. m.
"	"	arr. **Kristiania**		10.27 p. m.
"	"	dep. Kristiania		10.52 p. m.
5th day	arr.	**Bergen**		11.00 a. m
		daily service of steamers		
"	"	dep. Bergen		1.00 p. m.
7th day	arr.	**Newcastle**		in the forenoon

Petrograd-England in 7 days

via STOCKHOLM - BERGEN.

1st day	dep.	**Petrograd** Finland station		7.40 a. m.
"	"	dep. {Valkeasaari / Bjeloostrov} (custom)		9.41 a. m.
"	"	dep. Riihimäki		4.19 p. m.
"	"	dep. Tammerfors		7.07 p. m.
2nd day	dep.	Uleaborg		9.10 a. m.
"	"	arr. **Torneo** (custom)		12.20 noon
"	"	dep. Haparanda (custom)		7.30 p. m.
3rd day	dep.	Boden		7.33 a. m.
"	"	dep. Langsele		8.25 p. m.
4th day	dep.	Krylbo		7.39 a. m.
"	"	arr. **Stockholm** C.		10.19 a. m.
"	"	dep. **Stockholm** C. 9.21 p. m.		8.33 a. m.
5th day	arr.	Hallsberg 1.36 a. m.		12.28 p. m.
"	"	dep. Laxa 3.06 a. m.		1.24 p. m.
"	"	arr. Charlottenberg 7.10 a. m.		6.31 p. m.
"	"	dep. " (cust.) 7.18 a. m.		6.39 p. m.
"	"	arr. Kristiania 10.30 a. m.		10.27 p. m.
"	"	dep. Kristiania 10.52 p. m.		7.34 a. m.
6th day	arr.	**Bergen** 11.00 a. m.		9.15 p. m.
		daily service of steamers		
"	"	dep. Bergen		1.00 p. m.
8th day	arr.	**Newcastle**		in the forenoon

Russia to England Train & Boat Timetable 1917

177

9

Eastern Exploration

As British traders and travellers progressively pushed across Russia during the 17th and 18th centuries, there was one area that for them remained relatively unknown and unexplored – the northern Pacific coasts of Siberia and Russian Alaska. The area had been initially charted by the Danish navigator, Vitus Bering, working for the Russians in 1728 but the first British man to explore the region was Captain James Cook during his third round the world expedition of 1776. Cook had set out from England in the *Resolution*, later joined by the *Discovery* under Captain Charles Clerke and after exploring parts of the Indian Ocean and the southern Pacific, they sailed north along the North American coast. In April 1778 the two ships left what is now Vancouver Island, sailing around the Alaskan coast, improving on Bering's original charts and looking for inlets that might lead to a northwest passage to the Atlantic. By July he had rounded the Alaskan Peninsula and reached the Chukotskiy Peninsula, the most easterly point of mainland Russia, before heading out into the Bering Sea. After entering the Bering Sea on 11th August 1778, Cook crossed the Arctic Circle but was forced back by pack ice off Alaska. On the ice all around the ships were large numbers of walruses and some of these were killed to replenish the supplies of fresh meat and provide oil for the ships' lamps.

Still searching for a north-west passage, Cook turned west and worked his way down the Russian coast, eventually heading south and east into Norton Sound, Alaska, where they met with Russian fur traders in September 1778. Cook realised that it was too late in the year to make any progress and so sailed for warmer winter quarters in the Hawaiian Islands, arriving there in December 1778. On February 14th 1779, Cook was murdered by Hawaiian islanders and Captain Clerke took over command of the stunned British expedition and eventually set a northerly course once more searching for a northwest passage. They called at Petropavlovsk in April where a Russian clockmaker repaired their failed chronometer and continued north – but they did not get far. The *Discovery* was leaking and Clerke had become seriously ill from a tuberculosis infection caught in England some years before. The expedition headed south back to Kamchatka in August for supplies, landing at Bolsheretsk from where the news of Cook's tragic death was taken overland to St Petersburg, eventually reaching Britain in January 1780. Soon after, Clerke died from his infection and was buried near Petropavlovsk. The two ships now under the command of Captain John Gore finally returned home in October the same year.

The new information gained from the northern voyages of Cook and Clerke caused a spurt of interest in Tsarist Russia in the Kamchatka and Alaskan regions. Coming on top of explorations by its own subjects, the government was increasingly amazed at the discoveries of new islands and a continent, of which previously it had only a vague concept and certainly not any idea of its extent or proximity to its own territories. Frustratingly, these voyages had only confirmed the existence of these places without providing any details about their geographic or potential economic situation. Until now, the Russians had not considered these distant and barren regions of sufficient importance to justify the expense and trouble of exploring them. When William Coxe published his *Account of the Russian discoveries between Asia and America* in 1780, a copy of which was translated specifically for the Empress Catherine, a new exploration fever gripped the country. The staggering extent of the territories now coming under the control of Russia, both from its eastwards expansion as well as the acquisitions by conquest in the south became the main topic of conversation at the Russian Court. While Coxe was still in St Petersburg, he had suggested that Russia should undertake an expedition to complete the geographical knowledge of its most distant eastern possessions and the northern parts of the opposite continent that Captain Cook had not been able to explore. This idea was eventually taken up and in late 1784 the Russian Admiralty was ordered to prepare for such an expedition. They recruited the Englishman Lieutenant Joseph Billings who had been the Astronomer's Assistant in Captain Cook's last voyage and had joined the Russian navy the year before. Based on his experience with Cook and Clerke, the Russians thought he would be a suitable person to lead the enterprise, even though his leadership and navigation skills were unproven. In August the following year, an order, signed by the Empress, was sent to the Admiralty approving the expedition.

Billings, now promoted to Captain Lieutenant was appointed to the command of 'A Secret Astronomical and Geographical Expedition for navigating the Frozen Sea; describing its Coasts, and ascertaining the situation of the Islands in the Seas between the two Continents of Asia and America.' Whilst Coxe's idea was simple and easy to articulate, the planning and logistics needed for such an expedition were extremely complicated for the Russians. The government promised full financial support and orders to provide every possible assistance were sent to all the governors and military commanders across the vast extent of Siberia. Although Billings was given a free hand to select his own officers and crew, finding available men with the right experience and then co-ordinating their arrival at the chosen marshalling point of Okhotsk on the Russian Pacific coast was not an easy task. In addition, two new ships suitable for sailing in the Arctic waters had to be designed and built. The new vessels were designed by the English shipbuilder John Yeames and a team of his men were dispatched by sea to Okhotsk to cut the timber and construct the ships on the river Kolyma. Billings was instructed to travel overland so as to explore Siberia on the way and left St Petersburg in October 1785. Collecting supplies and expedition members as he went, his route took him to Moscow, Kazan where he celebrated the New Year, then on via Ekaterinburg, Tobolsk and Tomsk to Irkutsk where he arrived in February 1786. In Irkutsk, he purchased provisions which along with the rest of the expedition's supplies were then to be transported by specially built river boats to Yakutsk and then on pack horses across the coastal mountain range to the port of Okhotsk. Once again, the plans were sound but the practicalities of undertaking all this in such a remote and sparsely populated land were very different. Some 2,000 horses, along with many hundreds of men to act as drivers and guides, had to be found to transport Billings and his equipment to the coast.

Although Billings arrived in Yakutsk in May 1786, he was obliged to wait while his ships were built and the arrangements for moving his expedition forward to the coast were put in place. He used the time to make several exploratory trips into the surrounding area, recording something of the geography as well as the local nature and fauna. During this enforced delay, Billings apparently acquired a local mistress who lived with him in his rented quarters. Arriving back at Yakutsk from a trip in November 1787, Billings was surprised to encounter an old shipmate, John Ledyard, who had also been an officer with Captain Cook. Ledyard, an Anglo-American had since left the Royal Navy and come to Siberia with the intent of finding an overland route from Europe to America. He had managed to raise financial support for his one-man expedition from a number of people and organisations, including Sir Joseph Banks the famous and wealthy British naturalist. Having arrived in St Petersburg, Ledyard had then joined an overland convoy transporting supplies to Yakutsk for the Billings expedition. Ledyard stayed with Billings and his mistress but didn't get on well with either Billings or the rest of the expedition, despite many of them also having served with Cook. He found himself without support when trouble came a few months later. In late February 1788, a messenger from the governor arrived at Billings' quarters to say that orders had arrived from the Empress to immediately send Ledyard back to Moscow under guard for interrogation. Ledyard was accused of being a French spy although he protested his innocence and asked Billings to vouch for him but the latter refused to interfere. Ledyard was quickly bundled into a carriage escorted by two guards with only a set of wet linen clothes hastily grabbed from the washtub and a few roubles that Billings gave him. He was taken all the way back across Russia to Moscow and eventually deported across the Polish border.

Billings had spent the past twelve months waiting for the horses to transport from Irkutsk the expedition's guns and ammunition, anchors, cables, cordage, sailcloth, cloth and food for the voyage. In the summer, he decided to go to Okhotsk to check on progress there and set out with a few of his officers and some packhorses. When Billings eventually arrived at Okhotsk he was informed that his two ships would not be ready until the following summer, so he and his men returned to Yakutsk, the journey taking a further two months. In their absence, the impact of the expedition's spending in the town was clearly evident, with previously poor local officials suddenly become wealthy, now able to afford a carriage and enjoying a more opulent lifestyle. The delay in building the ships was partly due to a shortage of horses that were used to drag the felled timber to the dockyard, many of which had died from fatigue and a lack of food during the winter months. They were fed with brush-wood and the tops of willow trees as neither grass nor hay was available and many horses only lasted a couple of weeks before becoming worn out and dying.

At long last, in late May of 1789, the Billings expedition was finally ready and its two ships were launched and loaded on the river at Okhotsk. The spring meltwater was rising fast and had already flooded their riverbank homes so for a few days they lived in tents pitched on the roofs. With the countryside resembling a vast lake, Billings and his men boarded the boats. However, as they were about to set sail, a courier arrived from St Petersburg with orders that if they had not already left, they were to return immediately to the Russian capital. Due to the recent outbreak of war with Sweden, government funds for the expedition were running out and there was a shortage of naval officers and men. Billings ignored the order and immediately set sail for Kamchatka. However, soon after leaving, the expedition ran into a storm during which one of his two ships was badly damaged and sunk so Billings only went as far as the port of Petropavlovsk where he then spent the winter.

Whilst in the region, the Billings group encountered many who favourably remembered the visit by survivors of Captain Cook's expedition a decade earlier. According to the expedition's English secretary, Martin Sauer, the names of King, Bligh, Philips, Webbe and others were recalled and the locals had composed a Kamchatka song to their memory with a chorus to the tune of *God Save the King*.[127] With the return of milder weather in the late spring of 1790 and the lost ship replaced, the Billings expedition set sail again to explore the north Pacific. Travelling east along the Aleutian Island chain, they landed on Unalaska Island in early June and continued to the southern coast of mainland Alaska reaching Prince William Sound, named by Cook in 1778. Billings then decided to turn back and seek winter shelter in the Kamchatka peninsula but during the stormy return voyage his shortcomings as a navigator, combined with his arrogance and stubbornness, became increasingly apparent and caused disquiet among the crew. The following summer, Billings returned to the Aleutians but refused to explore the Bering Straits which was one of the main objectives of his expedition and chose instead to pursue his secondary task of mapping the north-eastern Russian coastline. This decision caused both disappointment and ill feeling amongst his companions. Martin Sauer, later wrote 'after so many years of danger and fatigue; after putting the government to such an extra ordinary expense; after having advanced so far in the attempt, even at the very time when we were in hourly expectation of our comfort, and, as appeared to me, being just entering upon the grand part of the undertaking, thus to abandon it, was the most unaccountable and unjustifiable of actions'.[128]

Billing's high-handed and peremptory attitude in this matter was described by Sauer thus: 'the representations of every officer who had hitherto presumed to have an opinion, were always treated by the commander with petulant and illiberal retorts. I have, indeed, had frequent opportunities of observing, that rank and power intoxicate the possessor'. Billings made for St Lawrence Bay on the Chukotsk peninsula where he disembarked to lead a survey party overland to the north-westward but his party ran short of food and were attacked by local tribesmen. His adventure produced little of value. Meanwhile the expedition's Russian surveyor, Gavriil Sarychev, sailed back in the other ship to continue exploring the Aleutians for the rest of the summer. The two halves of the expedition did not meet up again until the beginning of January 1794 at Yakutsk

---

[127] Martin Sauer, *An Account of a Geographical and Astronomical Expedition to the Northern parts of Russia*, 1802.
[128] Martin Sauer – ibid.

from where they returned to St Petersburg after nine years of absence. Billings' costly expedition had added little of any significance to Russia's geographical knowledge of the north Pacific littoral and it marked the end of Russian surveys in the eastern coastal regions of Siberia and Alaska.

In 1796 Billings was transferred to the fleet in the Black Sea, where he conducted coastal surveys. In 1799 he published his findings in an atlas which surpassed in accuracy and completeness anything previously available. In November of that year he was retired on full pension with the rank of captain-commodore. He died in 1806, leaving an uncertain record of achievement in Arctic and north Pacific discovery, but clearly having aided the process whereby Russian interests in Alaska were expanded, consolidated and eventually but importantly regulated. Prior to Billings' expedition, Russia's early conquest of eastern Siberia, the Aleutians and Alaska itself had been brutal and devastating for the natives. Many were killed or displaced by ruthless adventurers and whole settlements abandoned during a period when there was no effective Russian government. In the wake of Billings' explorations, the far east was steadily opened up and gradually a relatively more effective control and governance was established.[129]

Sauer's account of the expedition which was published in London in 1802 not only relates the expedition's trials and tribulations but provides a vivid and well-observed description of the wild, unspoilt scenery and the habits and customs of tribal life in Siberia at the time. He sets the springtime scene in the area: 'Yakutsk contains 362 wooden houses, five churches, and a cathedral ... on a shallow branch of the river Lena, ... producing chiefly wormwood, thistles, a few flowers and wild onions; here and there clusters of hawthorn bushes and osiers, with currants, dog-roses, and raspberries. It is bounded to the west by a ridge of inconsiderable but woody mountains, from which the inhabitants obtain firewood. Never was there a town in a worse situation than this. The branch of the river on which it is built is dry by the middle of July, and continues so all winter, the inhabitants having to go the distance of three versts for water. Although the river abounds with fish, they receive their supplies of that article, as also of meat, from about the Viluy, 40 versts down the river. Vegetables are brought them from the neighbourhood of Kiringa, 1650 versts up the river. In the month of June every necessity of life is brought hither down the Lena; and ... during this time every trader has permission to hire a public shop, and sell his ware; and this is the time when the opulent lay in a twelve month stock; for at the expiration of the month, the privilege of trading is only vested in the hands of the burghers, who make their own prices.'

A few weeks later in June, the party set out from Irkutsk for the coast and Sauer described what we now know as rhubarb (see also page 81):

'Here are extensive meadows, producing grass in abundance. The most prevailing plant that I observed was wild flax, some with white, and some with blue flowers; and a remarkable plant which the Russians call Zemlennoi Laudon, or frankincense of the earth; this is not a gum, but an aromatic root,

---

[129] A cape and a small settlement in Chukotka were later named after Billings by the Russian government.

given to children and to adults for pains in the bowels; its smell is very like that of snake root, though in appearance it is not so fibrous. The woods abound in wild beasts and game; and the plains are inhabited by very opulent Tartars, who possess immense numbers of horses and herds of cattle.'

Sauer's vivid descriptions of the daily lives, customs and rituals of the Yakut, Tungu and Yukaghir tribes people in Siberia were important, not only as the first detailed accounts to be recorded in English but also because at the time the native population was in severe decline, along with their traditions. At one Yukhagir settlement Billings and Sauer visited, they 'found that all their old customs were abolished, and that the race was almost extinct' largely due to the ravages of smallpox and venereal disease. The native women were definitely second class citizens, or rather third class, as the Russians dominated and exploited the local men who in turn took precedence over their women. The Tungus allowed polygamy with some having as many as six wives although the first wife was senior and attended on by the others. A Tungu man would give his daughter for a time to any friend or traveller that he took a liking to and if he had no daughter, then he would give a servant, but not his wives. This may well be how Billings acquired the local mistress referred to earlier. Girls were frequently married to the Russian Cossacks at the early age of twelve and 'as it is a slave that they want, it seems a matter of indifference to them whether she be Russian, Yakut, Tungoose (Tungu), or Yukaghir, provided she professes the Greek faith. Both sexes seem incapable of forming any tender attachment; the women are very inconstant to their husbands.' Sauer seems to have had little respect for the local shamans or holy men: 'I have seen their enchantments or incantations many times, I never could discover any of their feats equal to that of a common conjurer in England.' However, on a more positive note he stated 'I have not traced any atrocious vices among the Yakuti or Sakha. Robberies are seldom committed. They are extremely hospitable and attentive to travellers, especially to such as behave with a degree of good nature, and very inquisitive and intelligent.' Sauer evidently much admired the simple and independent life of the Yakuts and Tungus and took his leave with considerable regret, referring to them as 'Great Nature's happy commoners.'

Although the Russians largely gave up on any further exploration of the northern Pacific coastal region for the time being, the British continued, both in the Bering Sea and around the north of Canada in search of the elusive north-west passage. In 1825, Captain Frederick Beechey in command of HMS *Blossom* was sent to explore the Bering Strait and north coast of Alaska as part of a combined mission with the experienced Arctic explorer, Commodore Parry, sailing west in two ships from Greenland. In the summer of 1826, Beechey passed through the Bering Strait and sailed westward reaching a point less than 150 miles west of the mouth of the Mackenzie River in northern Canada. Although the two expeditions failed to meet up, their joint explorations left only some 500 miles of uncharted coast between the Mackenzie River and Prince of Wales Island to the east. Beechey's voyage lasted more than three years during which he discovered several islands in the Pacific and he named the three islands in the Bering Strait. The uncharted 500 miles were to lead to the tragic Franklin expedition which set out in 1845 to complete the navigation of the north-west passage.

The fate of Franklin and his men is now well known – their ships became stuck fast in ice in 1846 and the whole crew perished. By 1848, the lack of any news of Franklin and his ships led to several different expeditions being sent out search different parts of the Arctic Ocean and at one point there were ten British and two US ships engaged in the hunt for Franklin. One of these was led by Commander Thomas Moore in HMS *Plover* who left Plymouth in late January 1848 and, sailing by way of Cape Horn and Honolulu, made remarkably good time to reach the Bering Strait in mid October. Although Moore was an experienced polar sailor, the Strait's difficult currents and icy conditions forced him to abandon his plan of wintering in Kotzebue Sound on the east coast of Alaska and seek a closer, early winter haven. The following day, as they came in sight of the coast off the Chukotka peninsula in Siberia, they saw huts and local natives paddled out in dugouts to welcome them and guide the Plover into their harbour. Three days later, the ship was completely iced in and Moore's search for a winter base was decided by the weather. In fact, Moore and his crew ended up staying there for ten months, held fast in the grip of an especially long Siberian winter, but much appreciating the hospitality of their Chukchi hosts. One of Moore's officers, Lieutenant William Hooper, later wrote a book about the expedition and their fascinating encounters with the Chukotka natives who were effectively still living in the Stone Age.[130]

Life in this remote corner of Russia was primitive and hard, especially for the women. The winter diet was monotonous and simple, largely consisting of blubber, small raw fish, patties made from the contents of a reindeer's stomach and for desert, whale's gums. When the older members of the Chukchi family unit became too old to work, they were killed off by their children. They lived in two-roomed, skin-covered tents, an inner space for sleeping and an outer area for daytime shelter, cooking and storage. The tents were always erected facing the north-east, the direction of the early morning sun. Each morning, the housewife rose first to empty the night bucket and light a fire using a fireboard which normally took around twenty minutes to get going. The crew of the *Plover* with their matches soon found themselves very popular with the women who would do anything to get hold of them. Despite the length of their enforced stay, relations between the British sailors and the Chukchi seem to have been good and Moore at least took a local mistress. The crew of the *Plover* were neither the first nor the last British sailors to encounter the hospitality of the Chukchi as Cook and Clerke had met with some Chukchi during their 1778 expedition and in later years many British whalers spent time in the region. Apparently, English names such as Elizabeth and Robert became popular for Chukchi children, a habit that lasted well into the 20th century.

It was not until mid June 1849 that the ice around the *Plover* melted sufficiently to allow Moore to set sail for his original destination of Kotzebue Sound. Once there, he joined up with another British ship, HMS *Herald* under Captain Henry Kellett, which had already spent the past few months hunting for Franklin. The two ships then continued the search along the northern coast of

---

[130] Lieutenant William Hooper, *Ten Months among the Tents of the Tuski*, 1853

Alaska but finding no trace of the doomed expedition, the ships parted and Moore in the *Plover* left for England. Kellett remained in the region for a few more months undertaking a remarkable journey by sledge south from Kotzebue Sound along the Alaskan coast to St Michael and then continuing on to explore the Aleutian Islands. On his return to England, Captain Moore found himself under arrest and was court-martialled, accused of enjoying sleigh rides with his Chukchi mistress instead of searching for Franklin. The *Plover* returned to Alaska in 1852 to continue the search for Franklin but this time under a different commander, Captain Rochfort Maguire. He and his crew spent almost two years based at Point Barrow on the far north-west corner of Russian Alaska, fruitlessly seeking news of the missing men.

While the Royal Navy's ships explored the Alaskan coast, there were other occasional contacts between the British and Russians inland. During the fur trading boom, both Russia and Britain created outposts in this region, competing for its rich sources of beaver, bear, otter, mink and sea otter. However, in 1825 the two countries signed the Anglo-Russian Convention which allowed Britain to trade in Alaska and settled the border between Alaska and British North America (later Canada). Despite the 1825 Convention, men of the Hudson Bay Company in Canada continued to push westwards from the Mackenzie River and north into the upper Yukon River area to contest the region's fur trade with the Russians. In 1845, the Bay Company's chief trader John Bell set out from Fort McPherson near the Mackenzie and travelled west until he reached the Porcupine River. He then continued in a south-westerly direction for almost 500 miles through unknown territory until he arrived at the Yukon River in the area now called Yukon Flats in Alaska. This was the furthest west that anyone had yet penetrated by land from Canada.

The following year another trader, Alexander Murray retraced Bell's route until he reached the junction of the Porcupine and Yukon rivers where he constructed a trading post, now known as Fort Yukon. This was a bold, if provocative move by the Hudson Bay Company as Fort Yukon was the most isolated of all the Company's posts and was well west of the 141st meridian that had been agreed as the Russian's Alaskan territory boundary. The new post was in a good position to open up the relatively un-tapped fur trade with the Indians of the upper Yukon River. It took some time for the Russians to react to this invasion of their territory and it wasn't until 1863 that a Russian scout was sent east from St Michael up the Yukon to investigate the size and extent of the British presence. The scout, Ivan Lukin, was employed by the Russian American Company and was the first to travel up the Yukon to its junction with the Porcupine. When he finally arrived at Fort Yukon, he told the British that he had defected from the Russian-American Company and by this ruse was able to learn something of the Bay Company's trading activities. However, once Lukin eventually returned to St Michael, the Russians chose not to eject the British and enforce their border on the upper Yukon River. They were concerned to avoid another conflict with the British after the recent Crimean War and the idea of selling Alaska to the government of the USA was already starting to influence the Russians' thinking.

These journeys to Russia's Far East by British explorers were followed in the latter part of the 19th century by a very different visitor, the English nurse Kate Marsden, who came to Siberia to find lepers. Marsden was born in 1859, the daughter of a London solicitor but as both her parents died at a young age, she was obliged to find a job. Marsden started training as a nurse at the Evangelical Tottenham Hospital but after only eight months she was sent with a group of British nurses to Bulgaria to care for Russian soldiers in the Russo-Turkish war of 1877-78. Although she was only eighteen, this experience provided a familiarity with the Russian language and culture as well as her first encounter with leprosy. When she returned to England, Marsden continued training at the Westminster Hospital and then spent four years in charge of a convalescent home in Liverpool. In 1884, Kate went to New Zealand to care for her sister who was seriously ill with tuberculosis. After her sister died, Marsden remained in New Zealand where she worked as a nursing superintendent at the Wellington Hospital and helped establish the first branch of the St John's Ambulance Brigade in New Zealand. While there, she heard about a leprosy epidemic in the South Pacific and felt she had a calling to help the lepers herself. She returned to England with the intention of going to India to work with the lepers there. However, soon after her return to London, she received an invitation to visit Moscow from the Russian Red Cross Society. Her earlier services for the sick and wounded Russian soldiers had been recognized and the Tsarina wanted to present her with a medal. Marsden knew there were lepers in Russia, especially amongst the Yakuts in Siberia and saw this as her opportunity to go out to help them. But she couldn't do this out of her own resources; she needed a source of financial assistance so Marsden initially tried to raise funds in Britain for an expedition to Siberia. She also wrote to the Princess of Wales in the hope of patronage and was given a personal letter of introduction to the Tsar of Russia. But the publicity she received made her unpopular amongst some of the wealthy ladies from whom she was trying to raise money and there were insinuations that she was merely after an adventure holiday.

Marsden arrived in Moscow in November 1890 and after she had received her medal, she started to pursue contacts that might help with her intended project. She met with the Governor of Moscow, who was supportive and using her letters of introduction she also visited the Court in St Petersburg where she had discussions with the Tsarina. After several weeks of meetings, it was agreed that Marsden should go to Yakutsk to find out what she could about the conditions of the lepers there and also to search for a special herb that was believed to grow in the region that alleviated the effects of leprosy. Despite her already considerable experience and proven abilities, as a single woman, Marsden was obliged to travel with a female companion. She selected a young Englishwoman called Ada Field to travel with her who had the advantage of speaking Russian quite fluently. They set out on from Moscow on the Trans-Siberian Railway in February 1891 but were only half way into their journey to Yakutsk when they had to leave the train and transfer to sledges.[131] Enveloped in

---

[131] The completion of the Trans-Siberian Railway in 1890 boosted the numbers of foreigners travelling to Siberia. The first recorded British woman to complete the journey was Annette Meakin whose account of her travels, *A Ribbon of Iron*, was published in 1901.

layers of thick fur against the depths of the Siberian winter, they carried on, stopping off each night at post stations along the route. For female travellers, this mode of travel was especially difficult. The post houses offered little in the way of feminine comfort or amenities and the two women suffered considerably from the lack of privacy and the lack of hygiene. Little sympathy or understanding for their predicament was shown by the sledge drivers who seemed drunk most of the time. When they reached Omsk they spent two weeks recovering in the Governor's house. Field no longer felt able to continue with their journey so in her place the Governor provided Marsden with an old Russian soldier who spoke French and a little English.

Marsden however, continued and during the journey from Omsk to Irkutsk, she visited some of the prisons for exiled convicts. She estimated there were 40,000 people being held either in Siberian prisons or on their way to labour camps. She was appalled by the conditions in the prisons, the despair of the chained inmates and the suffering of the women prisoners some of whom had babies and young children with them. She gave them little packets of tea and sugar plus religious tracts but wished she could do more for them. By the time Marsden reached Krasnoyarsk, the snow had melted and she continued her journey in a *tarantass*, a four-wheeled wooden carriage, finally arriving at Irkutsk in the middle of May. She had brought with her letters of introduction and soon set about investigating the situation of the local lepers. At the time of her visit, there were eighty known lepers in the region of Yakutsk but there were probably many more unreported. A small hospital had been built in 1860 near Irkutsk to accommodate forty lepers but this had closed down for lack of funds just three years later. Since then nothing had been done to help lepers at all.

With the help of the Irkutsk Governor, Marsden organised a committee of influential people to raise sympathy and funds for the lepers and she was appointed as the official investigator on behalf of the Irkutsk authorities. Marsden then spent the next month travelling by *tarantass* and boat to Yakutsk, following much the same route along the Lena River as Billings almost a century earlier. The Yakuts had been told of her approach but she was described as being Russian with a 'frozen tongue' which was their way of saying that she could not speak Yakut. She was initially underwhelmed by Irkutsk, the capital of an area bigger than India or Western Europe finding it 'not a pretty place, with a dead and dreary appearance' but she soon found the locals very welcoming. Offers of help came from the bishop, who claimed he had heard about the curative herb and an old Cossack who lent her horses and men for the journey to visit the old abandoned leper hospital.

Marsden was unused to riding and this part of her journey was to prove a challenging experience. Yakut ladies rode astride wide wooden saddles and although this was considered indecent in Britain at the time, she was expected to follow local custom. Luckily, she had brought along an English tweed trouser suit that seemed to fit her needs but after a day riding on the hard wooden saddle, her inexperienced tweedy bottom felt very uncomfortable. The suit also not only proved of limited use in protecting her against the swarms of biting mosquitoes but was impractical for the Siberian summer with temperatures regularly rising to 40C. The plucky Marsden endured a very uncomfortable two-week journey to the leper hospital. She found it virtually in ruins, having been closed for thirty years. Despite this, there were still a few lepers living there, all severely handicapped and disfigured by their disease. She talked to them and found that anyone suspected of having leprosy, even small children, were driven out of their family and community and forbidden to approach within three miles of any village. Food was put out for them but it was mostly stale leftovers, usually rotten fish and they were given old clothes to wear. The lepers had no medical attention (the Yakutsk Medical Inspector told Marsden he would not go into the huts to see the lepers) and even the local priests would not visit. Over the next few days she visited eight different leper settlements and became increasingly appalled at their situation but it was the last visit at a place called Hatinach that was to distress her the most:

'Twelve men, women and children, scantily and filthily clothed were huddled together in two small huts covered with vermin. The stench was dreadful; one man was dying, two men had lost their toes and half their feet, and they had tied boards from their knees to the ground so they could drag themselves along. The fur of their tattered clothes stuck to their open, weeping sores. Two of the children were naked, having no clothes at all, and with the exception of a few rags they are in the same state in winter. As I sat there among them, the flies were tormenting their festering wounds and some of them were writhing in agony.'[132]

Marsden's travels showed that local people were aware of the appalling conditions of the lepers but their limited efforts to help had petered out through lack of organization and funding so she began a personal campaign across Yakutia. She organized the priests, officials and anyone with authority to help, threatening blackmail when necessary by using the report she would be making to the Tsarina. Those that helped would receive a favourable mention in the report; those that ignored the Imperial request to assist Marsden with alleviating the lepers' distress would also find themselves in the report to the Tsarina. Marsden also told local people about the quite small things they could do to help their lepers. In one village she persuaded the inhabitants to provide a sledge and horse so the lepers didn't have to crawl three miles across country to reach the food left for them. In another place she scolded the locals who only irregularly left out food for the lepers and that was rotten fish and stale milk. By the middle of September 1891, in her search for lepers, Marsden had journeyed some two thousand miles around Yakutia, mostly on horseback, through the heat of summer without washing or changing her sticky woollen clothes. Not surprisingly, she developed a painful abscess in her groin and a cart lined with hay was organised to transport her back to Yakutsk where at long last she was able to remove her filthy clothes and sink into a well-earned bath.

That autumn, Marsden began her return journey to Moscow which took three months. Her mission had been successful except that she never found the curative herb. In Tyumen, she met up again with Ada Field and they continued on together, arriving in Moscow in December. Marsden remained in Russia for a further six months, establishing a headquarters in St Petersburg for her leper

---

[132] Heather Hobden - Siberia: land beyond time, The Cosmic Elk.

charity, fund-raising and lecturing. When she left for England in May 1892, sufficient money had been raised to begin work establishing a leper colony in Yakutia and four nuns of the Sisters of Mercy were heading for Yakutsk to continue Marsden's pioneering work. The leper colony was eventually opened in 1897 with ten houses for lepers, two hospitals, a doctor, a laboratory, a church and a library. It was exactly what Marsden had campaigned for; her efforts were praised in Russia and she is remembered in Yakutia as a heroine. Once back in England, Marsden published a book about her travels,[133] the Royal Geographical Society made her a Fellow and Queen Victoria presented her with a brooch. Yet she found herself having to counter critics at home who insisted she had been funded for little more than an adventure holiday. Photographs in her book sitting astride her horse in her tweed trouser suit in Yakutsk did not endear her to some members of the public in Britain. The fact that some people did not take her efforts seriously caused her to become very depressed and in 1921 Marsden felt driven to defend her actions by publishing a second book *A Vindication of My Mission to Siberia*. Her health had never fully recovered after her Siberian trip and she was unable to ever return to Yakutia. Marsden died in 1931.

---

[133] *On Sledge and Horseback to Outcast Siberian Lepers*, 1892.

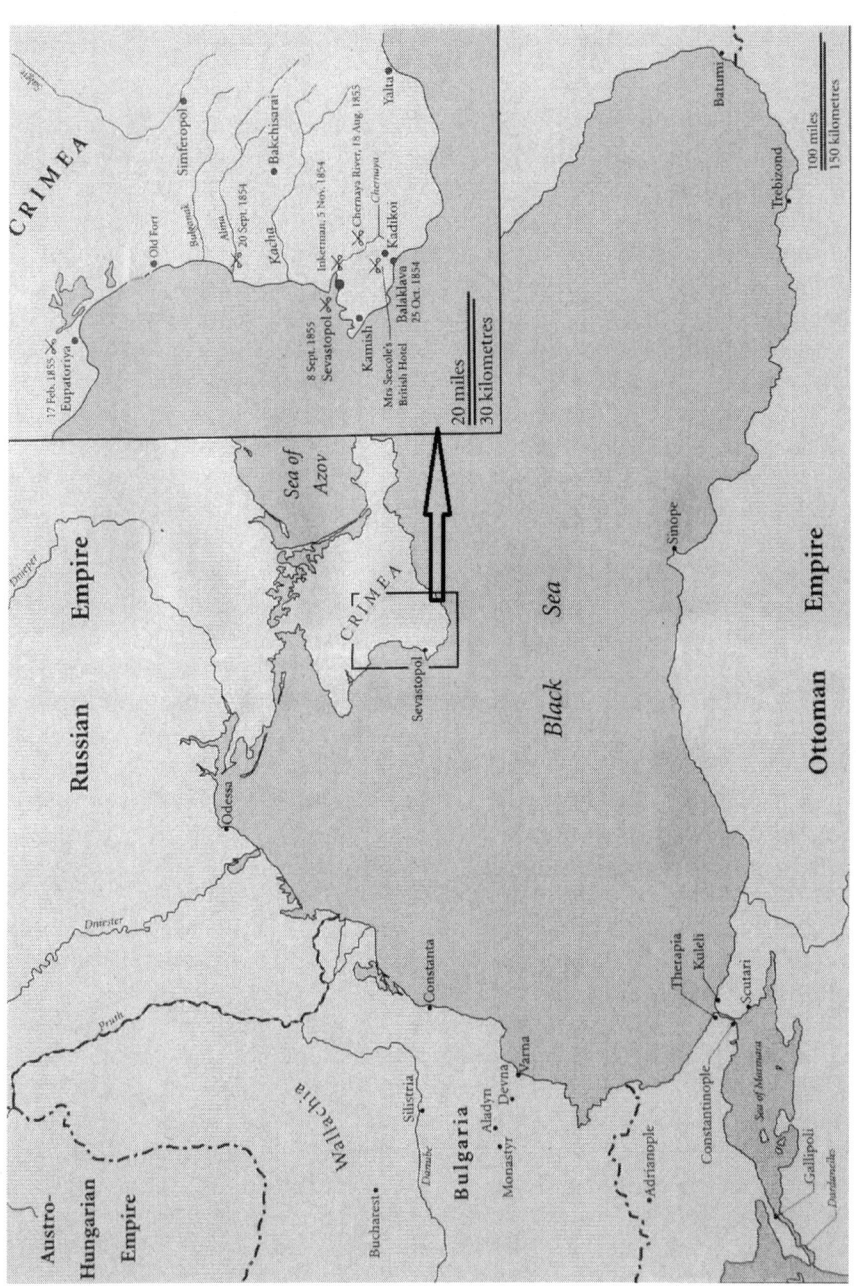

Crimea in 1855

191

10

The Crimean War

As we have already seen, the Crimean region featured regularly in the stories of many of the British that came to Russia in the 18th and 19th centuries but the year of 1854 saw the largest ever single British contingent to arrive on Russian soil. This time they came not for trade or travel but to fight in the Crimean War. The causes and prosecution of the war have been extensively dealt with by others so I do not intend to deal with these in any detail. Instead, this chapter concentrates on the impacts on those British in Russia at this time as well as the outcomes of the war and their subsequent effect on future British involvement with Russia.

In many ways the Crimean War was an accidental, largely unintended war, at least as far as Britain and Russia were concerned, as neither was really ready for nor wanted a war with the other. Although both countries had previously been aligned against each other in opposing alliances and had fought a couple of minor naval skirmishes, this was the first time during their three hundred years of relations that Britain and Russia had truly gone to war with each other. When hostilities broke out in 1853, initially between the Russian and Turkish empires, Russia was ill-equipped to fight a major war. It had fallen behind in the technological and social changes emanating from the industrial revolution and the consequent impacts on planning and organizing modern military campaigns. Even though Russia had a relatively large army, its equipment mostly dated from the Napoleonic War some forty years earlier. Crucially, in terms of logistical support, it had no railways south of Moscow and was forced to supply its Crimean forces by ox-carts.

The origins of this war lay in rather obscure events in Palestine where, in 1853 at the Church of the Nativity in Bethlehem, violent clashes had broken out between monks of the Orthodox Church, supported by Russia, and monks of the Roman Catholic Church, supported by France. The argument was caused by the Orthodox Church denying the right of the Roman Catholics to place a silver star over the manger and to possess a golden key to the church door. The Catholics prevailed but not before a serious riot occurred during which several Orthodox monks were killed. As Palestine was then a part of the Turkish Empire, the church was policed by Turkish Mohammedans who the Russians then claimed had stood by and allowed the Orthodox monks to be murdered. Whatever the truth of the matter, this religious quarrel provided a convenient excuse for Russia to attack Turkey – something the Tsar had been seeking for some time. In yet another round of the frequent Russian-Turkish wars, the Tsar's forces marched into the Turkish provinces along the Danube claiming to be the protectors of all Orthodox Christian subjects of the Sultan from Turkish persecution. By October 1853 Turkey and Russia were at war.

Although Britain was unhappy at the prospect of a further expansion of the Russian Empire at the expense of the Turks, it remained neutral. However, when in November the Russian Black Sea fleet sailed south from the port of Sevastopol and in a surprise attack annihilated the Turkish fleet, the mood in Britain changed dramatically. Anti-Russian sentiments were whipped up by parts of the British press, angry mobs paraded through the London streets and the talk of war with Russia was everywhere. Despite the popular agitation, grave doubts about the wisdom and the likely outcome of the war were held in many well-informed quarters; the Prime Minister, Lord Aberdeen, and *The Times* were against it and the Royal Family was uncertain. However, the British people were now intoxicated with an extraordinary bellicosity. Memories of past victories went to their heads, the triumphs of Waterloo and Trafalgar were on every lip and crowds paraded the streets delirious with excitement, inflated with national pride. 'When people are inflamed in that way they are no better than mad dogs,' wrote Cobbett and so in March 1854, shouting, cheering, singing, the nation swept into war.[134] The reasons for this unexpected and hitherto unlikely decision to declare war on Russia were hotly debated in Parliament and it seemed odd to now find the British fighting on the side of Mohammedans against fellow Christians of an old ally.

For the British, the Crimean campaign began in earnest when a joint invasion force, over 60,000 strong, comprising British, French and Turkish elements landed in Calamita Bay, south of Evpatoria, on the 14th September 1854. A few days later, the three armies marched south along the coast towards Sevastopol, thirty miles away. In their path lay the river Alma and on the heights to the south of the river, the Russian General Prince Menschikoff had prepared his defences. He had boasted that his troops would be able to hold their positions for at least three weeks, and the ladies of Sevastopol travelled to the Alma to enjoy both a picnic and the spectacle of the repulse of the invaders. On September 20th 1854 the Allies, under the joint commands of General Lord Raglan, Marshal St Arnaud and General Omar Pasha, reached the Alma and met the Russians in battle. A somewhat simplistic battle-plan was adopted, with the French being responsible for turning the left (or seaward) flank of the defenders, at which point the British were to make a frontal assault (across a stream and then uphill in the face of withering fire from Russian infantry and artillery). Due to the first of the catalogue of misunderstandings and misapprehensions which characterised this war, the British were forced to assault before the French had fulfilled their objective, with consequent slaughter. Lord Raglan (who was fighting his first battle since Waterloo, when he had been on the staff of the Duke of Wellington, and had lost an arm) moved so far in advance of his troops that he was actually directing the battle from behind the Russian front line. However, after some three hours, the Russians were completely routed and fled from the field in undisciplined retreat.

Lord Raglan wished to pursue the fleeing Russians, but his colleague, Marshal St Arnaud, refused. The Russian Army was allowed to regain Sevastopol, and a young genius of a military engineer, Lieutenant Colonel Todleben, began to prepare Sevastopol's defences.

---

[134] Cecil Woodham-Smith, *The Reason Why: The Story of the Fatal Charge of the Light Brigade*, 1953.

The Allied armies, deciding not to attack Sevastopol from the north, marched south-east, skirting the city, towards Balaklava harbour which was captured without bloodshed. The British took Balaklava as their supply base and the French occupied the undefended harbour of Kamiesch to the West. Siege weapons and ammunition began to be landed. The French took the left of the siege lines; the English the right. The Allies opened up their bombardment of Sevastopol on the 17th October 1854, and continued it for the next two days without noticeable success. On the 25th October 1854, Menschikoff made a major assault on the right of the besieging armies, whose forward defence works were a few half-hearted gun emplacements along the line of the road from Sevastopol to Prince Worontzoff's hunting lodge, manned by Turkish militia. Although the Turks fought bravely for over two hours, they were driven back as Lord Raglan arrived at his vantage point on the Sapoune Ridge.

The fleeing Turks reformed on either side of the four companies of the 93rd Highlanders under Sir Colin Campbell, which were the only troops between the oncoming Russians and the British base at Balaklava. Shortly afterwards a further two companies of the Highlanders, and a rag-tag of men from the port (including invalids from the hospital) joined this last line of defence, and these men came under Russian artillery fire. Campbell withdrew them a few yards to the comparative safety of the dead ground behind a low bank. A strong force of Russian cavalry moved in their direction. Campbell formed his men into line (not a square, which was the accepted way for infantry to face a cavalry charge) and the probing Russian advance was driven off with volleys of musket fire. This action gave rise to the famous phrase "*the thin red line*," from the account of *The Times* reporter, William Russell, to his readers wherein he described '*a thin red streak, tipped with a line of steel.*'

Another strong force of Russian cavalry was moving towards British forces, this time the Heavy Cavalry Brigade was the focus of its attention. General Sir James Yorke Scarlett led the men of the Heavy Brigade in a gallant uphill charge, and drove the Cossacks off. Whilst these actions were taking place, the Russians were calmly removing the British guns from the redoubts along the Causeway Heights which had been abandoned by the Turks, and Lord Raglan was desperately sending orders to his Light Cavalry Brigade and to his infantry to take action to prevent this. Finally, one of his orders was acted upon, and the Charge of the Light Brigade began but fatally in completely the wrong direction. From Raglan's viewpoint on the Sapoune Ridge it was possible to watch the vainglorious disaster unfold. Over 650 men charged; well over a hundred of them died within the next few minutes. As the Light Brigade went in, Raglan's infantry finally arrived on the battlefield but their only success was the recapture of the westernmost redoubts on the Causeway Heights. The British had lost possession of a considerable amount of ground, including the majority of their forward defences, as well as the only metalled road in the area.

Ten days later the Russians attacked again, in what came to be known as the Battle of Inkermann, or "the Soldier's Battle". The battle raged for almost the whole day, and was prosecuted in thick fog, heavy undergrowth, and with little if any generalship being shown on either side. As dusk fell, the British held the field (having received useful, if belated, help from the French). The numbers of the Russian dead left on the field exceeded the numbers of Allied troops that had been attacked. In total, over 17,500 men (mostly infantry and mostly Russian) were killed or wounded. After the battle of Inkermann, the weather deteriorated to such an extent that further action in the field was precluded, and the activities of the Allies were restricted to siege operations. During the winter of 1854/55 the shortcomings of the British military supply system were thrown into sharp focus, as thousands of men died from illness, exposure and malnutrition – four times as many died from disease as did from enemy action. One regiment, nominally over a thousand men strong, was reduced to a total of seven men by January 1855.

With the arrival of spring came the huts and winter clothing from England; too late to save the lives of the thousands who had died as a result of their absence. Military operations continued to be restricted to trench warfare until 7th June 1855 when the outer defences of Sevastopol were assaulted, with the British capturing the Quarries and the French the Mamelon. A coup de grace was planned for the anniversary of the battle of Waterloo, 18th June, as a way of cementing the new friendship between the British and their French allies. The assaults on the Malakoff and the Redan failed, partly due to incompetence on the part of the general officers commanding, and Lord Raglan sank into a decline, dying on the 28th June 1855. On the 16th August 1855, the Russian army under Prince Gortchakoff attempted to break through the Allied lines at the Traktir Bridge over the River Tchernaya, but was driven off by a combined French and Sardinian force a third its size. The Sardinians had joined the Allies in January 1855. On the 8th September 1855 the Allies again stormed Sevastopol, with the French successful this time at the Malakoff. The British attack on the Redan failed once more. The Malakoff, however, was the key to the town's defences, and at its loss the Russians evacuated Sevastopol, having made a spirited defence which had kept the best troops in the world at bay for over eleven months. After Sevastopol fell, the war in the Crimea was effectively at its end, although hostilities were not suspended until February 1856, and peace was not declared until the end of March.

The war was actually fought on two fronts, with the major land battles taking place in the Crimea and a series of naval actions fought in the Baltic Sea. The latter campaign essentially remained a backwater in the conduct of the war, largely turning into a stalemate with the outnumbered Russian fleet confining its movements to the areas around its coastal fortifications. The British and French commanders, even though they led the largest fleet assembled since the Napoleonic Wars, considered the Russian fortifications, especially the Kronstadt fortress protecting St Petersburg, too well-defended to engage. They spent most of the war blockading Russian trade and conducting raids on less fortified sections of the Finnish coast. However, as Russia was heavily dependent on imports for both the domestic economy and the supply of her military forces, the blockade seriously undermined the Russian economy and its ability to sustain the war. There were also limited naval engagements in the Black Sea which resulted in the British inflicting significant damage on the Russian fleet. After the latter's initial Pyrrhic victory over the Turkish fleet, the arrival of superior British and French naval forces caused the Russians to scuttle many of their ships during the siege of Sevastopol and they lost four major ships of the line, twelve frigates plus a large number of smaller vessels.

It was not only military tactics that evolved as a result of the Crimean War, the way in which war was actually reported also changed. At the forefront of this were two British men, William Howard Russell of *The Times* who was one of the very first modern war correspondents and the photographer Roger Fenton. Russell was born in Ireland in 1820 and he joined *The Times* in 1843 and covered various events in Britain as well as the brief war in Denmark in 1850. He was sent to the Crimea by his editor in early 1854 and reported on several battles and the siege of Sevastopol. Russell was not officially accredited as a British army reporter so he found himself largely unwelcomed and obstructed by senior officers. But being neither banned nor censored, he was able to make friends with junior officers as well as the ordinary ranks and by a combination of talking with them and keen observation, he obtained the information for his reports. The working conditions in the Crimea for newspaper reporters like Russell were difficult. They had to look after themselves as best they could, getting as close to the action as possible by their own efforts and once they had written their reports, they then had make their own arrangements for dispatching them. Russell also had to supply his own horse and tent as well as his own rations at times. Although he wore quasi-military clothes and carried a revolver he never became involved in any fighting. Russell was not a great writer but his vivid and convincing dispatches from the front line had a huge impact in Britain and around the world. For the first time the general public was able to read about the reality of warfare, almost as it happened. While writing of the heroism of the soldiers, he exposed the bungling and failure of high command as well as the suffering of the troops, particularly during the winter of 1854-1855.

The reactions to his accounts in *The Times* by both Queen Victoria and her government were very negative and he was accused of providing information useful to the enemy. However, the British public was shocked and outraged by Russell's reports and their angry reaction caused the resignation of the Prime Minister. When Russell arrived back in England he was treated like a national hero and he had become a household name among the reading public, a popularity he never lost for the remaining fifty years of his life. In 1856 Trinity College in Dublin awarded him an honorary degree and the same year on the advice of his friend, Charles Dickens, Russell published a book about the war[135]. He also pursued a highly successful lecture tour as well as later writing a series of books on military matters. In 1856 Russell returned briefly to Russia to cover the coronation of Tsar Alexander II for *The Times*. Russell was replaced in the latter stages of the war by another of *The Times'* reporters, Thomas Chenery. There is no doubt that their combined reporting on the plight of the sick and wounded in the Crimea not only convinced the British government to re-evaluate the treatment of its troops in the Crimea, it also ultimately led to Florence Nightingale's involvement in revolutionising battlefield medical care.

---

[135] William Howard, *The War: from the Landing at Gallipoli to the Death of Lord Raglan*, 1855

The collection of photos taken by Roger Fenton of the Crimean War were the first historic attempt to portray a war campaign with the help of the media of photography which was then still very much in its infancy. Fenton first went to Russia in 1852 to take photographs for the British civil engineer Charles Vignoles during the construction of a suspension bridge he was building over the Dnieper River in Kiev. This bridge took from 1847 until 1853 to complete and was the longest bridge in Europe at the time. During his visit to Russia, Fenton also photographed buildings and views in Kiev, St Petersburg and Moscow before travelling back to England. In 1855 Fenton was asked to return to Russia as a replacement for Richard Nicklin, another early photographer, who had been selected by the British government as the official Crimean campaign photographer. Nicklin had unfortunately been drowned, along with his assistants, photographs and equipment, when his ship sank during a hurricane that struck Balaklava harbour in November 1854. Fenton arrived in the Crimea in March 1855 and spent four months there as the British Army's official photographer, recording the soldiers and landscapes for posterity. Unlike the words of Russell, these photos never managed to capture the immediate drama of battles, the imagery of a cavalry charge or the harsh reality of broken limbs, blood and tears. This was partly due to the limitations of photographic techniques of the period but also because of the official wish to glamorize the war and shift public attention away from the shortcomings of government and military mismanagement which Russell has so effectively described. However, Fenton's series of photographs provide a level of realism and detail that could not be matched by Russell's written words.

The subjects of Fenton's fascinating photos are wide and varied with portraits of the leading allied commanders, officers of the Guards regiments with their fine horses, ordinary soldiers plus many of the army support staff such as orderlies, railway engineers, labourers and even the camp followers. He also photographed the bustling allied ports like Balaclava, brimming with shipping and the docks crammed with war materiel. Perhaps his most evocative photo is the one showing the Light Brigade's 'valley of the shadow of death'. Its stark dirt road leading up an empty ravine scattered with cannonballs still retains a haunting sense of the dramatic event more than a century and a half later. During his time in the Crimea, Fenton broke several ribs and contracted cholera so he had to return home before his goal of photographing the fall of Sevastopol could be achieved. His photographic work in the Crimea was subsequently continued by James Robertson. When the Crimean War finished, public interest in Fenton and his photos quickly faded and in 1862 he quit photography for good. He was not a well man and died several years later at the early age of forty-nine, penniless and almost forgotten. Now however, Fenton's remarkable work in the Crimea is recognised for its seminal role in establishing photography both as an artistic endeavour as well as an important part of professional war reporting.[136] There can be little doubt that it was the articles by Russell and his successor Chenery that convinced Florence Nightingale to travel out to the

---

[136] Many of Roger Fenton's fascinating photos can be viewed online at - http://allworldwars.com/Crimean-War-Photographs-by-Roger-Fenton-1855.

Black Sea and establish efficient and sanitary nursing facilities first near Istanbul and later at Balaklava in the Crimea.

The most famous non-military person from Britain associated with the Crimean War was Florence Nightingale who was born into a wealthy, upper-class British family in Florence, Italy in 1820 and was named after the city of her birth. Well educated and travelled, she refused to marry several suitors and at the age of twenty-five informed her parents that she wanted to become a nurse, a position then associated with working-class women only. Nightingale believed that God had called her to be a nurse and after a great deal of resistance from her parents, she finally overcame their objections and qualified as a nurse in early 1853, joining a women's hospital in London. A report by William Russell in *The Times* the following year that an estimated 8,000 troops in the Crimea were suffering from cholera or malaria[137] led to a surge of women volunteers wishing to go out to help as nurses. Initially, both the army and government rejected these offers, partly in recognition of the dreadful conditions at the front but mostly due to a considerable prejudice against women's involvement in medicine. Indeed, many soldiers in their letters home poured cold water on the nursing aspirations of their female family members. Captain Campbell wrote 'If you know any lady mad enough to come out here as a hospital nurse, use all your interest to put her into a straight-waistcoat as soon as possible'.[138] However, the growing public outcry forced the government to change its mind and when Nightingale offered her services she was eventually given permission to take a group of thirty-eight volunteer British nurses to the main British base in Turkey in October 1854. They were all trained by Nightingale and the group included her aunt, Mai Smith.

Nightingale and her fellow nurses arrived a few weeks later at the Selemiye barracks in Scutari near Istanbul. There they found large numbers of wounded soldiers being badly cared for by an overworked medical staff with an almost total indifference to the conditions and the men's fate by senior military staff. The men lay unwashed in rooms without blankets, still wearing their army uniforms that were encrusted with dirt and blood. There were only limited supplies of medicines, basic hygiene practices were ignored and mass infections, many of them fatal, were common. There was no equipment to prepare food for the patients. Nightingale used her own funds to buy fruit and vegetables for the sick and wounded soldiers as well as some elementary hospital equipment. Nightingale's attempts at change and reform in Scutari were met with little sympathy or encouragement by the senior medical staff who saw her ideas as a criticism of themselves. However, through the help of the editor of *The Times* she was able to publicise the appalling conditions and eventually the British government commissioned Isambard Brunel to design a prefabricated 1,000 bed hospital that was shipped out from England just five months later to the Dardanelles. This new model hospital was run as a civilian facility, not directly

---

[137] A large number of soldiers also suffered from scurvy; the Royal Navy's solution of giving its sailors fruit juice seems to have gone unnoticed by the Army Medical Corps.

[138] Helen Rappaport, *No Place for Ladies*, 2007.

under the control of the army or Nightingale and achieved a death rate less than one tenth that of Scutari.

The results of Nightingale's work during the Crimean War were mixed. Although definite improvements were made in the care, general comfort and well-being of the men, the overall death rate did not fall, indeed they actually rose. During her first winter at Scutari, over 4,000 soldiers died there and the death rate from illnesses such as typhus, cholera and dysentery was ten times higher than from battle wounds. The conditions at the barracks hospital were so deleterious due to overcrowding and the lack of effective sewers and poor ventilation. The death rate did not reduce until a Sanitary Commission was sent out from England to Scutari almost six months after Nightingale's arrival to organise flushing out the sewers and improvements to ventilation. However, the respect in which she was held by the troops is obvious from the fact she was dubbed 'The Lady with the Lamp' after her habit of making the rounds of the five miles of beds every night. During the war she did not recognise hygiene as the predominant cause of death and continued to believe the high death rate was due to poor nutrition and the overwork endured by the soldiers. It was not until after she returned to Britain in 1856 and began collecting evidence before the Royal Commission on the Health of the Army that she recognised that the poor sanitary conditions and inadequate medical supplies were the cause of most deaths at the hospital. To be fair, Nightingale never claimed any credit for helping to reduce the death rate in Scutari. She also shunned public praise in Britain and used her influence in high places, including Queen Victoria, to fight for effective reform of the entire system of military hospitals and medical care.

Having understood the real problem Nightingale, in her later career, stressed the importance of sanitary conditions, thereby helping to reduce deaths in the Army during peacetime and turned attention onto the sanitary design of hospitals. While she was in the Crimea, a public meeting to recognise Nightingale for her work in the war led to the establishment of the Nightingale Fund for the training of nurses. Through generous donations, she was able to establish a nursing school at St Thomas' Hospital in London which was the first secular nursing school in the world. The Nightingale Pledge was taken for many years by all new nurses in Britain and the annual International Nurses Day is celebrated around the world on her birthday. She also wrote several books on nursing and was also something of a statistician, using detailed charts developed from data she collected in the Crimea to press her case for reform. While she was in Turkey, Nightingale also took an interest in the broader aspects of health, visiting some of the spas in the Ottoman Empire and noted the conditions and treatments. She then recommended these spas for British patients as a much cheaper alternative to the then popular ones in Switzerland. In later life Florence Nightingale suffered from poor health and sadly, in 1895 went blind. Soon afterwards, the loss of other faculties meant she had to receive full-time nursing and although a complete invalid she lived another fifteen years until dying in London in 1910.

Florence Nightingale deservedly acquired an international reputation for her drive and determination in trying to improve conditions in the Crimea. But it is easy to overlook the contribution made to nursing during the Crimean War by other women such as Mary Seacole and the likes of Lady Alicia Blackwood and Elizabeth Davis, who still remain somewhat in Nightingale's shadow. When Blackwood and her husband, the Rev. James Stevenson Blackwood, read about the terrible events at the Battle of Inkerman they decided to go out to try to help. Dr Blackwood obtained a chaplaincy with the army and Lady Alicia plus two young female friends set out from England for Scutari where they arrived in December 1854. Lady Alicia immediately went to visit Florence Nightingale to offer her assistance in any way Nightingale thought suitable. From previous experience, Nightingale was rather sceptical of inexperienced ladies who came out to assist in the hospitals and she didn't think much of such well-meaning but dilettante women. However, after a brief discussion with Blackwood, Nightingale offered her the task of looking after more than two hundred soldiers' wives who were surviving in abject misery outside the hospital.

These women had sailed from England with their husbands with the intention of accompanying them to the Crimea but most had been disembarked at the Allied army assembly ports in Varna in Bulgaria or Gallipolli from where they had later been collected and brought to Scutari. Here they were largely left to their own fate; the luckier ones were reunited with their sick and wounded spouses while the less fortunate now found themselves widows. While conditions for the men were bad enough, there was very little provision for their wives who were now destitute, some of them ill and covered with vermin. Nightingale and her nursing staff had no time to deal with them and so she delegated to Blackwood the task of creating and managing an unofficial hospital for the wives, widows and children of soldiers in Scutari. In her later book[139], Blackwood described the appalling conditions in which she found them living and felt they were 'as much sinned against as sinning.' Nightingale had little sympathy for these women and there was some friction between these two strong-willed ladies, with Nightingale evidently regarding Blackwood as something of a nuisance. However, she did eventually allocate some of her funds and resources to Blackwood who was able to bring much needed relief to these unfortunate and abandoned people. Despite their differences, Blackwood's respect for Nightingale and her work are evident throughout her account.

Elizabeth Davis was born in Wales in 1789 but ran away to Chester and then Liverpool when only fourteen. After a varied and fascinating life in domestic service and as a nanny during which time she travelled widely in Europe, the West Indies and the Far East she returned to England and took up nursing. When she read one of William Russell's reports in *The Times* about the suffering of the soldiers in the Crimea, she volunteered in 1854 for army nursing service. She travelled out to Scutari in December with a party of some forty nurses and Irish nuns under Mary Stanley, a friend of Florence Nightingale. Unfortunately, the group had been sent out without the knowledge or agreement of Nightingale who was very annoyed not to have been consulted. There was no immediate room for this new party at the hospital, either in the sense of accommodation or in terms of work and this inevitably led to considerable bickering between

---

[139] Lady Alicia Blackwood, *A Narrative of Personal Experiences & Impressions during a Residence on the Bosphorus throughout the Crimean War*, 1881

Nightingale and Stanley's nurses and nuns. When it became clear that the Catholic Irish sisters were more interested in proselytising than taking care of the more immediate worldly needs of the troops the disputes worsened. Nightingale offered to resign and matters were only resolved by the intervention of the British Ambassador and the assignment of most of Stanley's group to another hospital.

The bickering and delays in Scutari did not sit well with Davis who became annoyed at being asked to do basic support work such as mending old shirts and sorting linen rather than being allowed to go to the Crimea to do real nursing. Davis was clearly a rather down-to-earth, argumentative person and did not get on well with Nightingale but the latter eventually agreed to allow Davis and several other nurses to leave Scutari and make their own way to the field hospital at Balaclava where they were quickly set to work treating the infested wounds of the soldiers. The men were in their last stages of exhaustion, verminous, filthy, clothed only in rags and as many of their wounds had received no attention for weeks they were full of maggots. Davis later wrote:

'I began to open some of their wounds. The first that I touched was a case of frost bite. The toes of both the man's feet fell off with the bandages. The hand of another fell off at the wrist. It was... weeks since the wounds of many of those men had been looked at and dressed... One soldier had been wounded at Alma.... His wound had not been dressed for five weeks, and I took at least a quart of maggots from it. From many of the other patients I removed them in handfuls.'

The problems lay not with the Army medical front-line staff who were mostly very conscientious and hard working – men like Dr Blake who was an experienced and enterprising regimental surgeon whose hospital was considered one of the best-run in the Crimea. Their difficulties were due largely to supply shortages plus the overcrowding and overwork resulting from the very high sickness rate. In Blake's hospital, the number of sickness cases was almost five times that of wounds. Davis cooked, cleaned and nursed, regularly working twenty hours a day and often for several days without a break and slept on a floor in a small room with seven other women. She later took charge of the kitchen and being a good cook was able to improve the soldiers' diet, making sure they had good food produced from fresh ingredients. When Nightingale later visited Balaclava and saw what Davis had achieved, she was full of praise for her work. Davis was in her sixties when she arrived in the Crimea and the desperate conditions took plus the heavy workload their toll on her own health and suffering from cholera and dysentery, she returned to Britain in 1855. Although Davis was very critical in her comments on the poor conditions in the Crimea and Nightingale's poor organisation, Nightingale did acknowledge her contribution and provided her with a recommendation for a government pension. Elizabeth Davis died in poverty at the home of her sister in London, in 1860.

Sarah Terrot was one of the nurses who originally accompanied Florence Nightingale to the Black Sea in October 1854. Born in 1820, she left school at fourteen and acted as a governess to her younger sisters before moving to London where she taught children and nursed the sick. Terrot volunteered to go out to Scutari with Nightingale's initial arty of thirty-eight nurses and although she didn't spend a long time there, her later memoirs[140] provide an interesting first-hand account of her early months at the hospital. Her views on Nightingale were very different from those of Davis as she says in her book that 'from the first moment I felt an impulse to love, trust and respect her.' On arrival at Scutari, she found the conditions were very primitive. The only food available was black tea with pieces of rough, stale bread and the nurses slept eight to a room. There were no tables anywhere, not even for performing operations and the corridors leading to the nurses' quarters were used as extra ward space with simple straw beds for the sick, wounded and dying. Terrot's first patient was the wife of a soldier who was dying of consumption and she '*looked after the woman till nightfall, but she died during the night. When I went to see her in the morning, her body had been wrapped in a blanket, and laid in a grave, the simple inscription "A Woman" on a piece of wood placed at the head of it, in the cemetery, where lie peacefully side by side Russians and English, rich and poor.*' Until Nightingale began to turn things around, the hospital seemed full of despair, although the soldiers were extremely grateful for the kindness and attention shown by the nurses. Terrot continued to work under the direction of Nightingale at Scutari for some six months until following severe illness, she was ordered back to England in the spring of 1855. Along with Nightingale, she was later awarded the Royal Red Cross medal for her services in the Crimea.

The last of this quartet of dedicated British Crimean nurses is Mary Seacole who was born in 1805 at Kingston, Jamaica. Her father was a Scottish soldier and her mother a local woman who ran a rest home for invalid soldiers which is where Mary first learned her nursing skills. Later, Seacole travelled widely in the Caribbean and Central America as well as visiting Britain, developing her knowledge of both traditional and herbal medicine. In 1851 she joined her brother in Panama where they opened a hotel and it was here that she first encountered cholera. While successfully nursing a patient with cholera, she contracted and recovered from the disease herself and thus gained detailed knowledge of its pathology. She was widely praised locally for her work in treating cholera and returned to Jamaica in 1853, where there was a yellow fever epidemic. The Jamaican medical authorities asked her to help provide nurses to care for the sick soldiers. In 1854, on hearing of the outbreak of war, Seacole returned to Britain at her own expense where she applied to the War Office, the Army medical department and the Secretary of War to be allowed to go to the Crimea as an Army nurse. She pointed out that she had extensive experience, excellent references and knew many of the soldiers and regiments, having nursed them while they were stationed in Jamaica.

Despite her undoubted capabilities and skill, she was rejected by everyone including Florence Nightingale, presumably because of her colour. In her frustration and disappointment, Mary wept openly in the London street after her unsuccessful meeting with Nightingale. But undaunted, she soon linked up with a distant relative of hers, called Day, with whom she established a firm called Seacole and Day. The pair purchased considerable stocks of medicines and provisions and then paid their passage out to the Crimea where they set up a

---

[140] Sarah Terrot, *Reminiscences of Scutari Hospitals*, 1898.

general store and hotel near the main British camp. Seacole opened her British hotel in the summer of 1855, near the besieged city of Sevastopol and soon the entire British army knew about 'Mother Seacole's'. Like Elizabeth Davis, Seacole was not a young woman when she went to the war zone but from the moment of her arrival, she set to, looking after as many of the sick and wounded as she could. She was well liked by the troops and was happy to sit up half the night with the patients drinking tea or just talking with them. Seacole was often on the front line, sometimes under fire, nursing the wounded and dying with little regard to her own safety.

Though some of the Army doctors regarded her as a "quack" despite her valuable contribution to the men's well-being, fortunately others were less bigoted and supported her efforts. It was William Russell who first drew public attention to Seacole's work in the Crimea and made her famous. He described her in *The Times* as *'a warm and successful physician, who doctors and cures all manner of men with extraordinary success. She is always in attendance near the battle field to aid the wounded, and has earned many a poor fellow's blessings'*. For a time, her reputation rivalled that of Florence Nightingale. Despite the fall of Sevastopol, the large numbers of Allied troops remaining kept the Seacole and Day hotel busy. But in the spring of 1856, with a peace treaty signed, the last of the troops departed and left Seacole and Day with a considerable amount of stores on their hands that couldn't be sold. They were both forced into bankruptcy and Seacole returned to England destitute and in ill health. The press took up her cause and in July 1857 a well-attended benefit festival was organized to raise money for her and later that year Seacole published her memoirs.[141] She became a masseuse to Princess Alexandra in London but her fame soon faded and she spent the last twenty-five years of her life in relative obscurity until her death in 1881.

Despite their remarkable achievements, official recognition was both limited and late in coming for the British nurses that served in the Crimean campaign. Nightingale received a personal gift from Queen Victoria, a brooch designed by Prince Albert, in gratitude for her devotion to the Queen's soldiers but it was not until 1908 that she was awarded the Order of Merit, just two years prior to her death. For the other 228 women recorded as nurses in the Crimea and Turkey plus all the unofficial nurses, mostly soldiers' wives, there was little in the way of honours. A few, including Sarah Terrot, belatedly received the Royal Red Cross medal in 1897, an award that had been created more than fifteen years earlier. Although Mary Seacole was given a Crimean medal by some of her supporters, she was never officially recognized. None of the graves of the many British men and women that died in the war survived the subsequent ravages of time, neglect and further wars, although there is now a British memorial to the fallen outside Sevastopol. The story of British nurses in Russia didn't end with the Crimean War and we will look at some of their later experiences in Chapter Fifteen.

While the Crimean War firmly established a new role for women as nurses with the British Army, it also marked the end of the tradition of large numbers

---

[141] Mary Seacole, *The Wonderful Adventures of Mrs Seacole in Many Lands*, 1857.

of ordinary soldiers' wives being allowed to accompany their husbands to war. Army regulations regarding women travelling with the troops 'on the strength' varied between regiments and application of the rules became arbitrary at the ports of embarkation, depending on the space available in the troopships and the determination of the women to get on board. So it is unclear how many women actually left Britain for the war zone in 1854 but it is likely to have been at least 750 and possibly as many as 1200.[142] Apart from a few senior officers' wives, only the most determined made it all the way to the Crimea. Some died during the sea journey but most found themselves abandoned at Army staging points along the Black Sea littoral in Bulgaria or Turkey with little prospect of finding onward transport to the front. Separated from their men, with no support, supplies, accommodation or money many of these women became destitute and suffered appallingly. Things were little better for those that eventually managed to get to the Crimea. Some like their men died from fevers and cholera. Others were left broken-hearted, stranded and penniless when their husbands were killed in battle. Probably only a quarter of those that set sail from Britain for the Black Sea ever managed to return home. The problems faced in the war zone by so many of these women were a major factor in persuading the British Army to later forbid the practice of allowing soldiers' wives to accompany the troops.

One of the British women present during the campaign was Frances Duberly who came out to the Crimea with her husband, Captain Henry Duberly, paymaster to the 8th Royal Irish Hussars. Frances was apparently a good horsewoman as well as being physically strong, daring, lively and quite at home in the company of soldiers. However, she refused to live in the camp tent that her husband shared with three other soldiers and spent much of her time in relative safety on board one of the British transports off Sevastopol. Being an officer's lady, she was told of battle plans in advance which gave her the opportunity to come ashore and find a good position to watch them which is exactly what she did at the Battle of Balaclava. Although her husband survived the day, many of her friends did not and she later wrote in her book *'Even my closed eyelids were filled with the ruddy glare of blood'*[143]. She witnessed the appalling scenes in the seaport of Balaclava where the dead and wounded from the battle were roughly manhandled onto steamships bound for the hospitals and graveyards at Scutari in Turkey. Wounded British soldiers were dying at the rate of eighty men a day and the losses were even greater among the Turkish army. On the beach, wounded and mutilated horses, mules and bullocks were abandoned to starve to death. This once picturesque little harbour had now become a seething cesspool for the dying, maimed, sick and destitute where the inadequacies of both military and civilian administrations were fully exposed.

In June the following year, along with William Russell and several other British Army wives, Duberly also watched the early stages of the battle for Sevastopol. The carnage was horrific with more than 6,000 French and British troops slaughtered in the unsuccessful initial assaults. Mary Seacole was there too, working tirelessly under fire trying to tend to the large number of wounded

[142] Helen Rappaport – ibid.

[143] Frances Duberly, *Journal Kept During The Russian War*, 1856.

men on both sides. Although it was a daunting and overwhelming task, she was certain that 'in scenes of horror and distress ... a woman can do so much'.[144] When Sevastopol finally fell to the Allies a couple of months later, Seacole was the first foreign woman to enter the ruined and desolate city. As ever, she was there to tend to the needy with supplies of food and drink. Duberly followed Seacole into the devastated city a few days later but her motives were less altruistic; her visit was made out of morbid curiosity and bravado. Her unsolicited presence disgusted many of the British officers who saw her riding around amongst the horrific and tragic scenes of the recent slaughter. With the end of the war, Duberly and her husband returned home but despite the horrors of the Crimea, her desire to be in the thick of things was insatiable. Despite Army objections, she managed to accompany her husband one more time when he was sent to India the following year. However, the wisdom of this decision came into question when in 1858, while watching the start of a cavalry charge, her own horse took off with the rest and she found herself racing forward into battle with the troops.

The war in the Crimean not only saw the arrival in Russia of the British troops, their wives and nurses but it also engendered an early form of war tourism. With the resumption of the campaign in the spring of 1855, a steady trickle of curious visitors from Britain made their way out to the Crimea to witness events. Initially, most were family or friends of serving officers and as such were generally welcomed and accepted as guests of the British Army. With the arrival of mild spring weather, these visitors joined a growing social scene that had developed behind the British and French lines. In an almost surreal country club atmosphere, there were horse races with crowds 'as large as that at Epsom or Ascot',[145] hunting parties on the steppe and the inevitable dinner parties and extended drinking sessions. In between the various social events, many of the tourists sought out the battlefields of the previous year, especially the 'valley of death' where the infamous charge of the Light Brigade had taken place. Now bright with early summer flowers, there was little to indicate the earlier carnage apart from fragments of cannon balls that still littered the ground. For the male visitors, an occasional visit to the siege lines around Sevastopol to see the action was permitted to satisfy their curiosity before returning home.

The experience of serving in the Crimea didn't put off all the British soldiers from later returning to Russia. Charles George Gordon from Woolwich in England was a second lieutenant in the Corps of Royal Engineers during the Crimean war and had the dangerous front-line task of mapping the Russian trenches. After the war, Gordon's ability as a surveyor helped him obtain a position as a Boundary Commissioner for the new frontier to be drawn between Russia and the Romanian principalities of Moldavia and Wallachia. Soon after completing this project, Gordon was sent to serve on the Boundary Commission deciding on the Russo-Turkish frontier in Armenia. After an extremely difficult journey to the frontier, he and the Commission's Russian and Turkish members then spent the next six months surveying and marking the new border. He spent

[144] Mary Seacole – ibid.

[145] Frances Duberly – ibid.

the winter of 1857-1858 back in England, during which time he was elected to the Royal Geographical Society. When he returned to Armenia the following spring, he found much to his surprise that most of the cairns erected to mark the border had been destroyed by the locals. As he discovered, for them the whole point of the border was that it should be as inaccurately defined as possible, thus guaranteeing work for both smugglers and customs officers. Gordon now realized the pointlessness of the project, especially as his Russian companions admitted they planned to take back everything they had lost to the Turks. He returned to England in December 1858.

The outbreak of the Crimean War had a varied impact on the British living in Russia. Many naturally returned home, especially the diplomats and those running their own businesses trading with Russia. However, a surprising number of the British that had settled in Russia remained during the War and in some cases the Russians actually encouraged them to stay. James Johnston, a principal engineer at the Admiralty yards at Kolpino, near St Petersburg, resigned at once when the state of war was announced. The Russians did not want him to go and offered him the post of Engineer in Chief at Kronstadt if he would become a Russian citizen but he still returned home. Many of the engineers on Russian naval ships at the time were of British origin and while no pressure was put on those who decided to leave, some stayed and became Russian citizens. Despite the reduced congregations, the British churches in Moscow and St Petersburg continued to function. The Russian police were unhappy at this but following a direct appeal to Tsar Nicholas, he confirmed the right of the British to meet for worship as they wished.

Many of the British owned or operated businesses were forced to close with the outbreak of war, especially those in Ukraine or the Crimea itself such as the large grain trading firm of William Yeames in Taganrog and the flour mill run by John Tandy at Kerch. However, some British companies continued in operation. For example, in December 1854 *The Times* reported that: '*Mr Baird's iron foundry is in full work again. He has contracted for five screw engines (four 300 horsepower and one 400 horsepower).*' The Baird Works, located just outside St Petersburg, had been founded in 1792 by Charles Baird (see page 235) and at the time of the Crimean War was the most important metal working and machine manufacturing business in Russia. Baird made a wide range of machinery for industry and shipbuilding, including steam engines, sawmills, sugar mills and bridges, employing some 900 workers in its foundries and machine shops. Baird's colleague, Charles Gascoigne also continued with his iron-making operation in Lugansk (see page 236). Many of the British employed by Russian companies however, lost their jobs and returned to Britain such as Joseph Platts who had come to Odessa from Derbyshire in 1837. He worked initially at John Tandy's flour mill in Odessa and then as an engineer with the Black Sea Steamboat Company. He married Tandy's daughter and they raised a family in Odessa and although they went to England in 1855, the family eventually returned to Russia some years later.

Apart from the advances in medical treatment for the wounded, the results and benefits of the war for the British were inconclusive and as unclear as its beginnings. For the Russians, the war demonstrated only too clearly the country's need to modernise and upgrade both its weaponry as well as its military and civilian infrastructure. Russia's failure in the Crimean War proved to be an important watershed in the future development and modernisation of the country. The defeat had three major impacts on Imperial Russia. It caused political unrest, especially among the peasants due to conscription into the militia during the war, contributing to the decision to emancipate the serfs in 1861. It caused severe financial problems – the Russian government was left with a debt burden of one billion roubles and it exposed the backwardness of the country's economy and its outdated military capabilities. The new Tsar Alexander II and his government took on board the lessons of defeat and steadily moved to tackle these three issues. From a British perspective, it was the decision by Alexander's government to aggressively follow a policy of industrialisation that would have most impact. In particular, the decision to dramatically expand the railway network and modernise the coal and metallurgical industries as well as manufacturing in general was to prove vital in paving the way for the arrival in Russia of a new breed of British people – industrial entrepreneurs and businessmen.

Post-war relationships between the two countries soon improved with diplomatic and trading contacts being quickly restored in 1856. Indeed, the Russian hero of the siege of Sevastopol, Colonel Todleben was fêted during a visit to London that same year. Todleben, now promoted to a general, visited England several times over the next few years to look at purchasing new armaments and also to meet with British entrepreneurs who might be persuaded to go to Russia to assist with its future industrial development. Two of the key people he invited to Russia during his visits were Captain Alexander Blakely and the Welsh industrialist John Hughes, who we will discuss in the next chapter. Blakely was among the earliest to apply theoretical science to the manufacture of ordnance and went on to obtain several British patents for inventions relating to cannon. He had been an artillery captain in the British Army until retiring on half-pay in 1852. During the Crimean War in 1855 he served as a major in the irregular cavalry of General Robert Vivian's 22,000 strong Turkish Contingent, a mercenary corps organized by the British Army. By the early 1860s he was a well-known expert on ordnance and started to manufacture large guns in partnership with a couple of British companies, supplying many foreign armies. Todleben invited him to Russia and in 1863 Blakely arrived in St Petersburg where he went into partnership with Francis Baird to tender for new Russian government contracts for large guns to upgrade the Baltic coastal defences. In November 1863, the Imperial Artillery Committee selected Baird and Blakely as the successful contractors for the supply of heavy ordnance for both coastal defences and the Russian navy. During 1864 the pair supplied around 160 guns and equipment to the value of £960,000 and by the end of their contract later the next year they had delivered over 220 pieces of modern heavy ordnance to the Russians. Blakely returned to England a rich man and moved into 1 Park Lane, overlooking Marble Arch in London but it was not to last. His business interests in Britain failed and he had an affair with a married woman who was subsequently divorced by her husband. His reputation and finances were in tatters so he fled the country with his mistress, ending up in distant Peru where he died of yellow fever in 1868, aged only forty-one.

11
Diplomats, Politics and the Great Game

From the moment of Chancellor's accidental first arrival in Russia, diplomatic relations with England and subsequently Great Britain over the ensuing three centuries were largely dominated by two things – trade and political alliances. It's not surprising therefore that many of the early English envoys were senior merchants of the Russia Company whose diplomatic roles were closely intertwined with their trading interests. Along with the merchants of the Russia Company, the various British envoys and ambassadors represent the longest ongoing link between the two countries, stretching in an almost unbroken chain from 1566 to 1917. The first exchange of official letters between Britain and Russia took place in 1554 between Queen Elizabeth I and Tsar Ivan and her correspondence continued with the two subsequent Russian Tsars until her death in 1603. Despite a break in relations for several years, at least ninety letters were exchanged during this period, typically two or three each year.[146] Although throughout this lengthy series of letters, the common thread was trade, the real intentions of the respective rulers remained different. On the Russian side, particularly for Ivan, the main objective was to use commerce as a lever to achieve some sort of alliance with England. For Elizabeth however, the concern was to protect the valuable trading rights granted to the Muscovy Company without becoming embroiled in an alliance.

As already outlined in Chapter One, Anthony Jenkinson was the first British diplomatic representative in Russia. Initially this was in an unofficial capacity with Jenkinson acting as a go-between in his role as principal agent of the Russia Company and the first formally appointed ambassador to Russia was Thomas Randolph in 1568. Born in 1523, Randolph was a professional diplomat having worked for many years for Elizabeth, mostly in Scotland during the difficult period of negotiations with Mary, Queen of the Scots. The English had become aware that rival foreign traders had been allowed to use Russia's Baltic ports new restrictions had been imposed on the Muscovy Company's merchants so Randolph was dispatched to Moscow to try to resolve these issues and negotiate new trading privileges. He was accompanied by the English poet, George Turberville, as his secretary and their time in Russia proved to be an unhappy experience for both of them. When Randolph arrived in Moscow he was treated coldly and made to wait four months before an audience with the Tsar was finally agreed. This first meeting took place in open court where Randolph, surrounded by some 300 courtiers, was made to stand and state his business – a position that was hardly conducive to negotiating confidential affairs. This treatment, combined with the delay did not sit well with Randolph

---

[146] Irina Lubinenko, The Correspondence of Queen Elizabeth and the Russian Czars, *American Historical Review*, 1914.

who as an experienced, senior diplomat was used to better treatment. A few days later, he was summoned late at night to a second meeting at the Kremlin for which Randolph, on Ivan's instructions, had to disguise himself as a Russian. Nothing was resolved until a third meeting some six weeks later when the mercurial Tsar was all smiles and quickly granted the rights Randolph was seeking, enabling him to immediately return to London in July 1569. Turberville found his Russian experience not at all to his liking; for him the Russians were boorish and uncouth and Moscow had little to offer a foreign visitor. On his return to England he published a series of poems about life in what he regarded as a rude and barbarous kingdom.

With Randolph's departure from Russia, the ambassadorial role was subsequently taken up again by Jenkinson. He had been such an effective negotiator and trusted communicator that he was appointed special ambassador and sent back to Russia in 1571. The cloak of diplomatic immunity offered an important level of protection for the British ambassadors in a wild country like Russia, especially with an unpredictable and violent ruler like Ivan. However, there was a limit to the power of diplomatic immunity, even for the British, as evidenced by Jenkinson's eventual replacement, Daniel Sylvester. The unfortunate Sylvester had gone out as a clerk in the service of the Russia Company and having become fluent in Russian he returned to England to act as interpreter for the Company as well as the Crown. He was appointed ambassador in 1575 and the following year on a return trip from England was struck by a bolt of lightning in the English factory at Kholmogory. The lightning strike caused a fire that burned down the factory and destroyed all Sylvester's papers as well as a personal letter from Elizabeth I to the Tsar.

The subsequent English ambassador, Sir Jerome Bowes, fared somewhat better but still ended up in prison and in danger of losing his life. Bowes was sent as ambassador to Russia in 1583 following the aborted discussions regarding the proposed marriage of Lady Mary Hastings to Tsar Ivan. After months of fruitless negotiations and foot dragging by Elizabeth, Bowes sailed to Russia with the Russian ambassador to tell Ivan that Lady Mary would not after all be coming to Moscow to be his next bride. Under the circumstances it wasn't surprising that the initial meetings between Bowes and the Tsar got off to a bad start. Ivan was rumoured to have recently nailed the French ambassador's hat to his head and Bowes was threatened with the same treatment as well as later being told he would be thrown out of the window. Bowes stood his ground with the irascible Tsar and eventually gained his respect. But this came too late as Ivan died soon afterwards and his successor, Feodor, favoured the Dutch. Bowes soon found himself under house arrest and for a few weeks was in real fear of his life until he was finally allowed to depart for England. As he embarked, in a defiant, undiplomatic gesture, Bowes sent back the new Tsar's introductory letters and his present for Elizabeth.

Bowes' ambassadorial duties were eventually taken over initially by Giles Fletcher in 1588 and then by Jerome Horsey two years later. Horsey had actually been in Moscow since 1573. He started as a junior employee and translator for the Russia Company and during his seventeen years in the country, he steadily worked his way up the corporate and political ladders. He led a colourful and eventful life until his departure in 1591 and came to know well many of the leading personalities at the Russian Court. Horsey was a somewhat vain and enigmatic character who clearly sailed very close to the wind in some of his affairs and in so doing made enemies of both Russians and English colleagues at the Company. It seems however, that he was well liked by Ivan who, after the untimely death of Daniel Sylvester, increasingly turned to Horsey as his main conduit for contact with the English. Horsey took advantage of his growing influence at the Court in Moscow to have some of the English who crossed him imprisoned and even tortured. Yet if his memoirs[147] are to be believed, he interceded with the Tsar to prevent him sending a young Baltic noblewoman, Madelyn van Uxell, to a brothel and helped over one thousand British mercenaries held in prisons in Moscow. These men had been in the Polish and Lithuanian armies and captured by the Russians in the recent wars. Horsey sent food to the gaols, arranged for many of them to join the Russian Army and even obtained permission for them to build a church.

Horsey successfully negotiated a new trading charter with the Tsar and at the Company's request, used his influence at Court to obtain additional land for the English factory compound. Conveniently, part of this extra land was then used to construct Horsey's own house where he regularly entertained his friends and contacts at the Russian Court. He also used his favoured position in Moscow to conduct private trading on behalf of senior members of the English Court, probably the Earl of Leicester and Sir Francis Walsingham, and thus went against the rules of the Company. On several occasions it seems he falsified the accounts of the Company, possibly to cover the traces of his private trading activities or simply to embezzle the money. Although when discovered, Horsey paid back some of the missing funds, his nefarious conduct resulted in formal complaints by the Company to the Russian and English Courts. However, with the support of Walsingham, Horsey managed to ride out the storm and eventually resolved his difficulties by giving up the property he owned in Moscow to the Company.

In his role as the Tsar's envoy and Russia Company agent, Horsey regularly travelled back and forth between Russia and England, conveying both written and verbal messages. In late November 1581, Horsey was asked by Ivan to carry urgent secret letters to Queen Elizabeth which due to their confidential nature, Horsey hid in his personal wine flask. Due to the time of year, the sea route was closed but an overland journey meant passing through several countries then at war with Russia. Horsey undertook this dangerous mission wearing different disguises or pretending he was an English fugitive from Russia and all went well until he reached Arensburg in modern day Estonia, where he was locked up as a spy. However, through pure luck, it turned out that Madelyn van Uxell, who he had earlier helped in Moscow, was the daughter of the local governor and so he was quickly released and allowed to continue his journey through Germany and on to England. Horsey explains in his memoirs that he did his best to straighten out the Tsar's letters and remove the lingering smell of alcohol before presenting them to Queen Elizabeth but apparently, she still noticed the strange odour.

---

[147] Jerome Horsey, *Travels of Sir Jerome Horsey*, 1856.

These letters, delivered under such difficult circumstances, probably related to the secret discussions between the two monarchs regarding the proposed marriage of Ivan to Lady Anne Hastings.

Horsey returned to Russia once more with nine ships laden with cargo, partly supplied by adventurers outside the Russia Company and he was clearly once again sidestepping the Company's monopoly position. A year later, Horsey was again back in England with letters from the Tsar, this time asking for help as the Tsarina was having difficulty conceiving. Unfortunately, the Tsar's message was poorly translated as Jerome returned to Moscow with a midwife and this misunderstanding led to a deterioration in relations with the Russian Court. England's position worsened further in 1588 when the Russians felt that Elizabethan England might be conquered by the Spanish. However, the welcome news of the defeat of the Spanish Armada soon led to a halving in the customs duty paid by the English.

As the Russia Company's chief agent and factor, Horsey worked closely with Giles Fletcher during the latter's short period as England's ambassador to the Russian Court and the two men seem to have got on well together. Fletcher was an experienced diplomat and was sent out to Moscow in 1588 to build on the trading agreement already negotiated by Horsey with the new Tsar Feodor. On his return to England, Fletcher published a book[148] about his experiences in Russia but its detailed and vibrant observations of life there were regarded as potentially inflammatory to good Anglo-Russian relations and the book was suppressed for several years. His opinions of Russian institutions and life in general no doubt simply reflected the views of most foreigners at that time but his description of the Tsar as a 'person of a mean stature, somewhat low and gross, of a fallow complexion, and inclining to dropsy, hawk-nosed, unsteady in his pace by reason of some weakness of his limbs, heavy and inactive, yet commonly smiling almost to laughter' was especially critical. Horsey's own memoirs, although clearly selective and self-promoting in parts, also provide an interesting first-hand account both of life in Russia under the mercurial Ivan as well as the relationships between the English merchants and the Russia Company. He describes some of the frequent atrocities committed by Ivan against his own people and indicates how difficult it must have been for the Russian people to live through this period of irrational tyranny. After returning to England in 1591, Horsey became a Member of Parliament, serving his constituency for thirty years and was knighted in 1603. He also translated the Slavonic Bible and was responsible for introducing the term 'White Russia' to England for the country of Belarus.

Fortunately for the sake of Anglo-Russian relations as well as the health and safety of the British ambassadors, the ensuing twenty-year period saw the restoration of more normal diplomatic contacts between the two countries. When James I succeeded to the English throne, he moved quickly to build relations with his opposite number in Russia. A large red velvet coach was constructed by craftsmen in London and shipped in sections to Moscow. Sumptuously decorated with fine carvings and detailed painted scenes, the coach

---

[148] Giles Fletcher, *Of the Russe Commonwealth*, 1591.

was reassembled and in 1604, it was presented to Tsar Boris Godunov by James' ambassador, Sir Thomas Smythe.[149] As with much of the beautiful silverware presented to the Tsars by the British, this impressive gift was intended to fulfil both a political and a commercial purpose. It clearly demonstrated the wealth of the English court, the skill of its craftsmen and the capability of the English fleet in delivering such a large object to Russia. In essence, the message to the Tsar was that England was a rich and powerful ally with which Russia would do well to maintain its trading preferences.

In 1612, John Merrick, then the chief agent of the Russia Company and effectively the English representative at the Russian Court, was asked by King James I to undertake an extremely sensitive mission. Since the death of Feodor in 1598, Russia had steadily descended into chaos with effectively no strong central government and considerable political unrest. There were concerns that Russia might not survive as an independent country with first Poland and then Sweden trying to seize control by supporting foreign pretenders to the throne. Such an eventuality would have had serious implications for England's trade and so consideration was given in England to establishing a protectorate over northern Russia. Merrick was tasked with secretly sounding out Russian nobles regarding possible support for such an idea but it soon proved to be impractical and would probably have resulted in war with Sweden. However, it is interesting to speculate how subsequent world history might have been altered had Russia become an English protectorate. Merrick did play an important role in negotiating the Treaty of Stolbovo in 1617 which, for the time being at least, resolved the differences between the Russians and Swedes.

The next formal ambassador to Russia, Sir Dudley Digges, was asked to go to Moscow by James I in 1618. The Russians were at war with Poland and the Tsar had sent ambassadors to England to negotiate a loan which at King James' direction, was furnished by the Muscovy and East India Companies. Digges, who was then a member of both companies, sailed to Archangel in June with £20,000 in bullion together with the returning Russian ambassadors who travelled in a second ship. However, on arrival at Kholmogory, Digges and his party found Russia was in such chaos that after only travelling halfway to Moscow Digges decided to abort the mission and return to England. Although he did send a few of his men on to Moscow with a part of the money, his trip to Russia turned out to be a failure.

The execution of Charles I in 1649 and the subsequent decade under the Cromwells left Anglo-Russian relations strained and there were no formal ambassadors until well after the Restoration. However, the visit to England by Peter the Great in 1698 led to a renewed interest in Russia and although there was a rise in trade as well as a significant increase in the numbers of British going to work there, Peter's Russia was still regarded by the British as backward and underdeveloped. The emphasis in Britain's policy towards Russia remained one of trade and this was evidenced by the two ambassadors around the turn of the 17th century who were both heavily involved in promoting trade, especially in tobacco. Indeed, the first British consul-general in Russia, Charles

---

[149] On his return to England in 1605, Smythe wrote *Voyage and Entertainments in Russia.*

Goodfellow, was appointed in 1699 precisely to handle the development of the tobacco trade following Peter the Great's controversial grant of a monopoly to his friend the Marquis of Carmarthen. In this capacity, Goodfellow represented British interests generally as consul-general and later resident minister while also running the tobacco trade for the Russia Company until 1714 when he returned to England and continued to trade with Russia as Goodfellow, Ransom & Parsons.

In 1704 Charles Whitworth arrived as British envoy to Russia, becoming ambassador in 1707 and despite the rather awkward situation of having both an ambassador and a consul-general in the same city, Whitworth and Goodfellow worked harmoniously together in Britain's interests. Later in Catherine's reign, the British adopted the practice of automatically offering the position of consul to the agent of the Russia Company, thereby formally reinforcing the links between British diplomacy and trade. The dual position of consul-general and agent of the Company proved to be both prestigious and powerful, giving the incumbent great influence at the centre of the British merchant community in Russia. However, this was not always an easy role. One of the consul-general's responsibilities was to safeguard the Company's trading rights and ensure that all trade between Russia and Britain was conducted by freemen of the Company. But as the Company's monopoly came under increasing threat both from independent British and Russian merchants as well as its own employees trading on their own account, there were frequent disputes, which occasionally led to serious diplomatic disputes between the two countries.

With Peter the Great's defeat of the Swedes at the battle of Poltava in 1709, Russia regained its outlets to the Baltic and re-asserted its control over the supply of tar, timber, hemp and pitch, so vital to Britain's naval interests. Although the British diplomats in St Petersburg now found themselves having to deal with Russian requests for reciprocity in trade treaties, the fact that British ships continued to handle most of Russia's exports kept the negotiating balance in Britain's favour for the time being. However, fearful of Peter's expansionist policies in the Baltic, Britain tried to redress the balance of power by allying itself with both Sweden and Prussia. But over the next decade, Russia's increased military power allowed it to continually push back the Swedes as well as thwarting Prussian ambitions and, in 1719, diplomatic relations with Russia were broken off by Britain. In 1728 the British sent Thomas Ward, a Russian speaker, as consul-general and agent of the Russia Company to St Petersburg to try to rebuild diplomatic relations. Ward, who was accompanied by his wife, Jane, sadly died in post in early 1731 but his wife stayed on and remarried, living in Russia for twelve years in total. [150]

Anglo-Russian relations were not fully restored until 1733 with the appointment of Lord Forbes as envoy extraordinary and minister plenipotentiary to the Russian Court of Empress Anna. George Forbes was an experienced Anglo-Irish naval officer whose primary objective was to finalise a new commercial agreement that had been under discussion for some years. During

---

[150] In 1775 Jane published an account of her time in Russia, *Letters from a Lady who Resided some Years in Russia, to her Friend in England*.

the last twenty years of ruptured diplomatic relations, German merchants had largely supplanted the British as Russia's main supplier of woollen cloth, especially for Russia's expanding military forces. As textiles were one of the few goods that Britain had to offer in exchange for Russia's vital naval supplies, the decline in the Russia Company's market share had resulted in a significant British trade deficit. According to the Company's own estimates at the time, the British were forced to pay for nearly seventy-five percent of their Russian purchases with gold and silver, an annual sum amounting to £225,000.[151] Although the negotiations proved protracted, due once again to the British solely wanting to discuss trade and the Russians seeking to widen the agreement to cover an alliance, a mutual understanding was finally reached in 1734 with Forbes achieving most of what the British wanted. This was the St Petersburg Court's first formal commercial agreement with any European state and it provided a comprehensive, legal basis for the renewed growth in trade between the two countries for the first time in the history of their long relationship. The new treaty granted the Russia Company's merchants exceptional economic benefits by favouring the re-introduction of British woollen goods and introduced better customs regulations. It also formalised their rights and privileges in Russia and marked a new era of power and influence for the Company in St Petersburg. By securing the supply of important raw materials for its navy, it ensured Britain's increasing dominance of the seas which was so vital for its security and commercial success. Commerce between Britain and Russia once again flourished and subsequent Anglo-Russian negotiators used this treaty as a model for all their later 18th century commercial agreements. After Forbes' return to England in 1734, Empress Anna, who had been very impressed by his performance during the difficult and lengthy negotiations, offered him the command of the Russian navy but he declined the position.

Following the accession of Catherine II in Russia, a new envoy, George Macartney, was dispatched to St Petersburg in 1764. Of Scottish-Irish descent, Macartney was not an experienced diplomat and was only twenty-seven when he was appointed but he had already coined the phrase that Britain now controlled '*a vast Empire, on which the sun never sets.*' Macartney felt Russia to be a very backward nation that had been held back by its despotic form of government and, although things were changing, the Russians 'still continue the least virtuous and least ingenious nation in Europe.' Given his relatively young age, it is perhaps not surprising that Macartney had an affair with one of Catherine's ladies-in-waiting. He was not the only British diplomat to become involved with a Russian lady and several of his successors were known to have had similar attachments. Despite Macartney's local dalliance, he proved himself to be a very capable and respected diplomat, holding the position in Russia for three years. At the time, Britain was trying to strengthen her European alliances and recognising Russia's growing power and influence, Macartney was tasked with exploring with Catherine the potential for an Anglo-Russian treaty. Catherine's focus was then more on Poland and Germany and although nothing was formally concluded with Britain, the discussions paved the way for

---

[151] Michael Bitter – Anglo-Russian Relations during the 1730s, Germano-Slavica 2007.

improved relations between the two countries as well as an agreement that was finalised by a later ambassador, Sir Robert Gunning.

Gunning was appointed as envoy extraordinary and minister plenipotentiary to the court of Russia in late 1771, although he didn't arrive at the Russian Court until the following summer. His initial instructions were to offer the services of the British as a mediator between the warring Russian and Ottoman empires to try to achieve a peace treaty as well as to support the policy of Catherine II in Poland. Gunning seems to have been well liked by Catherine who always treated him with great favour. When he dined with her she would address the greater part of her conversation to him, and she frequently admitted him to private audiences. His diplomatic efforts were also much appreciated by England's George III who nominated him as a Knight of the Bath in June 1773 and requested the Empress to carry out the investiture. Catherine readily agreed and chose the anniversary of her own accession for the ceremony at which she not only presented Gunning with the insignia of his knighthood but also gave him the gold-hilted sword set with diamonds that she had used to knight him. In the summer of 1775, Gunning was instructed to explore with the Russians the possibility of them providing troops for potential service in North America. After receiving positive responses, he successfully negotiated for a contingent of twenty thousand fully equipped Russian infantry who would be placed under the command of a British general and transported in British ships to Canada to serve against the American revolutionaries. However, when the British government indicated that that the principal Russian officers would have to take an oath of allegiance to the British crown, Russia's support for the operation waned and the agreement was called off.

Certain aspects of Gunning's time in Russia were mirrored by his successor, Sir James Harris, the 1st Earl of Malmesbury, who arrived in St Petersburg in the autumn of 1777 with his sixteen-year-old new bride, Harriet. He held the position of envoy extraordinary to Russia for five years and like Gunning was made a Knight of the Bath and returned home to England owing to the ill-health of his wife. He clearly established good relations with the Russians as Empress Catherine became godmother to one of his children. During his period as envoy, Harris had the delicate task of steering Anglo-Russian relations through the various problems surrounding what was called the first League of Armed Neutrality[152] which could have resulted in war breaking out between Britain and Russia. Harris felt greatly handicapped in trying to perform his role and communicate with London due both to the distance between the two Courts and the indolence of the Foreign Office. In summer it could take six or eight weeks to obtain a reply but in winter, with the northern ports frozen, it could take months. Harris estimated that he received only one reply for every forty dispatches that he sent to the Foreign Office but consoled himself for the infrequency of instructions with the reflection that he had *never received an instruction that was worth reading.*

---

[152] This was an alliance of several European naval powers between 1780 and 1783 intended to protect their neutral shipping against the Royal Navy's wartime policy of unrestricted search for French contraband.

He succeeded in building good relations with Catherine II and her first minister Prince Potemkin in spite of her predilections for France. In 1780, Harris was in negotiations to cede Minorca to the Russians as a bribe for them to ally with Britain. The Russians were attracted by the potential of a base in the Mediterranean for their expanding maritime ambitions but in the end declined the offer '*the bride is too beautiful*' Catherine told Potemkin and it would have been difficult for Russia to hold onto it. Harris was followed by Alleyne Fitzherbert and then Charles Whitworth who arrived at Catherine's Court when Russia was again at war with Turkey. Against the background of Russia's growing power in the Black Sea region a period of increased tension ensued between Britain and Russia. The British sent a fleet into the Baltic in a fruitless attempt to threaten the Russians to give back its conquests from the Turks but the Russian government replied with an uncompromising refusal to listen to the proposal of restitution. In the spring of 1791 Whitworth advised the British government that a French adventurer, named St Génie, had arrived in St Petersburg and was discussing with the Russians a plan for them to invade British India by way of Kashmir. In July he wrote an account of a circumstantial plot to burn the English fleet at Portsmouth by means of Irish and other mercenaries in Russian pay. These possible machinations helped cause the British government to rethink its policy towards Russia and although relationships remained strained for some while, Whitworth was gradually able to rebuild a position of trust.

A gradual rapprochement between the views of Russia and England then steadily evolved, mainly due to the shared fear of revolutionary infection from France. In February 1795 a new Anglo-Russian treaty of alliance was drawn up but Catherine died before it could be signed and it was not until 1798 that her successor, Paul I, finally accepted it. Whitworth was now at the zenith of his popularity in St Petersburg and when Paul pressed the British government to raise him to the peerage, the request was readily complied with. In March 1800 the ambassador was made Baron Whitworth but before the papers reached him, the Tsar allied Russia with France, seduced by promises of non-aggression by Napoleon and abruptly ordered Whitworth to leave Russia. A series of anti-British decrees by Paul then ensued. British ships in Russian ports were seized and their crews were marched off to detention camps. All goods and possessions of the British merchants, including their homes, were confiscated by the Russians and all trade with Britain was prohibited. Lastly, Paul decreed that any debts owed by Russians to the British should be cancelled. Paul's deceit and moves against the British led to the second period of Armed Neutrality between Britain and Russia that lasted until Paul's death in 1801. British mistrust of Russia deepened further when, in early 1801, Paul tried unsuccessfully to convince Napoleon to join forces with Russia and conquer India.

With the accession of Tsar Alexander I, political relations between Britain and Russia were again steadily restored. Alleyne Fitzherbert returned briefly to St Petersburg as ambassador to attend the coronation of Alexander and to arrange a new treaty between the two countries. The subsequent invasion of Russia by Napoleon once again brought Britain and Russia together as allies and in 1812, William Cathcart, the 1st Earl Cathcart was sent to St Petersburg as ambassador and military commissioner. He had already been to Russia twice; first in 1771 with his father, Lord Charles Cathcart who was briefly the British ambassador[153] and again in 1805 when he briefly occupied the role of ambassador. William Cathcart's initial primary role in St Petersburg was the challenging task of maintaining harmony and devotion to the common cause of defeating Napoleon amongst the generals of many nationalities. Cathcart also negotiated the fourth and final trade agreement between Britain and Russia which was signed in St Petersburg in 1813. His success in these roles was recognised by his elevation to an earldom in July 1814.

When Cathcart went to Russia in 1812, he took two of his sons with him – Captain Frederick Macadam Cathcart served as his private secretary and Lieutenant George Cathcart functioned as his aide-de-camp. Lord Cathcart not only performed the standard diplomatic duties at the Russian Court but he also became something of a cultural and recruiting advisor to Catherine as well. On several occasions she drew on his knowledge of British naval personnel to find officers for the Russian navy. Together with his wife, Cathcart also helped introduce the work of several British craftsmen and artisans to St Petersburg both by taking items to Russia and through personal recommendation as with Josiah Wedgewood. Cathcart remained as ambassador to Russia until 1820 when he returned to England. He was replaced by Sir Charles Bagot and his son Frederick was appointed an interim plenipotentiary at the embassy, a position he held for almost four years.

With the increase in Britain's trade and influence in Russia after the Napoleonic Wars, the need for additional diplomatic posts became evident. In Archangel, the Russia Company had effectively represented British interests since the 16th century and the first official consul there, Samuel Jenkins, was not appointed until 1819. Following the restoration of diplomatic relations in 1801 after the second league of armed neutrality, Henry Yeames was appointed the first British consul-general for the Black Sea region in 1803, based in Odessa. He was the son of John Yeames, the man who first forged the family connection with Russia as one of the Tsar's shipbuilders. Henry Yeames and his wife had four children in Odessa, one girl and three boys, Henry, James and William. James later married Elizabeth Whishaw and continued to reside in Odessa. The position of British consul-general in the Black Sea region became something of a Yeames family monopoly as after Henry's death in 1819, his son James took over the post and his youngest son William, became British consul at Taganrog, an increasingly important port at the eastern end of the Black Sea. William married Eliza, the daughter of Major John Henley from Kiev with whom he had seven children, all born in Russia. He carried on his work as British consul at Taganrog until his death in 1848 when the family relocated to London. His eldest son, also William, later became a successful watercolour artist and a member of the Royal Academy.

All three Yeames seem to have performed their consular duties with distinction and the role of consul general in Odessa continued in the Yeames

---

[153] Lord Cathcart had returned to Britain prematurely after the sudden death of his wife in St Petersburg during an outbreak of the plague in 1771.

family for fifty years until the outbreak of the Crimean War in 1854 when both the Odessa and Taganrog posts were temporarily closed. George Wigfall was vice-consul in Kerch in the Crimea in 1839, Charles Cattley in the early 1850s (he supplied vital intelligence on Russian military dispositions in the Crimea prior to the war), Eldridge in 1858 and Clipperton in 1863. Eldridge ad Clipperton also monitored and reported on the subsequent fighting between the Russian army and the Circassian tribes that led to tens of thousands of Circassian families fleeing the region through the port of Kerch for makeshift refugee camps in Turkey. However, most of their work revolved around assisting the large number of English merchants and their ships that were increasingly using the various Black Sea ports. British trade through this part of southern Russia rose steadily through the 19th century. In the decade prior to the start of the Crimean War, the number of British trading ships sailing to Black Sea ports increased sevenfold and the British market accounted for more than one third of the grain exports from Odessa.[154] A report from the British consul in Taganrog, Mr Hunt, which indicated 229 British steamers entered port in 1899, handling just over 50% of the port's total shipping trade.

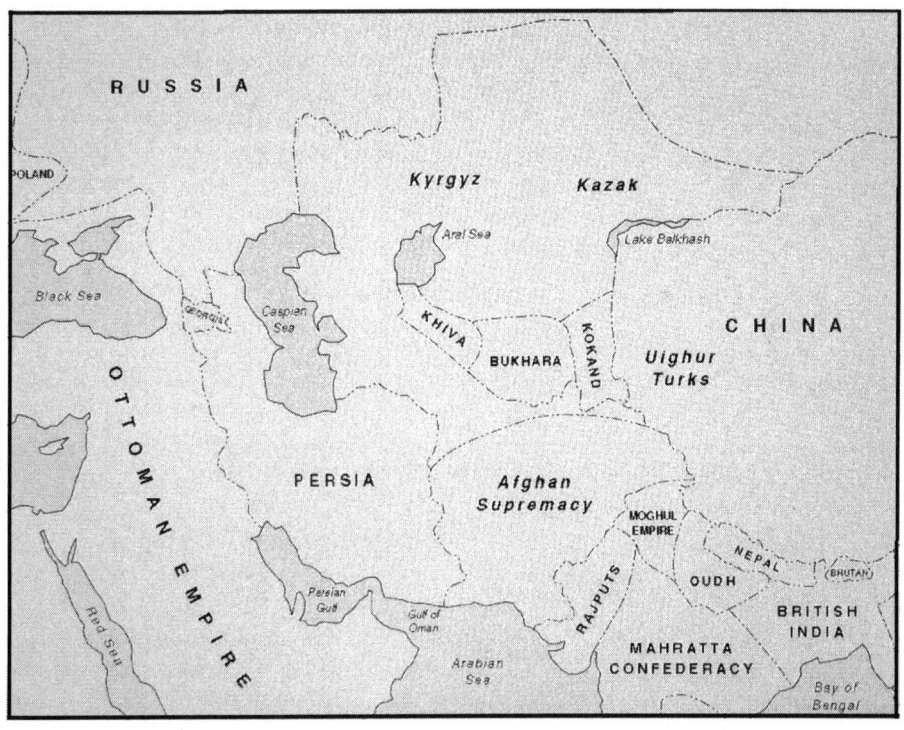

Asian Russia in the 1780s

---

[154] Edward Morton, *Travels in Russia*, 1830

As the 19th century progressed, the British government not only added these new diplomatic posts around the Black Sea but also became increasingly involved in less formal diplomatic activities further east in the Caucasus and central Asia. These were part of what became known as the Great Game, a term coined to describe the struggle between Russia and Britain for control and influence in central Asia, initially in the Caucasus and Persia, then later in Turkestan, Afghanistan and Tibet. As the Russian Empire pushed relentlessly further south and east during the 19th century, it increasingly posed a threat, both implicitly and at times explicitly, to Britain's interests in India. For the next one hundred years, the British and Russian empires participated in a shadowy struggle for control and influence in central Asia, a conflict that increasingly dominated Anglo-Russian relationships and which on several occasions almost led to war. A growing number of British diplomats, intelligence officers, soldiers, spies and travellers were drawn to the region to investigate what the Russians were up to and to try to develop political or trading links with local khanates or tribes. Most of these young men were drawn from the cadre of young British officers in the Indian Army and were among the brightest and boldest soldiers of their time, with many of them speaking several languages.

When the Great Game began, the high passes north of India that led into Afganistan and then on to Turkestan were largely unknown and unmapped. Similarly, the approaches to India from the Caucasus or northern Persia across the deserts to the east of the Caspian Sea were also unexplored. These were the two possible routes that a Russian army might use if it were to try to advance on India and both regions also seemed to offer new trading opportunities for the competing Russian and British merchants. The Tsarist Empire had expanded at a tremendous rate over the past four centuries, growing at the rate of some fifty-five square miles a day or 20,000 square miles per year. At the beginning of the 19th century, over 2,000 miles separated Russia from British India but by 1900, it was just a few hundred miles and at its closest it was less than twenty.[155] During the 19th century Russia's inexorable expansion in central Asia and the east regularly added areas bigger than the whole of Great Britain to the territories under its control with millions of new subjects. So it was not surprising that certain factions in London and St Petersburg believed that Russia could soon be at the gates of India.

Stretching eastwards from the shores of the Caspian Sea lay a vast region of mostly desert and mountains called Turkestan (containing modern day Kazakhstan, Turkmenistan and Uzbekistan). Its size and relative inaccessibility plus the ferocious reputation of its Muslim rulers had limited foreign incursions. During the 1700s, the occasional Western explorer or soldier that ventured into the region usually either disappeared or returned to die of some strange and virulent disease. The region seemed like a modern-day 'Bermuda Triangle'. By the early 1800s, the threat from Russia against British India seemed to be increasing. Paul I's abortive plan to invade with Napoleon and Russia's annexation of Georgia in 1801 caused alarm bells to ring in London and the government realized it knew very little about the lands to the north-west of

---

[155] Peter Hopkirk, *The Great Game*, 1990.

India. The British East India Company was also starting to eye the area as a potential new market in which to sell the goods being produced in India and to trade the fabulous rugs, silks and gems rumoured to be found there. So the British began to send men both east through Persia and north from India with four objectives in mind; to explore and map these tribal lands, to watch for possible Russian activity, to try to establish possible alliances and finally to investigate the potential for trade. The threat from Russia was real and in 1801, Tsar Paul, who disliked the British, proposed to Napoleon a joint invasion of India. Napoleon was sceptical about the chances of success of Paul's plan but the latter persisted alone and dispatched a force of 22,000 Cossacks south from Orenburg towards Afganistan. It is unlikely that this number of troops would have been sufficient to conquer India and oust the British but as they neared the frontier, a messenger arrived to say that Paul was dead and the Cossacks were recalled by the new tsar, Alexander.

One of the first targets for the British was the Khanate of Bokhara which was an important stop on the Silk Road. The British knew roughly where Bokhara was but had little idea of how to get there, who to contact or even whether they would be listened to. The only advice available at the time was not to travel there. After much deliberation, a small British mission was sent north from India in 1820 to travel the 2,000 miles to Bokhara. It was led by William Moorcroft, a young British vetinary surgeon, ostensibly looking for horses to buy for the Indian army. After almost five years of frustrating and arduous travel through the mountains, Moorcroft eventually arrived in Bokhara but although he was well treated, he found that the Russians had beaten him to it and were already trading there. Moorcroft turned back but within a few months, he and his companions all died on the route home from a combination of sickness and weariness. The tragic failure of Moorcroft's mission did not prevent Britain from sending further expeditions into the vast expanses of central Asia. Probably the most successful was that of Lieutenant Alexander Burnes who arrived in Bokhara in June 1832. He was an experienced and skillful negotiator who was able to counteract some of the Russian influence as well as gain useful intelligence about the areas he travelled through. Burnes was later sent to Kabul in Afganistan where he again successfully countered Russian political agents who were active in the region and laid the foundations for a British military presence there.

Sometime around 1841 the British sent a young Army colonel, Charles Stoddart, to Bokhara to try once more to open negotiations on a trading treaty. Although a good soldier, Stoddart was perhaps not the best choice for this difficult mission. He was deeply religious and held rather deep-seated views about the righteousness of his country's imperial might. More seriously, the British were unaware that Bokhara now had a new Emir, Nasrullah whose character was entirely different to that of his predecessor. Nasrullah had murdered several of his own brothers to secure the throne and this was simply the prelude to a reign that became increasingly marked by vice, venality and violence. This was the situation the unsuspecting Stoddart now rode into. Having made his way safely to Bokhara, he made the early mistake of riding up to the local Emir on his horse instead of dismounting and genuflecting. Then when introduced, the clueless Stoddart offered no gifts to the Emir. The response to these perceived affronts came quickly and within only thirty minutes after his arrival, Stoddart found himself tossed into the infamous 'bug pit'. This was a thirty-feet-deep hole in the ground infested with all manner of vermin, snakes, scorpions and rats plus the remnants of previous human occupants. Once a fortnight, the Emir would have Stoddart hauled up out of the pit, give him some food, jokingly tell him he was about to be released and then had him thrown back into the filthy hole. Although Stoddart didn't realise it, things could have been worse as most people who fell foul of the Emir were simply thrown to their death from the top of a minaret after Friday prayers. The awful situation continued for the best part of a year despite repeated attempts by Stoddart to escape.

Eventually a rescue mission was launched from India and a captain in the Bengal Light Infantry called Arthur Conelly was dispatched to Bokhara to effect Stoddart's release. Coincidentally, it was Conelly who first used the term 'the Great Game' in correspondence with the British government in 1839. He had visited Moscow in 1829 and then travelled through the Caucasus, central Asia and Afghanistan, reaching India in 1831 where he became a British intelligence officer specialising in central Asian affairs. On his arrival in Bokhara in 1840, Connelly did better than Stoddart – he lasted several hours before also ending up in the bug pit. The pair remained imprisoned in this manner for almost two years before one day being hauled out and told that if they renounced Christianity and embraced the Muslim faith, they would be freed. Conelly declined the Emir's offer but although after some hesitation Stoddart agreed, it was to no avail and both were made to dig their graves and were beheaded on the spot in front of the Emir's palace June 1842. A year later, the Rev. Joseph Wolff, an experienced Anglican missionary arrived in Bokhara seeking news of the two captives and was himself briefly imprisoned. Wolff only escaped death because as he claimed in his subsequent book[156], the Emir laughed uncontrollably at his appearance in full canonical garb. Wolff's story of his mission went through seven editions between 1845 and 1852 and made Stoddart and Conelly household names in Britain.

The Great Game now moved to the Caucasus, a region that held special interest for the British due its strategic position on the borders of the Persian, Ottoman and Russian empires. As we have seen, a few hardy merchants from the Muscovy Company visited the area in the 16th and 17th centuries to explore the potential for trade. In the early 19th century, as the Russians steadily expanded into the region, British interest and concern gradually increased. The struggles of the Caucasian mountain tribes, particularly the Circassians, against the Russian invaders generated considerable awareness and support among British observers and visitors to Circassia. The publication of books and press articles about the region by three British writers (Spencer, Longworth and

---

[156] Joseph Wolff, *Travels and Adventures in Persia, Bokhara, Cashmeer, etc.*, 1861.

Bell)[157] plus vociferous campaigning by the British diplomat David Urquart, brought about a much broader understanding of the region and much sympathy for its people in defending their land against Russian aggression.

Urquart was an outspoken critic of the Russians and his career suffered because of it. He actually designed the Circassian flag and later was responsible for the introduction of Turkish baths into Britain. Despite the arousal of the British public's interest in their cause, the British government decided not to intervene or even censure Russia. However, with the start of the Crimean War, the British government changed tack and considered the possibility of providing arms and money to the Circassians. James Longworth, who first went to Russia in 1838 as correspondent of *The Times*, was dispatched to Circassia in 1855 to try to levy Circassian cavalry to fight against the Russians but was unsuccessful due to tribal rivalries and a lack of interest in renewing the fight against Russians without the support of Allied troops. Once the Crimean War was over, the Russians returned with a vengeance to Circassia, pursuing a scorched earth policy and huge numbers of the Circassian people died in what today would be described as a genocidal war. Many fled the killing grounds, crossing the Black Sea in leaky and overcrowded ships, often to later die miserably in desolate refugee camps on the Turkish coast. Eventually, around half the Circassian population of two million perished during the 19th century as a result of the Russian invasion.[158]

Having largely subdued the Caucasus, the Russians turned their attention once more on their almost perpetual adversary, the Turks and in their war of 1877/78, there was the very real prospect of Russia occupying Constantinople and threatening British shipping to India via the Suez canal. In March 1878, the British and Russian governments reached an agreement to reduce tensions that was subsequently ratified at the Congress of Berlin in July. However, many Russophobes in London saw their government's position as a weak fudge. Their position seemed to be justified when Charles Marvin stepped onto the scene as probably Britain's first 'whistle-blower'. Marvin was born in Kent in 1854 and at the age of sixteen he went to Russia to join his father, who was an assistant manager of an engineering works near St Petersburg. He stayed in Russia for six years and acquired a good knowledge of the language and also worked for a time as the St Petersburg correspondent of the London *Globe* newspaper. When he returned to London he took the civil service examination and was eventually given a job as a writer in the Foreign Office in July 1877, while still working part time for the *Globe*. Almost a year later, he was entrusted to make a copy of a secret agreement that had recently been reached with Russia regarding spheres of influence in central Asia. Marvin learned that the government intended to leak the details to *The Times* so that evening he supplied the *Globe* with a summary of the document based solely on his extremely retentive memory, thus providing the *Globe* with a worldwide scoop. A political storm ensued and

---

[157] Capt. Edmund Spencer, *Travels in Circassia*, 1836 and *Travels in the Western Caucasus*, 1838; J.A. Longworth, *A Year among the Circassians*, 1840 plus James S. Bell, *Journal of a Residence in Circassia*, 1840.

[158] Oliver Bullough, *Let Our Fame be Great*, 2010

Marvin was arrested on June 26th on the basis of having stolen a copy of the secret document. However, when it transpired that the *Globe's* article was derived solely from Marvin's memory, he was released as he had not committed any offense known to the law at that time.

The affair proved positive for Marvin's subsequent career as a writer on Anglo-Russian matters. His concerns about Britain's position and lack of opposition to Russia's continued advances in central Asia led him to publish an account of the treaty a few months later,[159] followed by articles in some twenty publications. In 1880 he published his first book on the Russo-Indian question, *The Eye-witnesses' Account of the disastrous Campaign against the Akhal Tekke Turcomans* which was adopted by the Russian government for its military libraries and in 1881 he published *Merv the Queen of the World and the Scourge of the Man-stealing Turcomans. With an Exposition on the Khorassan Question* (he was clearly someone who liked long book titles). The following year he was asked to go to Russia to interview some of their leading generals and statesmen on the Russo-Indian question and on his return he wrote *The Russian Advance towards India: Conversations with Skobeleff, Ignatieff and other Russian Generals and Statesmen on the Central Asian Question*. In 1883 Marvin travelled to the Caucasus to explore the Russian petroleum region and the following year he published an account of his findings under the title of *The Region of the Eternal Fire: an Account of a Journey to the Petroleum Region of the Caspian*. He went on to write a further ten books about the region but the best-known of his works (possibly because of its shorter title) is *The Russians at the Gates of Herat* which was written and published within a week in 1885 and enjoyed a circulation of sixty-five thousand copies.

Probing expeditions into central Asia by the British continued to take place in the latter part of the 19th century, the most notable were those of the intrepid Captain Frederick Burnaby in 1875 and George Curzon's journey of 1888. They both travelled east across Russia with Burnaby reaching Khiva before he was stopped by the Russians and Curzon (subsequently a viceroy of India) who visited Bokhara, Samarkand and Tashkent. However, the signing of the Anglo-Russian entente in 1907 signalled the end of the thrusts and parries of the Great Game and political relations between the two rivals largely resumed a more normal pattern. The renewed amity between Britain and Russia was officially sealed in June 1908 at the Baltic port of Reval when King Edward VII met his cousin Czar Nicholas II to agree on an Anglo-Russian alliance. This was the first visit by a British monarch to Russia.

The historic visit by King Edward was followed up by the appointment of the forceful and dynamic George Buchanan as Britain's ambassador in 1910. He was the son of the British Ambassador to Denmark and followed in his father's footsteps as a diplomat. When he arrived in St Petersburg, he could not have foreseen that he would have the challenge of handling Anglo-Russian relations during the most tumultuous period in their history. Like most diplomats, he used a variety of sources to keep abreast of developments in Russia but was

---

[159] *Our Public Offices, embodying an Account of the Disclosure of the Anglo-Russian Agreement, and the unrevealed Secret Treaty of 31 May 1878.*

particularly close to Harold Williams, a journalist working for the British *Daily Chronicle* who was based in St Petersburg.[160] Williams helped keep him informed of political developments in Russia and arranged for him to meet some of the leading reformists in the country, especially those from the rising Socialist Revolutionary Party. Under Buchanan, Moscow finally became a consulate-general in 1913, recognizing both its growing economic importance as well as the sizeable British presence in the city. A new consul-general, Clive Bayley was appointed, additional staff were recruited and the delegation moved to larger offices. Bayley worked hard at boosting the image and reputation of his new posting and as a man of independent means, he used his financial resources to entertain in style. He was an imposing, man and wore an eyeglass which with his new approach to the role of consul soon brought him to the notice of the Russians who enjoyed his jovial company. He even proposed a special seat in the Moscow Anglican church to be reserved for 'His Majesty's Representative' (for which he was willing to make a significant contribution) but after a close vote, the church council rejected the idea. As a result of a serious illness, Bayley returned to Britain in 1916 and was replaced by the more mysterious Bruce Lockhart.

In 1913, Buchanan was joined in St Petersburg by Henry Bruce, who later became First Secretary at the Embassy. Bruce married the Russian prima ballerina Tamara Karsavina in 1915 and returned to London with her in 1918. Buchanan's work in Russia became much more demanding and complicated in the build-up to the First World War and his reports to the Foreign Office in London were increasingly important. In July 1914, Buchanan wrote presciently about his negotiations with members of the Russian government:

"As they both continued to press me to declare our complete solidarity with them, I said that I thought you might be prepared to represent strongly at Vienna and Berlin the danger to European peace of an Austrian attack on Serbia. You might perhaps point out that it would in all probability force Russia to intervene, that this would bring Germany and France into the field, and that if war became general, it would be difficult for England to remain neutral. Minister for Foreign Affairs said that he hoped that we would in any case express strong reprobation of Austria's action. If war did break out, we would sooner or later be dragged into it, but if we did not make common cause with France and Russia from the outset we should have rendered war more likely."

In 1916 Buchanan was granted the unexpected and unusual honour of the freedom of Moscow. This was a symbolic act but one that reflected both his own reputation in Russia as well as the strong relationship between the two allies in the early years of the First World War. During the 363 years of Anglo-Russian relations, he was the first British national to receive this honour.

As events in Russia continued to deteriorate, Buchanan began to fear that Nicholas II might be overthrown and urged him to change his policies and introduce much needed reforms. In his report to London on a meeting he had with the Tsar in January 1917 he wrote:

---

[160] St Petersburg was renamed Petrograd in 1914 but I have stayed with the city's original name for consistency.

"I went on to say that there was now a barrier between him and his people, and that if Russia was still united as a nation it was in opposing his present policy. The people, who have rallied so splendidly round their Sovereign on the outbreak of war, had seen how hundreds of thousands of lives had been sacrificed on account of the lack of rifles and munitions; how, owing to the incompetence of the administration, there had been a severe food crisis." [161]

The fact that Buchanan was able to have such a frank conversation with the Tsar indicated the strength of his relationship with Nicholas but his advice, like that of so many others, was ignored. Buchanan told his colleagues before the meeting that '*if the Emperor received him sitting down all would be well. The Tsar received him standing*'.[162] Over the next two months it became clear to Buchanan that the Tsar was in an increasingly untenable position and he was not surprised when Nicholas abdicated in March 1917. Although a man of deeply held conservative views, Buchanan was generally supportive of Russia's attempted transition to democracy in the form of the new Provisional Government. But by the summer it was clear to him that their experiment in democracy was not working and he reported to London that:

"The military outlook is most discouraging. Nor do I take an optimistic view of the immediate future of the country. Russia is not ripe for a purely democratic form of government, and for the next few years we shall probably see a series of revolutions or counter-revolutions. A vast Empire like this, with all its different races, will not long hold together under a Republic. Disintegration will, in my opinion, sooner or later set in, even under a federal system."

As a well-informed senior diplomat, Buchanan was well aware of the stresses and pressures faced by the country and understood the potential threat posed by the growth in support for the scheming Bolsheviks:

"The Bolsheviks, who form a compact minority, have alone a definite political programme. They are more active and better organized than any other group, and until they and the ideas which they represent are finally squashed, the country will remain a prey to anarchy and disorder. If the Government are not strong enough to put down the Bolsheviks by force, at the risk of breaking altogether with the soviet, the only alternative will be a Bolshevik Government."

When the Bolsheviks did indeed seize power, Buchanan was horrified by the brutality, terror and chaos ushered in by their revolution. However, in his book published shortly before his death in 1924, he recognised the talents of its leaders, Lenin and Trotsky:

"I readily admit that Lenin and Trotsky are both extraordinary men. The Ministers, in whose hands Russia had placed her destinies, had all proved to be weak and incapable, and now by some cruel turn of fate the only two really strong men whom she had produced during the war were destined to consummate her ruin."

Buchanan and his wife plus most of the embassy staff left St Petersburg in January 1918, travelling through Finland and Sweden and on to Scotland.

---

[161] George Buchanan, *My Mission to Russia and Other Diplomatic Memories*, 1923.

[162] Robert Bruce Lockhart, *Memoirs of a British Agent*, 1932.

Conspiracies, Intrigues and Espionage

British agents and spies, both professional and amateur, had been active in Russia almost since the start of the two countries' unexpected relationship but in 1916, British activities moved to an entirely new level. It was perhaps inevitable that during a period in history so crucial and full of turmoil that an abnormal level of intrigue and spying in Russia occurred. The Germans, keen to see Russia pull out of the war were busy fomenting dissent in Russia and supporting the Bolsheviks then outside of Russia. The British were on the opposite side, anxious to see the Russians maintain their war effort and thus prevent the Germans from releasing large numbers of troops onto the Western Front. For the British secret service officers in St Petersburg there were two main concerns. The first was the growing influence at Court of the infamous monk, Grigory Rasputin, who opposed Russia's continued involvement in the war. The second was the level of German intrigue and propaganda, both inside and outside Russia, attempting to persuade the nation of the futility of fighting on. In November 1916 one of the British agents in Russia summed up the situation thus:

"German intrigue was becoming more intense daily. Enemy agents were busy whispering of peace and hinting how to get it by creating disorder, rioting, etc. Things looked very black. Romania was collapsing, and Russia herself seemed weakening. The failure in communications, the shortness of foods, the sinister influence which seemed to be clogging the war machine, Rasputin the drunken debaucher influencing Russia's policy, what was to the be the end of it all?"

Rumours began to circulate that the Tsarina and Rasputin were leaders of a pro-German group at Court that was seeking a separate peace with Germany in order to help the survival of the monarchy in Russia. Much has been written about the subsequent plot to kill Rasputin and although the details will probably never be totally clear, it seems certain that members of the British Secret Intelligence Service in Russia played a key role. The SIS office in St Petersburg was under the command of Lieutenant-Colonel Samuel Hoare and members of his unit included Oswald Rayner, Stephen Alley, John Scale and Cudbert Thornhill, all of whom were probably involved in the plot to kill Rasputin. Rasputin was assassinated on 29th December, 1916 in the Yusupov Palace and a few days later Prince Felix Yusupov and four other senior Russian monarchists confessed to being involved in the murder. However, Russian suspicions regarding the role of the British SIS in the affair soon surfaced. Indeed, during a subsequent meeting between Buchanan, the British ambassador and the Tsar, the latter suggested as much, naming Rayner as a guilty party. Despite a vociferous denial by Hoare, it is likely that Tsar Nicholas was correct.

Although at the time of the murder, both Scale and Thornhill had conveniently arranged to be away in Romania, the two remaining officers, Rayner and Alley were in St Petersburg and knew Yusupov well. Rayner was an old schoolfriend of Yusupov and they had both studied at Oxford together. Alley was actually born in the Yusupov's palace in 1876 and the two families had close ties. Russian witnesses confirmed both that Rayner and Yusupov had met several times prior to the murder and that Rayner was present at the scene of the fatal shooting. Rasputin was killed after four shots were fired into his body. Later forensic evidence has shown that one of the bullets (which entered Rasputin's forehead at close range and was instantly fatal) was fired from a different gun from those responsible for the other three shots. The type of bullet fired was uniquely used by British officers in their standard issue Webley revolvers. In their testimony the five Russians involved in the killing seemed keen to retain the glory of Rasputin's murder for themselves and played down the presence of Rayner. If Rayner was the real killer he was never charged and he left Russia before the end of the war and in 1920 joined *The Daily Telegraph* as its Finnish correspondent. He never spoke about the events of that day and took the secret to his grave in 1961.

The Russian-born Stephen Alley was recruited by the British Secret Intelligence Service in 1914 and proved highly effective in countering the work of German agents in the Baltic region. There is little doubt that he was involved in planning the murder of Rasputin with Rayner, even if he wasn't actually present at the time of the killing. He later became involved in the British government's half-hearted attempts to rescue the deposed Nicholas and his family from Bolshevik captivity. Although both King George V and the government were initially willing to negotiate for the release of the Tsar, preliminary discussions soon failed to progress. The British government was concerned that the presence of the Tsar in England might prove awkward in terms of future relations with Russia. Alley prepared a plan for the SIS to help Nicholas and his family escape from the house in Ekaterinburg where they were held. He recruited four agents, obtained details of the layout of the house and surrounding area and prepared a plan for them to be taken by train to the British-held port of Murmansk and thence by a Royal Navy ship to Britain. Sadly, Alley's plan was never put into action.

John Scale was a tall, ex-Indian army officer who spoke fluent Russian, having trained as an interpreter in Russia in 1913. He was sent to the Western Front on the outbreak of war and then joined the SIS in St Petersburg in 1916. At the time of Rasputin's murder, he had been sent on a mission, along with Thornhill to destroy the Romanian oilfields and corn harvest ahead of the invading German troops. He later returned to St Petersburg until the Bolshevik revolution when he left for England, narrowly escaping capture by the Bolsheviks. In 1918 he became head of the British SIS station in Stockholm where, along with Rayner, he recruited Russian speakers to infiltrate Russia. Thornhill, who was born at a British frontier station in Tibet, was also an ex-Indian army officer. In 1916 Thornhill was made an assistant military attaché in St Petersburg, controlling the collection of military intelligence. One of Thornhill's agents was Arthur Ransome, the Russia correspondent of *The Daily News* (see below). Like Scale, Thornhill continued to operate in Russia for a few months after the Bolshevik revolution but was forced to go into hiding. He reported on the formation of units of the new Red Army and set up agent networks across the north around the White Sea and Murmansk in order to warn the British of any Bolshevik advances.

In addition to the SIS quartet above, there were other British men involved in espionage and propaganda in Russia during this critical period. Paul Dukes, originally came to Russia to study music and he subsequently found work at the Marinsky Theatre with the British conductor Albert Coates. Soon after the outbreak of war he became a member of the Anglo-Russian Commission, a British propaganda organisation and over the next two years he was involved in a variety of rather nebulous propaganda activities carried out by the Commission. In the summer of 1917 he was asked by the Tsarist secret police to spy on some of the Bolshevik leaders and he apparently prepared two detailed reports which he also submitted to London. In the summer of the following year Dukes was recalled to Britain and offered a role in the SIS. In his autobiography[163] he explained that the British government recognised that Russia would soon be closed to foreigners and they wanted someone there *'to keep us informed of the march of events.'* Dukes returned to Russia where as a fluent Russian speaker he passed himself off as a Ukrainian member of the Cheka (the Bolshevik's secret police). He then linked up with Scale and Alley for a while, joined the Communist Party and infiltrated the Comintern and the Poliburo, passing on details of their operations to London. In his new covert role in Russia, Dukes became a master of disguises, regularly changing his appearance and using more than a dozen names to conceal his true identity. He became known as 'the man with a hundred faces'. In later recalling the daily risks of his espionage work Dukes described how he worked:

"I wrote mostly at night, in minute handwriting on tracing-paper, with a small caoutchouc [latex bag] about four inches in length, weighted with lead, ready at my side. In case of alarm, all my papers could be slipped into this bag and within thirty seconds be transferred to the bottom of a tub of washing or the cistern of a water closet. In efforts to discover arms or incriminating documents, I have seen pictures, carpets, and bookshelves removed and everything turned topsy-turvy by diligent searchers, but it never occurred to anybody to search through a pail of washing or thrust his hand into the water-closet cistern. Only on one occasion was I obliged to destroy documents of value, while of the couriers who, at grave risk, carried communications back and forth from Finland, only two failed to arrive and I presume were caught and shot." [164]

Operating under the code name of ST-25, Dukes took enormous risks but survived the dangers and eventually returned to London in 1920 where his successful work for the SIS was marked with the award of a knighthood by King George V. He is the only person to have been knighted solely on the basis of their exploits in espionage.

By their very nature, spies remain somewhat shadowy figures, at least during their working careers and fully understanding what they were up to is often difficult. This is the case with Sydney Reilly, a Jewish, Russian-born adventurer and spy. His original name was Sigmund Rosenblum but under dubious circumstances he acquired a new British identity in 1898. Reilly first

---

[163] Paul Dukes, *Red Dusk and the Morrow: Adventures and Investigations in Soviet Russia*, 1922.
[164] Paul Dukes – ibid.

visited Russia the following year when he travelled to the Caucasus to covertly investigate its oil resources on behalf of the British government. A year later, Reilly turned up in Manchuria and operated as a double agent for the British and Japanese. Over the next few years he was involved in a variety of commercial and clandestine activities in France, Germany and the USA. In the spring of 1918 Reilly was recruited by the SIS and initially employed on counter-Bolshevik operations in Germany and Russia. However, a plan to strike at the Bolshevik leadership soon emerged from the SIS offices in London, probably conceived by Reilly and Bruce Lockhart, a former British consul in Moscow. Reilly was selected to go to Russia to implement the plan, the main thrust of which was to subvert disillusioned Latvian troops guarding the Kremlin and to employ them in a palace coup against Lenin's government. The goal was more to try to force a change in the Bolshevik regime's leadership rather than its total overthrow. However, on the eve of the coup planned for September 1st, unexpected events thwarted the operation. A military cadet shot and killed the head of the Cheka in St Petersburg and Lenin was wounded in a shooting in Moscow by a member of the Socialist Revolutionary Party.

These events were used by the Cheka to justify a major crackdown and thousands of political opponents were seized and executed. It seems likely that the Cheka had somehow found out about Reilly's plot as within days they had arrested many of those involved in the intended coup. The British Embassy in St Petersburg was raided and Francis Cromie, the British naval attache and one of Reilly's accomplices, was shot dead. Lockhart was arrested but later released in exchange for a Russian diplomat who had been arrested in London in a reprisal. Reilly was identified as the plot leader and the Cheka quickly closed in on him. They raided his assumed hiding place but Reilly was just ahead of them and using a German passport he avoided capture, eventually escaping north through Finland and Sweden. He returned safely to London on November 8th and the following January, he was awarded the Military Cross for distinguished services in the field.

Both Reilly and Lockhart were subsequently sentenced to death *in absentia* by a Russian Revolutionary Court for their roles in the attempted coup against the Bolshevik government. Incredibly, within a few weeks of his return to Britain, Reilly was sent back to Russia by the SIS posing as a British trade delegate to obtain information about the Black Sea coast. Reilly's activities over the next few years are unclear but in September 1925 it seems he was lured back to Russia, probably in a sting operation mounted by Soviet intelligence agents. As soon as he crossed the Finnish border into Russian territory, he was arrested and taken to the Lubyanka prison and later executed on the direct orders of Stalin.

Arthur Ransome who was mentioned earlier as a source for Cudbert Thornhill was involved on the fringes of espionage during the Bolshevik revolution. He was an English writer, mainly of children's stories and first went to Russia in 1913 to research Russian folklore for a book that he subsequently published in 1916 entitled *Old Peter's Russian Tales*. After the start of the First World War, he became a foreign correspondent for a left-wing British newspaper the *Daily News*, initially covering the War on the Eastern Front and then the Bolshevik revolution in 1917. Ransome developed some sympathy for the Bolshevik cause and built close relationships with several of its leaders including Lenin and Trotsky which is presumably how he obtained some of the information he passed on to Thornhill. During his time in Russia he also met the woman who would later become his second wife, Evgenia Petrovna Shelepina, who at that time worked as Trotsky's personal secretary. Despite the help that he gave SIS, there was a lingering suspicion in Britain that Ransome was too close to the Bolsheviks and may have been acting as a double agent.

After the Allied military intervention in Russia, Ransome moved to the Baltic region and built a yacht, the *Racundra*, in which he spent several months cruising around the Baltic coast. Later in 1919, he joined *The Manchester Guardian* and returned to Russia via the Baltic where he met the Estonian foreign minister who entrusted him with a secret message to the Bolsheviks. At the time Estonia was fighting for its independence alongside the Russian anti-Bolshevik counter-revolutionary forces and Ransome was asked to deliver an armistice proposal to the Bolsheviks. The message was not written down in order to preserve secrecy and so its authority depended solely on the high regard in which Ransome was held in both countries. After crossing the battle lines on foot, Ransome successfully passed the proposal to the Bolsheviks in Moscow. They accepted Estonia's offer and a few days later, he was asked to deliver their reply which meant Ransome had to return by the same dangerous path, secretly accompanied by his future wife, Evgenia. Bruce Lockhart provided official assistance to enable Ransome to smuggle her out of Russia, though he probably didn't know that she was carrying some two million roubles in diamonds and pearls for the Communist network abroad. As a result of his mission, Estonia withdrew from the war and Ransome then set up home in the Estonian capital Reval (now Tallinn) with Evgenia. He subsequently divorced his British wife and married Evgenia, later bringing her to live in England, where he continued writing for *The Guardian*. He later became famous for his children's book *Swallows and Amazons* published in 1929.

There is one name that links several of the above stories, that of Robert Bruce Lockhart. As his name implies, he came from a fervent Scottish family and after a few years in Malaya working on a family rubber plantation, he returned to Britain and joined the Foreign Office in 1912. Later that year he was posted to Moscow as vice-consul. At the time of his arrival, a rumour went round that a leading footballer had come to Moscow named Lockhart and Bruce Lockhart soon found himself invited to play football for Morozov, a cotton textile factory team in the Moscow area, managed by a man from Lancashire. Lockhart played for most of the 1912 season and the Morozov team won the Moscow league championship that year. However, the rumour was ill-founded as the great player was in fact Robert's younger brother John, who played rugby football for Scotland. Bruce Lockhart later admitted in his autobiography[165] that he barely deserved his place in the Morozov team and had played simply for the love of the sport. Although Lockhart was now acting consul-general in Moscow, he had another role during the revolutionary year of 1917, probably working for

---

[165] *Memoirs of a British Agent*, 1932.

the SIS as he reported directly to London rather than through the Ambassador. While in Russia, Lockhart met Moura Budberg, the widow of a high-ranking Tsarist diplomat, who soon became his mistress and their affair led to the British Ambassador sending Lockhart home on 'sick leave' so as to avoid any scandal, just before the Bolsheviks seized power. However, in January the following year he returned to Russia as Britain's first envoy to the Bolsheviks. He continued to work for the SIS there and was provided with over £600 worth of diamonds to fund the creation of a network of British agents in Russia. The results of his efforts are not public but it is known that an extensive and effective British spy network existed in Russia for several years from around 1919. Code named D-37, the spy or spies had access to the most senior levels within the Bolshevik government and sent back detailed reports to London. Following his involvement in the plot with Sidney Reilly in 1918 and subsequent brief imprisonment, he returned to London where he continued to work for the Foreign Office until 1922.

12
The Business of Money

The British involvement with Russia was, as we have seen, originally driven by trade and from the very early days of the Muscovy Company, it remained an important and essential backdrop to relations between the two countries. The Muscovy Company, or the Russia Company as it came to be known, was formed originally under a royal charter in 1551 and initially comprised 201 merchants with an elected governing court or board based in London that regulated its business of trade with Russia through a number of agents and merchants employed there by the Company. For almost one hundred years it held a monopoly on all trade between England and Russia. Technically, its operations were split into two – the Russia Company in London and the merchants or factors based in Russia who became known as the British Factory. Over time, as with any organization, there were differences in opinion between these two groups about the conduct of the company's business and relations with Russia. However, for convenience in this book, I have used the Russia Company to refer to both parts of the organization. The Russia Company derived its revenue principally from duties that it levied on the imports from Russia made by its merchants into British ports. During the period of its monopoly over Russian trade, it also benefited from monies raised from the seizure of interloping British and foreign ships and the sale of their goods. The Company's funds were largely spent on its offices plus a small staff in London, its large number of agents in Russia as well as paying for naval protection for the large merchant convoys that sailed from London twice yearly. The Company also had significant operating expenses, paying bribes and inducements to officials, providing gifts for the Russian Tsars and generally entertaining influential members of the Court. A private dinner in St Petersburg for one of the Russian Grand Dukes in 1839 cost the Company almost £300 (over £20,000 today). Later, the Company contributed heavily to the costs of the English churches and chaplains in Russia and St Andrew's Church in Moscow is still supported by the Company.

Aspiring merchants had to pay a fee to join the Company and also had to serve a period of apprenticeship in the business, either in London or Russia and most of the Company's merchants or agents mentioned in this book progressed through this system. The apprentices in Russia received a wage plus a small annual clothing allowance including three pairs of boots, one workday hat and one holiday hat. The merchants also received a salary but much more importantly, a share of the company's trading profits. Sir Daniel Bayley was paid £300 for six months' salary in 1814 while the company secretary received £200 for the whole year. In the early years, the Company's senior agent also often acted as the de facto representative of the English government in Russia.

The Company's headquarters in Moscow were in a small former palace, not far from the Kremlin, that had been given to the Company by Tsar Ivan.[166]

Around 1630 the Company changed its structure from a joint-stock basis to that of a regulated company which, subject to various rules, allowed the merchant members to trade on their own account. Although Tsar Alexis ended the company's trading privileges in 1649 after the execution of King Charles I, it retained its monopoly on Russian trade at home until 1698. After the loss of its monopolies, the Company's trade with Russia was gradually supplemented and then superseded by independent traders, entrepreneurs and businessmen who arrived in Russia in increasing numbers in the 18th and particularly the 19th centuries. The Company benefited from the revival of Anglo-Russian trade during the 18th century and was handling some two thirds of all Russian exports from St Petersburg by the 1750s. Although it lost its dominant position again during the 19th century, the Company survived as an influential and revered City of London institution until the Bolshevik revolution, since when it has mainly operated as a charity in Russia.

British involvement in manufacturing and industry in Russia also occurred early on as the merchants of the Muscovy Company were quick to build on their initial trading activities in Russian hemp, pelts, wax, tar and pitch. It soon became apparent to them that it was more economical (and profitable) to export Russian hemp in a processed form and they set up a rope works near Archangel, the first British manufacturing operation in Russia. British skills in iron making were also in demand by the Russians at an early stage as evidenced by a letter from Tsar Ivan to the Muscovy Company:

'*Also we haue of our goodnesse giuen and graunted to the English marchants, leaue to buy them a house at Witchida and there to search out mines of yron. And where they shall happily finde it, there to set vp houses for the making of the sayd yron, and to make the same, and of our goodnesse haue graunted them woods, five or six miles in compasse about the said houses, to the making of theire yron, and not to exceede those bounds and limits: And where they shall cut the saide wood, not to set vp any village or farme there; bringing the artificers for making of their yron out of their owne Countrey and to leame our people that arte, and so freely to occupy the saide yron in these our Dominions, transporting also of the same home into England... And if any of the said yron shal be needfull for our workes, then we to take of the saide yron to our worke, vpon agreement of price, paying money out of our Treasurie for the same.*'

It is uncertain where these early British ironworkers came from or where they were sent to in Russia, although it was probably somewhere close to the White Sea or Novgorod. However, it is known that specialists from Britain helped develop the first ironworks in the Urals, setting up the blast-furnace of the Nevyanski works in 1703 which mainly produced armaments such as cannons, guns and shells for the Russian military.[167] However, the high-grade

---

[166] The building, known as the Old English Court, still exists and was refurbished in 1994 and opened by Queen Elizabeth II.
[167] E...Zablotski - Russian Mining History - *Industrial Heritage*, Vol.27, 2001.

ore found in the Urals was also soon being exported to Britain and during the second half of the 18th century Russia was the main supplier of iron ore to Britain's rapidly expanding manufacturing industries. But by the late 1700s, this trade had all but disappeared as iron ore from English and Welsh mines supplanted that from the Urals.

The initial commercial contacts between Britain and Russia that flowed from the founding of the Russian Company really gathered pace with Peter the Great in the early 18th century. Many of the British sailors, engineers, mathematicians, technicians and doctors that he brought to Russia made important contributions not only in their own specific fields but also to the overall economic development of the country. Peter trusted British specialists and was impressed with their capabilities, appointing them to some of the highest posts in both government and industry. One of the earliest British owned and run factories in Tsarist Russia was that of the Welshman, John Lloyd who obtained a ten-year lease from Peter the Great on a glass factory in Moscow in 1709. With the lease came a monopoly on the sale of glassware and window glass throughout Russia as long as Lloyd trained Russians in the skills of glass making. Lloyd's qualifications for being offered this apparent gift horse are unclear but the fact that he was a member of a well-known British drinking society in Moscow that was frequented by Peter may have been prominent in Peter's decision. Lloyd brought in several British glass experts to run the factory but it failed to prosper and in 1713 the factory was destroyed by a fire. The British glass-makers moved on to St Petersburg which during the early years of its construction, had been largely glazed with glass imported from England. The Russians were now building new factories in St Petersburg to make window and looking glass and here the British glass-makers found a ready market for their skills. As the 18th century progressed, other British manufacturing ventures were set up in Moscow, St Petersburg, Archangel and Kronstadt with rope works and sugar refineries being the most numerous initially with breweries following later. As with Lloyd's business, Russian permission for these operations was usually granted on the same basis i.e. that Russians were trained in the relevant manufacturing techniques. These companies met with mixed success but some continued in operation well into the 19th century. The growing list of British manufacturing endeavours in Russia was not always welcomed by the rest of the British merchants, either in Russia or Britain. Such was the case with a wallpaper company set up in Moscow in the 1750s by George Thompson and Martin Butler which would clearly have an adverse impact on the lucrative export trade from Britain. The British envoy in St Petersburg was asked to look into the matter by furious English manufacturers but he found there was nothing that could be done to prevent Thompson and Butler proceeding. This minor trade dispute marked the beginning of a slow but steady shift in attitudes towards those British businessmen who established companies in Russia that competed with British exports. Opinion regarding their activities gradually swung from exasperation and irritation, through extreme annoyance to finally regarding them as traitors to the true cause of the British Empire.

The commercial ties between the two countries continued to flourish under Catherine II during the 19th century. The successful negotiation of a new commercial treaty with Russia in 1766 heralded a further acceleration in the pace and variety of both new British arrivals in the country as merchants and traders as well as the number of British companies being founded in Russia. Men like Timothy Raikes from Yorkshire who, after completing an apprenticeship with the Russia Company in 1753, went on to set up several businesses. He traded in linen and tallow from warehouses in St Petersburg, built a nail factory near the Finnish border and supplied silver to the Russian mint. His two younger brothers both became successful merchants with the Russia Company in the latter part of the century.[168] Another was Francis Gardner who in 1766 founded his highly successful porcelain works near Moscow. Despite initial difficulties, his business became a remarkable success, producing good quality tableware as well as figurines in the style of the Meissen works in Germany. The reputation of his products grew such that in 1777 Catherine ordered three dinner services from him for use in the Winter Palace, with a further order which was delivered in 1785. On the back of these orders, Gardner was able to further expand and opened retail shops in Moscow and Tver. His son later took over the running of the business and it remained a going concern in family hands until the end of the 19th century. The fortunes of others (both in terms of their luck and financial reward) were however not always as successful. The timber-exporting and shipbuilding business of William Gomm and William Ramsbottom in the area around Archangel and Onega experienced great success in the 1760s but a few years later it was in severe decline and near bankruptcy with large debts that the Russian government ultimately had to underwrite. By 1780, Gomm was surviving solely through the generosity of his friends and family but was fortunate to be offered a job in the British embassy until he was able to leave Russia a couple of years later.

In the 1770s, the British Government agreed a programme of aid to the Empress Catherine of Russia that was to lead to the arrival of two of the most well-known British entrepreneurs in Russia – Charles Baird and Charles Gascoigne. Both men were skilled senior engineers at the Carron Works in Glasgow which in 1774 shipped a steam engine (believed to be the first in Russia) for the naval docks at Kronstadt as part of the assistance programme. A decade later, Carron received another Russian order for cannons and over the next two years supplied a considerable quantity of equipment for the Russian iron foundry at Petrozavodsk, near Kronstadt. These orders emanated from Admiral Samuel Greig who had been asked by Catherine to acquire British men and machinery to modernise Russia's iron foundries in order to produce improved artillery. Greig focussed his attentions on the Carron Works and in early 1786 sent an invitation to both Gascoigne and Baird to come to work in Russia. Both men were experts in the design and casting of guns and whilst at Carron, Gascoigne had invented a new gun, called the Carronade which was used to great effect in the Napoleonic wars. The invitation was carried to Glasgow by Adam Armstrong, a graduate of Edinburgh University, who was then tutor to the Greig family. Following discussions with Armstrong, the pair

---

[168] Raikes' nephew, Thomas Raikes also visited Russia and published a book, *A Visit to St Petersburg*, 1838.

accepted Greig's offer and with the agreement of Carron, they left for Russia in the early summer of 1786. Neither was to return to Britain. Gascoigne who was originally from Yorkshire, remained in Russia until his death twenty years later. Together with Baird, he was responsible for greatly improving Russia's foundries and cannon-making capacity as well as building the first dry dock at the Kronstadt naval base. He created a new Russian unit of measure based on the inch (the distance between the top and knuckle of the thumb). He became director of the Alexandrovski Gun Works and Konchezerski Iron Foundry, where he taught metal casting to Russian workers and was made Head of Mines.

Gascoigne was also the first British entrepreneur to commercially exploit the rich coal and iron resources of Ukraine and he was instrumental in setting up the Lugansk iron works there. The Russian government had been aware for some time that there was coal in the Ukraine and the region's resources were one of the reasons behind the Tsarist Empire's struggles with the Ottomans for control of the area. In 1794 an expedition led by Gascoigne was sent to the Donbass region to explore the region's possibilities and to choose a site for building coal mines and an ironworks. Gascoigne was impressed by the area's potential and selected a location near the river Lugan. In November 1795, Catherine II approved a bill for the establishment of coal mining and an iron-smelting plant in the location selected by Gascoigne. Lugansk was to become the centre of a new metallurgical complex in this part of Russia using local coal and iron ore brought from the Urals. Coal mining was started in 1796 and construction of the new ironworks began under the direction of Gascoigne with a group of ten skilled British workers and some 200 locally recruited men.

It took more than two years to complete the plant and it produced its first iron for cannon shells in 1798. Most of the British workers stayed on in a supervisory role and to train the Russians. But hiring local workers was not easy and peasants were brought to Lugansk from many other parts of Russia and the jails were even used as a source of labour. As the population of Lugansk grew, other manufacturing operations became established in the town. There were three brick-making factories, one tile plant and five lard and candle-making factories, plus a hospital, a school, works police, a prison and a playhouse. There were 204 brick houses, twenty wooden huts and seventy-four barracks for craftsmen and workers. The British specialists lived in their own colony on the main street known at the time as English Street. In the first half of the 19th century, the works became an important part of Russia's armaments industry, producing guns, shells, grenades and other kinds of armament, mostly for the Russian Black Sea fleet. It is ironic that much of the munitions used by the Russians to fight the British during the Crimean War were sourced from this British-built and -run plant. However, the cost of production in Lugansk using iron transported from the Urals proved expensive and uncompetitive, limiting its further development.

Gascoigne and Baird were also involved in the development of a new steam-powered Imperial Mint in St Petersburg for Tsar Paul I. The original design and most of the equipment were supplied by Matthew Boulton whose Birmingham company specialised in steam-powered machinery for mills and minting coins.[169] On Gascoigne's advice, a team of Russian apprentices was sent to Boulton's works for training and in 1803 they returned to St Petersburg together with four of Boulton's English mechanics to begin the construction process. In addition, Boulton sent his nephew, Zacchaeus Walker, as his personal representative to oversee the project and work with Gascoigne and Baird on installing the new equipment. Walker remained in St Petersburg for four years until the Mint came into full production in 1807. James Duncan, one of the original Boulton mechanics also stayed on in Russia as a technical adviser at the Mint and in 1814 he reported to London that the Mint was coining ten million silver pieces a year. Boulton's equipment continued in operation until the 1840s, when more modern machinery was introduced.

Gascoigne's first wife died while they were in Russia and in 1797 he married a second time to Anastasia-Jessye, the daughter of Dr Matthew Guthrie, one of the many Scottish doctors then working in St Petersburg. Gascoigne was given many honours by the Empress and her successor, eventually becoming a State Councillor (he was known as Karl Karlovich Gaskoin) and a member of the Russian Government. He died at Kolpino, near St Petersburg, in July 1806, during the reconstruction of the Izhora works and in accordance with his will was buried in Petrozavodsk. Gascoigne was succeeded as director of metallurgical operations in 1807 by Adam Armstrong who held the position until his death in 1818 and was also buried in Petrozavodsk.

After a few years of working closely together with Gascoigne, Baird struck out on his own founding what would become Baird & Sons in Kronstadt (later relocated to Kolpino) and it became extremely successful, known for its orderliness and efficiency. Baird owned his own wharf on the River Neva and he built the first Russian steamship, the *Elizaveta*, using a brick chimney for a funnel. It plied between St Petersburg and Kronstadt and Baird had a ten-year monopoly on the route which made his fortune. His son, Francis, who joined his father in Russia at the age of seventeen, took over the business at his father's death in 1843. The Baird works produced the magnificent dome of St Isaac's Cathedral in St Petersburg, considered an engineering feat at the time, as well as all the decorative metalwork. The company also produced the cast-iron structures for the first iron bridges in St Petersburg which were designed by his fellow Scot, William Hastie. Several hundred skilled British workers were employed at the Baird factories during the 19th century. When Francis Baird died in 1864, he was followed by his son George who became head of the Baird Works and he was granted the extraordinary honour of being confirmed by Tsar Alexander II as a hereditary Russian nobleman in 1871.

There were other Scottish ironworkers at the Alexandrovski works before the arrival of Baird and Gascoigne. Alexander Smith arrived in Kronstadt in 1783 to operate the steam engine originally supplied by Carron and went on to become Gascoigne's right-hand man. Alexander Davy, a skilled mining

---

[169] Matthew Boulton was closely associated with James Watt in the development and manufacture of steam engines and more than 500 Boulton & Watt machines supplied to a variety of industries in the UK and overseas. A special act of Parliament had to be passed to allow the export of Boulton's machinery for the Russian Mint.

technician and metal worker from Scotland arrived to work in Tsarskoye Selo in 1784 before transferring a few years later to the Alexandrovski cannon-works where he was joined by Smith in 1793. Smith was employed as a mechanic and supervisor of the steam engines and Davy worked as a metalworker and a blacksmith until 1806 when he was transferred to the St Petersburg foundry. Davy was the founder of an important dynasty of Russian mining engineers of English origin whose Imperial service continued into the early 20th century. Many more British workers came to Russia during Gascoigne and Baird's time, some of whom also had quite remarkable careers and made important contributions to the country's industrial development. Jacob Wilson, a blacksmith, arrived in Russia 1784 together with his eight-year-old son, Alexander. Jacob easily found employment with various factories in the St Petersburg area and his son started work at Tsarskoe Selo in 1790 and then moved to the Sestroretsky Gun Works. A few years later, he worked as an assistant to Gascoigne in Lugansk and then the Alexandrovsky and Izhorsky plants. He was manager of both plants between 1827 and 1856 during which time he completely re-equipped them to manufacture steamboats, steam engines and marine machinery as well as artillery weapons. Alexander also became involved in various land drainage and civil construction works, including an urban landscaping project in the town of Kolpino, the building of both the town's St Nicholas' Church and its first girls' school. Wilson also designed a flax-mill in St Petersburg and helped establish two large cotton mills in Russia. He died in 1866 and was buried in Kolpino but his family stayed on and later some of his descendants married into Russian nobility.

Matthew Clark, a metallurgical engineer, also arrived in Russia with his father who was another of the Carron workers who came with Gascoigne. Matthew became an inspector at the St Petersburg Iron Foundry in 1824 and two years later, director of the Alexandrovski Foundry until 1842. Under his direction, the foundry cast several major sculptures designed by Russian artists that were installed at various public buildings in both St Petersburg and Moscow. Clark was also in charge of building the *Neva*, one of the first Russian steamboats and the first Russian submarine in 1834. He was also in charge of the reconstruction work at the Winter Palace after the disastrous fire of 1837. He died in St Petersburg in 1846. We do not know exactly how many of the hundreds of skilled British metalworkers that came to Russia during the 19th century stayed on beyond their initial contracts. As we have seen, a good number clearly did and often their sons followed in their fathers' footsteps such as those of Baird, Davy and Wilson; even their daughters seem to have married engineers.

The traveller Cochrane mentions in his book[170] a Mr Major, an Englishman from Birmingham that he encountered working near Ekaterinburg in the early 1820s who was running salt works there, installing new steam engines. He was also involved in panning for gold in the region and had invented a new machine to improve the recovery rate from washing the sands. He told Cochrane that he was earning 30,000 roubles annually and owned an estate of several square

---

[170] Captain John Cochrane - ibid

miles that had been given him by Tsar Alexander. He also had a small factory producing cutlery, a business that he was hoping to expand into the Siberian market. Major was clearly doing very well at the time from these Russian ventures but, unfortunately, his success laid the foundation for his untimely end. He was killed by a burglar who wanted to steal his gold. Another man who came to Russia from Birmingham was General Alexander Wilson, who was in charge of the Kolpino works near St Petersburg in 1848. He died in 1850 and his son, James took over his job. Wilson's descendants became quite wealthy businessmen in St Petersburg and later married into one of the longest established British families in Russia, the Wishaws.

The Wishaws had become involved with Russia in the late 18th century when William Wishaw arrived in St Petersburg from England. In June 1777, at the age of thirty-one he married Constancia Fock, a Russian-born descendant of a Dutch immigrant family. Constancia was one of nine children, five of whom eventually married into British merchant families in St Petersburg. William and Constancia also had nine children and four of them married into British families in Russia. Wishaw prospered as a merchant in Russia and by the early 1800s he was able to rent a summer residence in Mourino, an estate belonging to Count Vorontsov-Dashkov, some twelve miles north-west of St Petersburg. The estate became a popular summer resort for some of the wealthier British families in St Petersburg such as the Andersons, Cattleys and Higginbothams. Wishaw was popular with both the British and Russian communities and regularly entertained guests at Mourino until his death at the age of ninety-three in 1838. He was described as "*a temperate man but, as was the custom in those days, he drank his port after dinner, never exceeding half a bottle. He would then cover his face in a silk handkerchief and enjoy a short nap.*" After one of these sessions, his wife came to wake him only to find that the old man was dead.[171]

Wishaw's eldest son, Bernhard, was born in St Petersburg in 1779 and in the early 1800s, he co-founded Hills & Whishaw which would become one of the leading grain exporters in Russia. In 1819, Bernard married a lively, indomitable beauty from the British community in St Petersburg called Elizabeth Yeames (the granddaughter of John Yeames, the Tsar's shipbuilder) and they had ten children. The link between the Wishaw and Yeames families was further strengthened by the marriage of one of Bernhard's sisters, Elizabeth, to James Yeames. These family connections were also mirrored by common business interests as the Yeames family also ran an important grain-trading company in Taganrog in southern Russia. According to family legend, Bernhard was a strict father, regularly caning his seven sons and three daughters whenever they seriously misbehaved. He used to give the boys a cane each, instructing them to thrash each other and then whichever boy gave in first would then be taken out and caned by Bernhard. Apparently, he once walked through the winter snow all the way from from Mourino to St Petersburg to negotiate a deal and once the transaction was completed, he walked back again. He was seventy years old at the time. Around 1851, the company experienced financial difficulties and Bernhard and Elizabeth retired to live near Cheltenham, England where they

---

[171] James Whishaw, *A History of the Wishaw Family*, 1935.

both died. The link between the Wishaw and Yeames families was further strengthened in the early 1820s when James Yeames married Elizabeth Wishaw.

Bernhard's first child, William, was born in St Petersburg in 1820 and joined the family business around the age of seventeen. When he was twenty-one, he left his father's company and moved to Archangel to establish a business of his own. In 1846, he married Harriet Henley in St Petersburg and they subsequently had two children before Harriet unfortunately died from peritonitis, followed soon after by the death of their daughter. Understandably, the double tragedy left William very upset and in early 1854, he decided to leave Russia with his one-year-old son James and sailed for Britain. He returned to Archangel briefly in 1855 to liquidate his business affairs and went back to live in Warwickshire where he died in 1882. His son, James, was educated in England and went on to study medicine in London but he abandoned the idea of becoming a doctor in favour of a commercial career in Russia and in 1877, he joined Hill and Wishaw which was then run by his uncle Jem Wishaw. Unfortunately for James, his uncle died two years later and the firm was left in such a weak position that it failed in 1882. However, James was so enamoured with St Petersburg that he decided to stay and set up in business on his own, eventually becoming involved in a variety of activities, including shipping, banking and armaments. In 1880, he married Frances Anderson and over the next twenty-one years, the couple had seven daughters and a son and then in 1884 James adopted Russian nationality. Shortly afterwards, he received the Freedom of the City of St Petersburg and was also the British Vice Consul for more than twelve years.

Wishaw was able to take advantage of his Russian nationality by helping his British friends circumvent Russian law. At the time, foreigners were forbidden to own mining lands in Russia[172] but as a Russian national, James was invited to become a trustee by several of the British companies then taking an interest in Russia's vast wealth. He also forged a link with Lord Revelstoke, the founder of Barings Bank and through this important connection, Wishaw became involved with the newly developing Baku oilfields in Azerbaijan. He ended up with a substantial property portfolio registered in his name but held on behalf of British companies. Of course, the Russian government was not blind to what was happening and Wishaw was invited to a meeting with the Minister of Finance, the formidable Count Witte. The latter wanted to regularize the situation and he persuaded Wishaw to ensure that all those for whom he was acting applied to have their interests in Russia legalized immediately, offering his "*his powerful assistance*" in the event of any problem. Within a few months of this meeting, Wishaw secured Imperial recognition for all the British companies for which he had been acting. He essentially became the Russian legal representative for many of them and steadily moved away from his previous main interest of shipping.

In 1905, Witte became Russia's first Prime Minister and negotiated a loan of around £80 million from Britain and France, a large part of which was provided

---

[172] The only exception was the New Russia Company, founded by John Hughes in 1870 which had both coal and iron mines.

by Barings, probably with the help of Wishaw. Just three years later, he became the official representative in Russia of Barings Bank and shortly afterwards, Wishaw also joined the board of Azov-Don Bank in St Petersburg, the second largest Bank in Russia. In early 1917, he became an agent supplying platinum to the Russian Ministry of Munitions and Wishaw was now one of the most respected and popular figures in Tsarist Russian business circles. The rising tide of civil unrest and violence that year made Wishaw uneasy and when he was advised that he might be arrested, he fled Russia just days before the Bolshevik revolution of October 1917. Although he escaped with his life, he left everything else behind. All his property, including many family heirlooms, was subsequently confiscated by the Bolsheviks. At some personal risk, Wishaw returned briefly to the south of Russia in 1919 when he was involved in trying to organize munition supplies for General Denikin's White Army. When he returned to England, Wishaw became a popular figure in the Anglo-Russian Society and used some of his remaining wealth to help family members who had suffered from the Bolshevik revolution. He remained with Barings Brothers and was later employed as the manager of an office set up by the Cunard Company and the Hudson Bay Company to encourage young men to emigrate to Canada. He steadfastly refused to acknowledge the Bolshevik Government in Russia and in 1925 successfully applied to have his British nationality restored.

Another of the early British families to settle in Russia was the Cazalets. The Cazalets were a Huguenot family originally from France that had settled to England in the early 18th century. Noah Cazalet was born in London in 1757 and trained as a silk weaver. He moved to St Petersburg with his first wife, Charlotte Moore around 1785 and started a successful rope making business there. Charlotte died some two years later and Noah remarried, eventually having nine children in St Petersburg. Noah died in 1800 but both the business and the family continued to expand in Russia over the next 150 years, especially under Noah's grandson, Edward Cazalet. Through his marriage, he also linked the Cazalets with the merchant business of the Miller family. One of his sons, Edward Alexander Cazalet, born in 1836, was the founder of Anglo-Russian literary society and 1864 he joined the Russian Steam Navigation and Trading Company in Odessa which had a fleet of seventy-two steamships by the turn of the 20th century and was listed on the St Petersburg stock exchange. At the turn of the 20th century, the family was involved in several enterprises including St Petersburg's largest brewery, a tallow processing and candle factory (one of the firm's contracts was to supply all the Tsar's palaces with candles) as well as banking, railway development and the Muir & Mirrielees department store (see page 247). Lieutenant Cazalet (the son of William) was the first British man from Moscow to lose his life in the First World War at the battle of Loos in 1915.

The acquisition of Finland by Russia from Sweden in 1809 opened up yet further opportunities for British entrepreneurs in the Tsar's empire. One of the most successful in Finland was James Finlayson who was born in Penicuik, Scotland in 1772 which at the time was a small but thriving weaving and paper-making centre. It was here that Finlayson gained his initial experience of textile machinery as a mill engineer. However, by 1811, the Penicuik mills had closed and Finlayson was forced to seek work elsewhere and in 1815 he arrived in St Petersburg as a master machinist at Baird's Kolpino works. Finlayson held strong religious views and soon became associated with both the Quakers in St Petersburg as well as the British church where he became friendly with John Paterson, one of the founders of the Russian Bible Society. In 1820, the pair set off for a tour of Finland to investigate the potential for setting up Bible societies there. By pure chance, during his visit Finlayson came across the Tammerfors rapids and was immediately struck by the potential of the site's abundant hydraulic power for manufacturing. He returned to St Petersburg with a proposal to the Russian government to develop the area as a modern industrial centre.

His idea was enthusiastically accepted and following a visit to the site by Tsar Alexander, the plan was given the royal seal of approval. Finlayson was granted an interest-free loan, free land, customs concessions and rights to most of the rapids. Under Finlayson's skilled eye, the site steadily developed, initially making textile machinery based on the latest British designs and then textiles themselves. He moved there with his wife Margaret, who became very active in local charitable works and together they set up Finland's first provision for orphans. The company and settlement founded by Finlayson was the start of Tampere, now Finland's second largest city. After a decline in prosperity in Russia in the late 1820s, the company suffered financially and Finlayson's health also deteriorated. In 1837, he was forced to surrender his company to its creditors and returned to Scotland with his wife where he remained until his death in 1852. However, his company survived and Finlayson & Co later became the largest industrial enterprise in Finland until well into the 20th century.

Another British businessman who became involved with Russia and Finland was William Crichton who was born in 1827 at Leith in Scotland. He came from a ship-owning family and he trained as an engineer, working both on land and later at sea. In 1850, Crichton was offered a job by a family friend as the manager of an engineering business in Turku Finland. At the time Turku was a relatively small provincial town with only 13,000 inhabitants and Crichton was initially reluctant to take the position, believing that the opportunities were better in Russia itself. He had been in correspondence with his great uncle Sir William Crichton, the Tsar's personal doctor and had been encouraged to go to Russia to try his luck. However, the job in Turku was a chance for the young Crichton to build a career and make his mark. The company he joined was owned by James Cowie and was building the first steam engines for use in Finland. In 1852 Crichton met his future wife, Annie Owen who was then the beautiful nineteen-year-old daughter of Samuel Owen whose own father had moved from England to Stockholm in 1806 also to set up a company to build steam engines. Owen junior had subsequently relocated to Turku to work with Cowie. Crichton proposed to her in 1853 but before they could marry, the Crimean War broke out. Crichton planned to go to England and wait until the war was over but was arrested the day before his departure from Finland because he was a British citizen. Crichton was initially sent to St Petersburg where he was imprisoned. After a few days he managed to speak to the prison governor and explained that he was related to Sir William Crichton, the Tsar's doctor. He was released shortly afterwards and sent to Pavlovsk in the care and protection of his great uncle. Whilst in Pavlovsk, he managed to get the Owen family released to join him there and was thus able to link up again with his fiancée Annie. Once the war ended, Crichton decided to stay on in Russia and obtained a job at the Alexandrovski plant in Kolpino. He and Annie were finally able to marry in the English church in Saint Petersburg and they went on to have four children all born in the Russian capital.

Clearly, Crichton prospered in the Russian capital for when he learnt in 1862 that his old company in Turku was for sale, he was able to able to raise almost 33,000 roubles to buy it. The family moved to Turku and the name of the company was changed to Wm Crichton & Co with William taking over as managing director. His decision was a fortunate one as in the post-Crimean War period, industry in Russia was booming and Crichton's company grew substantially. He used the many contacts he had made over the years in both Finland and Russia to obtain new business. In the late 1870s he bought the shipbuilding company Åbo Skeppsvarfs AB in Turku and he built a large number of both naval and civilian ships for Russia. Crichton became highly respected in Russia and was awarded both the Great Gold medal and the Great Stanislaw decoration. As his business grew, so did his family. English governesses were brought out to educate and raise the children and the boys were also sent to boarding schools in England. Despite his success in Russia, he retained his British citizenship and was appointed British vice-consul for Turku. In 1882 Wm Crichton & Co was Turku's largest company with 1000 employees. Crichton died quite suddenly in 1889 when only sixty-two years old, leaving behind his wife and twelve surviving children. Unfortunately, none of them wished to take over the company and it passed to Crichton's friend and colleague, John Eager.

Finlayson and Crichton are good examples of the increasingly important role played by the British in providing both capital and technical knowledge to Imperial Russia during the 19th century, especially in the burgeoning manufacturing industries. They introduced the latest manufacturing techniques, brought over skilled men to Russia to run the factories and train the local workforce and often developed new markets for Russian products. As a result, the British companies were generally able to 'outstrip most of the local competition and to initially accumulate substantial profits'.[173] In the 1840s and 1850s several large British-owned companies were established in Russia, such as the textile businesses of John Thornton, Hubbard and Egerton plus John and Joseph Shaw. In the machinery and metallurgical sectors, names such as Carr & McPherson, Ellis & Butts, Wilkins and Isherwood were important in St Petersburg and Smith, Bromley and Williams were active in Moscow.

In the early 20th century, almost all the textile mills in St Petersburg and many of those in Moscow were either owned or run by the British and the Thornton mill was one of the largest employers in Russia. The business was founded by John Thornton, a Yorkshireman who was invited to Russia soon after the Crimean War to assist with the development of Russian mills and the

---

[173] William Blackwell, *The Beginnings of Russian Industrialization*, 1968

Thornton business developed from this. When Thornton died in 1870, the company was then run by his two sons, John and Daniel and at its peak, their huge mills on the banks of the Neva employed some 10,000 people primarily making cloth for Russian military uniforms. John Hubbard owned several large cotton and print mills near St Petersburg and was one of the first to establish trading agencies with the incipient cotton-growing regions in central Asia. His son, Evelyn Hubbard, who joined the business in 1875, was the last governor of the Russia Company.

As one of the largest companies in the international cotton thread business, J & P Coats was also very active in Russia and its factories in the country were the largest of some fifty-three investments it made outside the UK. Cotton thread in Russia was in high demand, primarily for the cheaper grades of cloth that ordinary Russians wore all year round and, by 1914, Coats held close to a 90% market share. In the 20th century Coats, like many other companies, suffered frequent strikes and lockouts due to the social unrest of the period, which adversely affected sales. Nevertheless the Russian subsidiaries were able to provide much higher returns than those of other Russian textile companies or of Russian industry as a whole.[174] There was also a British lace factory near Moscow, owned by the Peet family and over the years a considerable number of British men, especially from Lancashire and Nottinghamshire, came to work in these mills and lace works. The British textile factories were some of the largest employers in the St Petersburg and Moscow areas and as such were primary targets for the incipient Marxist movement's agitators. As early as 1895, Lenin wrote a pamphlet exhorting the Thornton workers to strike for higher wages and a decade later, Yosif Vissarionovich Djugashvili, who later became Josef Stalin, was employed there as a supervisor in its finishing room. In the revolutionary turmoil of 1917, the textile workers proved to be particularly active in the demonstrations that brought down the Tsarist regime.

The engineering business that eventually became known as Smith & Co was founded by Richard Smith, a Scot who left Greenock and arrived in Kolpino, Russia in 1847 at the age of twenty-three. He moved on to Moscow and soon found work in one of the British engineering businesses there. By 1850, through endeavour and good luck, he had formed a partnership with his employer and established Rodion, Smith & Co which he later took over completely and dropped his former partner's name from the business. The company made industrial boilers and was located in a manufacturing district a couple of miles west of Moscow's city centre where several other British owned or run companies were already established. Over the next sixty years, three generations of the Smiths were involved in the business, ending up with Harry Smith, Richard's grandson who was born in 1892.

Harry's father married the daughter of John Boon who had arrived in Russia in the 1860s and worked at the Morozov textile mills in Tver. Harry's cousin, William Boon was a manager at the large Nevsky mills in St Petersburg and one of Harry's sisters married George Whitehead, a prominent British businessman

---

[174] Kim Dong-Woon, *J. & P. Coats as a Multinational*, Department of Economics paper, Dong-Eui University, Korea.

in Moscow. In May 1916, the Smith family decided to take the opportunity to sell the boiler works to a Russian company for 275,000 roubles and this proved to be a prescient decision with the Bolshevik revolution just a year away. The Smith family stayed on in Russia after the sale but the deterioration in conditions after the Revolution forced them to leave Moscow. Harry and his mother fled north by train to Finland and then via Sweden to Scotland. The rest of the family (together with the female side of Whitehead family) left in June 1918 via Archangel and Murmansk, then under British control, where after three weeks they sailed for Britain in a troopship.

Many other well known British companies established subsidiary operations in Russia during the latter part of the 19th century in a wide variety of fields. It was a chance meeting with William Thornton that brought the Mather & Platt company to Russia. The partnership was formed in 1845 in Manchester, England, initially making engineering equipment for the textile industry. Colin Mather made several exploratory visits to Russia in the 1850s but nothing significant happened until 1859 when his nephew William Mather met William Thornton in England. At the time, the English textile machinery business was in recession and Thornton convinced Mather of the opportunities in the expanding textile industry of Russia. Mather paid the first of many visits to Russia the following year and within a few years, the company was actively involved in several large industrial projects, the largest of which was a new calico printing works at Schlusselburg near St Petersburg. Another engineering company, Babcock & Wilcox had a head office in a modern building near the Kremlin in Moscow managed by a Mr Metcalf plus a branch in St Petersburg. The company evacuated all its British staff after the October revolution in 1917 and closed the St Petersburg office, leaving three Russians to run the remains of their business in Moscow. The engineering and armaments firm of Vickers also set up offices in St Petersburg and Moscow in the early 20th century and did well during the First World War years supplying armaments to the Russians. The British automotive company Vauxhall Motors also had a small operation in Russia in the early 1900s.

During the latter half of the 19th century, there were several attempts by British entrepreneurs to exploit the rich iron and coal resources of Russia, initially in the Urals and later in the newly discovered Donbass deposits of Ukraine. One enterprising English company is even recorded as having set up in the distant Tobol River area of what is now Kazakhstan in the 1870s, developing the rich iron, coal and copper deposits in the Karkarali region.[175] In the Donbass, the industrial path was blazed by a Welshman called John Hughes who sailed from London in 1870 with one hundred skilled British workers in eight chartered steamships to lay the foundations of a modern coal and iron industry in Russia. The story of his eventual success[176] is quite remarkable for a variety of reasons. He not only had to bring everything needed with him in the ships from England, down to the last nut and bolt, he had to deal with official indifference and obstruction (despite being invited by the Russian Government

---

[175] Henry Butler Johnstone, *A Trip up the Volga*, 1876.

[176] Roderick Heather - *The Iron Tsar*, 2010.

to set up the enterprise) and he had to recruit and train a local workforce in a hitherto barren and under-populated part of the country. When he set sail from England, he was relatively old at fifty-five to be taking on such a challenge but he succeeded spectacularly. In its prime, the company he founded and later managed with his four sons was the largest producer of iron rails for the rapidly expanding Russian railway network as well as major coal producer. He also built and ran the city we now call Donetsk (it was known as Hughesovka in pre-Soviet times) constructing hospitals, schools, churches and houses for its inhabitants. In many ways Hughesovka was a much larger and more successful version of what Gascoigne had earlier achieved in Lugansk. Hughes combined modern industrial equipment, manufacturing and management techniques with the rich coal and iron resources of Ukraine and effectively introduced modern industrial capitalism to Russia. Of all the British businessmen and entrepreneurs who worked in Imperial Russia, Hughes was one of the most influential in terms of the country's economic and industrial development. Yet his involvement with Russia was quite accidental, coming as it did through a combination of unforeseen events.

John Hughes' initial contact with Russia also revolved around the ongoing improvements to the country's Baltic defences. In the 1860s Hughes was in charge of the Millwall Ironworks in London, a company that had a worldwide reputation for the new system of iron cladding for which Hughes held a patent. In 1864, Hughes' company obtained a contract to supply a large quantity of iron cladding for the Baltic forts and General Todleben visited the Millwall works to liaise on production. During his visit Todleben discussed with Hughes the problems Russia was facing as it tried to rapidly modernize its industry and expand the railway network. It is not known whether the challenges and opportunities outlined by Todleben struck a chord with Hughes at this time but he was doing well at Millwall and did nothing to follow up the conversation. However, the London financial crash of 1866 brought dramatic changes for both Hughes and the Millwall Ironworks. Although the company survived the crisis, largely thanks to the efforts of Hughes, the overall outlook for the business in London was poor. New competitors with lower cost structures had sprung up in Scotland and Northern Ireland. A year later, Hughes took up the earlier invitation of General Todleben to visit Russia and examine for himself the possibilities for industrial development that the country now presented. Various projects were discussed with him but following an exploratory visit to Ukraine where promising coal and iron deposits had been found, Hughes decided that this was where his future lay. Hughes was not the only British entrepreneur to have a significant impact on Russia in the 19th century. But he was exceptional in that he started a new business from scratch, away from the traditional centres of St Petersburg or Moscow and arrived literally under his own steam, rather than furthering an existing company's commercial expansion into the country. Hughes' achievements are all the more remarkable as he could barely read or write.

As well as playing a significant role in the development of a modern coal- and iron-mining industry in Russia, the British also invested heavily in gold mining, particularly in the Lena goldfields in Siberia around the turn of the 20th century and in the Caspian oilfields. During the latter part of the 19th century, oil became an increasingly important resource for the world's industrial economies and the British were involved from the beginning in the development of Russia's oil reserves in the Baku region of Azerbaijan. The British were aware of the presence of oil there as early as the 18th century. Jonas Hanway of the Russia Company wrote about the use of oil and gas in Baku following visits in 1741 and in 1784, another English traveller G. Foster wrote that the people in Baku used thick black oil to cover the roofs of their houses to protect against leaks.[177] By the 1880s, the commercial potential and strategic importance of the Caspian oilfields were being increasingly recognized in Britain and it was felt that 'the Russian oil business was too attractive for England to allow it to slip out of its hands' [178] and English businessmen were soon making substantial investments in the Caspian region. In order to fully exploit the Baku fields, the construction of a pipeline across the Caucasus to Batumi was begun in 1897 and completed exactly ten years later. In 1898, the Russian oil industry surpassed production levels in the USA and by 1901 Baku was producing more than half of the world's oil. Between 1898 and 1903 British oil firms invested some sixty million roubles in the Baku oilfields and there were twelve British companies operating in the region. In 1912, the Anglo-Dutch firm Shell acquired a major stake in the region by purchasing a local company from Rothschild's Bank its Caspian operations then produced a fifth of all Russian oil output up to 1914. Anglo-American investors also established the Caucasus Copper Company in Batumi at the turn of the 19th century and several British mining engineers came out to work there.

It was probably inevitable that the 'nation of shopkeepers', as Napoleon dismissively called the British, would also feature in the field of high-street commerce in Russia. Among the many British-owned shops that were established in Russia during the 18th and 19th centuries, the one founded by the Scottish partnership of Muir and Mirrielees in Moscow was the largest and best known. Archibald Mirrielees, originally from Aberdeen, came to Russia from London in 1822 to set up a St Petersburg office for his employers, Fisher & Co. Over the next twenty years, Mirrielees married twice, raised a large family and prospered in business such that by 1843 he had established his own trading company in Russia. It was his second marriage to Jane Muir in 1844 that brought him into contact with his eventual partner, Andrew Muir. Andrew and his elder sister, Jane, came from a family of successful merchants and entrepreneurs in Greenock, near Glasgow and it was probably Andrew's business background that persuaded Mirrielees to invite his brother in law to join him in his Russian enterprise in 1852. Despite the onset of the Crimean War, both Mirrielees and Muir remained in St Petersburg continuing to run their business, now known as Mirrielees and Muir, unhindered by the Russian authorities. In 1857, Mirrielees decided to retire after thirty-five years in Russia and he returned to Britain with his wife Jane, leaving Muir in charge of the company.

---

[177] Jonas Hanway, *Historical essay about English trade in Caspian Sea*, 1753.

[178] Charles Marvin, *The Petroleum of the Future; Baku, the Petrolia of Europe*, 1883.

Muir married in 1861 and like his former partner, he raised a family in St Petersburg and steadily expanded the trading business of M&M which was primarily based on selling imported European haberdashery to the wholesale trade from showrooms on the top floor of a prestigious building on St Petersburg's principle street, the Nevsky Prospect. Although the business was doing well in St Petersburg, Muir recognised the growing potential in Moscow and opened a branch there in 1867. Muir retired in 1874 and returned to England with his family, leaving the M&M business in the hands of his young stepson, Walter Philip together with his nephews, Archy and Fred Mirrielees who had by now also joined the company. Muir remained a partner in the business, continuing to periodically visit Russia and was involved in the important decision to purchase a three-storey building opposite the Bolshoi Theatre in Moscow which allowed M&M to open up their first retail outlet in 1885. The business prospered and by 1891, the original wholesale side of the company was closed so as to concentrate on the retail department store in Moscow. With the death of Andrew Muir in 1889, Walter Philip became the principal guiding hand in the continuing development of the M&M business, setting up a printing works and a highly successful furniture-making factory which became one of the leading manufacturers in Russia. In their 1898 advertisement, M&M now claimed to be 'Russia's first and largest universal stores' with close to 1,000 employees. By 1915, the number of employees had grown to 2,800, serving 40,000 customers each day and, despite the ongoing First World War, profits reached record levels. With the onset of the Bolshevik revolution, the store continued to trade, even though many of its customers were leaving Moscow. The British management team clung on until November 1918 when the company was effectively nationalised.[179] Walter remained in Moscow but died from bronchitis the following June at the age of seventy-three.

There was one other notable high street retailer with significant British involvement, the well-known confectionery business of Landrin in St Petersburg. Established by Georg Landrin in 1848 to manufacture and sell chocolates and sweets, the company became one of the largest and best known confectionery businesses in Russia. By 1883, Landrin had become one of only two confectionery suppliers to the Russian Tsar and the company traded from a prominent store on the Nevsky Prospect. However, in the latter part of the 19th century, the business ran into financial problems and the Hides, an English family in St Petersburg, stepped in to provide new finance. Charles Hide, possibly born in Yorkshire around 1782, had arrived in Russia around 1814 along with several other Englishmen to set up the new Imperial paper mill in St Petersburg. Hide was employed there until at least the 1840s and then possibly moved to the new Imperial Mint which like the Imperial Papermill was constructed using the latest machinery imported from Britian. The Hide family later became involved in the development of the important cotton textile industry in Narva, Estonia. It was Charles Hides' grandsons, Charles William and Charles Louis who bought shares in Landrin and subsequently joined the board, running the confectionery business very successfully until the Bolshevik

---

[179] The M&M store was renamed TsUM under the Soviets and continues to trade.

revolution in 1918. Unfortunately, like many other businessmen of that time, the Hides lost everything when their companies were nationalised by the Russians. Although the family later submitted a claim for compensation of almost three million roubles, nothing was ever received from the Soviet government. The Landrin name survived however, and the business has continued to trade to the present day.

As we have seen, virtually all the British businesses were run mainly by the British, either by members of the founding family or managers subsequently recruited from Britain. As these companies grew, an increasing number of key skilled workers were brought in to operate the modern equipment (often imported from Britain) and to train local workers.[180] A similar situation existed at many of the more progressive Russian-owned businesses where British (and other foreign) managers or skilled workers were employed. The opportunities and rewards for these foreign workers emigrating to Russia in the second half of the 19th century and early 20th century were considerable as, for much of this period, Russia was the fastest growing economy in Europe. But the potential was not widely appreciated and compared with the opportunities in North America, Australia and later southern Africa, the challenges of Russia's climate, language and culture dissuaded many. But of those that did come, a high proportion stayed on beyond their initial contracts, moving to more senior positions or setting up in business on their own and fanning out across the country. Barry[181] cites the example of an enterprising British man he met in the remote town of Tiumen in western Siberia:

'*I was a foreman in Glasgow seven years ago, when I had the offer of coming here. I wanted to better myself... I have got 15,000 roubles (about £2000) in the bank... and now I am going into building steam-boats, which I mean to run on the Siberian rivers.*'

It would have been almost unthinkable for such a man to accumulate this sum over the same period working in Britain. Much the same applied to the British women who arrived in Russia to work as nannies and governesses, many of whom came in the hope of earning enough money to lead a comfortable life back in England. Other than work as a nanny or tutor, it was difficult for British women to find jobs in Russia but one that did was Edith Kerby. Her parents left England for St Petersburg in 1875 where her father, Henry Kerby, joined the city's British-owned Waterworks Company. Edith was born there in 1892, the youngest of seven children and together with five aunts, the whole family lived in a rented house in St Petersburg. Edith spoke four languages, English and Russian acquired at home plus French and German which she learnt at her St Petersburg school. Edith also taught herself shorthand and when her father died unexpectedly in 1912, she started work as a translator for the newly arrived St Petersburg correspondent of *The Daily Telegraph* newspaper, Edwin Wilcox. The introduction was obtained through her brother Harry who was also working in Russia and Edith later became Wilcox's assistant and right-hand girl, the pair

---

[180] By the turn of the 20th century however, the number of Russian managers was increasing as a result of internal training programmes and the output of Russian technical schools.
[181] Herbert Barry - ibid

of them working closely together from a small office in Singer House on Nevsky Prospect. When Wilcox was recalled to London in late 1916, Edith was offered a similar job compiling daily press reports for the newly formed Anglo-Russian Commission, where her boss turned out to be the young writer Hugh Walpole.[182] Her evenings were often spent working in centres set up to help the thousands of refugees then pouring into St Petersburg. It was in this context that Edith met the Emily Pankhurst, the English suffragette leader who visited Russia to investigate the contribution of women to the Russian war effort. Edith was given the job of interpreter to Pankhurst during her ten-day visit.

As conditions deteriorated in St Petersburg during 1917 due to the mounting civil unrest, Hugh Walpole was transferred back to London to work in the Russian department at the Foreign Office and Edith was offered the opportunity to go with him to also work at the Foreign Office. She had never even been to England but always dreamed of going there to live and so eagerly seized this chance to go to England and fulfil her dream, though sad at having to leave many of her family behind in Russia. However, shortly after, Edith's mother and eldest sister escaped to China to join another of Edith's sisters who was living in Shanghai. They travelled on the last train from western Russia to arrive in China and her other sister reached Stockholm leaving only Edith's five aged aunts in St Petersburg. One of them was a companion to a Russian princess and the pair escaped from Russia, arriving safely in England late in 1917. The other four aunts chose to remain; all their savings were held in Russian banks and there was no possibility of transferring funds abroad during the Revolution. These four ladies suffered terribly in St Petersburg during the dark days of 1918 and 1919 and the eldest aunt died of starvation. The three remaining aunts were finally allowed to leave Russia in 1919 and were met by Edith on their arrival in England. They were a forlorn sight and in a desperate condition, having not only lost a great deal of weight but also their hair, teeth and nails. However, with months of careful nursing, they all regained their health (though sadly not their teeth) and lived on to a good age.

From very early on in the Anglo-Russian relationship, it is clear that the British provided finance to both the Tsarist government as well as members of the nobility. As we have already seen, the funds, whether loans or outright gifts, were initially from government to government but in the 18th century, private moneylenders entered the scene and the first of these was probably Richard Sutherland. He was the eldest son of Alexander Sutherland, a Scottish shipbuilder who had come to Russia in 1736 where he enjoyed a successful career working for the Tsar in Archangel. His son chose not to follow his father into shipbuilding but instead joined the Russia Company in 1763 as an apprentice. His decision to go into business seems to have been a wise one as he soon proved to have a sound commercial sense and financial acumen. He went into partnership with a John Watson and was later joined in the business by his three younger brothers, John, George and Alexander. The latter subsequently returned to England to run the company's London office. Sutherland became a favourite of the Empress Catherine and Prince Potemkin and in the early 1780s

---

[182] Walpole had originally gone to Russia as a volunteer stretcher bearer in the Russian Army.

was appointed court banker. In this role, he was responsible for administering official Russian financial transactions overseas and in particular those relating to the running of Russian embassies in Europe.

During a period of financial turbulence on international markets in 1788, Sutherland provided key advice both to the Court and the merchant community in Russia and later that same year he was created a Baron of the Russian Empire. Sutherland continued to prosper until early 1791 when certain financial irregularities came to light regarding his operations on behalf of the Russian state. A series of lengthy investigations followed which ultimately showed that some two million roubles had been embezzled by Sutherland. Conveniently perhaps, Sutherland died in October, before he could be accused and brought to trial and Sutherland's son, also Richard, essentially took over the running of the business. Initially, Catherine was unsure how to handle the scandal which was made worse by the fact that many senior Russians, including Potemkin, had sizeable debts outstanding to Sutherland. She ordered the Russian treasury to settle many of the debts while allowing enquiries to continue. Meanwhile, the young Sutherland, who had inherited his father's title, reorganised the company with new partners but by 1794 it was clear the game was up and the company was declared bankrupt. Most of Sutherland's personal assets were seized by the Russian government and although he later tried several new ventures, his commercial abilities were clearly limited and they ended in failure, leaving him deeply in debt.

Another Scottish financier was William Grey who throve as a trader and moneylender in Russia during the latter part of the 18th century. However, in the 19th century, the private merchant banks established in London became increasingly important to the Russians as a source of finance, largely due to the size of the loans now required, and the most pre-eminent of the British banks was Barings, founded by Francis Baring in 1762. The cost of the Napoleonic War nearly bankrupted the Russian treasury and this provided the opportunity to both the Barings and Rothschild to enter the Russian market in a major way. Between 1818 and 1850, Barings alone provided some £15 million in loans and bonds to the Russian government and they remained in contact even during the Crimean War. Their importance was recognized internationally and the prime minister of France, the Duc de Richelieu, is reputed to have remarked in 1820: *"There are six main powers in Europe; Britain, France, Austria-Hungary, Russia, Prussia and Baring-Brothers."* In the 1850s, Barings lent the Russian government over £5 million to pay for the completion of the first railway line between St Petersburg and Moscow. The British were also important players in the Russian insurance market, especially the Northern Assurance Company that would later become part of Commercial Union. It appointed its first agents in St Petersburg in 1856, underwriting its first life policy there the following year. They later expanded into Odessa and in 1864 the company took £7250 of premiums in Russia. Norwich Union also entered the Russian market around 1865, followed in 1883 by the Lion Fire Insurance Co., which later became part of General Accident.

Life in Russia for the British businessman was not always easy. Dealing with corruption and pettifogging administration were almost daily events; the periodic outbreaks of serious epidemics, especially cholera and occasional civil unrest were much more serious and potentially fatal as illustrated by the tragic story of Joseph Crawshaw. He was a manager in a factory in Teikovo, east of Moscow in 1895, when during a wage dispute a mob entered his house and murdered him, dragging off his body to be nailed to factory wall.[183] William Horwood Stuart, a British businessman and the British vice-consul at Batum, Georgia was shot dead there in 1906. It seems likely that his murder was related to some local corruption or extortion affair. A different problem experienced by businessmen was the frequency of religious holidays set by the Russian Orthodox Church. The Welsh industrialist John Hughes found a unique way to deal with the large number of religious holidays in Ukraine. He carefully cultivated a friendship with the local Orthodox bishop and once he felt the time was right, after a substantial genial dinner, Hughes made him a proposal. He explained to the bishop that:

'for the success of the new enterprise, so vital to the State, so advantageous to the people, it was absolutely necessary to increase the number of working days. Unfortunately, this could only be done by docking the Orthodox hierarchy in Heaven of some of their rights on earth.' [184]

The canny Hughes went on to explain that there were so many saints' days that surely some were more important than others to the church so would it not be possible to delete a few of the less important ones? In return, by way of compensation, Hughes offered to pay to the Orthodox church, in the person of the bishop, an amount based on all the extra steel produced as a result of this concession. *'The proposal was favourably met. The Calendar was sent for, and Welsh ex-miner and Orthodox priest went carefully through it, retaining all names of importance, striking out those of least significance, till in the end John Hughes had gained 10 or 15 per cent, of working days in the year.'* [185] How this substantial new income was to be split between the bishop and his church was left entirely to the bishop's conscience to determine.

In the 20th century, the increasing level of civil disorder and strikes caused considerable disruption to production. When the First World War broke out, British employers found their Russian workers called up into the Russian army quite haphazardly with no regard to the type of work they did and its importance for the war effort, with only the railways and munition plants protected. Also most of their younger British employees left to volunteer in the British armed forces resulting in key skill shortages, all at a time when many of the companies faced an increasing workload with high priority for government orders. During 1917, the situation for most of the British still working in Russia became increasingly threatening, occasionally turning to violence and it was often impossible to keep businesses running efficiently. Over the ensuing twelve months almost all the surviving British businesses in areas under the control of the Bolsheviks were nationalised without compensation. Initially some of the British company owners or workers stayed on but most soon found themselves

---

[183] Harvey Pitcher, *The Smiths of Moscow*, 1984.

[184] John Baddeley, *Russia in the Eighties*, 1921.

[185] John Baddeley – ibid.

being literally thrown out through the factory gates by their former employees or fellow workers. Those with any sense now quickly fled the country.

13
British Life in Russia

According to a recent survey, the British have the most positive attitude towards Russia of all major western countries.[186] Yet, from the earliest days of contact, the opinions of the majority of British visitors to Russia during the period covered by this book were generally not very favourable. The Elizabethan impressions of Russia were split in two. On the positive side lay an admiration of the country's size, the number of its people and the abundance of its natural resources. For most, this was more than counterbalanced by a dislike of the Russian manners and behaviour, viewed as highly uncivilised, violent and primitive according to Elizabethan standards. Also, the Russian government compared poorly against Elizabeth I's reign at home: *'the common people suffer and naturally are mean and coarse'.*[187] Despite the growth in trade and the numbers of Britons going to visit, work and indeed to settle in Russia, this view persisted well into the 19th century as the following selection of writers' comments show:

'When a foreigner arrives in St Petersburg for the first time, he is forcibly struck with two things the magnificence of the city, and the high degree of civilization of its inhabitants, contrasted with the wild natural state in which the greater part of the country around it still lies, and the rude uncultivated appearance of the natives.'[188]

'There is scarcely any nation in the world so deficient of decency as the Russians ....

'I know of no people more offensive for their unclean habits than the Russians'.[189]

'The influence possessed by Russia in the councils of Europe is a perfect incongruity, for though her extent of territory is enormous, her natural resources great, her court surrounded by all the insignias of civilisation, and her capital replete with all the luxuries of life, she is the lowest in the scale of those nations that have any claim or pretension to be called civilised'.[190]

Russia's system of government was held in equally low esteem as this comment made by Lieutenant-Colonel George Cameron shows:

'No despotism was ever so complete .... as that of the Muscovy Sovereignty!'
[191]

---

[186] Pew Global Attitudes Project, 2012.

[187] *Of the Russe Common Wealth*, 1591. The Muscovy Company worried that Fletcher's frank account and criticisms would offend the Tsar's government and thus damage trade so the book was suppressed and only reprinted in its entirety in 1856.

[188] Robert Pinkerton – ibid.

[189] George Keppel, *A Journey Across the Balcan*, 1831

[190] Captain William Jesse, *Russia, Circassia and the Crimea*, 1841

[191] George Cameron, *Personal Adventures in Georgia, Circassia and Russia*, 1845.

He went on to state that Louis XIV's famous saying *'L'etat c'est moi'* applied even more so to the Russian Tsars. British attitudes towards Russia moderated for a while after the Anglo-Russian alliance during the Napoleonic Wars. The Russians were now seen as important allies and friends of Britain and many of the Russian nobility visited Britain which helped develop personal relationships as well as an appreciation of British culture and the way of life. Indeed, many Russians became as at home in the drawing rooms of London as the salons of St Petersburg. However, the increasing competition between Russia and Great Britain for spheres of influence during the Great Game, followed by the Crimean War, stoked up Russo-phobia in Britain with British propaganda at times portraying Russians as uncultured Asiatic barbarians.

Despite the Anglo-Russian entente of 1907, the largely negative British attitudes towards Tsarist Russia continued until the First World War, with the country still widely seen as backward and ruled over by an autocratic government. Official British wartime propaganda focused on presenting a more positive image of Russia in Britain with writers and journalists trying to build on the reputation of Russian literature and ballet. Although many British people welcomed the abdication of Tsar Nicholas in 1917 and were initially supportive of the Bolshevik revolution, the subsequent tales of horror and violence that emerged once again swung public feelings against Russia. Even the influential British economist John Maynard Keynes, writing much later, claimed there was an inherent *"beastliness in the Russian nature"* as well as *"cruelty and stupidity"*.[192]

Yet behind and beyond this apparent antipathy towards Russia and many of its institutions, there lay a genuine warmth of feeling towards the people and their way of life, at least by those who spent some time in the country. Although many things were very different, the language, a strange alphabet, an extreme climate, the food and culture as well as the vast size of Russia, a glance through almost any of the books about travelling in Russia listed in Appendix II reveals descriptions of the hospitality of local people plus the fun and enjoyment of life that could be had in the country. Invitations to grand balls or dinners at Court, visits to the theatre or ballet, summer picnics in the countryside, a sledge ride through the deep snow, skating on the frozen rivers and lakes or simply walking through fields of wild summer flowers or in the vast expanses of forest all helped to make life in Russia bearable.

"Strangers are faced with many inconveniences, but also with much that is very desirable and enjoyable. Every effort is made on the part of the Russians to render the sojourn of foreigners amongst them as agreeable as possible. Peculiarities and caprices of strangers are regarded not only with patience, but with respect and indulgence, and they are on all occasions treated with such consideration and kindness as cannot fail to make a deep impression." [193]

Although topographically Russia is generally less remarkable than Europe or the USA, the vast expanses of the Russian landscape still had the power to impress. The urban centres of Moscow and St Petersburg also provided stunning

---

[192] *A Short View of Russia, Essays in Persuasion*, 1932.

[193] Amelia Lyons, *At Home with the Gentry*, 1998.

aspects to visitors. Sir Robert Ker Porter described the winter scene that lay before him from the top of a Russian church:

'The sun shone with unattempered splendor through an atmosphere, whose clearness cannot be conceived in England; the variegated colours on the tops of innumerable buildings; the sparkling particles of snow on the earth and palaces; the fanes and crescents of the churches flashing their blazing gold; and, added to all, the busy world beneath, passing and repassing in their superb dresses and decorated sledges, presented such a scene of beauty and grandeur, that I should have thought myself repaid for my disagreeable journey, had I even been obliged to return to St Petersburgh immediately, in beholding so glorious a view'. [194]

Life for the majority of British residents in the larger cities of Russia was generally a pleasant experience with the wealthier ones living in almost aristocratic comfort, at least until the First World War. By the end of the 18th century, St Petersburg's grand embankment facing the River Neva had become known as the English Embankment due to its large number of British residents. The distinguished Greig family lived at number 62 for more than a hundred years, a little further along was the large blue and white mansion once owned by Sir James Wylie, John Rogerson lived at number 21, the prominent merchant, Samuel Orchard Gwyer and his wife Ann, resided at number 70, number 38 was owned by Clarke the grain merchant and at number 6 was the wealthy Cazalet family. The English Embankment boasted a British hotel run by Miss Benson and the English Anglican church; elsewhere in the city, there were British boarding-houses and British shops selling vital imported foods such as marmalade and shortbread. The British shops also became popular with the Russians. Although in the late 19th and early 20th centuries most upper-class Russian women preferred to purchase their clothes in France, usually during their annual holiday there, for the fashion-conscious Russian man however, the style became increasingly English, satisfied by the English outfitters in St Petersburg.

A wide variety of British clubs and sporting facilities were established, including an English debating society and a monthly English literary review plus several English schools. The elite among both the British and Russian communities were even able to go hunting with imported British hounds. There was a branch of Britain's Bowlton & Co. Bank as well as a British bookshop and reading room, which were also very popular with the local Russians. The city's first English-language newspaper was called *Friendship* and there were a number of British charities and hospitals in the city. As the size of the British community in Russia increased in the latter part of the 19th century, so did the amount and quality of their social life, at least in the larger cities. The theatre, opera, ballet and music concerts were regular and of a high standard. Dances and parties which invariably started late were also popular.. The invitations might be for nine or nine thirty p.m. but people rarely arrived much before ten thirty or eleven p.m. It was quite normal to go to the opera or the ballet and then on to the dance which often meant returning home at four or five a.m. In the

---

[194] Sir Robert Ker Porter - *Travelling Sketches in Russia and Sweden*, 1809.

summer, many were able to enjoy country dachas or holiday homes on the coast and for the wealthy, a variety of servants, nannies and governesses eased the stresses and strains of day-to-day living.

The situation was similar, at least from the mid 19th century onwards, for the British living in the provinces. Even places like Odessa and Hughesovka had English hotels or clubs that offered decent dining and a bar plus access to English newspapers. Although the British communities had to organize much more of their own entertainment, they did so with gusto, arranging plays, music concerts and sporting activities. One visitor to the Hughes' family home in Hughesovka wrote:

'As I entered the house, a Chopin waltz was being played on the piano. ''You will find us in the billiard room after you have dressed'' said my host. It seemed like a dream, so much civilisation.' [195]

Comments about the social life in St Petersburg by both residents and visitors were almost without exception favourable. James Wishaw felt that:

"The English colony (especially those in society) was a large one, and one could dine out practically every evening without meeting the same people twice. No English people living out of their own country could have lived happier or more jolly lives than we did... It was a bright and comparatively care-free life - visitors from the old country always carried away with them happy and perhaps somewhat envious recollections." [196]

John Baddeley, news correspondent for *The Standard* in Russia for almost twenty years in the late 19th century was equally enthusiastic about the British community, which:

'at the time of my arrival in Russia (had reached) a stage that as far as regarded social amenity left really nothing to be desired. There were very few old people, the great majority of the leaders of the community being, by chance, young married couples, nearly all in receipt of good incomes and possessed of spacious apartments in St Petersburg and pleasant country quarters at Lígovo, Mourino or elsewhere – with tennis lawns – where they spent the summer months and where they delighted to entertain their friends. There were pretty girls about, too, and altogether a more pleasant society, for a young man, it would have been difficult to find anywhere.' [197]

The English Club in St Petersburg, which was founded in 1770 by the English entrepreneurs F. Gardner and C. Gardiner rapidly became the centre of social life in St Petersburg for British men. It was based on the example of similar clubs in London and although called the English Club, membership was open to all nationalities but women were not permitted. By the end of its first year, it had a membership of 250 and over the ensuing century, the club occupied several different buildings in the city. The club's income was based on annual membership fees, donations and income from card games played at the club. In the 19th century, the club steadily evolved from its initial, mainly local British merchant base into a broader and more aristocratic establishment, with

[195] Sir Henry Norman, *All the Russias*, 1902.

[196] James Wishaw – ibid.

[197] John Baddeley – ibid.

members of some of the most eminent Russian families, top officials and cultural figures. Despite its high profile membership, the club was closed on the orders of the Anglophobic Tsar Paul but reopened a couple of years later in 1800 with the agreement of Alexander I. By the middle of the 19th century, although membership had grown to 400 with almost as many on the waiting list, the vast majority of members were now Russian and it had become a centre for gambling. A new English club was set up elsewhere in the city towards the end of the century which catered more for the British. Both clubs finally closed their doors during the Bolshevik uprising.

Yet life in Russia could still be tedious, annoying and full of challenges. Apart from the climate – extremely cold in winter, hot and humid in summer – the thing that seemed to most irk the British was the widespread corruption in Russia. Although the problems relating to bribery, corruption and kickbacks for officials would have been familiar to most Britons prior to arriving in Russia, their endemic nature across the whole country was a shock. By the 18th century, corruption in Russia had effectively evolved into a national institution, involving some of the highest officials in the land and was difficult or avoid or evade.[198] It was therefore inevitable that the British became caught up in its web, whether Russia Company merchants giving bribes for trading privileges, visitors paying extra for travel documents or businessmen handing over shares in their companies in appreciation of services rendered. George Cameron described the situation he found in the mid 19th century:

'*in the most barefaced manner, bribery and corruption of the very worst description... of which no public department... is exempt*' and '*it is morally impossible for a poor man in Russian service to be an honest one; he must either be a rogue like others or starve*'.[199]

If possible, the situation in Russia became even worse during the 20th century when shortages and disruption added to the corruption. Although most Russians professed strong allegiance to the Orthodox Church, their religion was often only skin deep; true belief and morality were largely absent, taking a back seat to self-interest and survival as Tsarist Russia and its people moved inexorably towards total meltdown.

There were other very real downsides to living in Russia. Travelling outside the main cities, especially in winter, had always been difficult due to the climate, the poor roads and the threat from wild animals that roamed the steppe. In the latter part of the 19th century, the dangers increased with the possibility of attack by wandering, homeless peasants, escaped convicts or bands of robbers. Disease and epidemics were a regular and very real threat to life in Russia as the British army discovered during the Crimean war when its casualty rate from illness was higher than that from wounds in battle. The danger from periodic cholera outbreaks was especially serious during the 19th century and many of the British families resident in Russia returned home until the outbreak had passed. Although the mounting civil unrest, strikes and riots in the late 19th and early 20th centuries were not a direct threat to the British community, they disrupted

---

[198] Many would argue that it has remained a national institution into the 21st century.

[199] George Cameron – ibid.

life in general, as well as business and trade. Sometimes the riots were against the Jews who were unfairly blamed for many of Russia's problems and as they were often the shopkeepers, food shortages often resulted. In a few cases, all these events could occur at the same time as Leah Steel, the wife of a British worker in Hughesovka, experienced one Sunday in 1892:

'*I had just come home from Sunday school... people were running all over the place... a riot was in progress. An epidemic of Cholera was raging, and many people were dropping dead in the streets. The 'Cholera wagons' went through the streets picking up the dead. We were taken then to a military barracks... until the next day. We came home to find all the stores burnt down. Most stores were conducted by Jews, who were very unpopular with the Russians, so they were all burned and looted. Martial law was proclaimed until order was restored'.*[200]

Steel was to experience further riots and an outbreak of cholera in Hughesovka in 1905 and 1910. Amelia Platts (see page 263) also witnessed riotous attacks on the Jews in her home of Odessa. In a letter to her Aunt in England in November 1905 she wrote:

'*The hatred between the Russians and Jews has burst out again & fearful slaughter is still going on in the outskirts of the town... no troops have been out & the hooligans allowed to roam about and pillage at will (a mob of 10,00 at its peak) - they always made for the Jews, their houses and shops. The Jews were prepared and armed, fortunately & at every street about ten young men of a band of "Self Protectionists" to translate literally, have saved themselves.*' [201]

Not all the problems in Russia were quite as life threatening but they could still be extremely unpleasant, as the following description of an attempt to repel an invasion of locusts reveals:

'*An English lady gave us a very amusing account of the musical entertainments held in her house and gardens a few years before, at the time these swarms were in progress. Her husband (a British merchant) was, as of right, leader of the harmonious band, and for this purpose armed himself with a huge bell, which he swung with amazing effect. Next to him came the gardener with his watering-pan; after this zealous functionary came the footmen with the fire shovels; then the housemaids with their pots and kettles; and finally, the children of the family, equipped with teaboards and toasting-forks, which, assuredly, played no secondary part in this noisy concert'.*[202]

This was not an isolated event and a British visitor to Odessa described a similar noisy experience:

'*a fearful battle raging between the inhabitants and the ruthless enemies of vegetation. Every noisy weapon, from pistol to a mortar, from kettle-drum to a tin casserole, was rattling like thunder in the hands of the horrified citizens, for the purpose of defending their little domains'.*[203]

---

[200] Leah Steel – Memoirs, Glamorgan Records Office.

[201] Platts family memoirs

[202] Robert Bremner, *Excursions in the Interior of Russia*, 1839

[203] Edmund Spencer, *Travels in Circassia*, 1839

Another annoying problem was that although the British community received mail and newspapers regularly from home, they were often censored and certain books were banned completely by the Tsarist authorities. The British also had to be constantly wary in ensuring they abided by the myriad of rules and regulations governing daily life in Russia. A minor infraction could cause problems with the police and a major one might lead to prison or deportation. John Cole described how under Paul I, the dress of Englishmen was closely regulated by the police:

'They were ordered to wear a three-cornered ha.... a long queue measured to the eighth of an inch, with a curl at the end; a single-breasted coat and waistcoat; buckles at the knees and in the shoes instead of strings. Orders were given to arrest any person who should be found wearing pantaloons. An English servant was dragged from behind a sledge and caned in the streets, for having too thick a neckcloth, and if it had been too thin, that pretext would have been used for a similar punishment.' [204]

But not everyone obeyed the rules. Tom Wright, a friend of the Yeames family in St Petersburg, came very near to being banished from Russia around 1800. He had the temerity to refuse to stop his sledge and stand bareheaded in the snow, as all good Russians had to do when the Tsar passed by. One day when Wright was out on his sledge, he saw the Tsar's cavalcade approaching. Wright ordered his coachman to drive as hard as he could and not to slow down or stop until he reached the English Club. The Royal sledge with its three horses came alongside and the two sledges raced side by side for a while at full speed along the street until the Tsar eased ahead and drove on. Wright shortly arrived at the Club and descended full of pride at his prowess. His triumph, however, was but short-lived, for within ten minutes, officials arrived from the palace enquiring who was the Englishman who drove a troika with two bays and a grey and wore a fur coat with a sable collar. Wright was quickly identified but saved from any serious punishment by the personal intervention of the British Ambassador, who explained that Wright was very short-sighted. Soon after, the Tsar issued an order that in future Wright must wear spectacles, which he continued to do until he learnt a few months later of Tsar Paul's death. [205]

One of the unexpected complications that the British community in Russia had to deal with was the legality of British marriages in the country. The British community in Russia had been getting married happily (at least in most cases) for many, many years when in 1866 the question of whether these marriages were legal suddenly raised its head. The problem surfaced initially when a young man called Richard Webster decided to marry in Odessa. Webster was born into a Yorkshire farming family and he and his father became involved with a plausible English gentleman who persuaded them that a fortune could be made in Russia by salvaging the brass cannon left lying on the battlefield of Balaclava. Webster's father advanced the money needed to finance the enterprise and young Richard was sent to accompany their new partner to Odessa. A few days after arriving there, while Richard was negotiating with the

---

[204] JH Cole, *Russia and the Russians*, 1854

[205] M Stephen Smith, *Art and Anecdote*, 1927

Russian authorities, the English gentleman disappeared with the money as well as all their possessions, leaving Richard completely penniless and stranded.

Fortunately, Webster, who knew a little French, quickly found a job working for a Frenchman who owned a workshop for repairing agricultural machinery and a wool washing business. Webster settled in well and was soon promoted by the Frenchman to the position of chief clerk. A few months later, he wrote to his fiancée, Emma, in England asking her to come to Odessa to marry him, which she duly did and the pair were married shortly after her arrival in April 1866. The ceremony was conducted by the minister of the English Presbyterian Church at the British Consulate in Odessa in the presence of the Consul General, Eustace Murray and several witnesses. However, as they later discovered, the old adage 'marry in haste, repent at leisure' was not without foundation. By marrying so quickly after her arrival in Russia, Emma had fallen foul of the British residence qualifications and the marriage was deemed to be invalid. As it turned out, the Websters were not the only couple to have this problem, which was later blamed on Murray as he should have known the regulations and prevented the ceremony from proceeding. As a result of considerable correspondence between the English Church and the Foreign Office, a private member's bill, called the Odessa Marriage Act 1867 was passed by the British Parliament to resolve the situation and the Webster's marriage was declared valid. Although Murray was recalled to England the following year, the problem of the legality of British marriages in Russia lingered on.

The law in Russia was clear; persons of the Christian faith were allowed to marry freely as long as they either did so according to the rules of their church or used an Orthodox priest to officiate. For the British, this was all very well until following the Hambly case, it became evident that marriages had been conducted in Russia without the presence of a British consul. An attempt to clarify the position was made with the Foreign Marriage Act in 1892 but this only caused further confusion. The Act stated that British marriages in a foreign country could only be recognised if the British consul was present. If not, the marriage was not accepted as legal in Britain and all children born to this union were considered to be illegitimate. A wave of anxiety swept over those among the British community who had already married in Russia without a British consul present and an extended, agitated correspondence began between the concerned spouses, the Anglican Church and the British consulates. The Bishop of London became involved, since Russia was technically in his parish and eventually he issued a notice in 1895 to try to clarify the position. He decreed that marriages between British subjects were legal, whether or not a consul was present, as long as they were solemnized in church. However, civil marriages would have to be performed with a British consul present if they were to be recognised and for any British marriage in Russia to be registered at Somerset House, a consul had to be present. The Bishop totally failed to deal with the position regarding marriages between a British subject and a Russian and in his wisdom he left the matter to the Russian authorities. The chaos rumbled on until well after the Bolshevik revolution; Frank North, the British chaplain in Helsinki was still trying to sort matters out for one of his anxious parishioners as late as 1924.

It is hard to be precise about the numbers of British nationals in Russia at any one time as estimates vary considerably. In the first hundred years after Chancellor's arrival, the size of the British population in Russia was small, probably less than fifty. This original nucleus received a major boost with the arrival of large numbers British soldiers and sailors during the later part of the 17th century. It is likely that between two and three thousand came to Russia then, including wives and children. Many later returned to Britain and of those that stayed, their subsequent histories are largely lost to us as they Russified their names and merged into their local communities. The British population in Russia continued to grow through the 18th century and by the time Napoleon reached Moscow in 1812 a census showed at least 111 British living there[206] and in the 1820s there were more than 2000 in the St Petersburg region alone.[207] Around a third of these were merchants of the Russia Company and their families. If those living in other parts of Russia are added, the total number of British residents was likely to have been close to 2,500. By the outbreak of the First World War, there were probably around 6,000 British subjects resident in the Russian Empire with over 2,500 in St Petersburg, around 600 in Moscow and the rest scattered across the country (some sources give over 3,000 for St Petersburg and up to 1,000 for Moscow).

Over and above these figures, there were usually significant numbers of British visitors in Russia who would not have been counted in any of the surveys such as family friends and visitors, merchant seamen, travellers and tourists. Similarly, where British citizens had married Russians, their spouses and their children did not always take British nationality and so were not counted in the surveys, even though they formed part of the British community. In the same vein, there were liaisons between some of the British men working in Russia and local women and their offspring were also excluded from the numbers. By 1914, the unexpected original encounter of the British with Russia had developed into a relationship that had lasted for over 360 years. This was as long as their presence in North America and much longer than in their colonies in Africa, India, the Far East or Australia. Many British families had been in Russia for several generations like the Bairds, Carrs, Gibsons, Cazalets, Smiths and Hills and although they still maintained much of their British identity, they felt at home there and played an important part in the local communities.

As the numbers of the British community resident in Russia rose, this not only provided a steadily expanding base for an improved social life generally but also a wider choice of suitable local spouses. During the 19th century, many of the British families in Russia became increasingly interlinked through both marriage and common business interests. We have already looked at several examples of these influential Anglo-Russian dynasties such as the Yeames and Wishaws but as the following paragraphs reveal, there were several others. One of the most widely connected was the Webster family. Despite the problems described earlier surrounding his marriage in Odessa, Richard Webster prospered in Russia, setting up a successful shipping business in Kherson that

[206] Simon Sebag Montefiore, *Prince of Princes: The Life of Potemkin*, 1988
[207] Rev Knill – ibid.

operated two passenger steamers. Over the course of several years, Richard was joined by his sisters, Amelia and Mary-Rae, as well as his brother, Thomas. Richard Webster went on to have a large family in Russia though sadly, several of his children died during a cholera outbreak, along with their uncle Thomas. However, three daughters survived who also married in Russia and ultimately the extended Webster family was related to six other British families in Russia, the Wagstaffs, Woodhouses, Platts, Rogers, Macphersons and Staplebergs. When Richard Webster died at the good age of ninety-four, his son John took over the business which by now also included a coal business, a jute works and a champagne factory. John Webster was also Lloyd's assistant agent and Cadbury's representative for south Russia.

Richard's sister, Amelia, eventually married the British vice-consul in Odessa, William Wagstaff. His other sister, Mary-Rae, had married Arthur Slater Woodhouse several years earlier in England where they ran a hotel. When the business failed, they took up Richard's invitation and despite Mary-Rae being pregnant at the time, they sailed for Russia in May 1867. She ended up giving birth prematurely en route to her first son, William, during a storm at sea off the coast of Algiers. Arthur Woodhouse eventually joined the Webster business as their shipping agent in Nikolaev and later became the British vice-consul there, a position he held for many years. The Woodhouse's eldest son, William followed in his father's footsteps and joined the British diplomatic service and became vice-consul first in Batumi in 1891 and then Odessa in 1893.[208] That same year he married Selina Rogers, the daughter of Harry Rogers who owned an agricultural machinery import business in Odessa. He was one of the leading members of the British community in Odessa and a founder of the English Cricket Club as well as an excellent billiards player. William and Selina Woodhouse went on to have five children in Odessa before moving to St Petersburg in 1907 where William became vice-consul.

The Platts family in Russia into which the Websters also eventually married was started by Joseph Platts, an engineer from Derbyshire who came to work for the Black Sea Steamboat Company in 1837. He married Sarah Tandy and they had eight children in Russia. One of their sons, John, became the manager of the large locomotive works at Brianov near Moscow and was later employed as chief engineer at the Odessa Waterworks Company where he introduced the principle of bacterial filtration of sewage into Russia. His son, Theodore, later took over as manager of the Odessa Waterworks Company. Theodore married Amelia Webster and they in turn had four children in Russia. The size and extent of the Webster and Platts families in Russia were more than matched by the Moberlys. Their Russian roots go back to Edward Moberly from Cheshire who arrived in St Petersburg in the early 1780s to join the Russia Company. There he married Sarah Cayley, daughter of the British consul-general and the couple had eleven surviving children who in turn had ninety-three children and

---

[208] Like the Yeames family earlier, men from the Wagstaff and Woodhouse families filled several British consular posts in Russia during the late 19th and early 20th centuries.

256 grandchildren, many of whom went on to have distinguished careers in Russia and beyond.[209]

These long-term British nationals resident in Russia could be broadly split into two basic groups. Firstly, permanent residents who usually spoke at least some Russian, educated their younger children locally and were comfortable in Russian society. Some of these had lived in Russia for so long that their English acquired a distinctive accent peculiar to Anglo-Russians. Secondly, a smaller group of semi-permanent residents who made little or no attempt to integrate, usually because they knew their stay in Russia was of a limited duration. St Petersburg's British community was viewed as being more English while that in Moscow contained a higher percentage of people of Scottish origin. Apart from a few diplomats, the British community in the Russian capital was essentially middle-class, with a fascinating mixture of professions including merchant, accountant, jockey, ringmaster, cotton mill manager, clerk, weaving manager, banker, iron moulder, cotton carder, mechanic, electrical engineer, mining engineer, governess, foreman printer and head brewer. In Moscow, there was a higher predominance of business owners and factory or trading company managers who generally didn't socialise with the upper echelons of Russian society, each group going their own separate ways. The same was largely true for the working-class men that came to Russia. Although they might mix with the locals at public events on holidays, they mostly stuck with their own kind in organising their social lives. The language barrier was a significant hurdle, at least for the immigrant generation. Most of the children born to British parents in Russia learned the local language and in some cases were able to later act as translators for their elders. The number of marriages and liaisons between the British and the Russians does, however, indicate that the language barrier could be overcome.

One of the most important and enduring legacies of the British community in Russia was the introduction of recreational sports. As the numbers of British residents in Russia grew, they inevitably imported their own sporting habits. One of the first sporting events organized by the British was an annual boat race on the Neva between two crews drawn from the British diplomatic corps and the resident merchants. A St Petersburg newspaper report in 1851 stated:

'Now that we have a yacht club and horse racing we can honestly say English sport is here.'

Indeed, the English word 'sport' was then imported into the Russian language and the British led the way in the city's athletic life, founding its first clubs for rowing, biking, track and field, tennis and football. Tennis and cricket were probably the first with the founding of the Neva Lawn Tennis Circle in Saint Petersburg in 1860, followed by the Saint Petersburg Tennis and Cricket Club in 1868. By the end of the 19th century, lawn tennis courts had also been laid in several other cities, including Moscow, Kiev, Odessa and Taganrog. One of the earliest mentions of lawn tennis occurs in Leo Tolstoy's novel *Anna Karenina*, which was published in serial form in the years 1873-77. Tolstoy was known to be a keen player and had a tennis court at his country estate as was

---

[209] Anthony Cross – ibid.

Tsar Nicholas II who became a keen player. Towards the end of the 19th century, football arrived and teams quickly sprung up, mostly linked to the larger factories, first around St Petersburg and later in other cities where there were significant British residents. One of the earliest teams was set up in 1894 in Moscow by Harry Charnock who had played for Bishop Auckland in England and was reputedly the best player in Russia at the time. Another leading team was the Nevka team of mainly Scottish players from the Samson weaving mill in St Petersburg where football was apparently initially encouraged by the owners to distract the workers from drinking vodka on Sundays.

Most teams were a mixture of British and Russian players and matches, which were played in the summer only, soon attracted large crowds. A national league was established in 1901 and the first Russian intercity cup was played in Odessa in 1913 with twelve teams from across Russia, including Moscow, Rostov, Kharkov, Kiev, Sevastopol and Hughesovka[210]. The cup was actually won by Odessa who beat St Petersburg 4-2 in the final. The first international match between England and Russia took place in St Petersburg in September 1911 and the English team called *The Wanderers* won all four games convincingly – a result that would be highly unlikely today. Not all British sports met with the success of football or tennis in Russia. William Hopper tried to introduce rugby football in 1886 but an early game was stopped by police who considered it too violent and thought the game could potentially lead to rioting. Richard Smith who was employed at the Kolpino works tried to introduce curling to Russia and helped found the Moscow Curling Club in 1870 but the sport did not take off with the Russians. The same fate awaited golf and croquet, which were played almost exclusively by the British but disappeared with their departure after the Bolshevik revolution.

Probably the most influential and active of all the British community in Russia in terms of sports was Arthur MacPherson, born in St Petersburg in 1870. His grandfather had emigrated to Russia from Perth, Scotland in the 1830s and had built ships for the Tsar. MacPherson was a member of the Stock Exchange, a patron of the River Yacht Club, the Rowing Club and the Krestovsky Tennis Club where he organised the first international tennis tournament in Russia in 1903. In 1911, he was elected a member of the Russian Olympic Committee and in 1914, he received the Order of Saint Stanislaus from the Tsar, the first time anyone in Russia had been decorated for their services to sport. In addition, Arthur was a keen footballer, playing for a local team and became founder president of the Russian Football Federation in 1912. However, despite this distinguished record of service to sport in Russia, he was arrested by the Bolshevik secret police in 1917 and imprisoned in St Petersburg. The Bolsheviks later claimed that he had been shot for serving British interests. In fact, he had been taken from St Petersburg to a Moscow, kept in a miserable cell for many months where he contracted typhoid and without any medical treatment, he died towards the end of 1919. In a subsequent article, *The Times* reported 's*ome weeks later, three British soldiers, who had obtained permission*

---

[210] In his youth, the future Soviet prime minisiter Nikita Khrushchev, played for Hughesovka but not in this match.

to look for (his body), discovered it in one of the prison cells, buried beneath 40 others.'

Both of MacPherson's sons played tennis at the Krestovsky club and his youngest son, Robert, won the 1914 doubles title in Moscow with George Bray. The latter was an outstanding tennis player and won most of the Russian championships in the early 20th century. Born in St Petersburg in 1880, Bray became a director of the Russian-English Bank and treasurer of the Krestovsky tennis club. Bray left Russia for England during the Bolshevik revolution and settled in London. Robert MacPherson also returned to England to enlist when the First World War started and was appointed to the staff of Field Marshal Lord Kitchener as a Russian interpreter for a military mission led by Kitchener that was sent to Russia to try to persuade the Tsar to remain in the War. The mission sailed from the Orkneys in Scotland on board HMS *Hampshire* in June 1916 but the ship struck a German mine soon after leaving port and of the 655 men on board, only twelve survived. Nineteen-year-old Robert Macpherson and Lord Kitchener (whose body was never recovered) were among the dead.

14
Governesses, Nannies and Tutors

Since the arrival of the first English traders in the 16th century, the Russians had become accustomed to the presence of British men in their country. However, the unheralded arrival of an increasing number of British women seeking employment as nannies and governesses was certainly not expected by the Russians. This female invasion steadily gathered pace during the 19th century and these largely unassuming women were to have an impact right across the Tsarist Empire, most particularly on the upper echelons of Russian society. Although they were not quite as numerous initially as those from France or Germany, British governesses were to become the most highly prized and preferred of foreign domestic help and were employed by some of the most powerful families in Russia. Although popularly referred to as 'English' governesses or nannies, there were many who came from Scotland and Ireland as well as a few from Wales. We know very little about most of the thousands of these intrepid women in Russia but some of them did write about their experiences, which were published either in books or in letters and recollections that have survived in family records and archives.

Although the golden age for British governesses in Russia did not occur until the latter part of the 19th century, their roots can be traced back much earlier to the unfortunate Mary Hamilton who served at Court as a lady-in-waiting to the Empress Catherine I. Hamilton was a descendant of Thomas Hamilton who had emigrated to Russia during the reign of Ivan the Terrible. She became the mistress of Peter the Great and later, Count Orlov but was executed by decapitation in 1719 for abortion, infanticide, theft and slander of Empress Catherine.[211] Over the next three centuries there are periodic references to English governesses in both Russian and English publications. Alexander Paterson, the head of the Scottish missionary colony in Karass in the Caucasus described in his notes of June 1811 '*a Russian lady and her three daughters visited us. Her daughter spoke very good English. An English woman was with them as governess.*' Several of the early British travellers in Russia also mention in their books meeting young women employed as governesses. Captain Cochrane described how, when visiting a Russian family in Siberia, he met '*a very young and pretty Englishwoman, in the person of Miss Norman, who is going to educate the children of the governor of Kranojarsk; her accomplishments and amiableness duly fit her for the task, but her beauty will much expose her where she is going; so that she must shortly either marry well, or return to her family.*' [212]

---

[211] Hamilton was not the only English mistress of Peter the Great. The dubious honour was also enjoyed by the daughter of Colonel Munce, an English officer in the Russian army.

[212] Captain John Cochrane – ibid.

References to English governesses can also be found in Russian 19th century literature. Alexander Pushkin in one of a series of short stories published as *The Tales of Belkin* in 1830 described an English governess who he calls Miss Jackson. She is a dowdy, tightly corseted, forty-year-old spinster who is bored to death with her life in the uncivilised country of Russia but stays on because of the excellent pay. Like many other Russian descriptions of Englishwomen, Pushkin's Miss Jackson is a caricature but not too far from reality as many of the early British governesses were older single women who primarily came to Russia for the financial rewards. At a time when it was extremely difficult for single women to find employment in Britain, the job of a nanny or governess in Russia held out the prospect of earning sufficient money after some years to fund a comfortable retirement back in Britain. In fact, many of the British women found that they not only enjoyed the salary but also the life in Russia and stayed on with their host families, often looking after the next generation. However, some women had an additional motive for coming; the possibility of marriage to a wealthy Russian noble or military officer and for a few, the dream became a reality. Tolstoy employed an English nanny called Hannah Tracey for his three young children who arrived in 1866. She was the daughter of a gardener at Windsor castle and stayed with the Tolstoy family for six years but she suffered from consumption and moved to a new post in the warmer climate of the Caucasus where she ended marrying a Georgian prince. She was followed by other English governesses in the Tolstoy household. Tolstoy later wrote about an English governess in *Anna Karenina* who unlike her French predecessor does not have an affair with her employer. Chekhov mentions an English governess in two of his books, *The Cherry Orchard* and in an earlier short story *A Daughter of Albion*. In the latter, the unfortunate lady is described thus:

'a tall thin Englishwoman, with prominent eyes like a crab's, and a big bird-like nose more like a hook than a nose. She was dressed in a white muslin gown through which her scraggy yellow shoulders were very distinctly apparent. On her gold belt hung a little gold watch... she doesn't understand a syllable of Russian, whether you praise her or blame her, it is all the same to her! Just look at her nose! Her nose alone is enough to make one faint... the great stupid has been living in Russia for ten years and not a word of Russian!'

In *The Cherry Orchard* she is small but still thin, with long hair in pigtails and dressed in a man's suit, something of a lively tomboy. Neither description is very flattering but there is just a trace of reality about them.

The job of a governess ranged from being a nanny to the youngest children through to essentially being a companion or chaperone for the older girls in their late teens who were not allowed out on their own until the age of twenty-one. The ability of a governess to teach music was also highly regarded. The Russians employed their own nationals as nursery maids for the younger children but did not regard them as suitable for the position of governess. As the Russian nobility largely spoke French among themselves, Russian was only used to address local people of an inferior social status. It was therefore imperative for their children to be given the ability as early as possible to converse in French and later in the 19th century, to learn English. Many wealthy families would have both a British governess as well as a French or Swiss nanny. Salaries and working conditions varied and much depended on the whim of the Russian host family. But of all the foreign hired help, the British governesses were generally paid the highest salaries, usually ranging from £50 to £100 annually. In some families all meals were provided, in others the governess was expected to contribute towards her upkeep.

One of the earliest British governesses to arrive in Russia was Catriona MacKinnon who was born in the remote Isle of Mull in Scotland. MacKinnon's story is remarkable, not only because she eventually became governess to the Russian Imperial family but also the fact that her story was never written down at the time and largely only survived in the oral traditions of the islanders of Mull. MacKinnon was born around 1778, the oldest of four children, as a young woman she went to Edinburgh and lived with her aunt. Whilst there, she met a British lady whose husband held an official appointment in St Petersburg (possibly one of the Scottish doctors working at the Russian Court). MacKinnon was persuaded by this lady to return with her to Russia to become the family's governess. From her sheltered life in Scotland, MacKinnon, then aged twenty-six, was plunged into an entirely different world; Russia was then a nation at war and soon would experience the terror of Napoleon's invasion. At some stage, MacKinnon was introduced by her British employer to the Tsar's family and she subsequently entered the Imperial household, initially as a nanny to the future Alexander II who was born in 1818. She eventually became governess to the Imperial family and served through the latter part of Alexander I's reign into the first part of Nicholas I's reign. During her many years of loyal service to the royal household, MacKinnon was well paid and managed to accrue substantial savings. At some stage during her period with the Tsar's household, she met and then possibly worked for Princess Natalie Akazatoff Corsine from Odessa and in a will in 1836, the princess made a bequest of an annual payment of 2,000 roubles to MacKinnon. Five years later in 1841, the princess, clearly in some financial difficulty, borrowed 20,000 roubles at six per cent interest from MacKinnon and guaranteed her a second and equal amount, should MacKinnon survive her. Colonel Michael Kiriakoff, a member of the Tsar's Guard at St Petersburg and a landowner near Odessa, received the money from the princess and guaranteed repayment by giving MacKinnon two bills of exchange of 20,000 roubles each in his name – a substantial amount of money at that time.

Although she had now retired from her work as a governess, MacKinnon remained in St Petersburg throughout the Crimean War, seemingly under the protection of the royal family. She had been in the country for almost fifty years and felt at home there, although her financial arrangements were probably an additional inducement to stay. However, after the end of the Crimean War, Kiriakoff, now a general, ran into serious financial problems and his estate plus his assets were mortgaged to the Rural Bank in Odessa. With little prospect of receiving her money, MacKinnon then moved to Florence where she died a couple of years later in 1858. Her body was sent to Russia for burial and her funeral in St Petersburg was attended by Tsar Alexander II. According to Mull legend, as the coffin was lowered into the ground, the Tsar sang a Scottish lullaby in Gaelic that he had learnt as a child with MacKinnon. Unfortunately for her, the cemetery where she was buried was normally reserved for the Royal family and Russian aristocrats and was later completely destroyed by the Bolsheviks during the revolution. MacKinnon never received the money owed to her and for many years after, several of her descendants tried to claim the Russian debt but a combination of dubious documents, too many heirs and international conflict prevented the successful pursuit of a claim. [213]

Another of the early British governesses was a Miss Esterly who worked for the wealthy Davydoff family in 1815. They spent their summers in the south of France and Esterly went with them, possibly the first governess to enjoy the luxury of travelling abroad with a Russian family. Helen Pinkerton, a Scottish woman from Edinburgh was one of the pioneering British governesses with the Russian royal family. She was related to the Reverend Robert Pinkerton who had been part of the Edinburgh Bible Society's first mission to southern Russia in 1805. In 1835 when only seventeen, Helen married a German botanist employed by the Russians in St Petersburg and whilst still in her early twenties, she became governess to the young Grand Duke Nicholas, the third son of Tsar Nicholas I. Although Helen was later widowed, she remained in Russia living in a grace and favour apartment in the Duke's palace in St Petersburg until her death in 1905. She was not only one of the earliest British governesses to arrive in Russia but was also one of the youngest and longest British residents there. Soon after Pinkerton joined the royal family, Kitty Strutton became a nurse to Nicholas' younger brother, the Grand Duke Alexander. Strutton remained in Russia until her retirement when she was provided with a small apartment in the Winter Palace and her great niece, Millicent Crofts, followed in her footsteps as nurse to the Grand Duke Vladimir in 1876.

By the 1850s, the growth in worldwide demand for English governesses became so great that a vast galaxy of governesses began to migrate from the British Isles to countries across the world – a '*gigantic fifth column operated by a devoted band of genteel ladies and apple-cheeked nannies, which was to exercise enormous power and disseminate the traditional English way of life through European society.*' [214] During the rest of the 19th and early 20th century, the Russian market became one of the largest as well as the best paid for this genteel band. Britain's economic, cultural and political power was at its zenith and this was reflected in the worldwide interest in its social values, traditions and above all its language. Increasing wealth in Russia, especially amongst the rising group of industrialists, businessmen and professional people, combined with a growing interest in the ability to speak English, rather than French or German, fuelled demand for British governesses. This rising market coincided with a rising supply of young women willing and able to undertake the work overseas. In Britain, there were too many women chasing the limited number of positions available; more than 20,000 women were registered in the profession in England in 1850.[215]

---

[213] The Free Library, *Story of Scot and Russian Royals is Revealed,* 1999.

[214] Bea Howe, *A Galaxy of Governesses,* 1954

[215] Bea Howe - ibid

The main reason for the oversupply was the fact that this was one of the very few jobs that a respectable woman could do without losing her social status and as the type of family employing foreign governesses broadened, so too did the variety of British women taking up these jobs. With no state welfare support or pension for anyone unlucky enough to fall into hard times, a rising number of relatively well-bred and educated women found themselves with no alternative means of earning a living. The more traditional, well educated and older ladies were increasingly joined by younger women from a broader social background whose main quality was simply the ability to speak English. But as demand continued to rise, this skill was sufficient for them to be accepted into the best of Russian families. The fact that many of them had strong regional accents and did not therefore speak the 'Queen's English' was not considered a handicap in Russia. Prince Serge Obolensky, an Oxford-educated businessman, born in Russia in 1890, recalled his experience of learning English from his Scottish governess, Lizzie Arthur:

'Her English accent could hardly have been surpassed by Robert Burns himself. The result was that I learned to speak English like some Russian branch of a Highland clan, which highly amused my friends later at Oxford.' [216]

The emphasis in Russian families was on acquiring the ability to speak English, mainly as a social asset and at its extreme, there were some Russian children who learnt English before they had fully mastered their own language. The Russian writer Nabokov was an example of this strange phenomenon and in his early years, he had *'a bewildering sequence of English nurses and governesses'.*[217] However, the interest in English values and way of life often led to governesses being required to impart more than just the English language to their young charges. The governess became responsible for the moral, social and intellectual education of her charge and her ability to transfer the qualities of an English lady or gentleman were important. Since the Russian's approach to raising their offspring was much more relaxed and casual than in Victorian Britain, the English governess or nanny introduced discipline and structure into the household for the children, something that was not always welcomed by their charges.

Due to the oversupply, wages for those fortunate few who found a job were kept low in Britain and the typical wage for a governess in 1850 was only half the average annual wage of £48.74. In Russia, governesses could expect to earn at least £50 and usually a lot more. One aspiring young governess wrote: *'I intend to become rich myself, and then, oh! how gladly should I return.'* [218] As well as earning more money than they could in Britain, governesses in Russia were more highly regarded by their employers. *"At its best her position was that of an equal and respected member of the family, something that had not happened in England since the eighteenth century; and we shall hear of the English governesses attending important social functions on terms of complete*

[216] Harvey Pitcher, *When Miss Emmie was in Russia*, 1977.

[217] Vladimir Nabokov, *Speak, Memory*, 1951. The Nabokov family regularly spoke English at home, read *The Times* newspaper and closely followed the tennis at Wimbledon.

[218] E H Hamilton, *The English Governess in Russia*, 1861.

equality with the other guests. Even at its worst her position was still clearly differentiated from the upper servants." [219] It was not only easier to obtain a position in Russia, there were also significant additional benefits. A governess could also often supplement her wages by giving English lessons, summer holidays were usually spent with the host family by the sea or at their country estate and for those who stayed the course, there was the likelihood of a pension or invitation to live with the family free of charge for the rest of her life.

The motivation of some of the younger women that went to Russia as governesses was neither financial reward nor to seek a husband. Claire Clairmont, who worked as a governess in Moscow from 1825 to 1828, had an entirely different reason for leaving England. Clairmont was well educated and spoke several languages including French which no doubt helped her obtain the position in Russia. She had earlier been the mistress of the poet Lord Byron at the tender age of sixteen and bore him a child, Allegra in 1817. Their relationship did not last however and Byron rejected Claire and placed his young daughter in a convent in Italy where she died aged only five. Clairmont had been close friends with Percy Bysshe Shelley who also died a few months after her own daughter and these tragic events resulted in a distraught Clairmont moving first to Germany and then to Russia. Her period in Russia as a governess was simply a means of escape from the tragedies of her early life. For many of the younger women, the position of governess in Russia was seen not as a career choice but rather as a short-term experience or adventure during which they could save some money in preparation for a better life back home. Indeed, many of the young women who went to Russia were encouraged by the sense of adventure the trip promised. When Emma Dashwood (see page 279) carefully weighed the benefits and disadvantages of working in Russia, there remained *"the simple fact that she wanted to go, and was thrilled by the idea of this exciting new adventure."* [220]

Inevitably, the majority of British governesses and nannies were to be found in St Petersburg and Moscow and in the early 20th century, there were several hundred governesses working in these two cities each year. Although St Petersburg and Moscow were the preferred destinations for most British women that went out to Russia, a significant number tried their luck in the provinces. However, life in some of the more remote regions of the Russian Empire was less easy, especially for those in their first job who had not had the time to familiarize themselves to the Russian climate or customs. Those young women that had the misfortune to end up in places like Siberia, the Urals or the Caucasus found themselves cut off from the rest of the world and were often the only foreigner in the immediate area. Not surprisingly, many of them did not last long in these locations and moved to St Petersburg or Moscow to try to find better jobs or, totally disillusioned with Russia, they returned to Britain. One of the more remote assignments was filled by a young English widow who went out in the mid 1860s to Tashkent, the capital of Turkestan, which had only recently been captured by the Russians. She was employed as governess to the

---

[219] Harvey Pitcher – ibid.

[220] Harvey Pitcher – ibid.

family of General Kauffman, the Russian conqueror of Turkestan. She must have enjoyed her job and the exotic life in Tashkent as she was still there some fifty years later when Rosa Houston, an Irish governess arrived to work for another Russian family. Surprisingly, this remote corner of the Tsarist Empire also contained an English teacher called Smales who had married a Russian woman and had been living in Tashkent for fourteen years when Houston arrived.

Like many of the other governesses in Russia, Houston's hitherto quiet life changed dramatically during the Bolshevik revolution. In 1918, a British intelligence officer, Colonel Frederick Bailey, arrived in Tashkent on a mission to explore the Bolshevik's attitude towards India but was soon suspected of being a spy. Before he could be arrested, he went into hiding with the help of Houston and eventually escaped back to England. Houston decided it was time to leave and in September 1919 she applied for a new job as an English teacher at a Russian military school in nearby Askhabad from where she felt it would be possible to escape across the frontier into Persia. As soon as she reached Askhabad, she went into hiding while she sought a guide to take her across the mountains to Persia. She ended up paying an extortionate 240,000 roubles (which must have been her life savings) for a local guide and pony and duly set out. After three days and nights travelling through the mountains, Houston's guide suddenly deserted her, taking her pony and stealing her bag that contained her only belongings. Abandoned and totally alone in the middle of the remote mountains, she had no idea of where she was or how to continue her journey. Fortunately however, Houston met up with a band of smugglers the following day. They were initially understandably suspicious of this young foreigner wandering alone on foot in the mountains but eventually they agreed to take her to the frontier and true to their word they escorted her to the customs post at Jiristan. From there she was able to make contact with the British mission in Meshed, Persia who organized her eventual return home, where she presumably led a less stressful life.

During the 19th century, there were various agencies in both the UK and Russia that recruited governesses such as the Governesses Benevolent Society, formed in 1841 in London that effectively became an agency or clearing house for governess positions in the UK and overseas. Many of the governesses who arrived in the 19th century were strongly religious, often Methodists or Quakers, and in the 1830s Mrs Polly Scott started a clearing house for English Quaker and Methodist women in Moscow. Scott was the aunt of the novelist Nikolai Leskov who worked for several years at the British trading company of Scott and Wilkins which was then owned by Polly's husband, Alexander Scott. In Leskov's 1892 novel about Russian village life *The Vale of Tears*, he describes a Quaker governess whose great resourcefulness helped Russian serfs during a period of famine. She became so revered that they regarded her as a kind of saint. Another example was the enterprising Edith Sinclair from Norwich. She was the eldest of nine children and when she did not get on with her step-mother, she ran away from home. In the late 1890s, she finally ended up working as a nanny in an English family and when her employer decided to move to Russia, she accompanied them. There, she fell in love and married a

Russian naval officer and began to act as an unofficial employment agency for her relatives and friends. For example, she made arrangements for three of her sisters to come out to Russia to work; and Emma Dashwood was one of several family friends who also found a position as a governess in Moscow after first having worked for Edith herself. There was also a cafe in St Petersburg that was frequented by the English governesses and teachers where they exchanged information on new jobs and the desirability of prospective employers. By the end of the 19th century, the employment of governesses, at least in St Petersburg and Moscow became something of a closed system with good nannies and governesses being recommended and passed on between families and friends.

Finding a good job was one thing but with the rising number of young women seeking work in Russia, accommodation could also be a problem, either on arrival or when in between jobs. To help solve this situation, a women's hostel called St Andrews House was built next door to the Anglican church in Moscow, both largely privately funded by the McGill family. The large red-brick building opened in 1904 and was designed to normally accommodate around thirty women. The majority were transient residents, having recently arrived in Russia and looking for work or they were perhaps on their way back to Britain and breaking the long journey for a few days. Some were more of less permanent residents with their own rooms and would go out to work each day, returning for their evening meals. All residents shared a communal lounge and dining room, paying for bed and board as they went. The hostel even had its own lawn tennis court that was used in summer by both the residents and their pupils. Cats, dogs and smoking were all banned and any visitors were required to leave by eleven p.m.

Not all the English governesses actually came from Britain. The growing British community in Russia in the late 19th century also provided a recruitment source. As many of these women spoke some Russian and had experience of the country, they were able to fit into Russian family life much more easily than some young women straight from Britain. Also not all the British nannies and governesses worked for Russian families; some were employed by the growing number of British industrialists and businessmen in the country. One of the women who worked for a British family was Annie Gwen Jones from Wales who came out as a nanny and tutor for the family of Arthur Hughes in Hughesovka in 1889. She stayed there for three years and was fortunate to have enjoyed a relatively privileged life with the wealthy Hughes family but she also developed a concern for the less fortunate among the Russian people. She sympathised with the calls at the time for improved social conditions as well as the poverty of the peasants, the harsh treatment of the Jews and the suppression of the Polish people. She passed on her love of Ukraine and her high moral principles to her son Gareth Jones. He was born in Wales in 1905 after her return from Hughesovka and he became a famous journalist working for the *Western Mail* in Wales. The stories that his mother used to tell him as a child about her life in Russia made a deep impression on him and he visited Russia several times in the early 1930s to report for his newspaper on conditions under Stalin. Jones travelled through Russia and the Ukraine and was shocked at the conditions he encountered, especially the starvation and genocide in Ukraine and general repression in Russia. Although there were many western accredited journalists in Russia at the time, none had reported on this story. Jones estimated seven to ten million people died between 1932 and 1933 and was the first to reveal to the world the true conditions experienced by millions under the rule of Stalin. He was murdered in 1935 on the eve of his 30th birthday by bandits while travelling in Inner Mongolia, possibly at the instigation of the Russian government.

Despite being off the beaten track, Annie Jones found life in southern Ukraine both interesting and varied and she later recounted to her family back in Wales many stories of the happy times she spent there. She enjoyed going to the local market where the prices for most foods were very cheap and she was also intrigued by the signs hanging outside all the shops. These showed what was for sale in simple pictures not words, as most of the peasants were unable to read. There were occasional music concerts, skating on the lake in winter and one of her favourites, hunting foxes and hares out on the Steppe in the company of Cossack horsemen. The severely cold winters were hard to bear but the fun of sledge journeys across the glistening snow with the horses' bells ringing out in the clear air were a pleasant compensation. Such trips into the countryside were tinged with an extra sense of adventure due to the presence of wolves and occasional wandering bandits and robbers. The oppressive and stifling heat of the summers was also difficult with an increased risk from diseases like cholera or dysentery and Jones nearly died from the latter during her second summer. Like many of the other governesses in Russia, Jones also experienced a cholera epidemic and in 1892 she and the Hughes family had to flee the town following an outbreak of this serious disease and associated riots. However, despite all the problems, Jones *'had come to love the country and its people'* [221] and was sad to leave.

Perhaps the most prestigious and prominent of all the British governesses was Margaretta Eagar, who followed in the footsteps of Catriona MacKinnon and was employed in the Imperial household in St Petersburg. Eagar was born in Limerick, Ireland and went on to train as a nurse in Belfast. In early 1899 at the age of thirty-five, she obtained the position of nanny and governess to the four daughters of Tsar Nicholas II. In her role in charge of the Grand Duchesses Olga, Tatyana, Marie and Anastasia, Eagar was the most important and influential of all the governesses in Russia at the time. Her work at the centre of the Tsar's household also gave her exposure to the very highest levels of Russian society at a time of enormous political change, yet in her subsequent book[222] she largely ignored the dramatic events unfolding around her. Like many other British governesses in Russia, she seemed to have remained blithely oblivious to much of what was happening in the world outside her immediate surroundings of the nursery and schoolroom. In some ways, this was understandable as due to her position, her day-to-day life and personal freedom were relatively constrained. For example, she was not allowed to join the other British governesses for the Sunday ritual of tea at their club attached to the

---

[221] Annie Gwen Jones – BBC Radio interview, December 1943, Glamorgan Records Office.

[222] Margaretta Eagar, *Six Years at the Russian Court*, 1906.

English church and rarely travelled around St Petersburg on her own. The fact that she never bothered to learn to speak Russian was both a cause and reflection of her lack of interface with the Russian community. Although Eagar taught the Grand Duchesses to speak English well, they inevitably acquired a slight Irish lilt and in 1908, when their new English tutor Charles Gibbes arrived, one of his first jobs was to correct their pronunciation. Although Eagar built a close relationship with the girls, soon after the birth of the young Tsarevich Alexis in 1904, she left Russia and returned to England. The reason given in her book for her relatively abrupt departure was that it was a purely personal matter but it seems unlikely she would have voluntarily resigned such an important position. It is more likely that she was dismissed by the Tsar due to the political sensitivity of employing a British subject during Russia's war with Japan when Britain was supporting Japan. Sadly for her, after the murder of the Tsar and his family by the Bolsheviks, she lost her royal pension and despite subsequently working as a governess for several English families, she ended up penniless.

In the same way that Eagar had been the most prominent of British governesses in Russia, Charles Sydney Gibbes from Rotherham became the perhaps most famous English tutor. He taught Tsar Nicholas' children English from 1908 to 1917 and was well respected by the family who all called him Sydney. During his time in Russia, Gibbes, who was an academic and highly religious, became increasingly interested in the Orthodox Church as well as a strong admirer of the Tsar. When Nicholas abdicated the throne in March 1917 Gibbes lost his job but later bravely volunteered to join the Imperial family in exile in Tobolsk, Siberia where he continued to teach the royal children. After the murder of the family in 1918 Gibbes left for Omsk and briefly acted as secretary to the British High Commission in Siberia. As the Bolsheviks advanced across Siberia, Gibbes retreated with the British, eventually ending up in Manchuria working as an assistant in the Chinese Maritime Customs. He returned to England in 1928 to become ordained into the Church of England but decided this was not the right path for him and he returned to Manchuria where there was a large White Russian community and became an Orthodox monk, taking the name *Nicholas* in honour of the former Tsar. He eventually returned to England as an Orthodox abbot in 1937.

However, Gibbes was not the first official English tutor to royalty in Russia. In the late 17th century, the Scottish soldiers Menzies and then Gordon had acted as military tutors to the young Peter the Great and Henry Farquharson, a graduate of the Marischal College in Aberdeen had come to Russia to teach mathematics and geometry to Peter the Great. Also around the turn of the 19th century, Frank Cooke was a tutor to Prince Yusupov, the heir to immense family wealth and later to the Grand Duke Dmitri, cousin of the Tsar. Cooke then married and stayed on in Russia, renting a house near Moscow where he and his wife gave English lessons. As the English language became more important in Russia, several universities employed British teachers such as Charles Turner who was Lector in English at St Petersburg's Imperial University in 1864. His sister also worked in Russia as a governess and English teacher. Samuel Warrand, Thomas Shaw and Charles Heath all preceded Gibbes as royal tutors. Shaw, who was from Cambridge, spent twenty-one years in Russia as a tutor and lecturer of English at St Petersburg University and together with his father-in-law, founded the St Petersburg English Review of Literature in 1842, a monthly publication that was keenly read by both the British and Russians.

Of course, not all British governesses, nannies and tutors were perfect in the same way that there were good Russian employers as well as bad. But overall, the process worked well for both parties with most of the British being treated very fairly and delivering in turn a reliable, high quality service. Although as noted above, the portrayals of the British governess in Russian literature were rarely complimentary, most of these women proved to be faithful, honest and good humoured, displaying a remarkable level of common sense, courage and toughness in the face of the various crises that were to befall the Russian nation in the latter 19th and early 20th centuries. During these increasingly chaotic years, they provided a feeling of stability and social continuity for their families against a backdrop of wars, civil unrest, strikes, food shortages and pestilence. The period of Margaretta Eagar and Charles Gibbes represented the heyday for British governesses and teachers in Russia, both in terms of their numbers and the quality of life they experienced. In St Petersburg, most of their host families had luxurious holiday homes on islands in the Neva delta or around the Baltic Gulf. Others had large family estates in the country or rented homes around the Black Sea where the families plus their governesses would quietly spend the summer months. As well as the traditional pleasures of the theatre and ballet, the growth in leisure facilities in St Petersburg and Moscow allowed many of them to enjoy tennis, badminton, golf, yachting, skating and other winter sports. For those who wished to take advantage of the lively St Petersburg nightlife, there was plenty of choice; a night out in the capital did not start until ten p.m. and would usually go on until three or four in the morning. However, it was almost impossible for a young British woman to go out alone in such society and so most were unable to take advantage of the opportunities.

One of those who did manage to enjoy something of what St Petersburg could offer was Louisette Andrews who left her home in Wimbledon to go to Russia in the summer of 1912. She went not as a governess but to spend an extended holiday with her younger brother Emile, who had been working in Russia for several years as an engineer for the Westinghouse Company. Emile had arranged for his sister to stay with friends of his, the Tamplin family who originally came from Brighton where they owned a popular local brewery. The Tamplins were now well established in Russia, running a paint and enamel factory just outside St Petersburg and with family connections to the Thorntons, one of the largest mill owners in the country. Through her brother's extensive connections and intimate knowledge of St Petersburg, Louisette not only met a wide range of people in the city but was able to enjoy a lifestyle that for a young single woman would not otherwise have been possible. As it turned out, her time in St Petersburg proved to be so enjoyable that she decided to prolong her stay well beyond her original plan and was still there in early 1914 when her brother was recalled on business to London. As Emile did not expect to be away for long and Andrews was not yet ready to return to England, she felt it was time to find a job so that she could be independent and not reliant on the charity of his friends. She found a position with the distinguished family of Prince Andrei

Gagarin[223] as a companion and chaperone to their sixteen-year-old daughter, Kira. Andrews' duties proved to be fairly light, daily conversations and reading in English, regular tea parties and accompanying Kira occasionally to the ballet or opera concerts. Although Emile did not return to St Petersburg due to the impending outbreak of war later that year, Andrews was happy with her life and saw no need to return home. She stayed with the Gagarins for eighteen months and then moved on in 1915 obtaining a similar job for the summer with a Russian general's family on their large estate in Penza, almost 400 miles southeast of Moscow.

Ensconced in this semi-rural location with the family, Andrews had a most enjoyable summer. The terrible events that were taking place along the front line to the west, where the Germans were annihilating the Russian armies, seemed a long way off and were not spoken about. She returned to St Petersburg late that year and despite the worsening war situation for the Russians, she decided to stay and obtained a position as companion to the teenage son and two daughters of a very wealthy family called the Korniloffs. Andrews found them an easy family to be with and she was able to fully participate in their easy-going and busy social life in the city. The Korniloffs' fortune came from a large boat company they owned in Siberia and in the summer of 1916, the whole family left St Petersburg to go cruising on one of their own boats down the River Ob, visiting Irkutsk and Lake Baikal. Andrews must have been one of the very first from Britain to experience such a cruise on the Ob. The family ended the summer holidays at their house in Tobolsk but as it was full of prisoners of war at the time, they didn't stay long and returned to St Petersburg. A year later when the Bolsheviks exiled Tsar Nicholas and his family to Tobolsk, the Korniloffs' home was used to to accommodate the royal party. Tobolsk held another sinister connection with the Tsar's family as it was the province in which Rasputin was born. Apparently, the Korniloffs knew him and one evening after the family returned to St Petersburg, Rasputin was invited to dinner. Andrews was warned to be on her guard as Rasputin had a reputation when it came to women but she was totally unprepared for the sight of him eating his food at table with his hands. Like many others who met him, Andrews clearly found Rasputin repulsive and later aptly described him as '*greasy*'. [224] Andrews then joined many other governesses in St Petersburg doing voluntary work making bandages and dressings, initially at the Winter Palace and the following summer at Tsarskoe Selo, the Tsar's summer residence.

Andrews was not alone among the British governesses, nannies and tutors in choosing to remain with their families in Russia at the outbreak of the First World War in 1914. It was not expected to last long and there seemed no particular danger as the war zones were far away. General living conditions remained tolerable, at least until 1916 and although holidays in the south of France were no longer possible, visits to the Crimea or family estates in the provinces continued as before. However, the Bolshevik revolution in 1917 dramatically altered the picture with the rising violence and civil disorder

---

[223] One of his antecedents, Prince Nikolai Gagarin, was actually born in London in 1784.

[224] Harvey Pitcher – ibid.

causing both the governesses and their host families to rethink their position. Some of the governesses now followed the British government's advice and left Russia such as Rosamond Dowse. At the age of twenty, she had gone out to work in Samara in the spring of 1914, joining a Russian family that was already employing her brother as a tutor. Her brother was due to return to England that summer to take his law exams so Rosamond's job looking after three teenage girls was originally only for the summer months. Although the position in Samara was relatively remote, Dowse felt comfortable going to Russia as her aunt had also been a governess in St Petersburg for nine years and was now an English teacher there. Soon after Rosamond's arrival in Samara, her brother left for England but with the outbreak of war, he was unable to return and subsequently joined the British army. Rosamond was asked by the family to stay on which she duly did until 1916 when she took a new position with the Tolstoy family at Tsarskoe Selo near St Petersburg. This fortunate choice of location made it easier for her to arrange to leave Russia during the unrest of 1917 and she managed to return safely to her home in Norwich. However, Dowse never saw her brother again as, sadly, he was killed in the Battle of the Somme in 1916.

Many of the British governesses remained in Russia after the revolution, partly out of a sense of loyalty to their host families and partly because of the difficulties and dangers involved in trying to leave. Emma Dashwood was only twenty-two when she obtained a job as a governess with the Rahl family in Moscow in 1912, looking after their six-year-old son. The Rahls had a large estate near Staritsa, some one hundred miles north of Moscow and they treated Dashwood as one of the family. Although she intended to only go for a year, she so enjoyed her time with the Rahls that she ended up staying for two and a half years, returning to England in the summer of 1914. However, she was unable to settle and when the Rahls wrote her inviting her to return, Dashwood agreed to go back, despite the war and the difficulties of travelling to Russia. Early in 1916, after several months with the Rahls, she decided to move to St Petersburg where she found work with the family of a senior Russian naval officer. In April 1917, her new employers moved to the south of Russia to escape the civil unrest in Moscow, ending up in Yalta. Dashwood's family were not the only ones to have left for the south with their British governesses and it was all but impossible to find rooms for rent for the summer, everywhere was full, despite the troubled political situation. Although on the surface the days at the beach under the warm southern sun seemed normal, there was a tangible, underlying unease. Everyone seemed much more restrained than in earlier years, families largely kept to themselves and public social events were rare with the streets almost empty in the evenings.

As the pleasant summer weeks rolled by, the general feeling among the governesses was increasingly that it was time to leave Russia and it appeared that the best route out would be north via Moscow as the Black Sea was shut off by the Turks. Dashwood decided to make a move and left her family, paying her own train fare to Moscow. However, once there she was told by the British Consulate that there was no hope of leaving from Moscow and she would have been better off staying in the Crimea. Unsure now what to do, she took a job with a Russian family in Moscow but soon afterwards, she again heard from the Rahls who had also now moved to the Crimea and they invited her rejoin them in a rented datcha not far from Yalta. Thus Dashwood now found herself back where she had been the year before with no immediate hope of escape and no choice but to sit and wait.

Another British governess who became stranded in southern Russia was Helen Clarke. She had arrived in 1913 to work as a governess for the Petrovs, a Russian family on a 20,000 acre estate near the small provincial town of Bakmout in Ukraine. Clarke enjoyed both her work looking after the three youngest Petrov children as well as the relaxed life on the large estate. However, on New Year's Day 1917, the Petrovs were threatened with violence by local Bolsheviks demanding large sums of money. Although the Petrovs refused to pay, there was soon a complete breakdown in law and order in the area and like many other wealthy Russian families, they began to hide their valuables in the house and garden. Then local peasants arrived and occupied their gardens, trying to force the Petrovs from their home, probably hoping to seize their hidden assets. The children became sick and the family left their estate for Bakmout but Petrov was arrested there and only released when his wife paid what was effectively a ransom of 75.000 roubles. It became clear that it would be unsafe to remain in Bakmout so in the early winter of 1918, Clarke and the family fled to Kharkov, travelling initially by sledges across the steppe and then continuing on in a vastly overcrowded train. This proved to be a nightmare journey in a compartment meant for thirty passengers packed with one hundred people, many of them sick and screaming children. Clarke was nearly arrested and shot on the train for trying to open a door to let in fresh air and only saved by her nationality since the British were still popular in Russia as a respected partner in the war against Germany. With the help of the British vice-consul in Kharkov, Helen rented two rooms and looked after four of the Petrov children through what proved to be an extremely difficult and hot summer. Food was scarce and inflated prices were demanded for the little there was. The likelihood of Kharkov being soon overrun by the Bolsheviks forced the Petrovs to move again and late in the year, after yet another long and dangerous train journey, the whole family arrived in the Crimea.

After several months of anxious waiting as the Bolshevik forces moved progressively south, salvation for Helen Clarke, Emma Dashwood and the other marooned British governesses finally came in the unexpected form of British warships that started to arrive off the Crimean coast in March 1919. Both Clarke and Dashwood managed to board British Navy ships in Sevastopol and were evacuated to Constantinople from where they made their way home. The Petrovs also escaped by sea, taking a boat first to the Caucasus region and then some months later to Constantinople. Remarkably during this period, they remained in touch with Helen who had returned to England and at their request she journeyed out to Constantinople to escort the whole family to England. Unfortunately for the Petrovs, the British ship that Dashwood boarded was unwilling to take the Russians and she had to leave them to their fate on the quay.

In hindsight, Margaret Neame's decision in 1915 to leave Britain to become the governess to George, the son of the Grand Duke Michael (the Tsar's younger brother) and his step-daughter Tata was not a good one. Within eighteen months, Neame found herself caught up in the turmoil of the Revolution, a situation she could hardly have imagined when she left Britain. On his abdication in March 1917, Tsar Nicholas originally selected his brother Michael as his successor but the Grand Duke understandably refused the poisoned chalice. The Grand Duke together with his family and Neame were then placed under house arrest at their villa near St Petersburg. However, in September 1917, the house arrest was lifted and so Michael prepared to leave Russia with his family plus Neame and his English secretary Nicholas Johnson. He intended to drive everyone in his Rolls Royce car to Finland where the family had an estate. Unfortunately for them, the day of their planned escape turned out to be October 25th, the date of the Bolshevik revolution and their plan was discovered by Bolshevik sympathisers who became suspicious of the conspicuous Rolls Royce car. The family was taken back to St Petersburg, minus their Rolls and placed under house arrest again but in March 1918, the Grand Duke and Johnson were exiled by the Bolsheviks to the Siberian city of Perm.

The Grand Duke's wife, Natalia, concerned for her family's safety, approached the British to see if they would offer refuge but the government was unwilling to accept the royal group at that stage due to a lack of sympathy for the Tsar in the country generally. She then managed to persuade the Danish embassy in St Petersburg to help smuggle Neame and young George out of the country on a train carrying prisoners-of-war who were being repatriated back to Germany. They were issued with false passports, Neame posing as the wife of an Austrian officer and George as her son. If they had been discovered, Neame was in danger of being shot as a spy but they reached the Danish embassy in Berlin safely and were given shelter by the ambassador. The German government learnt of the fugitives but chose to ignore the fact that Neame was British and therefore an enemy and allowed the pair to continue their journey via Copenhagen to England. In June 1918, the Grand Duke and Johnson were shot dead in woods on the outskirts of Perm by the Bolshevik secret police. However, the murders were kept secret and the details did not become publicly known until some years later. Still believing Michael to be alive, the Duke's wife and George's half-sister Tata escaped from St Petersburg to Kiev, then occupied by the Germans. With the signing of the armistice in November 1918, Natalia and her daughter made for the Black Sea coast from where they were evacuated to England by the Royal Navy. They moved into a house in Sussex that had been rented for them by Johnson's mother where they were joined a few months later by George and Margaret Neame.

The resourcefulness and courage displayed by Neame in the face of extremely challenging circumstances were remarkable. But the situation of Neame and the Grand Duke's family was mirrored all across Russia through 1918 as the families of the nobility and wealthy tried to make desperate plans to move to the south or to escape the country entirely. As with Neame, the British governesses sometimes became involved in these plans, often at great personal risk, whether taking charge of the children, helping the families to try to hide their money and jewels or simply foraging to find food to keep the families alive. In a few cases, the Russians even entrusted their valuables to their governesses, knowing their honesty and the fact they were less likely to be searched or seized by the Red Guards. In the worst cases, the young governesses had to watch as members of their families were seized by the Bolsheviks, sometimes being immediately taken out and shot or murdered in more sadistic ways.

15
Wars and Revolution

Britain and Russia have fought each other twice, first in the relatively uneventful Anglo-Russian War of 1807-1812 when Russia was forced into war against its will by Napoleon and then the more serious Crimean War of 1854-1856. The two countries have been allies in war twice, during the Napoleonic Wars of 1812-1815 and the First World War from 1914 to 1917. They have also had two minor trade wars during the First and Second Treaties of Armed Conflict as well as the 'political war' known as the Great Game and Britain has intervened militarily in Russia once during the Russian civil war that followed the Bolshevik revolution. In terms of the volatile history of Europe, the armed conflicts between the two competing nations have been relatively few.

The First World War

The outbreak of the First World War In 1914 proved to be a catastrophe for Tsarist Russia. The government had not anticipated such a conflict and the country was poorly prepared for a major war. Although the embarrassing defeat by Japan nine years earlier had brought about some improvements to the nation's armed forces, the turmoil of the earlier 1905 revolution had shaken the Tsarist Empire and subsequent economic and political reforms were far from complete. However, as masses of workers and peasants rallied to the Russian flag in positive mood and marched off to fight, the initial outlook for both the war and national unity appeared good. But this early euphoria could only survive with victory and Russia's hopes were dashed very early in the war. At the battles around Tannenberg in September 1914, the Germans destroyed two entire Russian armies (more than 250,000 men were killed or wounded) and the survivors fled from the field. Although the Russians regrouped and had some later battle successes, they were relatively few and by 1917, much of the Tsarist army had literally been bled to death. Critics of the regime were asking whether Russia's misfortunes – including 1,700,000 military dead and 5,000,000 wounded – were the result of stupidity or treason. The regime seemed careless of such appalling losses and the Tsar said it was an honour to lose so many men in defence of their allies. By then the Tsarist situation was hopeless and beyond saving.

For most of the British community in Russia in September 1914, the outbreak of the First World War came as a surprise and, as in Britain, the general reaction was that it would not last long. The immediate impacts were limited and for the vast majority of the British community, life in Russia initially continued much as before. Trade was disrupted and contact with Britain rendered more difficult as the normal travel routes across continental Europe or via the Black Sea were now closed. But for some of the British companies operating in Russia business was brisk and profitable as orders poured in for armaments and war supplies. Although many of the younger men began volunteering for service in the British armed forces, making their way home through Scandinavia and then by ship across the North Sea, they generally left their families behind. Russia was Britain's ally in the war and there was no prescient intimation of the momentous events that would affect both them and the whole Russian nation just a couple of years later.

As soon as war broke out, the wife of the British ambassador, Lady Buchanan, immediately began mobilizing the British community in a range of charitable activities in support of the Russian war effort. She played a major role in setting up the British Colony Hospital (also known as the King George V Hospital) in St Petersburg which opened in September 1914. It was originally intended as a convalescent home for wounded Russian officers but soon became dedicated only to other ranks and provided a level of comfort not found in other hospitals. It continued to function until June 1917, when the deteriorating situation in the city led to its closure. The British also established the Anglo-Russian hospital in St Petersburg which was set up with the full support of the British government and partly funded by a high profile appeal in Britain headed by the King and Queen. An organizing committee was set up under the patronage of Queen Alexandra who was the aunt of Tsar Nicholas and led by Lady Muriel Paget and Lady Sybil Grey. The latter then travelled to Russia in October 1915 to coordinate the arrangements for opening the hospital. The site selected was the Dmitrievskii Palace on Nevsky Prospect and the hospital became known as the Dmitri Palace to the British.[225] It took several months to make the necessary alterations to the building and although it was not ready until the end of January 1916, when the hospital opened it had all the very latest equipment. The facilities included 200 beds, an operating theatre with adjoining anaesthetic and sterilising rooms, an X-ray department and bacteriological laboratory, a dispensary, a dental surgeon plus a fleet of twenty-two motorized ambulances. Most of the doctors and nurses were recruited from Britain and were led by Dr Andrew Fleming. Over each of the beds were plaques commemorating the names of the individual donors or those British towns and cities that had provided the money,

The Hospital admitted only the most seriously wounded and the number of casualties arriving at the hospital soon grew quickly so that it mostly operated at close to maximum capacity. A British visitor to the hospital in 1915 described what he saw:

'I was at the British Colony Hospital yesterday; out of the eighty-two wounded there over forty are on crutches, shot in the legs during the retreat. A Cossack was playing his guitar in the garden, and there were nine legs listening, with eighteen brains.' [226]

---

[225] Michael Harmer, *The Forgotten Hospital*, 1982 (Harmer's father served as a surgeon in the hospital).

[226] Philip Gibbs, *Diary of an Englishman in Russia*, 1919.

During the period from November 1915 to October 1916, more than 6,000 patients received treatment in the Anglo-Russian hospital.[227] There were several other British-run charitable activities in Russia during the war, including the British Womens' Maternity Hospital based at the Warsaw station in St Petersburg, the British hospital for children in Kazan that dealt with many severe cases of scarlet fever and double pneumonia, a hospital based in a large barracks at Lutsk run by Geoffrey Jefferson, a British surgeon and finally the British Committee for Relief of War Sufferers which worked under the auspices of the Russian Red Cross. During a visit to the Anglo-Russian hospital by Lady Paget in April 1916, it was agreed with the British medical staff that a mobile field hospital was needed at the front and this was quickly organized. By late May, a fully functioning mobile field hospital was ready to be sent to the front at Volynia. It comprised 100 beds in tents, forty-two ambulances and transport carts, 125 Russian orderlies plus eight British nurses. During 1917, the Anglo-Russian hospital increasingly admitted civilian patients who had been wounded in the street fighting but in late March, the hospital itself was attacked by Bolsheviks and its closure seemed only a matter of time. The medical staff struggled on with their work in an attempt to help the Russians but by January 1918 the conditions in St Petersburg were so dreadful that all the British staff were evacuated back home. The Union Jack that had fluttered so proudly on the hospital's roof for two years was torn down.

As Russia geared up its war effort in 1915, many of the British women there participated in a wide variety of charity work, some became involved in Red Cross work and a few even joined the Russian army as nurses. The idea of British women working as nurses with the Russian forces was not new. Having proven their value as nurses during the Crimean War, an increasing number of British women subsequently joined the profession and benefited from the improved training offered by a variety of new organizations that were being established. During the Russo-Turkish war of 1877-78, some of these nurses were sent out to Russia where they served with distinction. One of them was London-born Janet King who at the age of eighteen was so deeply moved by reports of the suffering during the struggle between the Turks and the Serbs for the latter's independence that she joined the Protestant Deaconesses's Institution to be trained for nursing the sick and wounded in war. King proved to be a quick learner and in 1877 she was selected to join a group of nine British medical staff sent out by the institution to help care for the troops in Russia. King's party, operating under orders from the Russian National Red Cross Society, travelled first to Bucharest and then crossed the Danube to Sistova (in modern day Bulgaria) where they had to wait for an escort to the front. The town was not only full of wounded soldiers but was being ravaged by typhus, so the nurses were kept busy while they waited. The British group was then moved up to the Russian front in horse-drawn carts where they spent the winter nursing the wounded. King was in charge of some 200 patients scattered in huts among the hills who suffered from both their wounds as well as the bitter cold. As the winter dragged on, conditions deteriorated, coarse black bread was the only diet,

---

[227] Doctors Waterhouse and Harmer – BMA Journal article, October 1917.

half the nurses went down with typhus and King was attacked by wild dogs and Turkish troops as she went about her duties. When the Turks finally capitulated the following spring, King was so worn out that she immediately returned to England, having received the Imperial Order of the Red Cross of Russia for her work. King later went on to serve in the Zulu War in South Africa and she was awarded the South Africa medal as well as receiving from Queen Victoria the decoration of the Royal Red Cross.

One of the first young British women to serve on the front line as a nurse with the Russian army during the First World War was Florence Farmborough who originated from Buckinghamshire and came to Russia as a governess in 1908 at the age of twenty-one. Her first job was in Kiev but she later moved to Moscow where at the start of the war she became a voluntary aide at a hospital. Farmborough went on to qualify as a Red Cross nurse and joined a front line Russian surgical unit in early 1915, serving in Poland, Austria and Romania. She survived the war and returned to England, eventually publishing a book of her Russian experiences when she was eighty-six.[228] But not all the British women who served with the Russian army survived to tell the tale. Margaret Ryle from Brighton volunteered as a Red Cross nurse with the Russian army and died from disease in Serbia in February 1915, aged only twenty-three.

In Britain, women were equally keen to do help the war effort and many patriotically volunteered as doctors, nurses and auxiliary staff to support the British and allied forces overseas. Several charitable organisations in Britain, including the Red Cross and what became known as the Scottish Women's Hospital (SWH) began to recruit female medical staff to go out to the front, mostly funded through public donations. In 1916 the SWH was asked if it could provide two field hospital units to operate with a recently formed Serbian division that was fighting with the Russians and had no medical support. The SWH was keen to assist and in August an initial volunteer group of some seventy-five female doctors, nurses and support staff sailed from Britain to Archangel. The unit was led by Elsie Inglis, a Scottish doctor who had graduated from Edinburgh University in 1899 and was an active supporter of the women's suffragette movement. Despite the organisation's name, the group actually contained only thirteen Scots, the rest were mostly English with a handful of Irish and Welsh. They arrived in Archangel and were immediately sent to join the First Serbian Division which was part of a mixed Russian and Romanian force fighting German and Bulgarian troops in the Dobrugda region of southern Romania.

After a tedious train journey of several weeks via Moscow and Odessa, they arrived in southern Dobrugda at the end of September. They set up two field hospitals, inland from the Black Sea port of Constanta and some twenty miles north of the front line. As well as their medical equipment, the unit had fortunately also brought out from Britain their own motorised transport and ambulances and so were able to operate independently of the Russians, transporting the wounded from the front line to the hospitals. After a month of heavy fighting, it was clear the Russians could not hold back the advancing

---

[228] Florence Farmborough, *Nurse at the Russian Front*, 1974

Germans and the SWH units were ordered to pack up their field hospitals and retreat northwards to Galatz where the Danube marked the Russian border. During a chaotic two-week period, the British medical staff first evacuated the wounded troops and then made their way north through the autumn mud, along with thousands of retreating Russian soldiers and civilian refugees.

Despite the speed of the German advance, all members of the SWH escaped over the Danube where they again set up their two field hospitals in early November, one in Galatz and the other in Ismail near the coast. The arrival of substantial Russian reinforcements aided by a division of British armoured cars [229] plus units of the British and French air forces temporarily consolidated the new front line. But when the Germans captured Bucharest, the Allied positions around Galatz were untenable and in mid December, the order was given once more to retreat. The shortage of Russian ambulances meant that the job of evacuating the wounded from all field hospitals, both British and Russian, fell largely to the SWH unit. Their task this time was considerably aided by the men of the British armoured car division who helped pack up all the equipment as well as providing additional transport for the move to their new bases.

Several of the women in the SWH units kept diaries during their time in Russia, including Elsie Bowerman who was born in Tunbridge Wells in 1889 and worked as an orderly. She had experienced more than enough drama in her life before she arrived in Russia. At the age of twelve, Bowerman and her mother had sailed for the USA on the *Titanic* when it sank on April 15th 1912. Both women escaped in Lifeboat 6 with around twenty-two others including Frederick Fleet, the lookout who had first spotted the iceberg. After this almost fatal adventure, it must have taken some courage for Bowerman to undertake the wartime sea voyage with the SWH to Russia. In her detailed pencil-written diary, Bowerman described pitching tents for the field hospital and serving meals to 250 people with the help of only one Russian, who could not speak English. She told of sleeping in the open just miles from the firing line, of having singing parties with soldiers around camp fires and of cross-country rides with Russian officers. Despite the privations and bitter winter weather, Bowerman clearly enjoyed the experience and excitement.

As 1916 ended, the intense cold of winter brought a temporary lull in the fighting but March 1917 saw both a resumption of the struggle as well as news of the dramatic political events in St Petersburg. Initially, life continued as before in the SWH hospitals but by April discipline among the Russian troops was clearly deteriorating and the hospitals saw a sudden rise in the number of conscripts admitted with self-inflicted wounds. Although for the time being the Russian provisional government remained committed to continuing the war effort, the British women noticed a subtle but steady change in the attitude of many of the Russian soldiers. Until now, the SWH women had always been treated with the utmost respect and even admiration for their work at the front

---

[229] This BAC division comprised some 500 men, largely made up of Royal Navy volunteers and was led by the British MP Oliver Lampson. Some of their equipment and vehicles had been donated by the British public and Lampson used his own converted Rolls Royce car at the front.

but that spring a growing distrust on the part of the Russians of any and all foreigners led to a dramatic change in relationships. There were increasing acts of insubordination by the Russian orderlies in the field hospitals and then suddenly several of the British women were arrested and accused of being spies for the Germans. Although the latter issue was soon resolved, it left a bitter taste and signalled that the SWH operations (as well as those of the British Red Cross) in southern Russia could be seriously at risk.

When a new Russian July offensive in nearby Galicia failed miserably within a few weeks, much of the southern front collapsed as Russian troops retreated rapidly in the face of a fierce German counter-offensive. A SWH field hospital in Galicia was left behind and only rescued by the timely intervention of a BAC unit. They were not the only ones to experience this sudden lack of care by the Russians and during the retreat many of the British medical staff found that they and their equipment were abandoned. Despite the valiant work performed by these brave and dedicated people, little help was provided by the Russian troops. Over the next few weeks, as mounting Russian casualties arrived for treatment, the SWH hospitals were kept extremely busy with the women working into the night. Being very close to the front line, they were also within range of the German artillery and on several occasions the hospitals were shelled, fortunately without casualties. Many of the British medical staff also suffered from bouts of illness, mostly malaria and typhus, which reduced the number of available personnel. Doctor Inglis also now fell ill, having caught a form of smallpox as well as suffering from gastritis and her condition gradually deteriorated.

By September, the likelihood of Russia withdrawing from the war and the deteriorating relationships with its allies led to serious consideration being given by the British government to the evacuation of the SWH and Red Cross units. After weeks of negotiation between British and Russian officials, it was finally agreed that the women of the SWH would be transported by rail to Archangel and from there by sea on to Britain. They were to return with 6,000 men of the Serbian First Division, the army they had originally gone out to assist which was now to be deployed on the Macedonian front, close to its Balkan homeland. The following spring the Serbs achieved spectacular success there, supported by a reformed unit of the SWH, retaking Belgrade and leading to the defeat of Bulgaria. Although the whole SWH unit arrived safely back in Britian, the health of Inlis had worsened considerably and she died within a couple of days of landing in November 1917. In recognition of her work, Elsie Inglis was given a full military funeral after lying in state in St Giles' cathedral in Edinburgh. By the end of the war, the SWH had provided fourteen hospital units staffed by one thousand women, operating in six different countries. [230]

The British Quakers were also active in relief work in Russia during the First World War. In 1916 the Society of Friends in London organized a relief programme for people in the Buzuluk region of Samara province where the effects of the war had disrupted the local economy, causing a severe food shortage as well as leaving many families without a breadwinner. The region

---

[230] Audrey Cahill, *Between the Lines*, 1999.

had also become flooded with tens of thousands of refugees fleeing the conflict further west a group of twenty-six volunteers from Britain was sent out in 1916 to help coordinate the provision of medical assistance as well as supplying food, clothing, education and library books. They also became involved in trying to find jobs for some of the displaced people. The small team operated at full stretch, trying to cover an area of over 1000 square miles, although they were later joined by American Quaker volunteers. They set up a children's home, ran several hospitals and workshops where they tried to teach people new skills so they could find employment. They carried on with their work through the chaos of both the revolution and civil war until spring 1919, when all the staff returned to their native countries.

The British and American Quaker Relief Committees continued to try to provide further relief and eventually, after many difficulties, they established a new relief unit based in Moscow. This was able to provide important assistance during the food shortages of the early years of Bolshevik rule. In March 1920, the unit reported that 8,338 children had been supplied with 9,249 articles of clothing in the past eight days, all handed out personally to the applicants. Later on, the Quaker unit made supplementary grants of food to 16,000 children in Moscow and provided iodine to the hospitals, which although only twenty pounds in total, was greater than the quota allocated as a year's supply by the Government for all the hospitals and pharmacies in the city. Fats, oatmeal and underclothing were supplied to maternity homes and sent to schools outside of Moscow. The Quakers also gave dried milk to feeding kitchens for infants and, as a result of these efforts, the local infant mortality was halved.

As we have already seen, units of the British armed forces saw action along the southern Russian front but the British were also involved during the latter stages of the war in other parts of the Tsarist Empire. In the Caucasus, a combined force of around 1,000 British and Dominion troops arrived from Persia in an attempt to prevent the advance of German and Turkish forces into the oil-rich region around the Caspian Sea. Known as the 'Dunster Force' after its commander, General Lionel Dunsterville, they helped defend Baku for several months in the summer of 1918 but the conditions in the city became so chaotic that the British were forced to retreat in September, losing some two hundred men. However, with the armistice in November, a much larger British force of 5,000 men under General William Thompson temporarily returned to Baku to try to restore order and set up a civilian Azeri administration. British troops also occupied the Black Sea port of Batumi in late 1918, expelling the Turks who had seized and ransacked the important copper mines run by the Anglo-American Caucasus Copper Company. The British forces again set up a local civilian administration under General Cook Collis who became governor. The town was handed over to the fledgling republic of Georgia in July 1920.

The Bolshevik Revolution

Russia's mounting battlefield losses in the war against the Germans and the rising civil unrest being stirred up by the Bolsheviks were simply too much for the Tsarist rule and in 1917, the government collapsed, plunging Russia into a chaotic, bloody revolution and ultimately, violent civil war. The Russian revolution occurred '*because the patience of the Russian people broke under a system of unparalleled inefficiency and corruption. No other nation would have stood the privations which Russia stood, for anything like the same length of time.*' [231] The period of the French revolution between 1793 and 1794 during which more than 16,000 people were killed by the Jacobins is often known as 'The Terror'. Yet compared with the events in Russia during its revolution and subsequent civil war, the French reign of terror was a relatively tame affair. In Russia, the chaos, disruption, brutality, horror, starvation and the number of people that died were all far, far greater. Most of the British in Russia were not unduly unhappy to hear of abdication of Tsar in March 1917 and indeed many, at least initially, supported the uprising.

The revolution did not come as a complete surprise, there had been clear warning signs of the awful abyss into which Tsarist Russia seemed doomed to disappear. However, the intensity of the struggle and the widespread casual violence on both sides took many by surprise. Most of the British who were in Russia at the time of the revolution had vivid memories of their traumatic experiences, many of which were expressed in either letters sent home at the time or in books written subsequently. One of the most vivid (and accurate) recollections of the early days of turmoil in the spring of 1917 is that written by Philip Gibbs, a British soldier and journalist who was a prolific writer about the First World War. [232] He described what happened one day in March when he was dressing in his hotel:

'*I had put on my boots and my trousers when I heard a sound which I knew, but couldn't recall. I opened my window wide and realised it was the chatter of a machine-gun; then I saw an indescribable sight all the well-dressed Nevski crowd running for their lives down the Michail Street, and a stampede of motor-cars and sledges to escape from the machine-guns which never stopped firing. I saw a well-dressed lady run over by an automobile, a sledge turn over and the driver thrown into the air and killed. The poorer-looking people crouched against the walls; many others, principally men, lay flat in the snow. Lots of children were trampled on, and people knocked down by the sledges or by the rush of the crowd.*'

Such scenes were to become an almost daily occurrence as the levels of violence escalated. With the breakdown in government control, chaos and looting ensued. Transport and distribution networks ceased to function effectively, banks and armament stores were ransacked and food shortages, especially in St Petersburg, became increasingly serious. The city's previously normal, everyday life steadily turned into an abnormal, day to day struggle for survival. Gibbs wrote:

'*there is only soldiers' black bread. The post comes fitfully, no news-papers have been delivered yet. Over a million letters were destroyed at the General Post Office.*'

---

[231] Bruce Lockhart – ibid.

[232] Philip Gibbs – ibid.

All the while, Russia's military losses in the war continued to mount and the threat of a German invasion of St Petersburg seemed a very real possibility, only surpassed by the more imminent dangers of summary arrests, imprisonment and executions.

As the events of 1917 unfolded – the Tsar's abdication, his murder, the collapse of the provisional government and the seizure of power by the Bolsheviks – it became increasingly clear to most of the British still in Russia that it was time to leave. The British consulates in Moscow and St Petersburg were besieged by crowds of refugees and distressed British subjects, all wanting help and advice. In St Petersburg, where the consulate was now run by William Woodhouse and his brother Clayton, a special office was set up to process the thousands of applications for exit visas. The staff all ended up with callouses on the palms of their hands from the constant use of the visa stamp. The Woodhouse brothers and the rest of the consular staff remained at the consulate even after the embassy closed and the ambassador left St Petersburg in January 1918.

There were essentially four potential avenues of escape; to Finland in the north via St Petersburg or Moscow, to the south where the Bolsheviks had not yet fully taken the Black Sea coast, to the south-east through the Caucasus to Baku and into Persia and finally to the east across Siberia and thence to China. Everyone had to make a choice about which route to select; staying put was no longer an option except for the elderly and infirm. Most chose the shorter northern route into Finland. Since the majority of the British were either in St Petersburg or Moscow, it was easier for them to obtain the necessary travel documents, at least while the British consulates were still in operation. This route was not without problems however, as the Calderwood family found when they left Hughesovka at the end of July 1917. Calderwood was a chief engineer at the Hughes' steel plant and together with his wife and four children, he travelled for nine days by train from southern Ukraine north to St Petersburg. They spent the whole journey in the corridor of the train as only Bolshevik soldiers were allowed in the compartments. The family was obliged to stay in St Petersburg for three weeks, waiting for the papers that would allow them to leave Russia and while there, all their money was stolen, their food supplies were almost finished and their youngest child became very ill with bronchitis. When they eventually received their papers they left by train and travelled through Finland and Sweden before arriving at Voss in Norway in early September. After two weeks in Voss, they were finally able to board one of two converted cattle ships in the port of Bergen. Although Royal Navy ships provided an escort across the North Sea, a German U-boat sank one of the transports but fortunately, the Calderwoods were on the other ship and arrived safely at Aberdeen. The German U-boat threat was to remain a constant menace for all those who escaped from Russia through Scandinavia until the end of the war in November 1918.

The journey undertaken in 1918 by the British vice-consul in Odessa, John Webster and his wife Marie, was equally traumatic and they spent almost two months travelling on trains and boats during their escape to London (see table below). They fled Odessa under threat from the advancing German army who took the city the following day without a shot being fired as most of the Bolshevik leaders had left on the same train as the Websters.

Itinerary of John and Marie Webster when they fled Odessa in 1918

ARRIVAL	DEPARTURE
	Odessa Wed 6th March 2.30 p.m.
Nikolaev Thurs. 7th March 5 p.m.	Nikolaev Friday 8 March 5 a.m.
Kherson Friday 8 Mar 8 a.m.	Kherson Fri 8 Mar 2 p.m.
Nikopol Sat 9 Mar 2 p.m.	Nikopol Sat 9 Mar 5 p.m.
Alexandrovsk Sat 9 Mar 8 p.m.	Alexandrovsk Sun 10 Mar 6.30 p.m.
Mariupol Mon 11 Mar 10 a.m.	Mariupol Monday 25 March 11 p.m.
Taganrog Wed 27 March 7.30 a.m.	Taganrog Friday 29 Mar 1 a.m.
Rostov Friday 29 March 4.30 a.m.	Rostov Friday 29 March 2 p.m.
Kozloff Sun 31 March 9 p.m.	Kozloff Sun 31 March 10.30 p.m.
Przarb Mon 1 April 8 a.m.	Przarb Mon 1 April 11 a.m.
Moscow Mon 1 April 7 p.m.	Moscow Thurs 4 April 12.40 a.m.
Bororga Friday 5 April 10 a.m.	Bororga Sat 6 April 11.15 a.m.
Zbarka Sun 7 April 8 a.m.	Zbarka Mon 8 April 7 a.m.
Hempozabodck Mon 8 April 8 p.m.	Hempozabodck Tuesday 9 April 12.05 a.m.
Kem Tues 9 April 10 p.m.	Kem Wed 10 April 2 a.m.
Kargaramka Wed 10 April midnight	Kargaramka Thursday 11 April 7 a.m.
Umargpa Thursday 11 April 11 a.m.	Umargpa Thursday 11 April 5 p.m.
Murmansk Friday 12 April 1 a.m.	Murmansk Saturday 27 April (evening)
Newcastle Friday 4 May 6 p.m. Landed Saturday 5 May 10 a.m.	Newcastle Saturday 5 May 1.19 p.m.
London Saturday 5 May 7 p.m.	

The eastern escape route across Siberia was the longest but had the advantage of avoiding the chaos of St Petersburg as well as passing through areas not yet fully controlled by the Bolsheviks. This was the exit path chosen by British residents in places like Ekaterinburg and Perm as well as Lady Paget early in 1918. She had already left the Anglo-Russian hospital before it closed to visit the British field hospital which had by then moved to Odessa. When news reached her that the St Petersburg hospital was closing and the British staff were being evacuated, she and the British nurses at the field hospital also decided it was time to leave Russia. They travelled by train from Odessa to Moscow and then across Siberia, fortunately without any serious problems and finally arrived safely back in Britain in May 1918. Lady Paget subsequently dedicated much of the remaining twenty years of her life to relief work for the many British citizens marooned in Soviet Russia.

Intervention and Civil War in Russia

The Allied intervention in Russia in the summer of 1918 brought about the last major arrival of substantial numbers of British people on Russian soil. The Allied intervention was a multinational expedition that involved troops from fourteen nations and its operations covered a large part of Russia. Initially, the military objectives were to prevent the Germans from seizing munitions held in Russian ports and to re-establish the eastern front after Russia's collapse. Later, after winning the war against Germany, the Allies expanded their operations in support of the anti-Bolshevik White forces in Russia. War was never officially declared and for a variety of reasons, the Allied intervention largely proved to be a failure, especially in terms of the latter objective. Some 40,000 British troops were sent to Russia, mostly to Archangel and Murmansk with smaller numbers going to Vladivostok, southern Ukraine and the Caucasus.[233] Royal Navy ships also operated in the Baltic and the Black Sea. The British soldiers landed in the north in the spring of 1918 were largely young and inexperienced troops but initially, with naval and aerial support, they made some limited progress against the Bolshevik forces. However by 1919, a growing war weariness in Britain, the refusal of some of the soldiers to fight and the collapse of the White army led to a general British withdrawal from the north in October.

When early in 1919, Baku was taken by the anti-Bolshevik White army, the British were requested to provide support and a volunteer group of some thirty Royal Navy sailors under the command of Commander Bruce Fraser was sent out. Their arrival in Baku led to one of the most infamous events relating to the Allied intervention when the group of British sailors was captured and imprisoned by the Bolsheviks in what was called the Black Hole of Baku. After a long, tortuous overland journey from Bagdad, the sailors ended up in Baku

---

[233] The polar explorer, Ernest Shackleton was one of the British officers in the military mission sent to Murmansk. He returned home in March 1919, full of plans for the economic development of northern Russia but when the region fell to the Bolsheviks, his plans foundered. Shackleton returned to the lecture circuit, and in December 1919 published *South*, his own account of the *Endurance* expedition to the south Pole.

where they tried to repair ships and guns for use by the White Russians. They found that the ships had not been used or maintained for several years and there was little they could do. The port of Baku was soon overrun by Bolshevik forces, who captured the sailors and lined them up on the quayside. They were then forced to strip naked while the Bolsheviks emptied their pockets of all their possessions. After their clothes were returned, the sailors were marched off through jeering crowds, to the local prison where they were joined by a small, assorted group of other prisoners, including the British vice-consul and placed into two adjoining cells, each measuring sixteen feet square. The cells had a bare earth floor and no furniture, blankets or bedding.

The next day, the Bolsheviks initiated a regime of the utmost cruelty and depraved torture. The British sailors were taken outside, where they witnessed the first of many periodic executions of other prisoners captured by the Bolsheviks (mostly White Russians and Armenians). The women were first disembowelled then shot, while the men were tortured with acid "so strong that when they moved their arms, the flesh hung down like huge gauntlets" before also being shot.[234] The sailors lived largely on a minimal diet of black bread and rice and were forced to work each day at heavy manual tasks. As time went on, many of the men became too weak to work and as a result, they were placed back in their cells on reduced rations. Water was only available for half an hour each day at a single tap in the prison courtyard and a hole in the ground in the same place provided communal ablutions. In the unsanitary conditions typhus and typhoid became rife and lice were a huge problem. Although the sailors did their best to try to remove them from their clothing using their teeth, the prison guards threw packets of lice into the cell through the grating in the door, so it remained a problem throughout their captivity.

The British vice-consul Hewelcke was periodically taken to the condemned cell where he was told he would be shot. Each time his life was spared but as a result of this torture he became seriously ill. No information was released about the Royal Navy prisoners by the Russian government to the British and the entire group was presumed dead. In these circumstances, it was not surprising that order and morale among the prisoners started to collapse but although Commander Fraser did his best to restore it, one of the sailors committed suicide by using a piece of glass to slit his wrists. The guards fought over his clothing, and the body was left in the cell with the other prisoners for four days. As more of the prisoners started to die from disease and maltreatment, the same thing happened with the body beginning to decompose each time.

After almost two years of captivity, a minister from Georgia came to visit the prison to discuss the possible release of Georgian prisoners who were held captive as a result of nearby fighting with the Bolsheviks. One of the prisoners in the cells with the British sailors was a Georgian interpreter and when it seemed likely that he would be released, Fraser persuaded him to smuggle out a message about their plight. The message was in the form of a locket containing a picture of Fraser's mother which the Georgian took with him by swallowing it. As a result of this action, news of the British sailors' situation reached the

---

[234] Max Arthur, *Lost Voices of the Royal Navy*, 2005.

British mission in Tblisi who eventually negotiated their release in November 1920. The men from the Royal Navy finally returned to Britain in Febraury 1921 but not without two more of their number dying on the journey home as a result of their appalling treatment in Baku. Only twelve survivors out of the original group of thirty volunteers finally made it home, one of which was Commander Fraser who was later promoted to the rank of admiral.

In Ukraine, there were several hundred British troops operating in support of the White Russian forces between late 1918 and 1920. They were mainly comprised of remnants of the British armoured corps (BAC) originally sent out in 1917 to assist the Russians along the southern Romanian front plus a couple of squadrons of RAF units. A small British military mission was also sent out to train and equip the White Russian army with the British Mk V tank which had proved to be extremely effective against the Germans in the last battles of the First World War. Britain supplied around seventy Mk V tanks to the anti-Bolshevist forces, most of them allocated to the White Russian forces in south Russia and their first combat deployment took place in May 1919 during an attack on the village of Kharunsk near Hughesovka. The British mission troops were forbidden from participating in any actual fighting but against their orders they did take part in an attack on Traritsyn (later called Stalingrad) in 1919. However, as the Bolsheviks gradually consolidated their control in Russia most of these tanks were captured and adapted for later use by the Red army. As the White forces fell back, some of the British liaison officers found themselves stranded when White units changed sides and went over to the Red Army. One such was Major Thorn who could only stand and watch when his turncoat unit joined the Reds, arresting all their officers and turning them over to the Bolsheviks. Thorn was also arrested but later released by the Bolsheviks.

The two RAF squadrons operated at various times from bases in Taganrog, Kharkov, Ekaterinodar and Djankoi. Although both units were very active, their results were limited, mainly due to the lack of secure bases. The front lines proved very fluid, with the Whites frequently forced to retreat leaving the British to quickly evacuate their bases, which on one occasion resulted in their planes being captured by the Bolsheviks. Their final sorties took place in March 1920, after which they handed over their remaining equipment to the Whites and were picked up by the Royal Navy from Theodosia. There were also various units of the British Indian army spread out around the Caspian Sea region and at one stage Winston Churchill urged the government to use these to assist the Muslim states in central Asia in their resistance against Bolshevik rule. In Bokhara, the local ruler made an impassioned plea to the departing British officers in 1920 to '*leave us at least one Englishman here; then my people will know that Great Britain will never adandon them and we continue to oppose the Bolsheviks.*' [235] But the British had their orders and left for India; the moment to change the course of history in Central Asia was gone.

For the remaining British citizens stranded in Russia at the time of the Allied intervention, life became even more difficult. The fact that Britain and Russia were no longer allies in the struggle against the common foe of Germany

---

[235] Tom Reiss, *The Orientalist*, 2005.

brought to a head the rising tide of anti-British (and -French) hysteria that had been sweeping across Russia, encouraged by the Bolsheviks. Notices started to appear in the Bolshevik press openly inciting the arrest and murder of British and French citizens.[236] In such an atmosphere, the possibilities of escaping the country for the British were made even more difficult and dangerous and with the later closure of the consulates in Moscow and St Petersburg, there was no diplomatic protection and no one to turn to for help. Although there are no accurate records of the numbers of British civilians remaining in Russia at this time, contemporary accounts indicate there were still over 1,000 in St Petersburg and Moscow with handfuls in Siberia, the Crimea and the Caucasus.

The unsurprising volt-face in official Russian attitudes was made amply clear during August 1918 when a series of armed raids were conducted against the British consulate in Moscow culminating in the arrest of all the diplomatic staff plus several other British nationals including several businessmen and Frank North, the chaplain of the English church. No formal charges were laid by the Bolsheviks, the men and women were simply rounded up and thrown in jail. Although they were released after a few days, Anglo-Russian relations nosedived when on August 31st, the British embassy in St Petersburg was broken into and ransacked by armed Bolshevik Red Guards. The naval attaché, Captain Cromie, shot dead three of the Russians as they forced their way in before he was in turn killed. A few days later, the British consul in Moscow, Bruce Lockhart was arrested and condemned to death. Although this was rescinded at the last moment after intense diplomatic pressure, further arrests of British and other foreign nationals continued in both Moscow and St Petersburg. Those foreigners detained in the capital were held in fortress of Peter and Paul where the prison conditions were extremely dire. For these one thousand or so prisoners there were just a few filthy beds and no sanitation or food and every night they could hear the sound of executions of Russian prisoners taking place in the prison courtyard. The cells were swarming with all kinds of insects that quickly attached themselves to the new inmates, causing even more discomfort. Gradually, the foreign community in St Petersburg was able to organise limited supplies of food and clothing for their nationals in prison. Although the great majority were eventually released by the Bolsheviks, some had to endure the horrors of Russian jails for several months.

However, not all the British arrested by the Bolsheviks survived and there are several recorded cases of them dying in prison from neglect and mistreatment or being killed. The British consul reported the death of Alexander Smith, a British worker who was arrested in Verkhoturye in the Urals and held in jail for several weeks before being shot in October 1918. His mutilated body was found abandoned on wasteland outside Verkhoturye a couple of weeks later when White Forces entered the town. A subsequent report from the Consulate cited two further deaths of British subjects in Perm in early 1919.[237] However, with the onset of the winter of 1918, the most immediate cause for concern for

---

[236] A Collection of Reports on Bolshevism in Russia – British Parliamentary Paper, HMSO 1919.
[237] A Collection of Reports on Bolshevism in Russia – ibid.

the surviving British (and many Russians) in Moscow and St Petersburg was not prison but famine. The situation in both cities was desperate as food supplies dwindled in the chaos of revolution. The combination of food shortages and Bolshevik violence led thousands to flee the cities and by 1919 the population of St Petersburg had fallen from around 2.6 million in 1916 to less than one million. The lack of food was compounded that winter by the failure of the electricity supply and fuel shortages; people were forced to burn their furniture simply to keep warm and stay alive. For the British still in Moscow and St Petersburg, there was nowhere to go, they were marooned in the Bolshevik heartland and the outlook for them became increasingly grim.

As conditions continued to deteriorate, the death toll of British residents steadily rose, especially the elderly and infirm who were most at risk. One of the many who died was Jane McGill who had helped fund the construction of the Anglican church and St Andrew's House in Moscow. Her death in 1918 was particularly tragic. Revolutionary Workers had been billeted in her house, and the sick, elderly lady was confined to one room. When winter came, they threw her out into the snow to die. Fortunately, she was recognized by passers-by and taken to St. Andrew's House, the hostel she had provided where she died a few days later aged 86. Her death certificate recorded 'paralysis of the heart', the usual polite euphemism for death by starvation. Her brother died in similar circumstances two months later.[238]

By the summer of 1919, St Andrews House, the women's hostel in Moscow was full to overflowing with a variety of British, German and Russian women, all deeply concerned about what the future might have in store. Their worst fears were realized when in early September, Russian soldiers arrived to arrest most of the British women who were taken off to the infamous Butyrki prison. The chaplain Frank North immediately bravely intervened to try to obtain their release but he was unsuccessful and the women, mostly young governesses, remained in prison for four months. Although they were released in January 1920, their ordeal was not quite over as they were still not allowed to return to Britain for a further couple of months. Their eventual departure, like that of most of the remaining British subjects in Russia hinged on the outcome of discussions that were held in Scandinavia between the Russian and British governments in 1919. A deal was finally reached in March 1920 whereby the remaining British citizens who wanted to leave were allowed out in exchange for Russians then held in Britain. In the absence of any British diplomatic representation in Russia, it fell on the shoulders of Frank North, the British chaplain, to act as the focal point for the British community and to try to arrange their safe evacuation. He and his wife showed great courage visiting those in prison and protesting about their treatment. They converted part of the parsonage into a canteen to feed the hungry and destitute and they persistently scoured the villages outside Moscow to try to buy food on the black market.

The indefatigable Norths also tried to help the increasing numbers of British military prisoners that were held in Moscow by the Bolsheviks following the Allied intervention. The first of these began to arrive in Moscow in early 1919

---

[238] Jean Coussmaker, The History of St Andrew's Church.

and by the end of the intervention in 1920, there were around thirty officers and 120 other ranks held there. The officers were kept in prison, some of them in solitary confinement but the men were in an open billet and allowed to wander around Moscow by day. The Norths visited the prisons, bringing the officers food and books to read from the church library. Once the Anglo-Russian deal was done, North worked hard to pull together as many of the British as he could from Moscow and the surrounding area to travel to St Petersburg to take the special trains for Finland. The main party from Moscow was packed into two cattle trucks and it took them sixty-eight hours instead of the normal twelve to make the journey to St Petersburg. Sadly, some of the British in Russia had by now died from cold and starvation but during the next few weeks around 700 British citizens were evacuated and the Norths finally left on the last official train. As the steady flow of British survivors arrived in Finland, many of them found that they were sent to a holding camp set up by the Finns to quarantine these refugees as a protection against typhus, which was then spreading fast in Russia. They were often half starved and arrived with nothing more than the clothes on their backs and, once back in Britain, a number of them were reduced to depending on charity. Many of these evacuees had been born in Russia and had spent the whole of their adult lives there, some of them couldn't even speak English properly.

For those British still in the south of Russia, conditions in 1918 were initially somewhat easier as they were in areas under the control of the White forces. However, as the Whites increasingly lost ground to the Bolsheviks, the outlook became far grimmer. For this small British group, mostly governesses plus a few diplomats and businessmen, the winter of 1918-19 proved to be exceptionally hard. Not only was it unusually cold but the availability of food that had previously been adequate, deteriorated considerably. Daily life became increasingly difficult and the daily forage for food grew more desperate and urgent. Talk amongst the small British community about how and when rescue might come kept their hopes alive through the dark winter months at the end of 1918. When British warships started to appear off the Crimean coast in early 1919, there was mounting excitement among both the stranded British as well as the fleeing Tsarist Russians. Although these first Royal Navy ships were unable to take any passengers on board, they sent word that there would soon be ships arriving that would do so and, by March, rescue for all at last seemed imminent.

The port of Sevastopol was secure under the control of the French and the rump of the White Russian army was holding back the Bolsheviks from crossing into the Crimea from the south of Ukraine. But within a few weeks, the White forces collapsed allowing the Bolsheviks to swarm south and a frantic, pell-mell rush towards the coast began. The ports of Odessa and Sevastopol became choked with thousands of anxious people desperate to escape the menacing Bolsheviks by boarding one of the few, newly-arrived British ships. In the chaos, luggage was abandoned, expensive cars were left with their engines running on the quayside and fights broke out as men jostled around the ships' gangways. The Royal Navy however, was under strict instructions as to who was to be given safe passage as space on board their warships was limited, making it impossible to evacuate all who wished to leave. Initially, priority was given to foreign nationals and as Emma Dashwood witnessed, the Russians were left in the ports. The exception was HMS *Marlborough* which was sent specifically to take off those members of the Russian royal family that had managed to reach Sevastopol, along with around one dozen British citizens. However, as more British and French ships arrived in the Crimean region, many more Russians were eventually able to escape. The final evacuation of the rump of the White Russian forces under General Denikin took place from the port of Taganrog along with the staff of the British consulate by HMS *Montrose* in December 1919.

Despite the life-threatening situation for any British national still in Russia in 1919, not all took the opportunity of leaving on the final trains or ships. A few remained, usually because they were too old or ill to make the journey home or because they were Russian women and their children who had married British men and either viewed Russia as their home or were not allowed to leave. One of these was Helen Clark, the daughter of a British father and a Russian mother. Her father had left Russia in November 1914 to join the British Army soon after she was born in Hughesovka. In 1917, when conditions really became difficult, the three-year-old Helen went with her mother to live with her family in a nearby village where she stayed for several years. Although Helen's mother managed to find a job, life was still very hard and many years later Helen wrote about the various problems the family faced during those difficult times:

'Shortages of food in those days were unbelievable... I remember seeing people sitting or lying on the ground by the roadside with their hands stretched towards us, begging for bread. They were grey-faced and emaciated and could hardly move. During the years of the Civil War money lost its value almost as soon as it was received and by the end of the War mother was receiving for her work as an accountant something like several million roubles a month, which was equal to almost nothing in purchasing power, but occasionally part of her salary was paid in kind – she might be given a bag of coal, a few pounds of flour or some potatoes.'

During the winter of 1923, Helen described how the whole family was evicted from their home without any alternative accommodation provided:

'grandfather received notice to leave his house within a week as it was needed for the club [for workers]*... It was absolutely impossible at that time to find another house... My uncle Konstantin had some weight on the* [village] *Council as an ex-commander in the Red Army, and he asked for some help in finding us accommodation, but the eviction took place. All our furniture was taken out of the house and dumped in the yard, and only the little back room where our servant slept was left for the whole family. It was the middle of winter, bitterly cold, with thick snow on the ground... This lasted for a few days, during which some of our belongings were stolen and the grand piano cracked with frost.'*

Despite the many privations she experienced, Helen survived and some years later, she was able to obtain permission to leave Russia and eventually settled in Wales. Another British citizen who stayed on was Mary Fellows who had gone to St Petersburg as a governess in 1911 and subsequently moved to Tbilisi in Georgia with her family. She was still with them when Fitzroy

MacLean, the British writer and military attaché came across her in 1937. Fellows was by then the governess to the son of her former pupil and had stayed with the family purely out of loyalty. At the time of MacLean's visit, they were all living in just one room of what used to be their house. It was a long way from the luxury and privilege she and the family had enjoyed in Tsarist times but at least they were all alive. Fellows remained with her Russian family until her death in 1941. It is clear that there were others like Clark and Fellows who were left behind in Russia as a trickle of refugees, penniless and often paperless, continued to arrive back in Britain through the early 1920s. A charity was set up in Britain to try to look after those few who remained in Russia. Little is known about their fate but records of the relief committee suggest that some were still dependent on donations from Britain as late as 1930. During the turmoil of the Russian civil war and the ensuing Soviet clampdown on contact with the West, most of those who stayed on Russified their names and kept their heads down, eventually merging totally into their respective local communities. As a result, this small British diaspora largely disappeared from the pages of history, effectively bringing to an end the remarkable and historic relationship between Britain and Russia that had begun so accidentally, in 1553.

Appendix I
Rulers of Britain and Russia

Russia
Ivan IV (the Terrible), 1547-84

Feodor I, 1584-98
Boris Godunov, 1598-1605
Feodor II, 1605
Dmitri I, 1605-06
Vasily IV, 1606-10
Dmitri II, 1607-10
Dmitri III, 1611-12
Michael I, 1613-45
Alexis I, 1645-76

Feodor III, 1676-82
Sophia (regent), 1682-1687
Ivan V and Peter I, 1682-96
Peter I (the Great), 1696-1725
Catherine I, 1725-27
Peter II, 1727-30
Anna, 1730-40
Ivan VI, 1740-41
Elizabeth, 1741-62
Peter III, 1762
Catherine II (the Great), 1762-96
Paul I, 1796-1801
Alexander I, 1801-25
Nicholas I, 1825-55
Alexander II, 1855-81
Alexander III, 1881-94
Nicholas II, 1894-1917

England / Great Britain
Edward IV, 1547-53
Mary I, 1553-58
Elizabeth I, 1558-1603
James I, 1603-25

Charles I, 1625-49
Oliver Cromwell, 1653-58
Richard Cromwell, 1658-59
Charles II, 1660-85
James II, 1685-88
William & Mary, 1689-1702
Anne, 1702-14
George I, 1714-27
George II, 1727-60

George III, 1760-1820

George IV, 1820-1830
William IV, 1830-37
Victoria, 1837-1901
Edward VII, 1901-1910
George V, 1910-36

Appendix II
A List of British Books About Russia

Alcock, Thomas. *Travels in Russia, Persia, Turkey & Greece*. London: Clarke & Sons, 1831.

Alexander, Captain James Edward. *Travels to the seat of war in the East: through Russia and the Crimea, in 1829*. London: H. Colburn and R. Bentley, 1830.

Armstrong, T. B. *Journal of travels during the last two campaigns of Russia and Turkey; an itinerary through the south of Russia, the Crimea, Georgia, and through Persia, Koordistan, and Asia Minor, to Constantinople*. London: A. Seguin, 1831.

Atkinson, George Franklin. *Pictures from the north, in pen and pencil: sketched during a summer ramble*. London: John Ollivier, 1848.

Atkinson, J. Beavington. *An art tour to northern capitals of Europe*. London: Macmillan and Co., 1873.

Atkinson, John Augustus. *A picturesque representation of the manners, customs, and amusements of the Russians: in one hundred coloured plates in three volumes*. London: W. Bulmer and Co., 1803-1804.

Atkinson, Lucy. *Recollections of Tartar steppes and their inhabitants*. London: J. Murray, 1863.

Atkinson, Thomas Witlam. *Oriental and western Siberia: a narrative of seven years' explorations and adventures in Siberia, Mongolia, the Kirghis steppes, Chinese Tartary, and part of Central Asia*. New York: Harper and Bros., 1858.

Atkinson, Thomas Witlam. *Travels in the regions of the upper and lower Amoor, and the Russian acquisitions on the confines of India and China*. London: Hurst and Blackett, 1860.

Baddeley, John F. *The Russian conquest of the Caucasus*. London: Longmans, Green and Co., 1908.

Baring, Maurice. *The Russian People*. London: Methuen, 1911.

Baring, Maurice. *What I saw in Russia*. London: T. Nelson & Sons, 1913.

Baring, Maurice. *A year in Russia*. London: Methuen, 1907.

Barrow, John. *Excursions in the north of Europe: through parts of Russia, Finland, Sweden, Denmark and Norway, in the years 1830 & 1833*. London: J. Murray, 1834.

Barry, Herbert. *Ivan at home, or, Pictures of Russian life*. London: The Pub. Co., 1872.

Barry, Herbert. *Russia in 1870*. London: Wyman & Sons, 1871.

Bell, James Stanislaus. *Journal of a Residence in Circassia*. London: Moxon, 1840.

Bell, John. *Travels from St. Petersburg in Russia, to diverse parts of Asia: in two volumes*.

Glasgow: 1763.

Bentham, Mary. *The Life of Brigadier General Sir Samuel Bentham by his widow*. London: 1862.

Birrell, C.M. Rev. *The life of the Rev. Richard Knill, of St Petersburgh with a review of his character*, by the late Rev.John Angell James. London: J. Nisbet and Co., 1861.

Bloomfield, Benjamin. *Memoir of Benjamin Lord Bloomfield*, edited by Georgina Lady Bloomfield. London: Chapman and Hall, 1884.

Boddy, Alexander A. *With Russian pilgrims: being an account of a sojourn in the White Sea Monastery and a journey by the old trade route from the Arctic Sea to Moscow*. London: W. Gardner, Darton & Co., 1892.

Bond, Edward Augustus. *Russia at the close of the sixteenth century*: comprising, the treatise "Of the Russe Common Wealth," by Giles Fletcher and the Travels of Sir Jerome Horsey. London: Hakluyt Society, 1856. Vol. Cxxxiv.

Bookwalter, John W. *Siberia and Central Asia*. London: C. Arthur Pearson, 1900.

Borrow, George Henry. *Letters of George Borrow to the British and Foreign Bible Society*; edited by T.H. Darlow. London: Hodder and Stoughton, 1911.

Bourke, Richard Southwell, Earl of Mayo. *St Petersburg & Moscow*, 2 volumes. Dublin: 1846.

Bourne, C. *Russian chit-chat, or, Sketches of a residence in Russia*, by a lady; edited by her sister. London: Longmans and Roberts, 1856.

Bremner, Robert. *Excursions in the Interior of Russia*. London: H. Colburn, 1839.

Brooks, Charles Shirley. *The Russians of the south*. London: Longmans, 1854.

Bruce, Peter Henry. *Memoirs of Peter Henry Bruce, esq: a military officer in the services of Prussia, Russia, and Great Britain*. London: Printed for the author's widow, and sold by T. Payne and son, 1782.

Bruin, Cornelis de. *Travels into Muscovy, Persia and part of the East-Indies*. London : Printed for A. Bettesworth 1737.

Buchanan, Meriel. *Petrograd: the city of trouble*, 1914-1918. London: W. Collins, 1918.

Buckinghamshire, John Hobart, Earl. The dispatches and correspondence of John, 2nd earl of Buckinghamshire, ambassador to the court of Catherine II of Russia, edited for the Royal Historical Society. London: Longmans, Green and Co., 1900.

Bunbury, Selina. *Russia after the war: the narrative of a visit to that country in 1856*. London: Hurst and Blackett, 1857.

Burnaby, Capt. Frederick. *A Ride to Khiva, a journey from St Petersburg to central Asia*. London: 1876.

Burney, James. *History of NE Voyages of Discovery*. London: 1819.

Bury, Herbert. *Russian life to-day*. London: A.R. Mowbray & Co., 1915.

Bush, Richard J. Reindeer, dogs, and snow-shoes: a journal of Siberian travel and explorations made in the years 1865, 1866, and 1867. London: S. Low, 1871.

Cameron, G, Lieutenant Colonel. Personal *Adventures in Georgia, Circassia and Russia*. London, 1845.

Carr, John, Sir. *A northern summer, or, Travels round the Baltic: through Denmark, Sweden, Russia, Prussia, and part of Germany, in the year 1804*. London: R. Philipps, 1805.

Cathcart, Sir George. *Commentaries on the War in Russia and Germany in 1812 and 1813*. London: J. Murray, 1850

Clarke, Edward Daniel. *Travels in various countries of Europe, Asia and Africa.* London: T. Cadell and W. Davies, 1810.

Cochrane, Captain John Dundas. *Narrative of a pedestrian journey through Russia and Siberian Tartary: from the frontiers of China to the Frozen Sea and Kamtchatka during the years 1820, 1821, 1822, and 1823*. London: J. Murray, 1824.

Cole, J,W. *Russia and the Russians*. London: Richard Bentley, 1854.

Collins, P. *Voyages*. London, 1860.

Collins, Samuel. *The Present State of Russia*. London: Printed by J. Winter for D. Newman, 1671.

Colmore, Lionel. *Letters from the Continent*. Published posthumously. London: 1812

Colquhoun, Archibald R. *The 'Overland' to China*. London: Harper & Bros., 1900.

Conolley, Arthur. *Journey to the North of India through Russia, Persia and Afghanistan* - (2 volumes.). London: Richard Bentley, 1834.

Consett, Rev. Thomas. *The Present State and Regulations of the Church in Russia*. London: 1729.

Cook, John, M.D. *Voyages and travels through the Russian empire, Tartary, and part of the kingdom of Persia*. Edinburgh: 1768.

Cottrell, Charles Herbert. *Recollections of Siberia: in the years 1840 and 1841*. London: J.W. Parker, 1842.

Coxe, William. *Account of the prisons and hospitals in Russia, Sweden, and Denmark*. London: Printed for T. Cadell, 1781.

Coxe, William. *Travels into Poland, Russia, Sweden, and Denmark*. London: T. Cadell, 1784-1790.

Coxwell, C. Fillingham. *Through Russia in war-time*. London: T.F. Unwin, 1917.

Craven, Lady Elizabeth. *A journey through the Crimea to Constantinople*. London: G.G.J. and J. Robinson, 1789.

Curzon, Hon George. *Russia in Central Asia and the Anglo-Russian Question.* London, 1889.

Curzon, R. *Armenia: A year at Erzurum.* London, 1854.

Daniel, W. *Bolshevism in Practice.* London: 1919.

De Windt, Harry. *Siberia as it is.* London: Chapman & Hall, 1892.

De Windt, Harry. *Through savage Europe: being the narrative of a journey (undertaken as special correspondent of the "Westminster Gazette"), throughout the Balkan states and European Russia.* London: T.F. Unwin, 1907.

Disbrowe, Charlotte Anne Albinia. *Original letters from Russia, 1825-1828.* London: Ladies Printing Press, 1878.

Dixon, William Hepworth. *Free Russia.* London: Hurst and Hackett, 1870.

Dobell, Peter. *Travels in Kamtchatka and Siberia.* London: H. Colburn, & R. Bentley, 1830.

Dobson, George. *Russia* / painted by F. De Haenen; text by G. Dobson, H.M. Grove, and H. Stewart. London A. and C. Black, 1913.

Dobson, George. *Russia's railway advance into Central Asia: notes of a journey from St. Petersburg to Samarkand.* London: W.H. Allen & Co., 1890.

Dodd, George. *Pictorial History of the Russian War 1854-56.* Edinburgh: Chambers, 1856

Drage, Geoffrey. *Russian affairs.* London: J. Murray, 1904.

Duberly, Frances. *Journal Kept during the Russian War.* London: Longmans 1856

Eagar, M. *Six years at the Russian court.* London: Hurst and Blackett, 1906.

Eastlake, Lady Elizabeth Rigby. *A residence on the shores of the Baltic: described in a series of letters.* London: J. Murray, 1841.

Eden, Charles H. *Frozen Asia: a sketch of modern Siberia: together with an account of the native tribes inhabiting that region.* London: Society for Promoting Christian Knowledge, 1879.

Edwards, H. Sutherland. *The Russians at home and the Russians abroad: sketches, unpolitical and political, of Russian life under Alexander II.* London: W.H. Allen, 1879.

Elliott, Charles Boileau. *Letters from the north of Europe.* London: H. Colburn and R. Bentley, 1832.

Eyre, Selwyn. *Sketches of Russian life and customs: made during a visit in 1876-7.* London: Remington and Co., 1878.

Fletcher, Giles. *Of The Rvsse Common Wealth, Or, Maner of Gouernement by the Russe Emperour.* London: Printed by T.D. for Thomas Charde, 1591.

Frankland, Charles Colville. *Narrative of a visit to the courts of Russia and Sweden, in the years 1830.* London: H. Colburn and R. Bentley, 1832.

Fraser, John Foster. *The real Siberia: together with an account of a dash through Manchuria.* London: Cassell and Co., 1902.

Fraser, John Foster. *Red Russia.* London: Cassell and Co., 1907.

Freshfield, Douglas William. *The exploration of the Caucasus.* London: E. Arnold, 1896.

Gibbs, Phillip. *The Russian Diary of an Englishman.* London: Heineman, 1914.

Gilder, William Henry. *Ice-pack and tundra: an account of the search for the Jeannette and a sledge journey through Siberia.* London: S. Low, 1883.

Glen, William. *Rev. Journal of a tour from Astrachan to Karass: north of the mountains of Caucasus.* Edinburgh: D. Brown, 1823.

Gordon, Capt Peter. *Fragment of the Journal through Persia in 1820.* London: 1833.

Gowing, Lionel Francis. *Five thousand miles in a sledge: a midwinter journey across Siberia.* London: Chatto & Windus, 1889.

Graham, Stephen. *Changing Russia.* London: J. Lane, 1913.

Graham, Stephen. *Russia in 1916.* London: Cassell, 1917.

Graham, Stephen. *Through Russia central Asia.* London: Cassell and Co., 1916.

Graham, Stephen. *A Tramp's sketches.* London: Macmillan, 1912.

Graham, Stephen. *Undiscovered Russia.* London: J. Lane, 1914.

Graham, Stephen. *A vagabond in the Caucasus.* London: J. Lane, 1911.

Graham, Stephen. *With the Russian pilgrims to Jerusalem.* London: Macmillan and Co., 1913.

Granville, Augustus. *St. Petersburgh: a journal of travels to and from that capital: through Flanders, the Rhenish provinces, Prussia, Russia, Poland, Silesia, Saxony, the federated states of Germany, and France.* London: H. Colburn, 1828.

Greener, William Oliver. *Greater Russia: the continental empire of the Old World.* London: W. Heinemann, 1903.

Green, George. An original journal from London to St Petersburg.and a vocabulary of the most useful terms, in English and Russian. London: T. Boosey and J. Hatchard, 1813.

Grenfell, Francis Wallace Grenfell, Baron. Three weeks in Moscow. London: Harrison and Sons, 1896.

Grove, Florence Crauford. *The Frosty Caucasus – walking in the Caucasus and ascent of Mt Elbruz.* London: 1875.

Guthrie, Katherine Blanche. *Through Russia: from St. Petersburg to Astrakhan and the Crimea.* London: Hurst & Blackett, 1874.

Guthrie, Maria. *A tour, performed in the years 1795-6.* London: T. Cadell, Jun. and W. Davies, 1802.

Hamley, Sir Edward Bruce. *The Story of the Campaign of Sebastopol.* Edinburgh: W. Blackwood, 1855

Hanway, Jonas. *An historical account of the British trade over the Caspian Sea.* London: Sold by Mr. Dodsley, 1753.

Hare, Augustus John. C. *Studies in Russia.* London: Smith, Elder & Co., 1885.

Harrison, Robert. *Notes of a nine years' residence in Russia, from 1844 to 1853.* London: T.C. Newby, 1855.

Hawes, Charles Henry. *In the uttermost East: an account of investigations among the natives and Russian convicts of Sakhalin, with notes of travel in Siberia, and Manchuria.* London: Harper & Bros., 1903.

Hayes, M. Horace. *Among horses in Russia.* London: R.A. Everett, 1900.

Heber, Reginald. *The life of Reginald Heber, D.D.: lord bishop of Calcutta with a Journal of his tour in Norway, Sweden, Russia, Hungary, and Germany, and a History of the Cossaks, by his widow.* London: J. Murray, 1830.

Henderson, Ebenezer. *Biblical researches and travels in Russia: including a tour in the Crimea, and the passage of the Caucasus.* London: J. Nisbet, 1826.

Henningsen, Charles. F. *Revelations of Russia, or, The Emperor Nicholas and his empire.* London: H. Colburn, 1844.

Henty, George. *Condemned as a Nihilist: a Story of Escape from Siberia* – although a novel, it contains an account of Siberia and life there. London: Blackie, 1893.

Heude, W. *A voyage up the Persian Gulf, and a journey overland from India to England in 1817.* London: Longman, Hurst, Rees, and Brown, 1819.

Heywood, Robert. *A Journey in Russia.* London: 1858.

Hill, S. S. *Travels in Siberia.* London: Longman, Brown, Green and Longmans, 1854.

Hodgetts, E. A. Brayley. *In the track of the Russian famine.* London: T.F. Unwin, 1892.

Holderness, Mary. *New Russia: journey from Riga to the Crimea, by way of Kiev.* London: Sherwood, Jones, 1823.

Holman, James. *Travels through Russia, Siberia, Poland, Austria, Saxony, Prussia, Hanover, &c: undertaken during the years 1822, 1823 and 1824, while suffering from total blindness.* London: G.B. Whittaker, 1825.

Horsey, Sir Jerome. *Travels of Sir Jerome Horsey* Hakluyt Society. London: 1856

Howard, Benjamin Douglas. *Life with Trans-Siberian savages.* London: Longmans, Green, and Co., 1893.

Howard, John. *State of Prisons; an account of visits to prisons in Russia and several European countries.* London: 1777.

Howe, Sonia E. *The false dmitri: a Russian romance and tragedy:* described by British eye-witnesses, 1604-1612. New York: F.A. Stokes Co., [1916]

Howe, Sonia E. *Real Russians.* London: S. Low, Marston & Co., 1917.

Hubback, John. H. *Russian realities: being impressions gathered during some recent journeys in Russia.* London: J. Lane, 1915.

Hume, George. *Thirty-five years in Russia.* London: Simpkin, Marshall, Hamilton, Kent & Co., 1914.

Hunter, William. *A short view of the political situation of the northern powers: founded on observations made during a tour through Russia, Sweden, and Denmark, in the year 1800.* London: J. Stockdale, 1801.

Jackson, Frederick George. *The great frozen land; a narrative of a winter journey across the tundras and a sojourn among the Samoyads.* London: Macmillan and Co., 1895.

James, John. T. *Journal of a tour in Germany, Sweden, Russia, Poland, during the years 1813 and 1814.* London: J. Murray, 1816.

Jefferson, Robert L. *A new ride to Khiva.* London: Methuen & Co., 1899.

Jefferson, Robert L. *Roughing it in Siberia: with some account of the Trans-Siberian railway, and the goldmining industry of Asiatic Russia.* London: S. Low, Marston & Co., 1897.

Jefferson, Robert L. A *wheel to Moscow and back: the record of a record cycle ride.* London: S. Low, Marston & Co., 1895.

Jenkinson, A. *Early Voyages.* London: Hakluyt Society 2v Nos 72, 73

Jesse, William, Captain. *Russia, Circassia & the Crimea.* London: Madden & Co., 1841.

Johnston, Robert. *Travels through part of the Russian Empire and the country of Poland.* London: J.J. Stockdale, 1815.

Justice, Elizabeth. *A voyage to Russia.* London: Thomas Gent, 1739.

Keeling, H.V. *Bolshevism.* London: 1919.

Kennard, Howard Percy. *The Russian peasant.* London: T. Werner Laurie, 1907.

Keppel, George, Major. *A Journey Across the Balcan.* London: Colburn & Bentley, 1831.

Ker, David. *On the road to Khiva.* London: H.S. King, 1874.

Ker-Porter, R. *Travelling Sketches in Russia and Sweden.* London: 1809.

King, Rev. John. *Rites and Ceremonies of the Orthodox Church.* London, 1772.

Knox, Thomas Wallace. *Overland through Asia.* London: Trübner & Co., 1871.

Lady, ten years resident in that country. *The Englishwoman in Russia: impressions of the society and manners of the Russians at home by a lady, ten years resident in that country.* London: J. Murray, 1855.

Lansdell, Henry. *Through Central Asia.* London: S. Low, Marston, Searle, and Rivington, 1887.

Lansdell, Henry. *Through Siberia.* London: S. Low, Marston, Searle and Rivington, 1882.

Lee, Robert. *The last days of Alexander, and the first days of Nicholas.* London: R. Bentley, 1854.

Lethbridge, Alan Bourchier. *The new Russia, from the White Sea to the Siberian steppe.* London: Mills and Boon, c1915.

Liddell, Robert. Scotland. *Actions and reactions in Russia.* London: Chapman and Hall, 1917.

Liddell, Robert. Scotland. "Sestra" (sister): sketches from the Russian Front. London: Hodder and Stoughton, 1917.

Longworth, J.A. A Year Among the Circassians. London: 1840.

Lumsden, T. *A journey from Merut in India, to London, through Arabia, Persia, Armenia, Georgia, Russia, Austria, Switzerland and France during the years 1819 and 1820.* London, 1822.

Lyall, Robert. The character of the Russians, and a detailed history of Moscow. London: T. Cadell, 1823.

Lyall, Robert. *Travels in Russia, the Krimea, the Caucasus, and Georgia.* London: T. Cadell, 1825.

Macartney, George. *Earl, An account of Russia: 1767 by the British ambassador to Russia.* London: 1768.

MacGill, Thomas. *Travels in Turkey, Italy, and Russia, during the years 1803, 1804, 1805, & 1806.* London: J. Murray, 1808.

Macmichael, William, *Journey from Moscow to Constantinople, in the years 1817, 1818.* London: J. Murray, 1819.

Macpherson, Georgina. *Upheaval! Reminiscences of Russia before and after the Revolution.* Oxford: Church Army Press, 1920.

Mahony, James. *The book of the Baltic.* London: E. Wilson, 1857.

Malmesbury, James Harris, Earl. *Diaries and correspondence of James Harris, first earl of Malmesbury: containing an account of his missions to the courts of Madrid, Frederick the*

Great, Catherine the Second, and The Hague edited by his grandson James Howard Harris, Earl of Malmesbury. London: R. Bentley, 1844.

Marsden, Kate. *On sledge and horseback to outcast Siberian lepers*. London: Simpkin, Marshall, Hamilton, Kent & Co., 1895.

Marshall, Joseph. *Travels*. London, 1772

Marvin, Charles. *The region of the eternal fire: an account of a journey to the petroleum region of the Caspian in 1883*. London: W.H. Allen and Co., 1884.

Maud, Renée Gaudin de Villaine. *One year at the Russian court*: 1904-1905. London: J. Lane, 1918.

Mayo, Richard Southwell Bourke, Earl. *St. Petersburg and Moscow: a visit to the court of the Czar*. London: H. Colburn, 1846.

Meakin, Annette M. B. *In Russian Turkestan*. London: G. Allen, 1903.

Meakin, Annette M. B. *A ribbon of iron*. Westminster: A. Constable & Co., 1901.

Meakin, Annette M. B. *Russia: travels and studies*. London: Hurst and Blackett, 1906.

Michie, Alexander. *The Siberian overland route from Peking to Petersburg*. London: J. Murray, 1864.

Miege, Guy. *A relation of three embassies from His Sacred Majestie Charles II to the Great Duke of Muscovie, the king of Sweden, and the king of Denmark: performed by the right honourable the Earl of Carlisle in the years 1663 & 1664*. London: Printed for John Starkey, 1669.

Moore, John. *A journey from London to Odessa*. Paris: Galignani, 1833.

Morley, Henry. *Sketches of Russian life before and during the emancipation of the serfs*. London: Chapman and Hall, 1866.

Morgan & Coote. *Early Voyages to Russia and Persia*. Haklyut Society: 1886

Morris, Isabel. *A summer in Kieff, or, Sunny days in southern Russia*. London: Ward and Downey, 1891.

Morton, Edward. *Travels in Russia: and a residence at St Petersburg and Odessa, in the years 1827-1829*. London: Longman, Rees, Orme, Brown, and Green, 1830.

Moser, Louis. *The Caucasus & Its People*. London: David Nutt, 1856

Mottley, John. *The History of the Life of Peter the First, Emperor of Russia.* London: 1739

Mummery, Albert. F. *My climbs in the Alps and Caucasus*. London: T.F. Unwin, 1895.

Munro Butler-Johnstone, H. A. *A trip up the Volga to the fair of Nijni-Novgorod*. Oxford: J. Parker and Co., 1875.

Neilson, Andrew, Mrs. *The Crimea: its towns, inhabitants, and social customs*. London: Partridge, Oakey, and Co., 1855.

Nevinson, Henry Wood. *The dawn in Russia, or, Scenes in the Russian revolution.* London: Harper & Bros., 1906.

Nicoll, Josephine. *Scenes from Russian life* by Josephine Calina. London: Constable and Co., 1918.

Nolan, E.H. *The History of the War against Russia,* 2 volumes. London: Virtue, 1855

Norman, Henry. *All the Russias: travels and studies in contemporary European Russia, Finland, Siberia, the Caucasus, & Central Asia.* London: W. Heinemann, 1902.

O'Donovan, Edmund. *The Merv Oasis: Travels and Adventures East of the Caspian.* London: 1882.

Oliphant, Laurence. *The Russian shores of the Black sea in the autumn of 1852: with a voyage down the Volga, and a tour through the country of the Don Cossacks.* Edinburgh: W. Blackwood and Sons, 1853.

Page, John Lloyd Warden. *In Russia without Russian: being the wanderings of an Englishman in Central Russia, by land and water.* London: G. Routledge, 1898.

Palmer, Francis H. E. *Russian life in town and country.* London: G. Newnes, 1901.

Pares, Bernard, Sir. *Russia and reform.* London: A. Constable & Co., 1907.

Parkinson, John. *A Tour of Russia, Siberia and the Crimea, 1792-94.* Edited by William Collier. London: Frank Cass & Co, 1971

Paterson, John. *The book for every land: reminiscences of labour and adventure in the work of Bible circulation in the north of Europe and in Russia.* London: J. Snow, 1858.

Paul, Robert. B. Rev. *Journal of a tour to Moscow: in the summer of 1836.* London: Simpkin, Marshall, & Co., 1836.

Pearson, Charles Henry. *Russia: its reforms, political and social progress and present state.* London: Bell and Daldy, 1859.

Perris, George. H. *Russia in revolution.* London: Chapman & Hall, 1905.

Perry, John. *The state of Russia, under the present czar.* London: Printed for Benjamin Tooke, 1716.

Phillipps-Wolley, Clive. Savage Svânetia. London: R. Bentley & Son, 1883.

Pinkerton, John. *Voyages and Travels.* London: 1811.

Pinkerton, Robert. *Russia, or, Miscellaneous observations on the past and present state of that country and its inhabitants.* London: Seeley & Sons, 1833.

Pollock, John. *War and revolution in Russia.* London: Constable and Co., 1918.

Poole, Ernest. *"The dark people":* Russia's crisis. New York: The Macmillan Co., 1918.

Porter, Robert Ker, Sir. *Travelling sketches in Russia and Sweden: during the years 1805, 1806, 1807, 1808: in two volumes.* London: R. Phillips, 1809.

Porter, Robert Ker, Sir. *Travels in Georgia, Persia, Armenia, ancient Babylonia, &c. &c.: during the years 1817, 1818, 1819, and 1820.* London: Longman & Brown, 1821-22.

Rae, Edward. *The White Sea peninsula : a journey in Russian Lapland and Karelia.* London: J. Murray, 1881.

Raikes, Thomas. *A visit to St. Petersburg, in the winter of 1829-30.* London: R. Bentley, 1838.

Ramble, Rayford. *Travelling opinions and sketches, in Russia and Poland.* London: J. Macrone, 1836.

Randolph, T. *Observations on the present state of Denmark, Russia, and Switzerland: in a series of letters.* London: Printed for T. Cadell, 1784.

Redesdale, Algernon Bertram Freeman-Mitford. *Memories by Lord Redesdale.* London: Hutchinson & Co., 1915

Redesdale, Algernon Bertram Freeman-Mitford. *Further memories by Lord Redesdale.* London: Hutchinson & Co., 1917.

Reynolds, Rothay. My Russian year. London: Mills & Boon, 1913.

Richards, John. *A Tour from London to Petersburg and on to Moscow.* Dublin: 1781

Richardson, William. *Anecdotes of the Russian empire: in a series of letters, written, a few years ago, from St. Petersburg.* London: Printed for W. Strahan and T. Cadell, 1784.

Ritchie, Leitch. *A journey to St. Petersburg and Moscow: through Courland and Livonia.* London: Longman, 1836.

Roth, H. Ling (Henry Ling). *A sketch of the agriculture and peasantry of eastern Russia.* London: Baillière, Tindall & Cox, 1878.

Royston-Pigott, G. W. *Savage and civilized Russia.* London: Longmans, Green and Co. 1877.

Russel-Cotes, Annie. *Letters from Russia.* London: 1914.

Ryan, George. *The Lives of our Heroes of the Crimea.* London: J. Field, 1855.

Sala, George Augustus. *A journey due North: being notes of a residence in Russia, in the summer of 1856.* London: R. Bentley, 1858.

Sarytschew, G.A. *Account of a voyage of discovery to the North-East of Siberia, the frozen ocean, and the North-East Sea.* London: 1806.

Salmon, Thomas. *The Present State of Moscovy, or Russia.* London: J. Crokatt, 1727

Sauer, Martin. *An account of a geographical and astronomical expedition to the northern parts of Russia performed by Commodore Joseph Billings, in the years 1785, &c. to 1794.* London: T. Cadell, 1802.

Seacole, Mary. *Wonderful Adventures of Mrs. Seacole in Many Lands.* London: J. Blackwood, 1857.

Seebohm, Henry. *Siberia in Asia: a visit to the valley of the Yenesay in East Siberia.* London: J. Murray, 1882.

Seebohm, Henry. *Siberia in Europe: a visit to the valley of the Petchora, in north-east Russia.* London: J. Murray, 1880.

Seymour, Henry Danby. *Russia on the Black Sea and Sea of Azof.* London: J. Murrary, 1855.

Simpson, James Young. *Side-lights on Siberia: some account of the great Siberian railroad, the prisons and exile System.* Edinburgh: W. Blackwood and Sons, 1898.

Sinclair, John, Sir. *General observations regarding the present state of the Russian Empire.* London: 1787.

Smith, Mary Ann Pellew. *Six years' travels in Russia by an English lady.* London: Hurst and Blackett, 1859.

Smith, Steven, *Art & Anecdote, recollections of William Yeames RA* London: Hutchinson

Spencer, Captain Edward. *Turkey, Russia, Black Sea & Circassia.* London 1855

Spencer, Edmund. *Travels in Circassia, Krim Tartary.* London: H. Colburn, 1837.

Spencer, Edmund. *Turkey, Russia, the Black Sea, and Circassia.* London: G. Routledge & Co., 1854.

Spilman, James, FRS. *A Journey through Russia.* London: 1742.

Spottiswoode, William. *A tarantasse journey through eastern Russia in the autumn of 1856.* London : Longmans, Brown, Green, Longmans, & Roberts, 1857.

Stadling, Jonas. *In the land of Tolstoi: experiences of famine and misrule in Russia.* London: J. Clarke & Co., 1897.

Stadling, Jonas. *Through Siberia.* Westminster: A. Constable & Co., 1901.

Stallybrass, Edward. *Memoir of Mrs Stallybrass; letters from Siberia to her family 1817-1833.* London, Fisher & Son, 1836

Stead, William. T. *The Truth about Russia.* London: Cassell, 1888.

Steuart, A F. *Scottish Influences in Russian History: from the end of the sixteenth century to the beginning of the twentieth century.* Edinburgh: 1913.

Steveni, W. Barnes. *Petrograd, past and present.* London: G. Richards, 1915.

Steveni, W. Barnes. *Things seen in Russia.* London: Seeley, Service & Co., 1913.

Steveni, W. Barnes. *Through famine-stricken Russia.* London: S. Low, Marston & Co., 1892.

Stevens, Thomas. *Around the world on a bicycle from San Francisco to Teheran.* London: S. Low, Marston, Searles, and Rivington, 1887-88.

Stevens, Thomas. *Through Russia on a mustang.* London: Cassell, 1891.

Swan, William. *Letters on Missions in Siberia.* London: Westley & Davis, 1830

Swayne, H. G. C. (Harald G. C.). *Through the highlands of Siberia.* London: R. Ward, 1904.

Swinton, A. (Andrew). *Travels into Norway, Denmark, and Russia, in the years 1788, 1789, 1790.* London: Printed for G.G.J. and J. Robinson, 1792.

Sykes, Arthur Alkin. *The coronation cruise of the "midnight sun" to Russia, Whitsuntide, 1896.* London: 1896.

Terrot, Sarah. *Reminiscences of Scutari Hospitals in Winter Experiences as a nurse during Crimean War.* Edinburgh: Stevenson, 1898.

Tilley, Henry Arthur. *The Pacific – a Circumnavigation.* London: Smith Elder & Co, 1861.

Tilley, Henry Arthur. *Eastern Europe & Western Asia.* London: Longmans, 1864.

Trevor-Battye, Aubyn B.R. *Ice-bound on Kolguev.* London: A. Constable, 1895.

Trevor-Battye, Aubyn B.R. *A northern highway of the Tsar.* London: A. Constable & Co., 1898.

Turnerelli, Edward Tracy. *Russia on the borders of Asia: Kazan, the ancient capital of the Tartar khans.* London: R. Bentley, 1854.

Turner, Samuel. *Siberia : a Record of Travel, XClimbing and Exploration.* London: T.F. Unwin, 1905.

Tweddell, John, Rev. *Remains of John Tweddell.* London: J. Mawman, 1816.

Urquart, David. *Progress of Russia in the West, North and South.* London: 1853.

Urquart, David. *The Secret of Russia in the Caspian.* London, 1863.

Venables, Richard Lister, Rev. *Domestic scenes in Russia.* London: J. Murray, 1839.

Vigor, Mrs. *Letters from a lady, who resided some years in Russia, to her friend in England.* London: Printed for J. Dodsley, 1775.

Walker, J. *Paramythia, or, mental pastimes: being original anecdotes collected chiefly during a long residence at the court of Russia.* London: Lawler and Quick, 1821.

Wallace, Donald Mackenzie, Sir. *Russia.* London: Cassell, Petter & Galpin, 1877.

Walling, William English. *Russia's message: the people against the Czar.* New York: A.A. Knopf, 1917.

Wellesley, Frederick. A. Col. *With the Russians in peace and war recollections of a military attaché.* London: E. Nash, 1905.

Wenyon, Charles. *Across Siberia: on the great post-road.* London: C.H. Kelly, 1896.

Westminster, Elizabeth Mary Grosvenor, Marchioness. *Diary of a tour in Sweden, Norway, and Russia, in 1827.* London: Hurst and Blackett, 1879.

Whishaw, Frederick. *Out of doors in Tsarland: a record of the seeings and doings of a wanderer in Russia.* London: Longmans, Green & Co., 1893.

Whitworth, Charles Whitworth, Baron. *An account of Russia as it was in the year 1710.* London: 1758.

Wilcox, E.H. *Russia's Ruin.* London: 1919.

Wilbraham, Richard, Captain. *Travels in the Trans-Caucasian provinces of Russia in the autumn and winter of 1837.* London: J. Murray, 1839.

Wilkinson, David. *Whaling in many seas, and cast adrift in Siberia: with a description of the manners, customs and heathen ceremonies of various tribes of North-Eastern Siberia.* London: H.J. Drane, 1905

Williams, Harold. *Russia of the Russians.* London: Pitman & Sons, 1914.

Wilson, William Rae. *Travels in Russia.* London: Printed for Longman, Rees, Orme, Brown, and Green, 1828.

Wilton, R. *Russia's Agony.* London: 1918.

Wood, Ruth Kedzie. *Honeymooning in Russia.* London: T.F. Union, 1911.

Wood, Ruth Kedzie. *The tourist's Russia.* New York: Dodd, Mead and Co., 1912.

Wraxall, Nathaniel William, Sir. *Cursory remarks made in a tour through some of the northern parts of Europe: particularly Copenhagen, Stockholm, and Petersburgh.* London: Printed for T. Cadell, 1775.

Wraxall, Nathaniel William, Sir. *A tour round the Baltic, thro' the northern countries of Europe.* London: T. Cadell and W. Davies, 1807.

Wright, George F. *Asiatic Russia.* London: E. Nash, 1903.

Wright, Richardson Little. *Through Siberia: an empire in the making.* London: Hurst and Blackett, 1913

Appendix III
British Companies

Union Bank of England and Russia Ltd. Incorporated in 1863. Dissolved before 1916

Rolling Stock Company of Russia Ltd. Incorporated in 1865. Dissolved before 1916

Russia Copper Company Ltd. Incorporated in 1871. Dissolved before 1916

Kharkow and South Russia Public Works Company Ltd. Incorporated in 1874. Dissolved before 1916

Russia Slate Company Ltd. Incorporated in 1874. Dissolved before 1916

South Russia Brewery Company Ltd. Incorporated in 1881. Dissolved before 1916

General Electric Light and Power Company of Russia, Ltd. Incorporated in 1882. Dissolved before 1916

Spratt's Patent (Russia) Ltd. Incorporated in 1886. Dissolved before 1916

Humber and Company (Russia) Ltd. Incorporated in 1895. Dissolved before 1916

Singer Cycle Company (Russia) Ltd. Incorporated in 1896. Dissolved before 1916

Starley (Russia) Ltd. Incorporated in 1897. Dissolved before 1916

Russia Commercial Development Company Ltd. Incorporated in 1902. Dissolved before 1916

Southern Oil Fields of Russia Ltd. Incorporated in 1904. Dissolved before 1916

South Russia Mining and Agency Company Ltd. Incorporated in 1904. Dissolved before 1916

Youla Wools (Russia), Ltd. Incorporated in 1907. Dissolved before 1916

William Stevens and Company (Russia) Ltd. Incorporated in 1910. Dissolved before 1916

Union Oil Fuel Corporation of Russia Ltd. Incorporated in 1910. Dissolved before 1916

Film Agency (Russia) Ltd. Incorporated in 1910. Dissolved before 1916

General Motor Service of Russia, Ltd. Incorporated in 1913. Dissolved before 1916

East Russia Corporation Ltd. Incorporated in 1914. Dissolved before 1916

A Le Coq (Russia) Ltd. Incorporated in 1904. Dissolved between 1916 and 1932

Commercial Trust Company of Russia Ltd. Incorporated in 1912. Dissolved between 1916 and 1932

Oddy Development Syndicate (Russia) Ltd. Incorporated in 1913. Dissolved between 1916 and 1932

Stuart A Curzon (Russia) Ltd. Incorporated in 1914. Dissolved between 1916 and 1932

Lachta (Russia) Constructions Ltd. Incorporated in 1914. Dissolved between 1916 and 1932

British Bank for Russia Ltd. Incorporated in 1918. Dissolved between 1918 and 1932

South Russia Banking Agency Ltd. Incorporated in 1919. Dissolved between 1919 and 1932

British Mercantile Bank of Russia Ltd. Incorporated in 1920. Dissolved between 1920 and 1932

United Western Russia Trading Company Ltd. Incorporated in 1923. Dissolved between 1923 and 1932
Oil Trust of Russia Limited.
Alfred Herbert (Russia) Limited.
New Russia Co. Ltd. Incorporated 1869. Dissolved 1970

Bibliography and Sources

In addition to many of the books listed in Appendix II, I have used the following for additional material:

Buchanan, Meriel – *Recollections of Imperial Russia*, Hutchinson & Co, 1923
Cahill, Audrey – *Between the Lines*, Pentland Press, 1999
Cross, Anthony – *By the Banks of the Neva*, 1997
Heather, Roderick – *The Iron Tsar,* Penpress, 2010
Holman, James – *Travels Through Russia, Siberia etc.*, 1825
Hopkirk, Peter – *The Great Game*, John Murray, 2006
King, Charles – *Odessa*, Norton & Co, 2011
Lockhart, Robert Bruce – *Memoirs of a British Agent*, 1932
MacGregor, Arthur – *The Tsar's Visit to England*, Ashmolean 2004
Montefiore, Simon Sebag – *Catherine the Great*, 2000
Parker, William – *An Historical Geography of Russia*, University of London Press, 1968
Pitcher, Harvey – *The Smiths of Moscow*, Swallow House Books, 1984
Pitcher, Harvey – *When Miss Emmie was in Russia*, Murray, 1977
Pitcher, Harvey – *Witnesses of the Russian Revolution*, Pimlico, 2001
Pitcher, Harvey – *Muir & Mirrielees*, Swallow House Books, 1994
Putnam, Peter – *Seven Britons in Russia*, Princeton University Press 1952
Rappaport, Helen – *No Place for Ladies*, 2007.
Reiss, Tom – *The Orientalist*, Random House, 2005
Scott, Richenda – *Quakers in Russia*, 1964
Whishaw, James – *A History of the Wishaw Family*, 1935

City of London Metropolitan Archives – The Russia Company Records

The London Library – The Baddeley Collection

I also acknowledge my indebtedness to various family websites, especially those of the Webster, Woodhouse and Platts families, as well a wide variety of articles published in various journals, most of which are referenced in the page notes of this book.

I am grateful to Antonin Grizenko for reviewing Chapter Seven, especially his input regarding the section on British missionaries in Russia.

Index